BOOKS BY G. C. BERKOUWER

Divine Election

Studies in Dogmatics

Divine Election

BY

G. C. BERKOUWER

PROFESSOR OF SYSTEMATIC THEOLOGY
FREE UNIVERSITY OF AMSTERDAM

WM. B. EERDMANS PUBLISHING COMPANY
GRAND RAPIDS, MICHIGAN

© Wm. B. Eerdmans Publishing Co. 1960

All rights reserved

Library of Congress Catalog Card No. 58-7568

Translated by Hugo Bekker
from the Dutch edition, *De Verkiezing Gods,*
published by J. H. Kok N.V., Kampen, The Netherlands

Printed in the United States of America

Contents

LIST OF ABBREVIATIONS

BC   Belgic Confession. English translation found in the *Psalter Hymnal* published by the Publication Committee of the Christian Reformed Church.

CD   Canons of Dort. English translation found in the *Psalter Hymnal*.

ET   English translation

HC   Heidelberg Catechism. English translation found in the *Psalter Hymnal*.

Inst.   *The Institutes of the Christian Religion* by John Calvin. Translated by Henry Beveridge, published in 1845 by the Calvin Translation Society and reprinted by Wm. B. Eerdmans Publishing Company.

K.D.   *Kirchliche Dogmatik* by K. Barth.

T.W.N.T.   *Theologisches Wörterbuch zum Neuen Testament.* ed. by G. Kittel.

P.R.E.   *Realencyklopädie für protestantische Theologie und Kirche*

CHAPTER ONE

THE BOUNDARIES OF REFLECTION

WHEN reflecting on the confession of the Christian
Church regarding election, one must be well aware of
the many dangers that surround this doctrine. A look at the
history of the doctrine will convince us of that. These dangers
are not merely theoretical; they touch upon the religious life as a
whole. It has happened more than once that a misinterpretation
of this doctrine has made its results felt for generations.

These results have at times been so obvious in the history of
the Church that they have given rise to the opinion that it might
be better to be as silent as possible about the doctrine of election
in order to avoid frightening the simple of faith. It has been felt
that perhaps the doctrine of election should remain in the background in preaching and catechetical teaching.

Great responsibilities, therefore, rest on him who discusses the
doctrine of election. To be sure, the treatment of any doctrine
harbors its dangers, and caution is always necessary. With
regard to the doctrine of election, however, a warning to caution
seems even more valid, and Scripture reminds us: "Put off thy
shoes from off thy feet, for the place whereon thou standest is
holy ground" (Ex. 3:5).

We remember that this word of God came to Moses on Mt.
Horeb and that it was preceded by the warning: "Draw not
nigh hither." We certainly do not mean to suggest that the doctrine of election should be discussed simplistically. What we
want to point out is that we may — and can — approach this
doctrine, provided we do it with great respect. The all-important
question is how to approach it and how to understand this caution and respect. How can we discuss election without marring
this mystery?

The seriousness of this question impresses us especially when
we recall that in the history of the Church and theology all kinds
of speculations and deviations have occurred. It need not surprise us that precisely the doctrine of election has been the cause

7

of bitter polemics.   One realizes intuitively that in the area of
this doctrine decisions are made that are of great importance for
a full understanding of God's plan of salvation.   We touch here
upon the profoundest aspects of human life, for whenever the
doctrine of election is discussed it is followed by the question
regarding the certainty of salvation.   We are confronted with the
fact that on the one hand we adhere to the doctrine of election as
the profound, unassailable foundation of salvation, while on the
other hand it is the most serious threat to that certain foundation; and as such it has acquired an ominous character in the
thinking of many people.

Nevertheless, it is impossible to explain the resistance to the
doctrine of election merely by pointing at the caricatural forms
which it sometimes has assumed.   It cannot be denied that in the
background of much of the criticism of this doctrine there is
something of the resistance to the *skandalon* of the gospel itself.
It is the resistance to the nature of election, which is often seen
as arbitrary and as making man completely dependent on God's
election.   It is the resistance to the loss of man's autonomy and
freedom, and this becomes evident in many forms of criticism
against this doctrine.   It is a rebellion against the apriori character of the doctrine; this doctrine seems to clash with the dignity
of man and to make man hardly more than a pawn in the divine
decision.

That explains why in the resistance to the doctrine of election
one motif especially becomes prominent: the appeal to man's free
will over against the sovereign election of God.

But if all the resistance to the doctrine of election cannot be
explained by pointing to its caricatural outgrowths, still we must
not overlook the influence of these developments which have
put their mark on many a phase of the history of the Church.
Man's resistance to the doctrine of election cannot be explained
by merely pointing to his reluctance to accept and bow before the
skandalon of sovereign grace.   In the course of the centuries
much resistance has been offered to what can only be called a
mutilation of the Biblical message, a caricature of what in the
Bible is placed in the context of glorification and thanksgiving.
We must always remember, therefore, that criticism of various
types of presentation of the doctrine of election does not necessarily mean that resistance is offered to the true doctrine of
election.   It is possible that this criticism is motivated — consciously or unconsciously — by a truly Biblical mode of thinking.

It is not always easy to differentiate between resistance to the doctrine itself and resistance to the caricatures of it, because, more likely than not, reaction to caricatures leads to one-sided formulations.

Bullinger and Groen van Prinsterer discussed these questions at length. Bullinger often warned against modification of the doctrine of election; he was very much concerned about mere speculation concerning this doctrine and he insisted on the necessity of remaining within the boundaries of the revealed Word. Of Groen it was said by Kuyper that he never gave his devotion to Calvinism without some reservation. "The doctrine of election remained for him the stumbling block. . . . Until the last days of his life the struggle between Calvinism and Methodism was continued in him, and not until just before his death did the full confession break through for him, and [then] he found rest in God's unsearchable election."[1]

One wonders sometimes whether the doctrine of election really was a stumbling block for Groen, for he often said that in the time of the Synod of Dort the foundations for the true faith were laid,[2] and that then unbelief chose "an advantageous position" in the denial of predestination in order to aim at the core of the gospel; but, he went on to write, "those times are gone." Today unbelief reveals itself in completely different forms. Predestination is a doctrine about which — perhaps largely through misunderstanding and prejudice — differences remain, also between those who are united in brotherly love on the justification of faith by free grace only.[3] Groen spoke of "an

1. A. Kuyper, *Anti-revolutionaire Staatkunde* (1916), I, 597.
2. Groen van Prinsterer, *De Nederlander,* July 9, 1852, no. 623.
3. Groen van Prinsterer, *Grondwetsherziening en Eensgezindheid* (1849), I, 435. Groen adds: "With the indisputability of the agreement as to what belongs to the foundation of the hope for life eternal, even the most important dogma, as shibboleth, falls away" (p. 436). This shibboleth returns also elsewhere. What in the time of the Synod of Dort came legitimately before that assembly — against attacks — has, says Groen, in his days been unjustifiedly put in the foreground as shibboleth. See also: *Het Regt der Hervormde Gezindheid* (1848), where Groen says that the doctrine of predestination "against which also a good-hearted Christian sometimes objects, was brought to the fore at a time when with the rejection of this doctrine all of the gospel truth was thought to fall" (p. 27), but that "certainly in our days doubt or prejudice against this dogma would give no reason for expulsion if this doubt and prejudice went together with a consciousness of one's own sinfulness and inability, of free grace and one's need of renewal by

unevangelical use of the doctrine of predestination" which had a bad effect on the Dutch national spirit.[4] Such an unevangelical use occurs especially whenever the doctrine of election is speculatively modified and the Biblical message is obscured and placed on a narrower basis, whenever the "fatherly countenance of God" (CD, V, 5) is hidden behind the concept of the "absolute power of God" or behind the frightening idol of a mechanistic-deterministic causality.

Resistance to such an interpretation of the doctrine of election is not only understandable but — in the light of the gospel — also completely legitimate. We are not concerned here about far and abstract possibilities, about dangers that threaten from afar, but about real and close transformations and deformations that obscure the consoling truth of God's election. In theology and preaching the doctrine of election has often been interpreted from a deterministic point of view. This has had serious results in the life of the Church and has often ended in disdain of and vexation about the doctrine of election itself. In the background

---

the Holy Spirit" (Groen speaks of this in connection with the adherence to the formulas). See also p. 131 (about Dort and the doctrine of election): "As a result of the particular developments in our church . . . any defense of the gospel causes almost vexation, although the doctrine that was discussed two centuries ago was not put on the agenda." Groen speaks of the schoolbooks "in which this mystery of Scripture presented in the kaleidoscope of a number of reading lessons, is served to the poor children as genuine milk of which perhaps the apostle makes mention." See also Groen: "Le parti antirevolutionnaire et confessionel dans l'Eglise Reformée des Pays-Bas," *in Etude d'histoire contemporaine* (1860), pp. 18-20, where Groen answers the question: "Do you approve of the famous canons?" and where he says that at that time — that is, of the Synod of Dort — the protest was against the Arminian subtleties and was for "the defense of the central truth of the gospel, the granting of salvation." If the same were done now "one would err gravely and commit a deplorable anachronism." Nevertheless, those of the seventeenth century were "perfectly correct in insisting on the doctrine of election" because "negation of election was the first link of a logical deduction that ended with conditional salvation." All this must be remembered when we discuss the question whether for Groen the doctrine of election was a "stumbling block," and whether he did not until the last days of his life find rest in God's unsearchable election. I owe the references to Groen's words regarding election to Prof. Dr. H. Smitskamp, Amsterdam. They form an important contribution to the complicated discussions around the doctrine of election. The complications around this doctrine return with great regularity. For Groen, see also: *Verspreide Geschriften*, II, 125-128.

4. Groen, *De Nederlander*, September 8, 1852, no. 692.

of the doctrine of election — and of the preaching of it — a
dark concept of God then becomes visible, which originates from
the mutilation of Biblical testimony, no matter how often one
appeals to all sorts of Biblical references. The counsel of God is
then discussed in a deterministic or even fatalistic manner so
that the faithful have no choice but to draw their conclusions of
passivity, quietism, and tormenting uncertainty. And that uncertainty is then not ascribed to the result of littleness of faith
or of unbelief — this is the crisis of certainty — but to the unavoidable correlation of the fact of an election which is and
remains hidden in complete mystery.

No connection can then be made between election and consolation, but only between election and fear and uncertainty.
The tension between election and certainty becomes very profound and finds its way to the depth of man's heart. This tension may be expressed in the form of a question that can be asked
in many variations: Is the certainty of salvation not harmed and
threatened by the hiddenness of election? Does not God's decision
always fall beyond the circle of all our certainties and of all we
have acquired? Is there in the span of our lives one single instance that is able to stop the stream of questions arising in us?
With these ever recurring considerations we find ourselves in
the midst of the questions that surround the doctrine of election.
It will be the test of the legitimacy of that doctrine if it can
answer all these questions. For in the doctrine of election the
issue cannot be a speculative knowledge of theology which penetrates all depths, but which remains incomprehensible to the simple
of faith; rather, the questions and answers of the children bear the
greatest weight. Christ, when speaking of the Father who has
kept these things from the wise and understanding while revealing them unto babes, spoke of God's "good pleasure" that
determined this structure of revelation and mystery for His
children (Matt. 11:26).

And if the doctrine of election is not without justice called the
core of the Church, will not the rights of the simple, the children, be safe here and come to light? Therefore, the most important question which presents itself to us at the very beginning
of our inquiry into the nature of the doctrine of election is
whether this doctrine can be made clear; whether we can show
that here the heart of the Church truly does, may, and can
beat, or whether we are dealing with a reflex which cannot
make that heart beat and which cannot be a consolation in life

and in death for the congregation — for all of the congregation.
Can we really speak of the consolation of election, or must we
conclude that this doctrine undermines the basic foundations of
our lives, devastating all certainty and stability? Is that perhaps the last and unavoidable consequence, when the apriori character of the eternal counsel of God, of predestination, is so much
emphasized, and when not only theology but Scripture itself
keeps us spellbound with the words "before the foundation of
the world"?

It is often apparent that even an emphatic reference to the
words of Deuteronomy 29:29 cannot take away the tension in
which many live. We read there that the secret things are for
the Lord our God, but the revealed things for us and our children. And this hiddenness, which is unknown to us, but as the
unknown does not altogether remain out of our field of vision,
can for that very reason become the source of the tension. For
although we do not attempt to penetrate into that which, according to God's revelation, must remain hidden for us, the fact
of that hiddenness remains known to us and we wonder whether out of this hiddenness — this *deus absconditus* — a shadow is
not also cast where the *deus revelatus* is preached with emphasis.

Has it not often happened that we, called upon to accept in
faith the promise of God in Jesus Christ, have had great difficulty in avoiding the question whether we have the right to apply that promise to ourselves, and whether we should not be convinced by another way — a roundabout way — of our personal
election? Around the halo of God's mercy always remains the
dark edge of the inscrutable election, of an eternal decision which
cannot be altered, the counsel of God's absolute freedom. Is
there still a possibility in this short life to answer the burning
question regarding our election with the certainty of an unswerv-
ing faith?

This connection between election and certainty does not tend
toward anthropocentrism. Concern for man's salvation and
searching for the "we know" is not opposed to a theocentrical perspective. Soteriology is immediately evoked by and connected
with an emphasis on God's free will. If we separate these two
from each other we can speak of election only in an abstract
manner. Our salvation is then causally and objectivistically
"derived" from God's sovereignty, and the consolation of election

gives way to a powerless submission which cannot be distinguished from submission to destiny and fate, and in which the Savior of the world can no longer be detected.

It is surprising that the explicit relation between election and the certainty of salvation has often become the great problem of the doctrine of election, for this tension is nowhere found in Scripture. In Scripture the certainty of salvation is never threatened or cast in shadows because of the fact of election. Rather, we always read of the joy of God's election and of election as the profound, unassailable and strong foundation for man's salvation, both for time and eternity. Election functions nowhere as a background to the order of salvation, a background that creates uncertainty, or as a shadow of the *deus absconditus* over the revelation of the *deus revelatus*. On the contrary, we hear with it a hymn of praise and gratitude for the foundation of salvation. Election does not loom as a problem, as an unbearable tension. It completely lacks those aspects, and we meet election in emphatically doxological and soteriological contexts, as when Paul writes that God "chose us in him [Christ] . . . foreordained us unto adoption as sons . . . according to the good pleasure of his will" (Eph. 1:4, 5). There is nothing mysteriously problematic here: "to the praise of the glory of his grace, which he freely bestowed on us in the Beloved" (Eph. 1:6). Nor does Romans 8 leave room for the possibility that the order of salvation can be broken down into disorder, or that the election of God may be instrumental in distorting the way of salvation. Rather, our attention is called to the interrelations in the numerous saving acts of God, and to the consolation which lies anchored in Christ for time and eternity. The revealing of the plan of salvation gives "a last message for the eschatological certainty."[5] To be sure, the plan of God, which is free and sovereign, is discussed in Romans 8:28, and history is seen as having its roots in eternity, but this is a basis for salvation, not a threat to it. The correlations in which Paul thinks are not obscure. They are filled with the light that is the source of that certainty which resounds in a song when Paul knows with the congregation that nothing can separate us from the love of God in Jesus Christ (Rom. 8:35ff.).

We wonder, therefore, where — in spite of this testimony in Scripture — the origin lies of the problematic aspect of revela-

5. O. Michel, *Der Brief an die Römer* (1955), p. 180.

tion and "hidden" election. We do not yet want to seek an
answer to this important question, but we pose it now to emphasize how necessary it is that we remain within the boundaries of
the gospel when we discuss election. We are conscious of the
fact that it is easier to give this warning than to heed it. But
it is necessary to understand that every speculation apart from
faith and the gospel threatens the congregation and confronts
it with insoluble questions which can turn the preaching of the
gospel into objective lectures. Only when the boundaries of reflection are respected can we be saved from a doctrine of election
that hangs over us like a dark cloud, and only then will it be
possible to continue to speak of election as the *cor ecclesiae,* and
to separate the confession of the doctrine of election from the
disturbance of faithful hearts by a menacing secrecy ascribed to
God.[6]

It is clear that in the light of Scripture we never can or may
seek an escape simply by not discussing the doctrine of election.
This solution may be recommended for pastoral considerations,
but it can only lead to new, insurmountable difficulties, for it
leads to a doctrine held in dormancy but fed by the fear that if
it is brought to life it will become a menacing factor in the or-

6. It seems to me undeniable that much of the terminology in theological
discussions has caused misunderstanding. We think especially of the
use made of the term *fatum* in the doctrine of election. Otto Weber
is correct when he writes: "It certainly is deplorable that at times even
orthodox believers identify *providentia* with *fatum*" (in *Grundlagen
der Dogmatik,* 1955, p. 563). He points especially to Gerhard
and reminds us of the fact that Calvin rejected this identification (*Inst.*
I, xvi, 8). Calvin deemed the word "fate" unacceptable because it belongs to the class of words "of which St. Paul teaches us to avoid the
unholy novelty" (I Tim. 6:20) and "because they endeavor to load the
truth of God with the odium attached to it." See for the use made of
the term *fatum*: K. Barth, *Kirchliche Dogmatik,* III, 3 (1950), p. 183,
and my *The Providence of God* (ET, 1952), Chap. VIII. More than
once in this connection Calvin's term *decretum horribile* has been mentioned (*Inst.* III, xxiii, 7). According to Bavinck, Calvin has, "completely unjustified, been reproached for the use of this word" (*Gereformeerde Dogmatiek,* II, 357; ET, *The Doctrine of God,* 1951). We
shall come back to this point, but we want to remind the reader now of
what Bavinck adds to it: "The *decretum* as doctrine of Calvin is
not *horribile,* but the reality is terrible, which is the revelation of that
decision of God and which is thus taught by Scripture and history"
(*ibid.,* p. 357).

der of salvation. Thus to hold the doctrine of election is to have a certain concept of the doctrine itself. Moreover, the doctrine thus held can unexpectedly make its effects felt, and with serious results, precisely because it has been alive all the while. Calvin has warned against suppressing the doctrine of election. Nobody is allowed to avoid mentioning predestination in order to avoid danger (*Inst.* III, xxi, 3). To be sure, he respects a cautious modesty in the discussion of such great mysteries, but he points out that man's mind does not permit itself to be laid in chains. He reminds us of the word of the Lord and attempts to indicate distinctly the boundaries of our discussions: "For Scripture is the school of the Holy Spirit, in which, as nothing necessary and useful to be known is omitted, so nothing is taught but what is of importance to know. Everything, therefore, delivered in Scripture on the subject of predestination, we must beware of keeping from the faithful lest we seem either maliciously to deprive them of the blessing of God, or to accuse and scoff at the Spirit, as having divulged what ought on any account to be suppressed." Precisely out of respect for the wisdom of God which comes to us in revelation, Calvin declines to shun the doctrine of election.

Indeed, it is impossible to adhere to a doctrine without mentioning it. It will be good to remember that Calvin warns us to keep our eyes and ears open for all of God's words and to do that "with this moderation — viz. that whenever the Lord shuts his sacred mouth, he [we] also desists from inquiry. The best rule of sobriety is not only in learning to follow wherever God leads, but also when he makes an end of teaching, to cease also from wishing to be wise" (*ibid.*). In this context Calvin quotes Deuteronomy 29:29; this text may never lead us to be silent about election, but rather must teach us to distinguish where the boundary of God's Word lies. As usual, Calvin's warning is twofold. On the one hand, we may not be silent where God speaks; on the other hand, we must not speculate beyond the boundaries which God in His wisdom has set us. Only by observing these two points will the doctrine of election not be harmful to God's congregation. They who for pedagogical reasons want to leave the doctrine of election in the background of the life of the Church — "so that it will not bring the weak into confusion" — are accused by Calvin of shamelessly criticizing God's pedagogy of revelation. Over against unbridled criticism Calvin sets the deciding limits for all our reflections: the revelation of God.[7]

This warning to observe the limits set by God is of great importance. But that does not mean that now all problems can be easily solved. That would be the case if Scripture would give us a number of truths in systematic context, so that it would be possible clearly to indicate the boundary between the truths that are mentioned in Scripture and those that it does not mention. But it is clear that for the recognition of the boundary of God's Word we must not expect a directly comprehensible and a simple spacial and quantitative boundary. Rather, the comprehension and consideration of the boundary depend upon our total comprehension of the Biblical message. It does not give us a doctrine of election which without further ado can eventually be taken up in our dogmatic system in a more systematized form. The Biblical message serves to make us understand the marvelous and inexhaustible liveliness which is so typical of the message Scripture brings and in which we hear the message of the sovereignly electing God.

Only when we recognize with Calvin the boundary of our inquiry into election does the hermeneutic question about the structure of Biblical testimony arise. Recognition of the boundary is not a goal in itself, but only the beginning of the correct form of questioning. Only in the concrete does the inquiry into the boundaries which we must observe become meaningful. At all levels of doctrine and theology it has become apparent that it is possible to come to very different conclusions, even though there is a common recognition of the boundary. This confronts us with the dispute over the purely Scriptural light on election, over the function of this message in the whole of Scripture. The point at issue is not a merely formal recognition of the authority of Scripture, for such a recognition often does not exclude the possibility of speaking and thinking of election speculatively. It is possible to respect the boundary of speaking of election while at the same time trespassing that boundary, because one may be handling the contents of the gospel in an illegitimate way and yet remain unconscious of

---

7. See A. D. R. Polman, *De Praedestinatieleer van Augustinus, Thomas van Aquino, en Calvijn* (1936), pp. 387ff.

his trespassing. When Calvin warns against the *sacrilegium*[8] we agree with him that silence is necessary where the Holy Spirit is silent.

It is clear that we touch here upon a profound problem that may be thus formulated: What can be deduced from the testimony of Scripture, and what consequences does it imply? This question, important in all doctrinal reflection, is of particular importance regarding the doctrine of election. The Westminster Confession has specifically connected it with the counsel of God: "The whole counsel of God concerning all things necessary for his glory, man's salvation, faith, and life, is either expressly set down in Scripture or by good and necessary consequence may be deduced from Scripture."[9]

It is not surprising that here the question arises how to interpret those "good and necessary" consequences. For these consequences have often played an important role in the caricatural deviations from the Scriptural givens. A certain teaching about election has often been defended with an appeal to man's courage to accept its consequences, while those who thought that the issue was no longer one of good and necessary consequences and who therefore refused to accept the consequences were accused of hesitation.[10]

The importance of the question posed here is sharply revealed in the light of the problem that played such a big role at the Synod of Dort, that of the *phrases duriores* (the hard sayings). In that conflict the issue lay not with minor questions but with a very important problem relative to the doctrine of election. Some delegates were of the opinion that via good and necessary consequences one had to come to certain strong statements about election, especially with respect to rejection. The question came to the fore especially in connection with Maccovius about whose *phrases duriores* there was so much ado, and it strikes us that he himself appealed to the rightful

---

8. See Calvin on John 6:44: *"ut altius inquirere sacrilegium sit"*; cf. *"non quod praeter simplex verbum quicquam desideret"* (*ibid.*).

9. Müller, *Bekenntnisschriften der reformierten Kirche* (1903), p. 545.

10. See A. D. R. Polman, *Onze Nederlandse Geloofsbelijdenis,* II, 207, who writes that Calvin rejected any operation with and speculation about God's decisions, and never adopted the apriori deductive methods of the later supralapsarians. With St. Augustine he rejects the *praescientia* as solution but "nothing can tempt him to go further." (Cf. p. 208 on Beza.)

use of the *bona consequentia*[11] and defended the thesis that
what can be deduced from Scripture by way of that good consequence has the same authority as Scripture itself.

The Word of God, Maccovius says, is related to the consequence as the premise is to the conclusion.[12]   Man's reason
is the instrument of faith, said Maccovius and thus he came
to all sorts of conclusions that culminated in the well-known
phrase *"destinare ad peccatum."*[13]   It is understandable that
this and other *phrases duriores* have been much discussed.

The heart of the matter was not simply a formal epistomo-
logical debate about the range of man's logic and about his
right to draw conclusions concerning election, but the structure of the whole doctrine of election.   It is known that especially the Remonstrants repeatedly appealed to such *phrases
duriores* in order to show that the Reformed doctrine of election revealed its untenability in precisely such phrases. This reproach shows the urgency of the problem of the *phrases duriores.*
Fundamentally, it is the problem of the boundary of our speaking
in the light of the entire Biblical message.   Also he who
rejects the Remonstrant doctrine of election can nevertheless
regret that certain *phrases duriores* have made it more difficult
for them to interpret the meaning and significance of the Reformed doctrine of election correctly.   We touch here very concretely on the boundary problem.   Even if one accepts that certain *phrases duriores* have repeatedly been taken out of their context, one nevertheless cannot remove himself from the question arising here by merely speaking of a pardonable extremism.   For in that extremism the divine revelation regarding election is immediately implicated.   Dijk, who agrees with
the decision of Dort not to condemn expressly the *phrases
duriores,* does say of Maccovius that he went to extremes with
the *decretum horribile.*[14]

It is impossible to imagine a sharper distinction where the
counsel of God is concerned.   But this criticism makes it understandable that repeatedly voices arose that demanded a con-

---

11. Cf. A. Kuyper, Jr., *Johannes Maccovius,* p. 149; cf. the chapter "Het
    recht der bona consequentia verdedigd" : *"quicquid per bona consequen-
    tiam ex scriptura deducitur, illud ipsum est scriptura."*
12. *Ibid.,* p. 155.
13. K. Dijk, *De Strijd over Infra- en Supralapsarisme in de Gerefor-
    meerde Kerken in Nederland* (1912), p. 219.
14. *Ibid.*

demnation of the *phrases duriores* to make it clear that the
Reformed doctrine of election wanted to differentiate itself from
such extremes. That the Synod saw the danger is evident not only
in the warning to Maccovius but no less in the epilogue which
took such an important place in the discussions. In this epilogue a warning was given to refrain "from all such manners
of speaking that go beyond the boundaries of the correct meaning of Scripture, and which could give the sophists righteous
cause to revile and/or defame the doctrine of the Reformed
churches." The danger of giving offense was mentioned with
emphatic reference to Maccovius.[15]

The question may arise why the Synod of Dort did not em-
phatically and concretely condemn these phrases. According to
Dijk the Synod would then have weakened its criticism of the
Remonstrant errors.

About the third and final draft of the epilogue which does
not contain an explicit condemnation, Dijk writes: "The decision which the Synod took in this very serious matter is of
great importance. The Synod stood its ground over against the
more tolerant group — from England, Bremen, and Hesse —
showing that it would not be moved by the reproach of the
Remonstrants, namely, that the Synod condemned them while it
absolved others whose teachings had caused the Remonstrants to
stumble. If the Synod had accepted the proposal of the English
there would have been a victory for the Remonstrants, and the
danger of such a decision was clear to the delegates from the
Netherlands, the Palatinate and Switzerland."

It cannot be our intention to judge what the Synod should
have done in these concrete and difficult circumstances, full of
threatening misunderstanding, and whether its decision regarding the *phrases duriores* was historically justified or not.
But from the purely doctrinal point of view it can be positively
defended that the existence of the Reformed doctrine of election would not be threatened or weakened by an emphatic rejection of the *phrases duriores*. Such a rejection is found in the
second draft of the epilogue in which it is acknowledged that
such phrases were employed.[16] Because of the difficulties in
formulating the special phrases that were here and there em-

---

15. *"Ne utatur phrasibus, quae scandalum praebent iunioribus."*
16. *"Nonnulli tam veterum quam recentium, scriptorum in explicatione
horum doctrinae Christianae capitum formalis loquandi incommodioribus
et in speciem durioribus nonnumquam usi sunt."* Dijk, *ibid.*, p. 196.

ployed, and which often needed all sorts of interpretations, the explicit rejection of the *phrases duriores* was omitted in the final draft,[17] so that Dort does not contain such a rejection in the official decisions.[18]   But this course of events in the history of the Church should not make us forget that the position of the Reformed doctrine of election is not weakened but only clarified and strengthened when it is made clear that the conclusions drawn from the *phrases duriores* are not true consequences.

The position of the Remonstrants is further undermined when it is clear that the Church, in refuting the Remonstrants, at the same time refused to move in the direction of any form of determinism with respect to the doctrine of election or to go to extremes with respect to the counsel of God.   The transition from the second to the final draft of the epilogue may, speaking historically, be understandable — in view of the complicated and diverse nature of the *phrases duriores* —; speaking doctrinally, however, the warning of the epilogue implies a warning against all conclusions that go beyond the boundaries of revelation. We must remember that the final draft of the epilogue emphatically rejected the attempt to make the people believe — against all truth, fairness, and love — that all sorts of terrible consequences are implied in this Reformed doctrine of election.   It was said, for instance, that this doctrine would be an accommodation to the flesh and that it would make God the author of all sin,[19] a tyrant and hypocrite, that this doctrine is nothing but a "renewed stoicism," that God "has predestinated and created to damnation the greatest part of the world by the mere inclination of his will without reference to or consideration of any sin," and that "rejection is the cause of unbelief and godlessness, the same way that election is the cause of belief and of all good works."

In all this the epilogue apparently saw nothing but a disastrous caricature, of which it spoke in Reformed intuition and wih the pathos of the pure preaching of the gospel of God.   The issue was always the nature of the conclusions drawn, as it was with Maccovius, whom Dijk said was the "most consistent

17. Dijk, *ibid.,* p. 203.
18. *Ibid.,* p. 209.
19. This rejection of the caricature we find also in the Canons, e.g.
    CD, I, 5 and I, 13.

of the supralapsarians"[20] and who developed the doctrine of the decree "more sharply." Granted that Maccovius, according to Dijk, has gone to extremes with the doctrine of election, the question remains whether we face the sharpness of the Word of God (Heb. 4:12) and the heart of the gospel.

It is thereby clear that the problem cannot be solved by saying that the one wanted to be more consistent than the other. After all, the point at issue was not a more or less logical and consistent mode of thinking so that the one draws every possible conclusion while the other refuses to go beyond a certain point and for no apparent reason suddenly stops drawing conclusions. The polemics about election cannot be interpreted as only a difference in the extent of consistency. The addition of the good and necessary consequence indicates a profound problem. The question is whether one speaks in the light of the full context of the gospel message. Nobody can or may deny and neglect this context, but it is possible that in drawing certain conclusions from references in Scripture we lose our way. It has often happened, for instance, that from the doctrine of divine sovereignty the conclusion was drawn that man could not be held fully responsible for his deeds, while from the acceptance of man's responsibility as Scripture presents it the conclusion was drawn that there could be no mention of an absolute sovereignty and of a truly apriori and sovereign divine election. It was believed that only logical consequences had been drawn, while actually the correct insight had been abandoned from the very beginning because divine sovereignty and human responsibility had been seen as factors that limited one another on one and the same level, and this view meant a deviation from the message of Scripture.

Therefore, the *phrases duriores* may never be rejected for fear of conclusions in one or the other direction. The issue in rejecting the *phrases duriores* can only be the inquiry into the structure of the message of Scripture in which man stands face to face with the sovereignly electing God. It is not so that at a completely arbitrary moment the line of conclusions can be broken off because they become unacceptable. When at the Synod of Dort the *phrases duriores* were discussed some argued that with a possible rejection of the *phrases duriores* all sorts of "harsh-sounding expressions" in Scripture could be

20. Dijk, *op. cit.,* p. 219.

rejected.[21]   This argument cannot be taken seriously, for the
protest of the Synod was not against such hardness as referred
to by the Jews who said of Jesus' words, "This is a hard saying; who can hear it?" (John 6:60).   Such a protest comes
from hearts that are hard.   The discussion of the *phrases
duriores* dealt, however, with formulations quite possibly not
really warranted by the Biblical message.   That is the reason the
epilogue warns against the not imaginary danger of giving occasion for scoffing at the pure doctrine because then a *skandalon*
would be posed that would not coincide with the *skandalon* of
the cross of I Corinthians 1.   There are profound interrelations
in the truth of God but we are not to think that they are to be
seen and understood by drawing some logical consequences from
a number of presupposed truths about election as they are revealed to us in Scripture.   It is good to remember that the
Westminster Confession does not only speak of good and necessary consequences but also of "the high mystery of Predestination," a doctrine which "is to be handled with special prudence
and care."[22]

This shows, then, that the seemingly simple matter of indicating the boundary of our speaking is a profound matter. Only
in the concrete can it become clear — in the light of God's
gospel — whether the boundaries are respected.   Calvin was
correct when he said that that boundary lies in the revelation
of God.[23]   But that does not mean that determinism is correct

21. *Ibid.*, p. 200.
22. Müller, *op. cit.*, p. 552. See what Bavinck writes about the Reformed:
"Once the justice and the honor of God were acknowledged, all the
Reformed advised the most careful and tender treatment of the doctrine
of predestination and warned against vain and curious investigations"
(*Gereformeerde Dogmatiek*, II, 359).   In this connection we also refer
to Maresius, who, when discussing Article 16 of the Belgic Confession,
speaks of carefulness and who is of the opinion that if the carefulness
of Article 16 had been observed, history might have taken a different
course (S. Maresius, *Foederatum Belgium orthodoxum sive Confes-
sionis Ecclesiarum Belgicarum exegesis*, 1652).
23. Miskotte has discussed my interpretation of theology as a science or
philosophy which may not go "beyond the boundaries of Scripture" in
"De triomf der genade" in *Kerk en Theologie*, 1955, p. 13.
He sees it as a profound problem to define the boundaries of the task
of theology in what Scripture leaves unclarified.   He wonders whether
he who poses that view "has really considered what that means with
respect to the old traditional theology."   It is indeed my opinion that
this limit is the boundary of speculation.   When Miskotte says that

when it speaks so emphatically of the sovereign will of God
that decides everything; nor can the Remonstrants convince us
when they refer to Scripture for the "conditions" that man must
fulfill to obtain salvation. The acceptance of the boundary of our
thinking immediately and repeatedly evokes questions that will
have to stay with us at all times. The boundary-concept is not
a simple solution that can be employed as if it were apriori clear
to everyone. Rather, the argument about the boundary plays a
role, also in the discussion between those who appeal exclusively to Scripture for their doctrine of election. All sides usually
want to adhere to Scripture but that does not mean that there
is no difference of opinion regarding, for instance, Romans 9-11.
Such a difference regarding the doctrine of election does not
mean that the confession of the exclusive authority of election
would not be of decisive significance for the purity of this doctrine. But we do see that in the midst of all our thinking the
urgency of the boundary problem meets us everywhere. That
is the hermeneutic question about the function of the message
of election throughout Scripture. We face the fact that even a
formal agreement with respect to the authority of Scripture has
not always led to an agreement regarding the doctrine of election. Therefore, when speaking of the boundaries of our thinking we must remain fully aware of our responsibility to return
always to Scripture and to understand its meaning and intention.
Against the background of the authority of Scripture election
has been interpreted in many different ways. Roman Catholic
and Protestant theology, theological determinism and Remonstrantism — they all appealed to Scripture, and the influences
of these different interpretations have been felt among the believers.

In the time just prior to Biblical criticism there was
still agreement about the formal establishing of the boundary,
but the concrete ways that were followed differed greatly. When
Luther opposed the *theologia gloriae* in order to pose the *theo-*

---

theology — in the light of the exegesis — is confronted with something
more than a "repetition of Holy Scripture" then it all depends how
such a "repetition" is understood. But the boundary — which also
with Miskotte comes to the fore — remains unaffected where he, too, is
confronted with a "plus" on the basis of exegesis and speaks of the
"border-theses" that are useful media in "making an approximate and
(theological-) reasonable interpretation of the absolute and universal
significance of the gospel" (*ibid.*, p. 14).

logia crucis, his anti-speculative protest did not touch the question of Biblical or extra-Biblical givens; he was concerned with a boundary for our speaking and believing which the full content of the Word of God indicated to him. The recognition of this boundary was not for a moment detached from the recognition of the boundaries of the Word of God (*sola scriptura*), even as Calvin's warning to remain within the boundaries of Scripture was in full harmony with his argument to keep solely to Christ in the discussion of election, and not to go beyond Him. The accentuation of the boundary is not a formalistic device employed to develop a closed system. It is quite possible that someone, speaking of Scripture and its doctrine of salvation and rejecting all extra-Scriptural argument, may go beyond Scripture in spite of that rejection. Later we shall speak of the clear definition of the boundary by the Reformers who constantly discussed election in the light of God's Word and in unbreakable connection with the Christ of Scripture.

The seriousness and danger of trespassing the boundaries was seen not only in the conscious combination of Scripture with another source of knowledge (tradition or reason) but also in the "curious" inquiry (BC, XIII) into eternal predestination by those who are not content with the Christ and therefore seek their own and others' salvation in the labyrinth of predestination.[24] The road of faith is thus left whereby the boundary becomes something concrete for us; it is not an abstraction, but a boundary revealed in the way that man can walk. In the history of the doctrine it has often become apparent that men wanted to penetrate ever deeper and higher into election and in so doing trespassed the boundaries. Luther and Calvin both gave solemn warning not to forget and neglect the Christological content of the boundary in order that precisely that content might protect us against all investigation beyond the simple Word of God.[25]

24. Calvin on John 6:40.
25. The transition from the boundary-concept to the idea of "content" may find criticism. However, the meaning can hardly be prescribed anywhere else but in this connection, and is linked up with the impossibility of a formal confirmation (*Vergewisserung*) of the authority of Scripture, detached from the content of salvation in Scripture. See for the Reformed warning also the *Confessio Helveticum Posterior* of 1562, p. 182, about the "curious" inquiry into the question *an sint ab aeterno electi? "Audienda est enim praedicatio evangelii eique credendum est."*

Thus, in all our thinking about election we shall be reminded of this boundary. All abstraction has been taken away from it when in the light of the concrete Word of God we see the place from which, without rashness, we are to listen to the revelation which is for us and our children. A "haughty heart" is not fitting here, nor a walk among things "too great" and "too wonderful" (Ps. 131:1), but we may hope in the Lord "from this time forth and for evermore" (Ps. 131:3). Who does not think here of the pronouncement that called the doctrine of election the heart of the church? Only if we are and remain warned men will it be possible to speak responsibly of what Scripture surrounds with praise and gratitude and to understand something of the fact that the doctrine of election is not the dark background of the preaching of the gospel but a confession that may not be suppressed because it speaks to us of God Himself in Jesus Christ, and because nowhere in Scripture is such preaching a menace to the veracity and trustworthiness of God's gospel.

It cannot be denied that in the history of the doctrine and in the preaching of the Church the doctrine of election has at times assumed such menacing aspects. Those were dark times. The solace of election was then no longer understood. The way to the doxological connections of the gospel had to be rediscovered in a maze of deformations and caricatures. In this rediscovered way God's sovereignty was confessed, unobscured by determinism and fatalism; and in the light of this sovereignty of God it became possible to understand the significance of His sovereign grace, grace that could be explicated in the light of divine commiseration and mercy and not as the result of a synthesis between God's act and our work. Therefore, it is clear in the light of the gospel that we cannot discuss the election of God apart from faith.

We are far from the Church's confession of election if we think to discover in it a metaphysical system of cosmology. This mistake has often been made and has always ended in determinism or — in reaction — in synergism. In the case of synergism, man claims autonomy for himself in defense against the pressure of determinism. With this, man comes to see God as a jealous God who in His overpowering might does not want to

grant man his freedom and holds him as a pawn.[26]   In this
presentation we no longer can discover the true God.

It is not incidental and unimportant that in this study we
discuss not *election* but the *election of God*. About this election
—God's election — one can speak only in the knowledge of Him
who is the God of Israel, the Father of Jesus Christ.   Apart
from Jesus Christ — the boundary and the Way — one cannot
but fall into the errors on the right or on the left side.   Everything changes when man's outlook on God becomes warped. But
if this outlook is correct, the faithful stand in silence, as Israel's praise waited in Zion (Ps. 65:1). "Blessed is the man
whom thou choosest, and causest to approach unto thee, that he
may dwell in thy courts" (Ps. 65:4).   Here the electing God
is also the hearer of prayers (Ps. 65:2), and His forgiveness of
transgressions is known and confessed (Ps. 65:3).   Apart from
all these connections, nothing can be known of this divine election.   The way of the confession of the election of God is the
way of faith.   That does not imply a correlation which makes
the election of God dependent on our act of faith.   Such a
correlation would affect the core of the doctrine of election, and
against such a relationship of dependence the Synod of Dort professed the sovereign election of God in the deep insight that
fides — in the form of the *praevisa fides* — could not be the
solution to the doctrine of election!

But there is another correlation between faith and election
in which the election of God is not made dependent on man's
faith, but is recognized and confessed by way of his faith.   In
this way the confession of sins is made and *hubris* finds no place.
Here God's sovereignty is confessed and man kneels before God.
Wherever the doctrine of election is detached from these connections of faith, it becomes a foreign element in the preaching of
the gospel, it loses its consoling character and becomes nothing
but a source of unrest.   Theological reflection on the veracity of
God's election must, in true surrender to the Word of God, make
it increasingly clear that the preaching of the gospel does not
intend to lead believers to mute submission to a hidden and
unapproachable Being but to adoration and praise.   If anything
is clear from Scripture it is this correlation.   In this study we
shall not want to loose sight of Psalm 65.   For, if anywhere, then

26. See the discussion of Otto Weber in *Grundlagen der Dogmatik* (1955),
    p. 492.

here — in this Psalm of nature — the way is opened that leads to the world, to the nations, and to full life. This Psalm on the election of God says it so beautifully: "O God of our salvation, Thou art the confidence of all the ends of the earth" (Ps. 65:5).

CHAPTER TWO

THE DOCTRINE OF ELECTION IN HISTORICAL PERSPECTIVE

W E do not aim in this chapter to give a complete survey of the history of the doctrine of election. We only want to speak of one perspective that urges itself upon us when we become engrossed in its history and that in all variations of the thought of the centuries proves that "there is nothing new under the sun." For we see that in the great number of problems that present themselves to us there is one that comes to the foreground repeatedly. It can be thus formulated: Where falls the decision of man's redemption? Does it fall exclusively in God Himself, in His electing act, or does it fall — albeit against the background of the generative grace of God — in man's free will? Does our redemption depend on God's decision or does it depend on ours?

Many answers have been given in the course of the centuries. These answers have usually not been a choice of one or the other possibility but an attempt to avoid this choice by trying to establish a synthesis between the divine and the human decisions. On the one hand, God's grace cannot be denied, God cannot be made dependent in the granting of salvation on man's decision; but on the other hand, the significance of man's decision — his belief or unbelief — is to be fully honored, and should not be allowed to be obscured by the overpowering character of God's working all things by Himself.

The effort has usually been made to bring God's grace and man's freedom (*liberum arbitrium*) into harmony and a balanced relationship with each other, in order to establish a synthesis, so that there is no danger that the exclusiveness of one or the other brings serious consequences to a living faith. For if the decision of man's salvation were thought to be dependent exclusively on God, man's decision and choice would become insignificant, and fatalism and determinism would result. Or at least we should be left with a concept of the exclusiveness of God's activity whereby man's endeavor would sink into nothingness. If, however, the decision were laid in man, God's grace would come into question.   Indeed, would it be possible to maintain it as real grace, as His merciful act?   Would not grace be deprived of its merciful aspect if it were overshadowed by the final active deed, the free choice, of man?   And would not God's grace then take on the aspect of an offer of grace — to be accepted or declined — rather than that of a gift granted by the free, sovereign Giver?   To avoid these extremes a synthesis was sought in which both God's grace and man's decision were given a full place.

This theme of a synthesis runs like a red thread through the history of the doctrine of election.   It is the theme of harmony, of cooperation.   Of course, within the limits of this solution it is still possible to establish all sorts of variations, depending on whether the grace of God or the decision of man is accentuated. But no matter how radical these variations may be, they always lie within the circle of synergism, which occupied such an important place in Protestant as well as in Roman Catholic theology. There are, for instance, the synergistic polemics in Lutheran theology of the sixteenth century, the polemics of the Remonstrants in the Reformed churches of the same time, and the quarrel between the Molinists and Thomists, in which the relationship between God's grace and man's freedom played such an important role.[1]

The question regarding this relationship between God's grace and man's decision arose already in 418 when at the Council of Carthage Pelagianism was condemned because it was based on man's free nature and it emphasized man's decision to such a degree that God's grace did not actually go beyond the granting of that free nature.   Pelagianism is based on an "exaggeration of the forces of free will"[2] and on "the essence of freedom as the opportunity to choose between good and evil."[3]   In Pelagianism the Church saw grace deprived of its primary significance, of its decisive value.   It was still spoken of, but it had actually been abandoned.[4]   In such a view, grace was no longer absolutely necessary, and the Church at the Council of Carthage con-

---

1. G. C. Berkouwer, *Conflict with Rome* (ET, 1958), Chap. IV, and
   Triumph of Grace in the Theology of Karl Barth (ET, 1956), Chap. VII.
2. *Dictionnaire de Théologie Catholique*, XII, 1, 675.
3. *Ibid.*, p. 683.
4. *Ibid.*, p. 684.   See K. Steur, *De Vrije Wil* (1935), pp. 11ff.

fessed its belief in the necessity of grace.[5]   It is not that grace
makes it easier to do God's will, but that without grace it is impossible to do God's will.   Christ does not say, "Without me it
is more difficult to do this"; He says, "Without me you can do
nothing."[6]   That word "nothing" conveys that there is a certain
absoluteness in this emphasis on the necessity of grace.

The Council of Orange (529) condemned not only Pelagianism but also semi-Pelagianism, a condemnation to which the
Roman Catholic Church still adheres for the reason that even
semi-Pelagianism thinks too depreciatively of the necessity of
God's grace.   To be sure, semi-Pelagianism rejected Pelagianism
and did not teach an inviolate *liberum arbitrium,* but it still
maintained a belief in a free will — although a weakened free
will (*infirmitas liberi arbitrii*).   It taught that man retains his
free will, but because it has been weakened by sin it is in need
of God's helping grace, so that a cooperation between God's
grace and man's freedom is necessary.[7]   Rome rejects this doctrine because she does not think the necessity of grace is sufficiently confessed by it.

At the Council of Orange Scripture was again quoted
to show clearly the necessity of grace.   Not only Christ's statement that we can do nothing without Him, but also God's words
in Isaiah were cited, "I am inquired of by them that asked not
for me; I am found of them that sought me not" (Isa. 65:1).[8]
This very citation from Isaiah seems to exclude any possibility
of synthesis because the simple relationship between seeking and
finding is here incurred by the sovereignty of God's grace.   One
wonders how it is possible that Rome still adheres to the decision of 529 and nevertheless rejects the Reformation because
it accentuates too much the *sola gratia.*   We cannot now, however, go into this question.   We only want to emphasize that
the Church of Rome — in spite of its polemic struggle with the
Reformation — adheres to the necessity of grace.   According to
Trent, the "power of nature" is not able to bring about redemption.   The starting point of justification lies with grace.[9]

---

5. See Denzinger, *Enchiridion,* pp. 101ff.
6. *Ibid.,* p. 105.   *"Sine me difficilius potestis facere"* — *"sine me nihil
   potestis facere."*
7. See Seeberg, *Dogmatische Geschichte,* II, 572.
8. Denzinger, *op. cit.,* p. 176.
9. The *"exordium justificationis"* (Denzinger, *op, cit.,* p. 797).   Cf.,
   "nisi in Christo renascentur, numquam justificarentur" (*ibid.,* p. 795).

On the other hand, the Roman Catholic Church confesses the free will of man, defends it emphatically against the Reformation and places it over against the *sola gratia*. Grace is necessary and active, but man must cooperate with it and affirm it. Grace comes first (*praeveniens*), but it is not irresistible. "Scripture never teaches that grace works all things by itself in the sense that man's free will can contribute nothing to the salvation of man. Both factors work in such interrelation that neither of the two will encroach upon the other."[10]   The Roman Catholic Church wants to emphasize that in relation to salvation man cannot be completely passive and it supports its position by quoting Scripture passages that call man to activity. From this position arises the problem of whether grace is, or is not, decisive in character.

In the polemics between Thomism and Molinism the point at issue was "the origin of this infallibly certain connection between active grace and the result that is willed by God."[11]   According to Molinism grace works by way of man's free will only, while Thomism holds that grace works in its own power. In support of this latter view the Council of 529 may well be quoted, in its definite statement that God does not wait[12] for man's decision.

It is strange, however, that criticism of the Thomistic view was always based on the argument that with saving grace overshadowing the natural free will of man, his free will could no longer be maintained,[13] and that Trent's position could no longer be valid since it taught that man's will is a decisive factor.[14] This places us in the midst of the tensions of synergism. Over against the "either . . . or" a "both . . . and" is placed which forms the core of synergism and this turns out to be of decisive significance for a correct understanding of the election of God.

10. F. Diekamp, *Katholische Dogmatik nach den Grundsätzen des heiligen Thomas,* II, 452.
11. *Ibid.,* p. 457.
12. Denzinger, *op. cit.,* p. 177: *"expectare."* Here reference is made to a place that contradicts "await," namely, Prov. 8:35. According to the LXX, this says: *"praeparatur voluntas a Domino."* Leaving aside the meaning of Prov. 8:35, it can be said that the Council of 529 wanted to accentuate the prevenient character of grace as it appears in the N.T., e.g., I Cor. 2:9.
13. See Diekamp, *op. cit.,* II, 408.
14. *"Posse dissentire, si velit,"* Sess. 6. Can. 4. This canon is especially illustrative because it treats the *liberum arbitrium,* but then *"a Deo motum et excitatum,"* and so *cooperatio* comes to the fore. See Denzinger, *op. cit.,* p. 814.

However, it is not only in Roman Catholicism that synergism plays a role. The Reformation, too, was confronted with a profound problem when it sought the connection between the function of man's freedom and responsibility, and the doctrine of election. The Reformation met with questions similar to those in Roman Catholic theology.

We think especially of the Remonstrants in their opposition to the Reformed doctrine of election. They wanted to account for the significance of man's freedom and activity and to emphasize that man's activity could not be meddled with. We meet here a striking parallel to the problems of the Roman Catholic Church, and we may well question whether we are not dealing here with a religious problem of great significance. Is that perhaps the reason why after the Synod of Dort there was room for some sympathy between the Lutherans and the Remonstrants? Did both perhaps feel that in the process of salvation — in order to escape fatalism — man's share could not be overlooked? Is it possible that this common position indicates the inescapability of synergism?[15]

In Lutheran theology the problem appears especially in the development of Melanchthon's thinking. As did Luther, he at first declined all synthesis or cooperation between the acts of God and of man, and based conversion exclusively on the deciding grace of God.[16] Later, however, Melanchthon began to emphasize the factor of man's free will "and with that he began to reflect on the relation between the human will and offered grace."[17] Accordingly, in his *Loci Communes* (1535), he speaks of three causes of salvation — Scripture, the Holy Spirit, and the will of man who does not reject Scripture but accepts it.[18] In this

15. See J. Loosjes, *Luthersen en Remonstranten in de Tijd van de Dordtse Synode* (1926), p. 24: "As far as rejection of the doctrine of election was concerned, the Lutherans agreed fully with the Remonstrants, so much so that a well-meant warning to all Lutheran Christians in Bohemia, printed by the strongly Lutheran faculty at Wittenberg, said that at the Synod of Dort, where the argument about election occurred, 'the Arminians defended our view.'" And Episcopius, although he did not want to merge with the Lutherans, said, "We Remonstrants nevertheless agree with the Lutherans concerning the doctrine of predestination" (*ibid.*, p. 29). Cf. Bavinck, *Gereformeerde Dogmatiek*, II, 318 (ET, *The Doctrine of God*, 1951).
16. See G. Kawerau, "Synergismus," in *P.R.E.*
17. *Ibid.*, p. 230.
18. "*Verbum, Spiritus Sanctus et humana voluntas assentiens nec repugnans Verbo Dei.*"

reflection on the human will[19] a direct interrelationship among the questions regarding predestination becomes visible. For the issue with Melanchthon is the how and where of the decision of man's salvation.   The issue is Melanchthon's rejection of any interpretation of human decision in which the superiority of God's predestination and sole activity would leave no room for any activity on man's part. This development in Melanchthon is clear in that he at first rejected the anthropological aspects (*liberum arbitrium*) in justification and predestination (the two terms by which the sovereignty of grace is necessarily indicated), but later resisted any viewpoint which made man "passive" and ruled out his responsibility. The Word of God, the Holy Spirit, and man's will — this was Melanchthon's combination, a combination which has well been called "suspect."[20]

To be sure, Melanchthon did not intend to give up the sovereignty of grace, or the *sola gratia* of justification, but he came nevertheless to this co-ordination whereby a synergistic equalization could no longer be avoided.[21] The predestination that Luther accepted was not completely disregarded; rather, it lost its prominence through this co-ordination. Such a loss, according to Melanchthon, cannot be avoided, for when one person believes while the other does not, the reason for this difference must be "within us."[22] Melanchthon's defense against determinism is understandable, but we must agree with Kawerau when he writes, "As commendable as the practical direction was which Melanchthon by this doctrine gave, it was nevertheless in error since by the combination of the three causes he combined the divine and human activity in such a way that salvation comes to pass by the addition of a human activity to God's. This resulted in synergism. . . ."[23]

19. Melanchthon also cites Chrysostom: *"hode helkoon ton boulomenon helkei."* About this statement, see Calvin's *Institutes,* II, iii, 10: "We must, therefore, repudiate the oft-repeated sentiment of Chrysostom, 'Whom he draws, he draws willingly"; insinuating that the Lord only stretches out his hand, and waits to see whether we will be pleased to take his aid."
20. H. E. Weber, *Reformation, Orthodoxie und Rationalismus* (1937), I, 166.
21. See for the attempt to protect Melanchthon against the criticism of synergism, Weber, *op. cit.,* I, 161.
22. *"Necesse est in nobis esse aliquam discriminis causam."* See *P.R.E.,* p. 230.
23. *Ibid.*

This synergism also appears in Pfeffinger's development of
Melanchthon's theology. Man is not completely passive in the
process of conversion. According to Pfeffinger, too, there must
be a "cause" within men for their different reactions to hearing
the gospel.[24] This does not mean that Amsdorf is correct when
he calls Pfeffinger a Pelagian. Pfeffinger did not attempt to deduce man's salvation from his nature. He wanted an organic synergism resulting thus in this mode of cooperation and in bringing
about a certain change of viewpoint of election. A pastoral emphasis on man's responsibility does not imply criticism of the
monergism of grace,[25] but Melanchthon's "three causes" certainly do imply this.

This short resume indicates how radical the problem of synergism is with reference to the doctrine of election. Synergism
does not confront us with a different problem than the one of
sovereign election. It is concerned with the same question; it
inquires into the prime cause of man's salvation. Synergism
does not merely attempt to give a solution to the problem of the
cooperation between God and man in time, so that it is without
significance for the doctrine of election. That this is not the case
is indicated fy the fact that synergism has an immediate reper-
cussion on the doctrine of election.

This is especially apparent in the enormous significance which
the idea of prescience, *praescientia* (or *praevisio*) has acquired
in the doctrine of election. We may say that synergism wants
to direct our attention to the real cooperation between God and
man in time, but that this view, projected back into the counsel
of God, leads — must lead — to the idea of prescience. Many
attempts have been made to solve the questions around the doctrine of election with this idea. Prescience has been placed between God's election and man's final destiny, for example, by
distinguishing between the *voluntas antecedens* and the *voluntas
consequens* in election, thereby placing between the two wills
man's freedom to choose and his reaction to the offer of salvation
as foreknown and foreseen by God, thus forming the basis for
the *voluntas consequens*.

The *voluntas antecedens* is of a universal character, it is a general decision of God — whoever believes is saved. And by way

24. *Ibid.*, p. 281: *"Sequitur ergo in nobis esse aliquam causam, cur alii
assentiantur alii non assentiantur."*
25. Weber, *op. cit.*

of the human link in this chain, namely, man's decision —
in the *praescientia* — the initial decision of God is followed
by the particular decision of granting salvation.[26]   What
happens in time — the human reaction — becomes the condition under which election occurs and is realized.   Conrad
Vorstius put it clearly and without disguise.   According to him,
election and rejection must be interpreted in such a manner that
God "always regards these two preceding conditions, faith and
unbelief" and "thus faith always precedes the election to salvation, while unbelief precedes the election to rejection."[27] The
idea of condition constitutes the link between a universal decision
and its realization.   This is the projection of synergism into the
counsel of God.

We often encounter this influential idea.   We find it in Molinism, with the Remonstrants, and with many Lutherans.   But at
the same time it is clear that the idea of prescience casts shadows
on the sovereignty of God's election and is a flagrant contradiction of the nature of Christian faith.[28]

Calvin saw this.   He knew synergism for what it is.   He rejected the *praescientia* as an explanatory device.   He did not deny
God's knowing beforehand (*Inst.* III, xxi, 5), for God sees
in fact all things as present before Him and His knowledge is
extended over all of history and over all of creation.   But the
question is whether predestination may and can be made dependent on this as its cause and basis.   Calvin found this relationship of dependence present in Ambrosius, Origen, Jerome, and
"almost all church fathers" (*ibid.,* xxiii, 6).   They taught that

26. Bavinck, *op. cit.,* II, 330.
27. C. Vorstius, *Doodsteek gegeven aan de absolute praedestinatie, die
voor of na den val Adams gesteld wordt* (1676), pp. 9, 10.
28. We find a recent example in Gaston Déluz' *Predestination et Liberté*
(1942) : "The decree of election is universal in its elaboration but not
necessarily in its realization" (p. 114).   He speaks consistently of
"the condition of election" in these words : "Faith is the condition without which election cannot be realized" (p. 109).   "God has posed a condition.   This condition is faith" (p. 110).   Déluz attempts to distinguish
this interpretation from the one of foreknowledge but he cannot really
escape it.   He describes the *praescientia* in these words : "According to
these authors predestination is based on the foundation of an ideal and
conditional ordinance: God declares that He will grant salvation to those
who believe.   This conditional decree has a universal validity" (p. 113).
And he adds — therein is supposed to lie the difference — that God
does not leave it at that, for through the help of the Spirit He makes
us fulfill the condition, a conception which certainly does not guarantee
the correct relation between election and faith.

God distributed His grace among men depending on His "fore-knowledge" of who would use it correctly (*ibid.*, xxii, 8).

Augustine, too, supposedly taught the idea of prescience, but he rejected it after gaining more knowledge of Scripture. Then he called it vain reasoning to defend God's foreknowledge over against His grace and to say "that we were elected before the foundation of the world, because God foreknew that we would be good, not that he himself would make us good" (*ibid.*)[29]

The reason for Calvin's opposition is clear — this *praescientia* implies justification by works. "For if you say, Because he fore-saw they would be holy, therefore he chose them, you will in-vert the order of Paul. We may safely infer, then, If he chose us that we should be holy, his foresight of our future holiness was not the cause of his choice" (*ibid.*, xxii, 3). According to Calvin, the idea of prescience does not solve any problem. He re-ferred to Valla, who taught that life and death are more the out-come of God's will than of His prescience. God sees beforehand, "but since he foresees the things which are to happen, simply be-cause he has decreed that they are so to happen, it is vain to debate about prescience, while it is clear that all events take place by his sovereign appointment" (*ibid.*, xxiii, 6). Furthermore, we could ask why God did not counteract the evil which he foresaw (*ibid.*).

Calvin resists the idea of prescience just as he resists the inter-pretation of God's providence as "bare permission."[30] He sees in it an attack against God's greatness. It supposes a waiting God whose judgment and final act depend on and follow upon man's acceptance and decision, so that the final and principal de-cision falls with man; it teaches self-destination instead of divine destination (*Inst.* I, xviii, 1). It is the same defense which we

---

29. For St. Augustine, see *De Praedestinatione Sanctorum*, XIX, 38, where St. Augustine refers to John 15:16, "*Non vos me elegistis, sed ego vos elegi; nec fides ipsa praecedit. Non enim quia credimus, sed ut credamus elegit nos.*" See also X, 19. In spite of the clarity of St. Augustine's word about *praedestinatio* and *praescientia* it has several times been attempted to interpret him in the direction of *praescientia* and *praevisio*. See about this, K. Barth, *Die Freiheit der Entscheidung im Denken Augustins* (1935), p. 162.

30. See my *The Providence of God* (ET, 1952), Chap. V. This often comes concretely to the fore in Calvin's writings, most centrally in connection with God's counsel and the cross of Christ where the simple idea of prescience is not sufficient to answer all questions. "And, in truth, if Christ was not crucified by the will of God, whence is our re-demption?" (*Inst.* I, xviii, 3).

meet later with Kuyper[31] and others, and which is summed up by Bavinck in words that convey that replacing predestination with the idea of prescience is emphatically contradicted by Scripture, religious experience, and theological thinking.[32]

Nevertheless, the influence of synergism was and remained so great that — reprojected into the doctrine of *praescientia* — it repeatedly invaded the Church and theology. Bavinck goes so far as to call this solution "general," for it is accepted by the Greek Orthodox, Roman Catholic, Lutheran, Remonstrant, Anabaptist, and Methodist churches.[33] In one way or another at-

---

31. For instance, A. Kuyper, *Dictaten Dogmatiek*, Lcus I, part III, 7, p. 340, in connection with the *scientia medio* of the Jesuits, and the Arminian *fides praevisa*, and Locus III, part V, 4, p. 481, about God's decision and the *praevisio rerum*. Kuyper rejects the thought that the *praescientia* could contribute to the *theodicee* (p. 116). See also his criticism of the distinction between *decretum generale antecedens* and *decretum particulare consequence*, a combination of the conditional decision and the Arminian *praevisa fides*.

32. Bavinck, *op. cit.*, II, 339. There is no *praescientia nuda* because the *praescientia* comprises the predestination (p. 340). These problems can be studied in connection with the *universalismus hypotheticus* in Amyraldism. Important for more than one reason is the article by J. Moltmann, "Prädestination und Heilsgeschichte bei Moyse Amyrant. Ein Beitrag zur Geschichte der reformierten Theologie zwischen Orthodoxie und Aufklärung" in *Zeitschrift für Kirchengeschichte* (1953/54), pp. 207, 303. Moltmann received his degree in 1951 in Göttingen on the dissertation, *Gnadenbund und Gnadenwahl* (unprinted), of which the article mentioned is a part. See especially the words by Camero (quoted by Moltmann, *op. cit.*, p. 284): *"Petrus credens efficit ut Christus, qui tantum moriebatur conditionaliter pro Petro antequam crederet, incipiat esse mortuus revera absolute pro Petro postquam in Christo credidit."* In the center of hypothetical universalism and of the doctrine of predestination in all its forms, the emphasis is the place and function of faith. In order to avoid the results of the function of faith as it occurs in Amyraldism, Camero declares: *"Est enim fides, quae morti Christi reddit efficaciam, non ulla quae ei insit dignitate aut merito, sed quia Deus voluit nos inseri per eam Christo capiti"* (quoted by Moltmann, p. 284). It is clear that already on the basis of this concept of faith the system "of the conciliation between Arminianism and Gomarism" (E. Haag, quoted by Moltmann, p. 284) should fail, while the whole idea of prescience inserts an un-Reformed view of the function of faith into the doctrine of election.

33. Bavinck, *op. cit.*, II, 339. Illustrative is the development in the Anglo-Saxon world. See, among others, the Confession of the Cumberland Presbyterian Church (1883) and the changes prior to that in the Westminster Confession on the point of election (see Müller, *Bekenntnisschriften*, pp. lxx and 928ff.). For the problems in general see: E. J. Bicknell, *A Theological Introduction to the Thirty-Nine Articles of the Church of England* (1935), especially pp. 250ff.

tempts have been made to clarify election as the sovereign act of
God and to make transparent its relation to man's act and decision, a relation which must be a synthesis.[34]

So far we have spoken of synergism with reference to the doctrine of election. It is clear, however, that although synergism
always functions in connection with salvation, the idea of prescience can also be connected with man's other possible decision,
the decision of unbelief. It has even happened that prescience
was rejected with respect to salvation while it was accepted in
connection with man's choice of unbelief. This brings us to a position quite different from that of Vorstius, the Remonstrants,
and many others. For Reformed conviction about *sola fide —
sola gratia* rejects the idea of prescience in the sense of *praevisio
fidei.* The Reformed theologians were too convinced of the instrumental character of faith to make election dependent on that
faith and to base election on a foreseen faith, i.e., the quality of
that faith as the *habitus* of man which — at least in God's sight
and knowledge — would have to precede election. For in that
case this faith would have been detached from its real relationship to salvation, and would have become the foundation or cause
of election.

But there have been those who thought it possible to speak of
prescience concerning the decision of unbelief, but not concerning
that of faith. We find the best example of this in the Formula
of Concord which makes a sharp distinction between predestination and prescience. Predestination is only brought to bear on
God's children, elected to life eternal. It is impossible to think

---

34. The polemic over prescience is exegetically often linked up with the
interpretation of Romans: "For whom he foreknew, he also foreordained . . ." (Rom. 8:29). See also (in connection with Christ)
I Peter 1:20; and on Israel, Rom. 11:2. In his exegesis of Rom.
8:29 Calvin discusses again the concept of *praescientia* and rejects it as
unsuitable. For Calvin this *praescientia* is undetachably connected with
human "dignity," while St. Paul, he thinks, is concerned with referring
us to God's counsel and thus rules out all dignity on the part of man.
See Zahn's criticism of the "untenable concept" that God "knew beforehand that they will hearken in belief to the call to salvation, and will
remain faithful to their belief until the end, from which then further
follows that God has predestined these individuals to salvation of whom
He foresaw the obedience in faith, in contrast to others whom He also
has called through the same gospel" (*Der Brief des Paulus an die
Römer,* 1910, p. 418). See also his criticism about "mere knowing"
(p. 419).

here of election based on prescience. Election (predestination) is not a foreknowledge of the salvation of the elect "but through God's gracious will and pleasure in Jesus Christ is also a cause of our salvation, and creates, works, helps and furthers all that belongs to it on which our salvation, therefore, is founded."[35] This election does not find its basis at all in our piety or virtue,[36] and it is impossible to speak of prescience as the foundation of election.

A problem does not arise until the decision to unbelief becomes real. For if there is unbelief, it is not by God's will but by our own fault. "For all preparation for damnation comes from the devil and from men, from sin and not at all from God who does not want one person to be damned: how, then, would He prepare a man for damnation?" [37]

That is the reason why here the idea of prescience enters in whereby God "foresees and foreknows evil also, but not as though it were His gracious will that it should happen."[38] In this prescience God also limits evil. The situation is different here from the one which relates election to faith. With reference to the decision to choose unbelief the Formula of Concord quotes Hosea 13:9: "It is thy destruction, O Israel, that thou art against me, against thy help.[39]

The object of the Formula of Concord is clear. It wants to reject the parallelism between election-rejection and faith-unbelief. The Lutheran Confession wants to speak pastorally in this rejection, and to emphasize the consolation of election. We are reminded here of Bullinger who also completely rejected the idea of prescience with reference to election but employed it with reference to evil. Both Bullinger and the Formula of Concord want to show that election lies anchored in Christ, and is apart from any merit on man's part.

But the decision to unbelief evoked other questions. The Formula of Concord says of man's resistance that man "obstructs the Holy Spirit so that the Spirit cannot work in him,"[40] and

35. J. T. Müller, *Die symbolischen Bücher der evangelisch-lutherischen Kirche* (1928), p. 705, with reference to Acts 13:48.
36. *Ibid.*, p. 720.
37. *Ibid.*, p. 721.
38. *Ibid.*, p. 705.
39. In addition to Hos. 13:9, reference is made to Ps. 5:4, "For thou art not a God that hath pleasure in wickedness." The text of Hos. 13:9 is often quoted in connection with this problem.
40. J. T. Müller, *op. cit.*, p. 555.

therefore we cannot but speak of prescience instead of predestination. This confronts us with the profound problem of this Lutheran Confession.

In this connection, and not incorrectly, Schlink put the questions: "Does not the Holy Spirit always meet with man's
resistance? . . . . Must not enslaved man resist the Holy Spirit
until he is conquered and on the last day is entirely renewed?"
And, most important, "Is maybe this rejection of a double predestination in the distinction between election out of grace and
foreknowledge, in spite of all hesitancy and respect regarding the
mystery of divine election, the beginning of a rational solution
to its problems as it afterwards came to light in Lutheran
orthodoxy?"[41]

It is interesting that in later Lutheran orthodoxy the idea of
prescience regained more general significance, especially again
in connection with the doctrine of election, although it remained
limited to its relationship to unbelief and guilt in the Formula
of Concord. It seems that wherever the idea of prescience has
gained admittance as a solution, it has grown in power and has
finally broken through the boundaries to which it was at first confined. It could be asked whether such danger was perhaps already implicit in the Formula of Concord. For when it is said
that God with respect to the elect "*clementer praescivit, ad
salutem elegit et decrevit. . .*,"[42] then it cannot be said that the
preceding "*praescivit*" is intended to be a decisive explanation of
the "*elegit et decrevit*" that follows.[43] However, it was not a-
priori certain that this was fully understood and would be understood in the future in analogy to Romans 8:29. It was at least
possible that later on it would be broken down into the distinction between "knowing" and "election" and thus end up with the
voluntas universalis antecedens (over all men), which then was
followed, via foreknowledge, by the *voluntas consequens* in connection with the faith which had been foreseen by God.[44]

At any rate, we see in the development of Lutheran orthodoxy
the imperialism of the prescience play its role. Schmid thinks
that this Lutheran view means (in connection with election and

---

41. E. Schlink, *Theologie der lutherischen Berkenntnisschriften,* p. 392.
42. J. T. Müller, *op. cit.,* p. 708.
43. I think that Barth goes too far when he says that the preceding word
praescivit already indicates the direction "in which the composers intended
to develop this thought further."
44. Schlink, *op. cit.,* pp. 392ff.

faith) that according to the concept of the *voluntas universalis* salvation is intended for everyone, but that the decision of salvation concerns only part of mankind.[45]   The basis for that is found in the *voluntas specialis* by which only those receive salvation who accept it.   God knows beforehand, from eternity, "who these will be, and this foreseeing is then the basis upon which the counsel of God, encompassing only a certain number of people, is an eternal counsel."[46]

It should not surprise us that Lutheran orthodoxy attempts to show that the *sola gratia* is not endangered by man's decision and that faith does not become something of merit.   This is done by means of a correlation-concept which is supposed to solve the difficulty.   But the manner in which the correlation is treated in this impasse can no longer be helpful because the real correlation is abolished by the ideas of prescience and condition.[47]

The transition from the idea of a limited foreknowledge, in connection only with unbelief and guilt, to the later idea of foreknowledge, once again in connection with the *praevisa fides,* is clear and informative.   We may disregard the historical question whether Samuel Huber was justified in appealing to the Formula of Concord to defend his universalism.   It is a fact that the problem of the *praescientia* plays an important part in Lutheran theology.   Gerhard says that Christ is the *causa electionis* but *"etiam fidei intuitum decreto electionis esse includendum."*[48] Faith must enter in here and that can only happen if only those are elected of whom God has foreseen that they would truly believe and would persevere in that belief till the end.[49]

Gerhard did not see faith as a *causa meritoria* or *efficiens electionis."*[50]   God has not elected us *"propter fidem";* He elects us *"intuitu fidei"* in Christ.   That is the reason why Gerhard argued against Zanchius, who had declared that when Scripture speaks of election, it does not add one single condition.[51]

45. H. Schmid, *Die Dogmatik der evangelisch-lutherischen Kirche* (1893), pp. 193ff.
46. *Ibid.,* p. 195.
47. So, for instance, Quenstedt (in Schmid, *op. cit.,* p. 207).   See also P. Althaus, *Die Christliche Wahrheit,* II (1948), p. 434.
48. E. V. Gerhard, *Loci Theologici,* II, 86ff.
49. *"Quos — vere credituros et in fide usque ad vitae finem permansuros praevidit"* (*ibid.,* p. 86).
50. *Ibid.,* p. 89.
51. *"Numquam addit conditionem ullam, ergo praeter Scripturam non est addenda quaedam conditio,"* (*ibid.*).

When it is said that election does not find its basis in man's works and therefore not in his foreseen faith, Gerhard answers that we do not teach that it does, but *"intuitum fidei ingredi electionis decretum."* And in this Gerhard sees a radical difference.[52] That is the systematization of the synergistic influence, which has been recognized by Lutheran theologians in later times, among others by Althaus. "Under the influence of Melanchthon the old Lutheran orthodoxy abandons unconditional predestination."[53] Althaus does not even hestitate to refer to Molinism as a parallel, with only this difference that Molinism speaks of merit and Lutheran theology speaks of foreseen faith. No matter how much Althaus criticizes Calvinism, he also criticizes the Lutheran notion of the priority of prescience in predestination.[54]

In such a notion God's decision is made dependent on man's decision. The initiative and the majesty of God's grace is overshadowed. Even if we reject the idea of God being a mere spectator in man's decision, once we yield to the priority of man's decision, we are no longer competent to resist the pressure of the idea that God is a mere onlooker. *Sola gratia* and foreknowledge must be connected in a synthesis. It is the synthesis of synergism in which the significance of the doctrine of election is violated.

In no form of synergism is it possible to escape the conclusion that man owes his salvation not solely to God but also to himself. Still more accurately, he may thank himself — by virtue of his decision to believe — that salvation actually and effectively becomes his in time and eternity. To be sure, synergism is constantly seeking to avoid this conclusion, and it is seldom expressed in so many words that salvation really depends partly on man.[55] Nevertheless, this conclusion cannot in the long run be avoided and it is clear that we actually are confronted here with the real problem of synergism as it results in a certain amount of human self-conceit.

52. *"Inter quas propositiones magna est differentia"* (*ibid.*, p. 90).
53. Althaus, *Die Christliche Wahrheit*, II, 433.
54. *Ibid.*, p. 434.
55. An example of this is found in C. J. de Vogel, *Ecclesia Catholica*, pp. 34ff. "Eternal salvation certainly depends on us. And God's forgiveness, given to us out of sovereign grace in our acceptance as children depends definitely on us." Note the combination of this "depending on us" and "out of sovereign grace."

For if synergism is accepted as a serious solution, man's share in this cooperation must receive attention. For that reason synergism confronts us with a serious religious problem, one that touches on all aspects of the Christian life. For is it possible that this self-consciousness, unavoidable in connection with man's cooperation, still leaves room for a full recognition of God's sovereign grace? Is not grace, as God's decree and gift, limited and obscured by such cooperation and self-consciousness?

These important questions find their illustration in a significant statement by Bavinck. In dealing with the doctrine of God's counsel he speaks of Pelagianism as opposing the sovereign grace of God and adds that "in doctrine one may be Pelagian, but in the practice of the Christian life, especially in prayer, every Christian is Augustinian, for then he declines all glory and gives all the honor to God alone."[56] Bavinck gives here a remarkable, existential application to his argument in connection with man's prayer. There is in it something of Luther's *"coram Deo,"* man before God. Bavinck wants to show that the main concern lies not with a number of logical conclusions drawn from a certain point of view, but that Pelagianism takes an irreligious position which comes into conflict with the nature of true Christian faith and prayer. Obviously he means that Pelagianism implies a view of man which is incompatible with Christian prayer. According to Bavinck it is contrary to the nature of true prayer that man meet God with this feeling of self-consciousness and self-esteem, and with the focus — partial though it may be — on himself, which receives its theological expression in Pelagianism, but also in semi-Pelagianism and in synergism. Such self-esteem is possible in the prayer of the Pharisee but not in the prayer of the publican. Man does mention himself in his prayer, but only as the object of God's mercy. The share of man is his recognition of the one-sidedness of grace, its sovereignty and lack of indebtedness.

With synergism the situation is different, for here one cannot — even if one wants to — escape the contradiction between true prayer and self-esteem. It has been posed that there is a cooperation in grace which, although it is a factor in salvation, does not evoke inordinate self-esteem. This is the same distinction as the one encountered in the doctrine of the meritoriousness

---

56. Bavinck, *op. cit.,* II, 339.   See A. Kuyper, *Calvinisme en Revisie* (1891), pp. 23-24, for exactly the same trend of thought.

of good works, i.e., between merit and achievement by one's own power.[57]

But if we take synergism seriously, then it has never been explained where the difference lies. Nor is it clear why man's decision may and should not be honored — even in his self-esteem — once synergism has been accepted. It is precisely at this point that synergism displays its irreligious character. For it indicates more or less emphatically the function of man as constituent in salvation without fully realizing that the essence of true faith is precisely that faith does not know such a function, but knows only God's sovereign grace. For that reason synergism must have its effects on the confession of the doctrine of election. It will always make it an election based on foreknowledge, i.e., the *praevisa fides,* and so a conditional election, whereby the "high tension" of God's sovereign election is reduced to the level of human decision.

We are the more struck by the frequent occurrence of the synergistic motif in the history of the Church when we remember that synergism always entails the problem we have just discussed. Yet it is encountered nowhere in Scripture. For if anything is clear in Scripture, it is that it nowhere presents the idea of a human-divine complementary relationship. Scripture speaks of the call to faith, conversion, and sanctification, but it never speaks of component factors, functioning side by side, as synergism must and does.

Roman Catholic criticism of the Reformation often says that the Reformation teaches a monergism of grace, an exclusive activity on God's part against which all human endeavor becomes mere nothingness,[58] a divine superiority in which human decisions are no longer of any consequence. But this characterization is unjust and incorrect. The Reformed position is different, opposed as it is to a cooperation which manifests itself in the idea that God's and man's acts are complementary. It is exactly such a complementary relationship that perverts the correlation between faith and grace.

57. See J. v. d. Steegt, *Geef Rekenshap* (1955), p. 53. He says that the Protestant confuses the meaning of the word "merit" and that he sees therein a depreciation of faith. Against that he poses that merit does not disparage grace, "for it is precisely through grace that the works of the believer are meritorious."
58. See especially E. Przywara, *Ringen der Gegenwart* (1929) II, 543ff.

It is understandable that the polemics often concentrated around Paul's admonition: "Work out your own salvation with fear and trembling; for it is God who worketh in you both to will and to work, for his good pleasure" (Phil. 2:12, 13). Paul speaks here of divine as well as human activity, and it is clear that it is not sufficient to call this a paradox, because man's act is connected with the divine act with the word *for*. It is also clear that that word excludes the idea of a complementary relationship and of cooperation. With respect to this and other Scriptural references Calvin argued against "the advocates of free will" who take up those words "as if [they] implied that we are kept partly by the power of God, partly by our own, whereas the very keeping of which the Apostle speaks is itself from heaven" (*Inst.* II, v. 11).

Hulsbosch thinks that Calvin made a mistake here. He, too, with the Roman Catholic Church, emphasizes the word *for* and he adds that "we definitely decline the concept of salvation as coming partly from man and partly from God and we acknowledge with Calvin that our preservation comes from heaven."[59] One could expect that this implies a radical rejection of synergism. But another look shows the opposite to be true, for Hulsbosch seeks the solution for the criticism against the partial activity of man in the concept of the free will. "There is a freedom which man loses in sin, the freedom to direct himself in his own power to God, for all of him is inclined toward evil; alongside of that there is the anthropological freedom of will which is man's own and which cannot be taken away from him.[60] According to Hulsbosch, it is this free will as a human element, an anthropological given, which is "accounted for in grace" and which the Reformation does not even consider.[61]

The Roman Catholic interest in man's activity repeatedly brings synergism to the foreground. It takes the place of the Reformed involvement of salvation with faith. In this involvement faith is really human activity, but it is utterly impossible to speak of this as co-ordination, as a both-this-and-that arrangement, whatever the form into which it is cast.

Reformed theology has been correct in quoting Philippians 2 in answer to this partially-by-God-partially-by-man interpreta-

59. A. Hulsbosch, "De genade in het nieuwe testament" in *Genade en Kerk* (1953), p. 75.
60. *Ibid.*, p. 76.
61. *Ibid.*, p. 77.

tion. This *eudokia* in Scripture must always be understood as an absolute gift, as God's gift "free and independent of all human influence."[62]

To be sure, there is a connection between the divine and the human act. The divine act makes room, leaves open the possibility for man's act. That possibility is not absorbed or destroyed by divine superiority, but created, called forth, by it. And within that "room," that possibility, God's work is honored according to His sovereign pleasure. It is here, within this real realm of possibility, that man's act receives its form, such a form that the nature of his act excludes cooperation; and a relation, altogether different from the one between grace and freedom, becomes visible. This relation has nothing to do with a Reformed dislike for the ontic, as Hulsbosch — as well as Van der Pol — suggests, as if everything develops along ethical-religious lines in contrast to the real aspects of human nature.[63] This contrast is not part of Reformed thought. Rather, religion is no stranger to reality and does not stand antipodal over against the ontic. That does not mean, however, that interest in the anthropological freedom of will may ever become a factor for solving the questions that arise in a discussion on the process of salvation. In the room, the possibility, for man's act, the outlook on the *eudokia* is preserved.

In the light of the evidence of Scripture, Hulsbosch acknowledges with Calvin that "our salvation comes from heaven"[64] This acknowledgment has its legitimate basis in the Reformed rejection of synergism, and it is not accidental that Calvin in his defense against the preachers of free will quoted not only the *for* of Philippians 2, but also I John 5:18, which says that "he that was begotten of God keepeth himself" (*Inst.* II, v, 2). Nor is it surprising that the Reformation — as its confessions show — was very much impressed by Christ's word, "Even so ye also, when ye shall have done all the things that are commanded you, say, We are unprofitable servants; we have done that which it was our duty to do" (Luke 17:10).

62. Kittel, *Theologisches Wörterbuch zum Neuen Testament,* II, 739. Also in Gal. 1:15 the *eudokein* reflects the idea of sovereignty. See Luke 12:32, Luke 2:14 and the whole article by Kittel.
63. Hulsbosch, *op. cit.,* p. 77. Hulsbosch thinks he sees a parallel with the Reformed doctrine of incarnation in which Christ's divine nature does not enter into His human nature.
64. *Ibid.,* p. 75.

Now that we have discussed this striking perspective in the history of doctrine that became visible in the doctrine of election and in the order of salvation that is based on it, we want to point out that in this synergism may be seen a theological formulation of the opposition to the sovereignty of God's grace. To be sure, there is not — except in a few instances such as Pelagianism,[65] which is generally rejected — a denial of election and the necessity of grace. But within the synergistic idea of cooperation the sovereignty of election and grace is in danger.

It is difficult to comprehend the frequency of the synergistic motif when we see how often both Old Testament and New Testament warn against obscuring God's electing grace. We think, for instance, of the warnings against the self-praise of Israel, against Pharisaism and Judaism. Each of these aberrations does not in the first place concern a moral shortage, a formal disobedience, but a stumbling over the *skandalon* of grace. On the other hand, Scripture makes perfectly clear where the origin and preservation of our salvation lies. How can the solution of synergism — also in its interest in the anthropological freedom of will — maintain itself over against the unequivocal words of Christ spoken in a moment of crisis for His people: "No man can come to me, except the Father that sent me draw him" (John 6:44)?

The word *draw* which Christ uses here has always attracted much attention. Kittel says that when it refers to man it has the meaning of *to compel,* of *irresistible superiority,* as in James 2:6

---

65. In Pelagianism we find the clearest idea of free will. It is true that not all grace goes unrecognized in a complete humanism that expects everything from man himself. But this "grace" (in man's own nature, in the law of Moses, and in the example of Christ) does not really close the road to self-esteem because grace and man's nature are practically identical. Pelagianism — usually criticized for its radicalism — can therefore always regain its influence, in its more moderate form, in a practical form of religion in which man has the decision in his own hands. Bicknell writes concerning England: "Pelagianism, however, is very common today. It flourishes especially upon its own native soil. The ordinary respectable Englishman is often a Pelagian at heart, though he has never heard of Pelagius. Apparently he has very little idea of God's intense holiness and the absolute consecration and self-sacrifice that God requires of him. He confuses the standard of Christ with the standard of decent society" (*A Theological Introduction to the Thirty-Nine Articles,* p. 250). It seems unfair to reproach England alone. Where sovereign grace is no longer understood, a view of life prevails of which Pelagianism can be called the theological formulation.

where the rich *drag* the poor before the judge, and as Paul and
Silas are *dragged* into the market place in Acts 16:19.

Criticism of synergism has often — and not incorrectly —
proceeded from the radical, the unequivocal nature of this word
draw. And indeed, the word touches the core of the doctrine of
election. The history of the doctrine shows that the danger of a
deterministic interpretation of the word was often feared. But
this fear often led to a tempering of the altogether merciful and
sovereign superiority of the divine act of election, and to the establishing of the "counterpoise" — man's freedom to decide —
which was to be a component factor in bringing about man's salvation. Thus, the "room," the possibility, for man's activity
had to be created.

We certainly do not lose sight of this idea of "room" in the
gospel.[66] As a matter of fact, it is emphatically pointed out to
us in John 6:37: "All that which the Father giveth me shall come
unto me; and him that cometh to me I will in no wise cast out."
See also John 6:44. But he who would draw the conclusion here
of synergism and the concept of cooperation forgets how much
that "coming" rests upon and finds its cause in the "being
drawn" and "being given."[67] This indeed is the marvelous and
inscrutable work of the Holy Spirit, that in and through this
superiority man really comes, is placed, in this realm of possibility, in this freedom. This "drawing" of the Father is not
at all an act that rules out all human activity; rather, says Kittel, it rules out all that is coercive and magical. It is the profound
reality described in the joyful words of Jeremiah: "O Jehovah,

66. Compare with this frequent Roman Catholic criticism of the Reformation the words by Barth about the fear-complex: "As if God were
a stranger to His creature, an opponent, perhaps even an enemy; as if
the more the creature could find a space of his own which he could keep
securely barricaded against God the better it would be for the liberty
and justice, honor and dignity of man; the more this space were diminished, the worse it would be; and were it taken from him completely
it would be still worse" (*Kirchliche Dogmatik,* III, 3, 166). "As if man's
freedom could be endangered by God, as if it would be good to protect
oneself against such intrusion under the safe shelter of some form of
synergism!" (*ibid.*).

67. Not only the word *to drag* deserves attention but also *to give,* since it
occurs as a central word in Scripture, e.g., God's *giving* (of Christ's
works), John 5:36; the *gift* of faith, Eph. 2:8; the *gift* of grace in Jesus
Christ, Rom. 5:16; etc. See further Kittel, *op. cit.,* II, 168ff., and
Christ's *giving* as in Matt. 20:28, Mark 10:45.

thou hast persuaded me, and I was persuaded; thou art stronger than I, and hast prevailed" (Jer. 20:7).

There is a superiority which is not that of a mechanical causality or of a coercion that obstructs man's activity; it is the personal superiority of love and grace, which in man's experience is making room for him to act by not destroying his freedom. And within this "room," the "thou" of Jeremiah is understood as the exclusive and profound source of all salvation.

It is good to observe that Christ employs the word *draw* when human resistance against His gospel seems at its strongest (John 6:41, 42). In that situation Christ knew that "everyone that hath heard from the Father, and hath learned, cometh unto me" (John 6:45).

To hear, to learn, to be drawn, to be given, and *then* to come — that is the evangelical incursion of all synergism. It is the reference to God's electing grace (cf. John 3:27), which in faith and experience is understood, not as a coercion and an annihilating superiority which takes away man's very breath, but as divine liberation.

This absoluteness of giving, drawing, and learning we meet not only in John, but also in the radical and exclusive testimony of Paul when he says, for instance, that *"no* man can say, Jesus is Lord, but in the Holy Spirit" (I Cor. 12:3). The message of Scripture repeatedly accentuates that human inability. The impotence of man is not something pessimism has discovered; it is most literally described in Scripture (cf. John 3:27, I Cor. 2:14, Rom. 8:5, 6, 7, 8). The Jews thought themselves to be free but they were to be free only after having been liberated by Christ. Until then, they live in slavery, in spite of all their activity. Their activity is not irrelevant. Rather, their activity proves that they are *willing* slaves. Paul says that men present themselves as servants to iniquity (Rom. 6:16), as the servants of sin (Rom. 6:16), and as servants of lust and sensual pleasure (Titus 3:3). It was the time that man lived in bondage to gods that were no gods (Gal. 4:8), man went his own way, in his so-called freedom, unconscious of his slavery but nonetheless subject to it in all of his existence. "No man can come to me, except the Father draw him."

It is not difficult to realize that synergism usually originated as a defense against and reaction to fatalism and determinism. But the fact that a defense is necessary does not make synergism

legitimate. Scripture fully honors man's activity; it calls for it
and stimulates it, but never makes it part of a synergistic synthesis. The relationship between the source of salvation in God
and the decision of man can never be presented as a co-ordinate
relationship, no matter how refined and ingeniously construed
it may be. Rather, the sphere of human activity and decision is,
and remains bound to be, the exclusive and gracious act of God.
in which faith finds rest. This activity of man — crowned by
beatifications (cf. Matt. 11:6, 16:17, 15:28) — is nevertheless
subject to the gift of grace.

In the light of the gospel it is foolish to let man's acts and
decision shrink to nothingness in a system of monergism. But
it is the nature of the relationship between God's grace and
man's act that is at stake. In the struggle of the Church to
understand this relationship the influence of the Scriptures repeatedly made itself felt. When the Formula of Concord rejected Melanchthon's synergism, it did mention "cooperation,"[68]
but at the same time it immediately limited this cooperation
and made it free of synergistic motifs. To be sure, man does
not receive grace in vain, but the Formula of Concord rejects
the notion "that converted man worked alongside of, cooperated
with, the Holy Spirit the way two horses pull a cart together."[69]

We realize that there are many who essentially adhere to the
synergistic concept but nevertheless say they agree with this
rejection because it is a rejection of an oversimplified formulation. Hulsbosch certainly will not recognize such a sharing of
activity as his view. He thinks in terms of a "mystery" rather
than a "distribution of work." But no matter how refined synergism is, the force of the opposition cannot be weakened and
undermined.

Paradoxical as it may sound, one can truly speak of cooperation only when synergism has been completely denounced.
Only then will it be possible to prevent tension between sanctification and justification; and only then will sanctification not
lead to the self-conceit which can be correlated with the merit
of good works. Only when we reject synergism — also in the
form of prescience — shall we be able to obtain the correct
religious insight into the sovereignty of God's merciful election.

68. J. T. Müller, *op. cit.*, p. 604.
69. *Ibid.*

As we shall later see, in Scripture the election of God is always characterized by its own special formulation — it does not come out of works but out of grace. It is wholly on the basis of His calling, Paul writes (Rom. 9:11), and this holy calling is "not according to our works, but according to his own purpose and grace, which was given us in Christ Jesus" (I Tim. 1:9).

The doctrine of election has often been called the heart of the Church. There are some who see in it rather a menace for the Church because speculative thinking can so easily overshadow it and rob it of its comfort. But we shall not hesitate to continue to speak of the *cor ecclesiae*. For we are not concerned with the copestone of the structure of our speculation, but with the "lovingkindness" and the "tender mercies" of Psalm 33 and Psalm 25.

This is not the presentation of a kind, humanized God, removed from the fullness of divine revelation; but of the true grace that appeared in Christ Jesus. This is no monergism in the sense that all life around this gift is empty and meaningless. On the contrary, Scripture bears testimony in doxological terms to the grace that brings salvation (Titus 2:11) through Him who gave Himself to set us free. (Titus 2:14).

Nowhere in Scripture does election take on the character of an abstraction. The point in electing grace is God's "tender mercy and lovingkindness" which *by faith* is understood as a miracle, as a light shining in the darkness, as the sovereignty of God. The doctrine of election is a continual reminder that all human glory, all self-conceit is impossible.

That is the reason the doctrine of election has repeatedly become the focal point of contention in Church and theology. Now and then it may have been put aside as a speculative doctrine, as a menace to the consolation of salvation and to the simplicity of faith, but it has repeatedly returned to the foreground to ask all our attention. And this is not a matter of a Reformed peculiarity which somehow can be understood as a desire for a metaphysical system of cosmology in which everything is derived from God.[70] Nor should it be understood as the courage

---

70. Cf. *Bijbels Kerkelijk Woordenboek*, "De Kerk," p. 309: "Only the Reformed still adhere to predestination"; cf. *Religion in Geschichte und Gegenwart*, IV², 1375, on "Prädestination": "It could only have developed on Reformed soil."

to draw dire consequences from an apriori concept of God[71] or from the pessimistic view of man who in his state of damnation can do nothing but bend silently and submissively to the hidden God.[72] If all that — or some of it — were true, we could scarcely speak of the doctrine of election as the heart of the Church. We suggest that in the midst of the polemics that surround election — synergism in all its aspects — we can still discover how the heart of the Church is involved because the heart of God is involved.

This explains why election has not been discussed apathetically as if it were the same as fate. It explains why so much opposition could arise against this *skandalon*. To be sure, that opposition could also rise against caricatures. But our concern is that there has been opposition to electing grace, to the grace which — for all time — frustrates all human vanity and yet evokes a gratitude akin to adoration.

He who is not altogether unfamiliar with the questions that have come up in the course of a long history and with the dangers that have threatened the doctrine of election will understand that we must direct our attention to two questions that have been decisive in guiding the thinking of many theologians. First of all, many have questioned whether in considering the electing God we do not discover arbitrariness in God (see Chap. 3). And when — except at the periphery of the Church and theology — this question is answered in the negative, another question comes up. It concerns the relationship between election and mystery (see Chap. 4), a question which has always come to the fore in connection with the certainty of salvation. Along these two roads we want to approach the election in Christ (see Chap. 5), the center and the mystery of the Biblical message of election.

---

71. See about Calvinism: J. de Zwaan, *Jezus, Paulus en Rome* (1927), p. 27: "That vertigo before God, that feeling of God's infinite majesty vibrates as keynote through the harmonies of Calvin's logic. Calvin is really a theologian of feeling. The feeling of nothingness in the face of the Infinite dominates everything he says," while "the God of his thinking is different from the God and Father of Jesus Christ."

72. Cf. M. Beversluis, *De Dwalingen van het Calvinisme* (1906), p. 7: "This root of the Reformed teaching, or Calvinism, is the doctrine of man's damnableness."

CHAPTER THREE

ELECTION AND ARBITRARINESS

ONE of the most profound questions which repeatedly confront us in the confession of our faith is the question concerning the difference between God's election and arbitrariness. Frequently in the course of the centuries the free and sovereign election of God has been attacked with the argument that this doctrine leaves us at the mercy of an arbitrary God.

This form of criticism has been nourished by a frequent presentation of God's election in a manner that made it difficult to distinguish it from arbitrariness. A survey of the history of the doctrine in relation to arbitrariness recalls the Occamistic nominalism, which posed that God was the great *Exlex*, and, more common, the concept of *potentia absoluta,* the power before whose completely inscrutable arbitrariness man has no choice but to bend.

We pose these questions at the very beginning of our inquiry because the issue of arbitrariness is not a minor question. Its implications are far reaching. For if we identify God's election with arbitrariness we do not bring this arbitrariness into one locus of the dogmatic system while we speak in other loci of God's faithfulness and immutability, but the identification of the election of God with arbitrariness would influence our entire mode of thinking and speaking of God. In other words, we must make a decision here which is of importance for the whole dogmatic system, for all preaching, and for all of man's religious life. The immediate discussion of these questions may be indicative of their urgency. This urgency becomes more apparent since there is apriori evidence in the message of the gospel that God in all His acts is a reliable, not an arbitrary, God. We want to discuss that apriori evidence in this chapter, for it is good to be conscious, right from the beginning, of the fact that at this juncture we can joyfully and undauntedly choose only one road to travel.

When the question is asked what we must understand by arbitrariness and why the Church has an intuitive aversion to speaking of arbitrariness in God, it is not easy to find an answer. This becomes especially evident when we attempt to distinguish sovereignty from arbitrariness. Yet, it is necessary to do so because they who want to avoid any thought of arbitrariness in God want at the same time to continue to speak of His sovereignty, of that sovereignty which is not bound to any law.

When we speak of arbitrariness in a man, the meaning of it is clear. Arbitrariness becomes visible in the actions of a man who decides and chooses without taking into account any norm or law above himself, with the result that at one time he acts this way, at another, that way. Human arbitrariness is always without norm. That explains why to our mode of thinking arbitrariness is something objectionable. Man's life is not protected against arbitrariness; it is in constant peril of it. It loses the stability and safety, the orderliness and protection, on which it could thus far rely in the non-arbitrariness of good regulation.

Thus in the arbitrary totalitarian state man's life is principally given over to legal insecurity. In this manner life is in danger in every state where the idea of *princeps legibus solutus est* rules. Defense against arbitrariness is therefore only possible when one has his life anchored to a law or authority that stands above life, a law to which also the authorities are subject. Only in such non-arbitrariness life can find stability and restfulness. In the light of Biblical testimony it is precisely by virtue of the authority established by God that arbitrariness is ruled out and condemned by God's sovereignty, which forms the enduring foundation of all authority. We can see that clearly in the King's Law of Deuteronomy 17. When Israel was to have a king, sitting on the royal throne, he was to have a copy prepared of the King's Law, which he had always to carry with him and in which he was to read all his life, "that he may learn to fear Jehovah his God, to keep all the words of this law and these statutes, to do them" (Deut. 17:19).

No danger could be greater than that his heart be lifted against his brothers and that he turn aside from the commandment "to the right hand, or to the left." All arbitrariness in royal authority was excluded by the warnings in the King's Law. Such arbitrariness would only be possible in flagrant illegality and disobedience. Royal authority could only be a blessing when it was and remained non-arbitrary, bound by law and put under norms — *auctoritas normata,* and only for that reason *auctoritas normans.* In the history of Israel's kings we repeatedly see evidence of terrible arbitrariness, when the violation of the King's Law led to the dislocation of social life down to its lowest stratum.

However, it is quite impossible to gain any clarity in this or a similar manner about arbitrariness in God. The argument that suffices to rule out human arbitrariness is completely insignificant with respect to God, for it is impossible to subject Him to a law above Himself to curb His arbitrariness. There is no norm above Him by which His sovereignty could be limited. If we think of the law as an entity above and beyond someone, then we can certainly speak of God as *exlex.*

The curbing of arbitrariness, sufficient and clear in the case of man by virtue of the law above him, is meaningless with respect to God, unless we should assume that He, too, is subject to all sorts of norms and ordinances, to authorities of all kinds, to concepts, eternal ideas, and truths. That, of course, is a thought which cannot be supported by any single reference in Scripture. On the contrary, Scripture definitely rejects such a thought. For that very reason it is difficult to find the words with which to distinguish between sovereignty and arbitrariness in God. For with respect to God there is no authority that can call Him to account, and it is precisely this "calling to account" that is characteristic of and essential to the defense against arbitrariness.

That is the reason why it is impossible to protest against the concept of arbitrariness in God by comparing it to arbitrariness in man. That is perhaps also the reason why in the history of Church and theology the concept of arbitrariness has been applied to God. The intention was not to indicate thereby something objectionable in God, something inferior in analogy to human arbitrariness, but to accentuate the radical independence of God from every norm or law placed above Him. The attempt was not to carry over and apply to God the arbitrariness and anarchistic traits of man but to speak of that which was sovereign-divine, and to point out that the essence of His sovereignty lay precisely therein that He never could be called to account.

What with man became a horror in his arbitrary actions without norm, with God would be nothing else but the riches of His unlimited will and majesty, uncurbed by any norm. When Paul finishes chapters 9 to 11 of Romans, he says, "For who hath known the mind of the Lord, or who hath been his counsellor?"

(Rom. 11:34).[1] The word *counsellor* indicates someone who co-
wills, who participates in the making of plans. Such willing is
impossible for man with respect to God. The question, "Who
hath been his counsellor?" needs no answer. For the question
refers to the depths of the riches of the wisdom and the
knowledge of God (Rom. 11:33), and there is no counsellor
possible, and consequently no authority which could from the
outside protect the sovereignty against the strain of arbitrariness. For this reason some people have not hesitated to speak
of divine arbitrariness.

It is striking, however, that in spite of the above reasoning,
seemingly so clear, the history of Church and theology has often
seen violent opposition to the use of the idea of arbitrariness with
respect to God Men have been unanimously averse to it and apparently were afraid that the use of this term would disparage
the holiness and trustworthiness of God. This protest did
not originate from the desire to subject God after all to a law
beyond and above Himself. On the contrary, confession of God's
unfathomable sovereignty went hand in hand with this protest
against the idea of arbitrariness in Him. It is therefore necessary
to go further in order to understand this protest.

The protest motif came sharply to the fore in Calvin's resistance to the idea of God as *exlex* (*Inst.* III, xxiii, 20). It is
important to investigate what Calvin meant with this resistance.
Did he want to see God after all as subject to laws and norms and
did he want to counteract divine arbitrariness in the same manner as human arbitrariness, i.e., by pointing to a higher law?
Did he perhaps want to decree a divine "King's Law" in order
to curb sovereignty by means of an absolute world order to
which even God would be subject? On the contrary, Calvin attempted to reject all human audaciousness. They are, he said,
foolish people who contend with God as if God would be subject to their accusations. He referred here to the accusation of
arbitrariness — the *libido tyranni* — and opposed it by saying

1. Cf. Isa. 40:13, 14: "Who hath directed the Spirit of Jehovah, or being
his counsellor hath taught him? With whom took he counsel, and who
instructed him, and taught him in the path of justice, and taught him
knowledge, and showed to him the way of understanding?" Cf. the
divine irony in Job 40:7: "Gird up thy loins now like a man: I will
demand of thee, and declare thou unto me." The exclusion of a counsellor has its basis in "of him, and through him, and unto him, are all
things" (Rom. 11:36).

that it is presumptuous "to inquire into the causes of the Divine will." This, he said, is impossible, for if God's will has any cause, there must be something antecedent to it "to which it is annexed; this it were impious to imagine" (*Inst.* III, xxiii, 2).[2] For God in His will is the cause of all things that are and His will is "the supreme rule of righteousness; so that everything which he wills must be held to be righteous by the mere fact of his willing it" (*ibid.*). The question why God has done something can only be answered by referring to His will. If you want to go still further and know why He has so willed, "you ask for something greater and more sublime than the will of God, and nothing such can be found" (*ibid.*). This bridle is necessary in the light of all human audaciousness.

In acknowledging God's will as the last and highest cause, Calvin protected his opinion against the fiction of the "absolute power" of God. "We, however, give no countenance to the fiction of absolute power, which, as it is heathenish, so it ought justly to be held in detestation by us. We do not imagine God to be lawless. He is a law to himself; because, as Plato says, men laboring under the influence of concupiscence need law; but the will of God is not only free from all vice, but is the supreme standard of perfection, the law of all laws" (*ibid.*).

This reference of Calvin to the *potentia absoluta* is unexpected. It is clear that in his attack against that notion he did not want to diminish the absolute power of God. He was apparently thinking of a special "absolute power" which he rejected as unholy. He resisted the idea of arbitrariness in the *potentia absoluta*. It is the concept of the *exlex* which he opposed with the remark that God is a law unto Himself. Calvin did not reason by starting from a law standing above God; he wanted to point to the God who is above all arbitrariness. By *potentia absoluta* he did not refer to the confession of the unfathomable will of God, but to a notion which he, as he said elsewhere, had encountered in scholastic writings and by which — as he saw it — the true sovereignty and trustworthiness of God is seriously violated.[3]

2. "*Nam si ullam causam habet, aliquid eam antecedat oportet, cui veluti alligeretur: quod nefas est imaginari*" (III, xxiii, 2).
3. In the *Institutes* Calvin does not further describe this notion, but in his commentary on Isa. 23:9 he discusses the same matter. "*Nam commentum illud de absoluta potentia Dei, quod Scholastici invexerunt, execranda blasphemia est,*" and he continues, "*Idem enim est ac si Deum tyrannum quendam esse dicerent, pro libidine, non aequitate quidvis*

On the one hand Calvin rejected arbitrariness and lawlessness, and on the other hand he denied that God must give an account of Himself.[4] He never accepted a law above God, but he
definitely refused to detach God's power and sovereignty from
His justice by using the idea of arbitrariness. Nor would he understand the divine will to be a power in itself, which could only
be curbed by a formal omnipotence. Whenever Calvin spoke of

---

statuentem. Talibus blasphemiis refertae sunt eorum scholae: neque
absimiles sunt ab Ethnicis qui Deum in rebus humanis ludere aiebant."
He opposes the idea of arbitrariness in God with: "Iustas igitur causas
tanti excidii refert propheta, ne Deum sine ratione quidquam agere exis-
timemus." About the notion of the absolute power of God Calvin also
speaks in "Altera Responsio de occulta Dei providentia" in Corpus
Reformatorum, IX, col. 288. Here we find an answer to the accusations against Calvin's teachings. "Itaque quod de absoluta potestate
nugantur Scholastici non solum repudio, sed etiam detestor, quia justi-
tiam eius ab imperio separant . . . Ego Dei arbitrio humanum genus
subiiciens clare affirmo nihil eum decernere sine optima causa, quae si
hodie nobis incognita est, ultimo diei patefaciet." Finally we refer to
Calvin's Institutes I, xvii, 2, where he speaks of the depths of the providence of God: ". . . let it be our law of modesty and soberness to acqui-
esce in his supreme authority, regarding his will as our only rule of
justice, and the most perfect cause of all things, — not that absolute
will, indeed, of which the sophists prate, when by a profane and impious
divorce, they separate his justice from his power, but that universal
overruling providence from which nothing flows that is not right,
though the reasons thereof may be concealed." In Calvin's commentary
on Rom. 9:21 he says of St. Paul: "He intends not to claim for God
any arbitrary power but what ought to be justly ascribed to him,"
cf. the expression "potestas inordinata," arbitrary power.

4. See Calvin's words quoted by P. Marcel, "La conception de la loi chez
Duns Scotus," in Philosophia Reformata, II, 244-47. According to Calvin, God's sovereignty does not imply an arbitrarily turning of His will
in all directions because he knows that God's goodness is undetachably
linked up with His power. See what Calvin says in Institutes, II, iii, 5:
"The goodness of God is so connected with his Godhead, that it is not more
necessary to be God than to be good." It is clear that we are here far
removed from any deterministic idea of necessity. The word necessitas
does not indicate a law above God, but the fullness of His attributes.
Calvin's thought is very different from the one of the late Scholastics
with whom the infinity of divine possibilities find their boundary in the
logical contradiction. See W. Link, Das Ringen Luthers um die Freiheit der Theologie von der Philosophie (1940), p. 275. Such a hyposta-
tization of the law of logic is impossible for Calvin. This "order" cannot be seen as standing above God in order thus to limit His possibilities.
Rather, each law has its basis in the will of God. To pose this has
nothing to do with nominalism. It all depends in which manner and in
which connection one speaks of the will of God.

these things he repeatedly spoke of the impossibility of separating God's power from His justice and holiness. That is what he opposed in the horrible notion of the *potentia absoluta,* which entailed for him something altogether different from the fullness and riches of divine sovereignty. For that reason he employed the expression that God is a law unto Himself, an expression in which he rejected the *potentia absoluta* as well as a law above God (*Inst.* III, xxiii, 2). It is the will of the God who is a law unto Himself that Calvin called "pure" and perfect. In other words, in his rejection of the *potentia absoluta* he pointed to the perfection of all God's virtues. This, in all modesty and reverence, is the ultimate of what can be said.[5]

The same problem that occupied Calvin[6] engages Bavinck's attention. He speaks of it especially when he discusses the concept of absolute freedom in nominalism. He acknowledges at the outset that the Christian Church has always spoken of the freedom of God's will.[7] With Calvin he points to Augustine who saw in the will of God the last and most profound foundation of all things, so that it is not permissible to inquire after a more fundamental basis.

Then Bavinck discusses the view of Duns Scotus who, he says, made the mistake of applying the Pelagian concept of free will, *liberum arbitrium,* to God, and who thus arrived at a total irrationality on the part of God. In the dis-

5. See J. Bohatec, *Bude und Calvin, Studien zur Gedankenwelt des französischen Frühhumanismus* (1950), pp. 325ff. on "Der Autoritätsgedanke in der Gotteslehre Calvins" and especially pp. 333ff, about "absolute power" and the *exlex.*

6. Repeatedly Calvin has been accused of adhering to the concept of arbitrariness in God, for instance, by A. Ritschl in *Geschichtl. Studien zur Chr. Lehre von Gott* (*Jahrbücher für deutsche Theologie,* 1868). In spite of Calvin's opinion as presented above, Ritschl brings Calvin's theology in direct connection with the differentiation between *potentia ordinata* and *inordinata* (*absoluta*). But Bohatec states that Schleiermacher attempted "to turn away the reproach of arbitrariness from Calvin's concept of God" (*Calvins Vorsehungslehre* [*Calvinstudien,* 1909], p. 398). Schleiermacher's trend of thought *ad hoc* (also about Calvin) can only be understood if his discussion of *arbitrariness* is considered with it. He offers it in *Der Christliche Glaube,* (6th ed., 1884), II, 261, where he attacks the idea of arbitrariness in God from his point of view on election. Otherwise the "appearance of divine arbitrariness of an immutable divine decree over the individual" cannot be avoided. One wonders whether there is essentially a great difference between Schleiermacher's and Ritschl's judgment on Calvin.

7. Bavinck, *Gereformeerde Dogmatiek,* II, 203.

cussion on Scotus we again encounter the problem of the difference between sovereignty and arbitrariness. Bavinck quotes
many of Scotus' statements which are similar to those of Augustine and, later, of Calvin; for example, that we must not try
to go beyond the will of God who wills it thus. He also cites
Scotus when the latter says that there is no reason more
basic to be found than the decision of God.[8] But Bavinck's
criticism begins when he encounters a concept of sovereignty
in Scotus which elevates this decision of God so much that the
means that lead toward the goal become entirely arbitrary.[9]
Later — according to Bavinck — Occam went still further, and
it was especially nominalism that caused Christian theology
to be on its guard against this accentuation of the sovereignty of
God. The actual objection comes down to this that God's sovereignty was presented as a strictly formal one, detached from all
God's virtues and taking on the nature of arbitrariness.

Over against every thought of arbitrariness and lawlessness
Bavinck poses the wisdom of God and, like Calvin, speaks of
reasons which, though we cannot trace them, do nevertheless
exist. This reference to the wisdom of God and Calvin's statement that God is "a law unto himself," do not assume a cause
more basic than the will of God, but rather is the pertinent denial
of such a cause. Bavinck wants to say with Thomas and Augustine[10] that there is no *cause* for the will of God, but that this will
is nonetheless not without *ratio*. This does not mean a *ratio* independent and apart from God; it is a reference to the riches and
harmony of all God's virtues.[11]

The great problem with which we are confronted in the
questions regarding arbitrariness is concentrated in the fact
that the protest against arbitrariness in God does not imply an

8. *Ibid.*, p. 204: *"voluntas Dei vult hoc."* There is no cause *"prior ratione
voluntatis."*
9. *Ibid.*, p. 205. Bavinck speaks of "formal arbitrariness," a term in which
the profoundness of the problem is reflected.
10. *Ibid.*, p. 209, on St. Augustine, Thomas, and Calvin.
11. *Ibid.* To be sure, says Bavinck, the point at issue is an "absolute
sovereignty," but then the sovereignty of "a wise, just, holy, merciful, and
omnipotent God." For arbitrariness with respect to the unlimited power
in the Islam, see S. L. Bakker, *De Verhouding Tussen de Almacht Gods en
de Zedelijke Verantwoordelijkheid van den Mensch in den Islam* (1922),
pp. 192ff.

attempt to limit His power and sovereignty; this protest is
raised to place the nature of the divine will and power in a
clear light.[12] We touch here immediately upon the questions
that have always arisen in connection with the power, the omnipotence, of God. He who employs a purely formal concept
of omnipotence and approaches God's omnipotence from the aspect of that formal power has difficulty imagining that Scripture can speak so calmly and freely of what He cannot do, for
instance, when we read that God cannot deny Himself (II Tim.
2:13). On the basis of a formal concept of omnipotence —
omnipotence *in abstracto* — one could see in such speaking a
limitation of God's power, or even an abolishing of His omnipotence. But in the Biblical message about God there is no
mention of "limitation"; there is only a revelation of the riches
and full power and magnificence of God.[13] That we can do
things which God cannot do certainly does not indicate man's
superiority or prerogative. On the contrary, God's unchangeability is just the opposite of the uncertainty, the arbitrariness,
and the "capabilities" of man. "God is not a man, that he
should lie, neither the son of man, that he should repent"
(Num. 23:19; see also I Sam. 15:29, Ps. 89:36, Titus 1:2,
Heb. 6:18). He is the complete opposite of all untrustworthi-
ness and inconstancy, as Balaam testified of Him when he said

12. See for Bavinck's point of view also his *Gereformeerde Dogmatiek*,
II, 218, where he discusses the distinction between *potentia absoluta* and
normata. This distinction was recognized by Reformed theology only
to a certain degree. Bavinck points out that Calvin did not deny that
God could do more than He did, but he refused to accept a *potentia absoluta* not bound to His essence and virtues and for that reason
capable of engaging in contradictory works. When we reject
this kind of arbitrariness then the distinction mentioned can
serve to indicate that, in contrast to pantheism, not all characteristics of
contingency can be taken from the world (p. 219). This recognition
has nothing to do with an existential concept of contingency because
with Bavinck the "contingence" functions over against the thought that
non-existence of the world would mean a logical contradiction (p. 219).
By "contingent" Bavinck does not mean "the accidental" over against
"the inevitable" (E. Troeltsch, "Die Bedeutung des Begriffs der
Kontingenz" in *Gesammelte Schriften*, II, 771ff.); he means by it what
Troeltsch calls "the creative freedom of God (*ibid.*, p. 778).
13. Cf. the *"non potest mori"* of Augustine and his *"non potest non
amare"* (H. Deppe, *Dogmatik* [1861], p. 78). Bavinck also emphatically
declares that God's not being able to does not imply a lack of power but
a true, absolute power (*Gereformeerde Dogmatiek*, II, 218). See also
K. Barth, *Kirchliche Dogmatik*, II, 1, 635ff.

to Balak, "Hath he said, and will he not do it? Or hath he spoken, and will he not make it good?" (Num. 23:19).

Scripture defines in many ways what John would sum up later in the words "in him is no darkness at all" (I John 1:5).[14] Here, in opposition to heresy and lack of appreciation, John uses a negation in order to point to Him who will not lie and is called the Strength of Israel (I Sam. 15:29). This unchangeability does not contradict that inability (as to deny Himself) or the impossibility spoken of in Hebrews 6:18 but coincides with it. If God is different from man (Num. 23:19, I Sam. 15:29) then our ability to do certain things does not mean that we have more power than He; but if we do things which God cannot do, then our importance and inability stand therein in contrast to his unchangeability and faithfulness.

According to Scripture our salvation can be said to lie not only with what God can do and does, but also with what is "impossible" for Him. We must not think that these are paradoxical expressions that should not be taken too seriously. For it is precisely in these expressions that Scripture offers us a clear view of the fullness of God's true power, of His holy and unassailable acts, of His elevation and trustworthiness. In this view of God all apriori resistance against arbitrariness in God is born and grows strong in the knowledge of this God.

It all depends, then, on what we understand by absolute power. The protest against the term *potentia absoluta* was not directed against the absoluteness of divine power, but against its unbiblical formalization. Because of this formalization — the formal omnipotence we have been discussing — the divine will and power as "absolute" *liberum arbitrium* obtained the features of arbitrariness and automatically became a menacing shadow in the background of the historical order of salvation. God certainly did will and ordain (*potentia ordinata*) that order of salvation, but what He ordained can never be considered apart from the *potentia absoluta* which not only could have done things very differently, but is still able to affect the *potentia ordinata* at any time.

This shows us the reason for the protest against arbitrariness in God. In spite of the emphatic declaration that what is meant

14. See R. Schnackenburg, *Die Johannesbriefe* (1953), p. 67. After the statement "God is light" comes "the continuation in the negative" (no darkness at all) to bring out "the shadowless holiness of the divine essence."

is not the kind of arbitrariness found in man, His will is still spoken of in such a manner that the stability and trustworthiness of God's revelation become a controversial issue. The way which God went was His way and the revealed will His will; but that which came to us via this way was after all *hic et nunc* His way and work only in point of fact, and it was possible for this order of salvation to have been abolished by virtue of the absolute freedom of God. In such a situation we may be admonished to adhere to the revealed order of salvation, but counteracting that admonition might be the notion that God could still will and decide differently.

Hence, it should not surprise us that in the nominalism of the late scholastic period the idea of arbitrariness, with the menace of the accompanying uncertainty, loomed so large that the theologians, seeking compensation for it, looked for support to the factually absolute authority of the Church. Once reflection had begun on the basis of the formal and absolute power of God, it was practically a matter of course that divine predestination was also taken into consideration. That is the reason why Feckes was justified in summing up Biel's nominalistic theology in the words, "Also with respect to predestination one must not forget that it is contingent, because it rests on a contingent act of the will of God and on a contingent merit. For that reason the predestinated could not be predestinated and subsequently be damned; nor is the reverse possible."[15] The concept of divine arbitrariness is not placed parallel to the order of salvation; it makes an incursion into it and affects the certainty of salvation to its very roots. And not one compensation, neither the authority of the Church nor the merit of good works, is able to furnish

---

15. Carl Feckes, *Die Rechtfertigungslehre des Gabriel Biel und ihre Stelle innerhalb der nominalistischen Schule* (1925), p. 88. In order to have a clear understanding of what is presented in the text, it must be remembered that predestination in nominalism is weakened to the level of *praescientia*. See on the "contingent predestination" S. U. Zuidema, *De Philosophie van Occam in Zijn Commentaar op de Sententiën* (1936) pp. 168ff., and further the entire chapter for the concept "incidentally gracious" (p. 167). This nominalistic doctrine is very closely connected with the concept of the so-called *acceptilatio* in the doctrine of reconciliation and also with the certainty of salvation and the merit of good works in semi-Pelagian fashion. It is not surprising that in this atmosphere the semi-Pelagian notions could take root. With reference to divine arbitrariness and human activity — *meritum* — Zuidema says correctly: "Thus the certainty of predestination is suffocated by divine and human arbitrariness" (p. 169).

a counterweight to what happens here. Arbitrariness in God makes human life arbitrary also, without foundation and without perspective. Normativity is sacrificed to the factualness of contingent being; consequently, the theological concept of arbitrariness in God can be secularized into a change-contingence in which there is no ground for comfort. It must be acknowledged, therefore, that the intuitive aversion of the Church and theology to the concept of arbitrariness in God has been of decisive importance for the recognition of the dangers that threaten the road that leads to salvation.

It has repeatedly been asked whether the idea of arbitrariness in God is not clearly present when Scripture speaks of the relationship between God and man. Is it not unavoidable here to speak of divine arbitrariness and is it not also an unavoidable subjective correlate that we in mute submission — or in defiance and fear — are subject to this divine arbitrariness? In this connection the Biblical idea of divine election has often been pointed out in particular. Does not divine election place us before an arbitrary God who decides, acts, and wills, not in reaction to human deeds, and not on the level of good order and morality, but according to the absolute *liberum arbitrium* in which He elects and rejects? It is not difficult to see that especially this concept of arbitrariness seems to be meant here.

This is specifically the case with respect to some references in Romans 9-11, especially chapter 9, where there is mention of the potter and the clay and of a divine distinction between the destinies of Jacob and Esau, the latter accompanied by the words, "being not yet born, neither having done anything good or bad" (Rom. 9:11 and 9:20ff.). It has been asked whether this was not an arbitrary act of God, without any order, form, or meaning. Are we here not asked to submit to divine arbitrariness because, after all, we *are* subject to it? "But, O man, who art thou that repliest against God?"

Does not Paul say emphatically: "Shall the thing formed say to him that formed it, Why didst thou make me thus? (Rom. 9:20). Do we not have the impression that Paul is presenting the idea of divine arbitrariness when he says, "Hath not the potter a right over the clay, from the same lump to make one part a vessel unto honor and another unto dishonor?" (Rom. 9:21). Is not this free decree, this *exousia,* a decree which may well be identified with what we call arbitrariness? Or is there a profound and essential difference?

It cannot be denied that these words of Paul place strong emphasis on God's sovereign decree, His divine freedom, and His mighty acts, which are completely beyond all human criticism. In this divine *exousia* it is a matter of that absolute divine freedom "over against which every inquiry into the relationship between the power and the righteousness of this *exousia* is futile because He is the source of both."[16]

Indeed, we are dealing here with an unassailable and undeniable freedom, and there can be no doubt that Paul thinks this freelom is not in any way limited by human pretentiousness. The deciding question is whether it is correct to identify this freedom and sovereignty with arbitrariness. When we reflect on this question we must remember that Paul's reference to the freedom of God is correlated not with mute submission and fear, but with adoration! For although God is unsearchable in all His ways, this unsearchableness is not coolly and abstractly stated; it is inserted in a song of adoration: "O the depth of the riches both of the wisdom and the knowledge of God! how unsearchable are his judgements, and his ways past tracing out!" (Rom. 11:33). Precisely in this passage, where Paul rejects the notion of man as counsellor (Rom. 11:34), this jubilant praise is given. That is for us men — with all our problems — the profoundest exegetical secret of Romans 9 to 11. That this is possible and real — the secret of this relationship between human adoration and divine freedom — that is as far removed from any correlation to an arbitrary God as the east is from the west! To Him be the glory for ever! (Rom. 11:36).

Evidently Paul is not concerned in Romans 9 to 11 with an *exousia* that is an arbitrary act without meaning, an act on which one cannot depend because the human mind cannot find a single point of contact with that which is utterly contingent. On the contrary, these chapters are brimful with meaning. They do not speak of the obscure secrecy of a far and enigmatic God, but of the awe-inspiring, meanginful mystery of the unsearchable and merciful God, of "the mind of the Lord" (Rom. 11:34). The depth of which Paul speaks is not the depth of the precipice, full of horror and terror and disaster, but the depth of God's riches.

16. Kittel, *Theologisches Wörterbuch zum Neuen Testament*, III, 563.

There *are* menaces that threaten life and all that regulates it; they become visible in the lives of those who say that they have come to know the deep things of Satan (Rev. 2:24). Their lives are uprooted by the arbitrariness of libertinism — *liberum arbitrium*. But the depth of God's riches corresponds to the deep things that are searched by the Spirit (I Cor. 2:10). In the revelation of the mystery the depth of Christ's love is revealed (Eph. 3:19), and this love is so trustworthy, so non-arbitrary, so far removed from all untransparent contingency, that neither height nor depth can separate us from the love of God in Jesus Christ (Rom. 8:39). The depth of the riches — that is the theme that summarizes Romans 9 to 11.

All arbitrariness is excluded here, implicitly and explicitly. Now the non-arbitrariness of the meaningful acts of God becomes visible in the history of salvation.

The meaningfulness and purposefulness clearly appears in these chapters of Romans. To make that clear, they would have to be discussed at greater length. But we do want to remind ourselves here of the teleology of God's acts made clear in the relation between the rejection of Israel and the acceptance of the heathen (Rom. 11:11, 15, 25), and then again between this acceptance of the heathen and the re-acceptance of Israel, after it has been aroused to jealousy (Rom. 11:11, 12). Unsearchable are all these ways, but they are the ways, not of an arbitrary God, but of a God who guides all things toward the goal that He has set. Where there is eschatological perspective, arbitrariness is ruled out. Arbitrariness, contingency, which does not recognize consequences and therefore has no final direction or goal, no longer finds a place here. We encounter arbitrariness only by way of man's pride and in the complete arbitrariness of sin.

In view of his corrupt condition man may well go on to ask about the meaning of his powerlessness in the face of the electing God. Paul saw that man's heart is often open to this temptation. Human pride before God is tempted to construct an idea of a power-arbitrariness in God, whereby man excuses himself: "Thou wilt say then unto me, Why doth he still find fault? For who withstandeth his will?" (Rom. 9:19). Man is busy drawing his own conclusions here. His vision of God's glory is obscured by an excuse, and the excuse is based on his defense against a fancied divine arbitrariness which eliminates all man's responsibility. Such arbitrariness is only a projection of the disobedient and unbelieving heart in an abstract demonstration against God.

It must be noted that Paul does not answer the assertion that God is arbitrary with a counterargument on the same abstract level[17]; rather, he rejects this abstract projection because he sees the situation to be altogether different. He unmasks the argument with great indignation and points to the meaning and the purpose of God's acts. Already before he answered this reproach he had posed a question in connection with what he had written about God's plan of election: "What shall we say then? Is there unrighteousness with God?" (Rom. 9:14). In this question, too, Paul meets the reproach directed against God in His act of election. This unrighteousness, this disorder and arbitrariness, this crisis and tension in the domain, indeed, in the very being of God is nothing but blasphemy in Paul's eyes. "God forbid!" he exlaims.[18] This unrighteousness which Paul negates is close to the arbitrariness, the lack of order, the incalculable fitfulness, the rebellion against God's elevation, that wholly obscures God's holiness and trustworthiness. Paul opposes such a possibility, and he does so not by avoiding the electing plan of God but by referring to it. He wants to show from Scripture and the history of salvation that in the electing plan of God there is meaning, order, a powerful clarity, and freedom from the capriciousness and fitfulness of arbitrariness. The man who places himself defiantly before God discovers nothing but arbitrariness, the arbitrariness of a *potentia absoluta*. But Paul points to another possibility, a possibility whereby man can understand that God's elective plan is not arbitrary. It is the discovery that God's purpose is "not of works, but of him that calleth" (Rom. 9:11).

God's election has nothing to do with sinister arbitrariness, but

---

17. A. Nygren, *Der Römerbrief* (1951), p. 263, is correct when he says that Paul "poses a question, not to answer it, but to solve it." Cf. the "O man!" in Romans 9:20 which indicates an altogether different level than the one of an objective answer to the question posed. See also O. Michel, *Der Brief an die Römer* (1955), p. 211; E. Kühl, *Zur paulinischen Theodicee, Römer 9-11* (1897), p. 22.

18. See Rom. 3:5, which indicates the same rejection of the question: "Is God unrighteous who visiteth with wrath? God forbid!" Also in this connection only human *adikia* can be meant (Rom. 3:5). See also Rom. 3:4, where Paul exclaims "God forbid" with respect to the nullifying of God's faithfulness: "yea, let God be found true, but every man a liar." Notice that Paul is horrified at the thought of unrighteousness in God and has to add, "I speak after the manner of men."

points out the order of salvation the way God intended it to
be understood. God's electing plan prepares the way of salvation
in which man learns that salvation is obtained only as a divine
gift and never as an acquisition because of good works. The
issue is God's plan (*prothesis*), but this plan is in form and
measure the principle of election (*eklogē*),[19] and this election
is not an arbitrariness in which no meaning can be discerned,
but the purposeful way in which God's plan is realized in
history. According to Michel "the actual meaning of this
section comes to light in Romans 9:11," and Michel speaks, not
unjustly, of a "watchword."[20] Everything which, in line with
God's electing plan, determines the course of history has the
mark of this divine purpose, and for that reason there can never
be a conflict between God's plan and His acts in history or His
interference in the lives of individuals and nations. The plan is
not a menace to what occurs in history. Rather, in the manner of
God's choice we encounter God's plan.[21] And that is what Paul
wants to indicate when he shows us that in the course of the
history of salvation God's acts contain nothing of the arbitrary.[22]

It is clear that Paul poses a very concrete problem respecting
the unbelief in Israel in Romans 9. If we consider the riches,
the glory and promises that were given to Israel (Rom. 9:4, 5),
we might assume that all this had grown so sterile in the presence of Israel's unbelief that the Word of God remained without

---

19. See B. Holwerda, *Dictaten*, Part I, *Historia revelationis Veteris Tes-
tamenti* (Kampen, 1954), pp. 33ff.

20. O. Michel, *op. cit.*, pp. 202-3.

21. See besides Rom. 9:11 also II Tim. 1:9 about the holy calling "not
according to our works, but according to his own purpose and grace,
which was given us in Christ Jesus before times eternal." Notice the
decisive meaning of all this, not only where Paul speaks of justification
(Rom. 3ff.), but also here in Rom. 9 with respect to election. See
Rom. 11:6, "But if it is by grace, it is no more of works; otherwise
grace is no more grace" and Rom. 9:32 in connection with "the law of
faith" (Rom. 3:27).

22. Kühl in *Zur Paulinischen Theodicee* (1897), p. 31, calls the guilt of
Israel "the refusal to acknowledge this principle." This formulation
sounds rather theoretical but is concretely meant and as such perfectly
correct as the description of Israel's apostasy at its core. See Rom.
9:30-32 about the stumbling block and the rock of offense. The abstract
misunderstanding of God's promise is a misjudgment of what Kühl formulates with these words: "The principle of the absolute free initiative of
God and the electing predestination to salvation is thus equally inherent
in the acts of promise and the words of promise" (p. 18).

effect and had "come to naught." But Paul denies that this is possible: "It is not as though the word of God hath come to naught."[23]

He refutes this "possibility" when he says, "For they are not all Israel that are of Israel: neither, because they are Abraham's seed, are they all children" (Rom. 9:6, 7). More than once this text has been interpreted to mean that God's election is a menace to or limitation of God's historic covenant and promise. All sorts of tensions in the history of the doctrine of election can be connected with the exegesis of these words of Paul. A deep shadow falls over the promise of God whenever they are interpreted to imply that one would first have to know of his election before one could consider himself the addressee of God's promise.

But it is clear that Paul does not want such a devaluation of the Word of God. He wants to indicate that it was not at all in the nature and purpose of God's word of promise that apart from faith it would be possible to conclude automatically that anyone truly belonged to Israel — merely on the basis of descent from Abraham. The Jews may have thought this conclusion to be self-evident,[24] but they misunderstood the promise and God's election. Out of the promise they constructed a claim, and in doing so did not recognize that there is an Israel in the flesh and an Israel in the spirit. Paul protests against such a claim. Election is not a threat against faithful listening to God's promise; it is a threat against the faithless claim.[25] That is the reason for the statement "not all" in Romans 9 which unfolds as such a powerful warning.

23. See Kittel, op. cit., VI, 169: "to become feeble, to lose its power and authority." Cf. I Sam. 3:19, "Jehovah did let none of his words fall to the ground" with Josh. 21:45, "There failed not aught of any good thing which Jehovah had spoken unto the house of Israel; all came to pass."

24. See John 8:33, "We are Abraham's seed"; see also John 8:37, 39. Jesus cuts across the matter-of-course conclusions of the Jews. On the one hand He acknowledges, "I know that ye are Abraham's seed (John 8:37), but on the other hand, "If ye were Abraham's children, ye would do the works of Abraham" (John 8:39ff.). They do not do these works but those of their father (John 8:41), and "ye are of your father the devil, and the lusts of your father it is your will to do" (John 8:44). See in this connection Matt. 3:9.

25. See O. Michel, op. cit., p. 199. "The plan of election gave certainty to the elect, but it does away with the certainty of Israel that boasts of the preference they think they enjoy."

In order to show us that God's Word does not "come to naught," Paul directs our attention to the divine choice, a choice which does not contradict God's word of promise or make an incursion into it, but the meaning and the content of which casts a light over the course of Israel's history. Paul shows us the kind of choice according to which God acts. It does not turn out to be an election — as realization of God's plan — of obscure arbitrariness, changeable and irrational, accidental and inaccessible, but an election which, while resting in God's freedom and sovereignty, is clear, irrefutable, and consistent in content and definiteness.[26]

Already in the history of Isaac it becomes clear what the choice is about. There is no arbitrariness when the choice is revealed in history: "It is not the children of the flesh that are children of God; but the children of the promise are reckoned for a seed" (Rom. 9:8). The birth of Isaac is the miracle, in contrast to the birth of Ishmael out of Hagar and Abraham. In these two sons of Abraham election is mirrored; it is not Ishmael, who was born "after the flesh," but Isaac who is the child of the promise.[27] It is not a matter of arbitrary choice or rejection, but of the revelation of God's plan in the choice — God's free act, His grace, to which only faith can correspond, without the works of the law. There is here, as in Genesis 21:12, a limitation, but it is not arbitrary and is revealed in history in the very words of God.

After this election of Isaac the electing plan of God continues in effect. Paul indicates this when he refers to the history of the two sons of Rebecca. With Ishmael and Isaac it was still a matter of two mothers, but the case of the sons of Rebecca concerns the children of the same mother. It is precisely in their history that the meaning of the choice is revealed. We touch here upon the words that have so often been quoted as a definite proof of the "arbitrariness" of election: "For the children being not yet born, neither having done anything good or bad, that the

---

26. See G. Schrenk, *Die Weissagung über Israel im N.T.* (1951), pp. 26ff.: "If one inquires into the way of salvation one always encounters election. That is why natural man goes through the crisis of the promise."

27. See Gal. 4:23, 28ff. The distinction within "Israel" already became apparent in the beginning when he "that was born after the flesh persecuted him that was born after the Spirit" (Gal. 4:29).

purpose of God according to election might stand, not of works, but of him that calleth, it was said unto her [Rebecca], The elder shall serve the younger. Even as it is written, Jacob I loved, but Esau I hated (Rom. 9:11-13; cf. Mal. 1:3). *Before* they had done good or bad — in that phrase men have seen a moral indifference, the outgrowth of arbitrariness and a violation of morality.

Now it is clear that Paul does intend to refer to a separation. Before their birth, that is, before they were ethically qualified in any way, the choice intervened decisively in God's words to Rebecca. This birth takes on special significance in the light of the divine intervention of salvation. This is the answer Rebecca received when she asked why the children struggled together within her: "Two nations are in thy womb, and two peoples shall be separated from thy bowels: and the one people shall be stronger than the other people; and the elder shall serve the younger" (Gen. 25:23). Paul refers back to this free ordinance of God, an ordinance that precedes this birth. It is generally agreed that Paul does not want to indicate here that *everything* has already been decided from eternity or that the eternal decision has been made about the individual salvation or rejection of Jacob and Esau; he wants to accentuate and illustrate the nature of election — out of grace and not out of works. He is not concerned here with the temporal problem as such; but with this temporal predestination — in the choice — in God's word to Rebecca as a demonstration of the freedom of God's decree, independent of man's activity. Here the way of God's sovereign grace in the world becomes visible. In this history salvation is shown to be a matter not of work and merit, but of grace freely granted.[28]

This choice is far from any sort of arbitrariness. It is pur-

28. See Gerhardus Vos, *Biblical Theology* (1948), pp. 108-110. "Election is intended to bring out the *gratuitous* character of grace"; and, in connection with Jacob and Esau ("neither good nor evil"), "even at the risk of exposing the divine sovereignty to the charge of arbitrariness, the matter was decided prior to the birth of the two brothers." In this important discussion Vos points out with respect to Romans 9 that the "revelation of the doctrine of election, therefore, serves the revelation of the doctrine of grace." In the election there is no question of "a blind unreadable fate" or "an impersonal mystery." Rather, "this one reason we *do* know, and in knowing it we at the same time know that, whatever other reasons exist, they can have nothing to do with any meritorious ethical condition of the objects of God's choice."

poseful, full, clear, and indisputable, as is shown in Malachi 1 where not Jacob and Esau as individuals, but the nations (Israel and Edom) experience the electing interference of God in their history — God's preference of Jacob above Esau. In their history as nations the choice becomes evident: "but Esau I hated, and made his mountains a desolation, and gave his heritage to the jackals of the wilderness" (Mal. 1:3). Nor can God's love for Jacob be related to Jacob's (Israel's) works, or be traced to any personal merit. The history of salvation does away with any personal glory.

In the choice revealed to Rebecca the freedom of God stands in contrast to any merit, be it good or evil, on the part of man. Israel repeatedly misunderstood that. It interpreted the fact of election — seen as preference — as a claim. Such deduction contradicts and violates the true election and shows that the history of Genesis 25 and the prophetic word of Malachi were misunderstood.[29] Such a position does not know of the divine electing plan, for the true meaning of election is always and without exception revealed as the most unarbitrary imaginable.

With this understanding one can walk in faith and find rest in God's election, precisely because God's ordinances, though unsearchable, are in no way detrimental to this assurance — not

---

29. G. Doekes, "De betekenis van Israels val," in *Commentaar op Romeinen* IX-XI (1915), p. 61. Doekes warns not to minimize hatred and he adds that here is meant a positive hatred and not one of less loving. "In vain many opponents of the doctrine of predestination have attempted to demolish the power of this *hemisesa.*" Doekes is right in saying that the positive force of Rom. 9 has often been weakened. But the real dilemma is not "positive hatred" vs. "less loving." It is a matter of divine "preference," a sovereign ordinance of unique character. This "hatred" is revealed in the prophecy of Malachi, in the devastation of the land of Edom, the domain of godlessness (Mal. 1:4). See C. Hodge, *Commentary on the Epistle to the Romans* (1875), p. 310: "The meaning therefore is that God preferred one to the other or chose one instead of the other." See also O. Kusz, *Die Briefe an die Römer, Korinther und Galater* (1940), p. 81, who also refers to Gen. 29:30ff., Luke 14:26, etc. The idea of (divine) preference has nothing to do with a weakening of the sovereignty of God or with any Arminian evasion (Doekes, *op. cit.,* p. 61). Besides, it seems to me incorrect to mention infralapsarianism — as Doekes does here (p. 62). Strangely enough, and in spite of the phrase "neither having done anything good or bad," Doekes concludes from the damnability of the human race: "Therefore, this *emisesa* is only understandable from an infralapsarian point of view."

out of works, but out of grace.   Because of this statement Paul
rejects any idea of arbitrariness.   He does not think of a *potestas absoluta;* his eyes are on God who in His freedom and
sovereign pleasure reveals the prospect that "it is not of him
that willeth, nor of him that runneth, but of God that hath
mercy" (Rom. 9:16).

That is what comes to light in the examples quoted by Paul
and therein lies the foundation of the road that leads to salvation — to trust oneself to God's mercy.   With such trust one
does not fathom the freedom and sovereignty of God, but neither
need he fall into the temptation of interpreting Romans 9 "indeterministically."   For it is no longer useful or necessary to
plead for man's freedom over against the freedom of God (in
mutual limitation), once one has seen the only way, the way of
God's mercy.

Paul applies the same standard when he begins to speak
of "the remnant." Of this remnant he writes that they are left
over "according to the election of grace" (Rom. 11:5). This is
not just an unqualified remnant, a number of individuals who
by a decision of flagrant arbitrariness and "without further ado"
have escaped judgment.   Rather, here again election reveals
itself.   That is also manifest in the fact that the attitude of man
is referred to in relation to election.   It is not only Paul who
speaks of the remnant who have not bowed the knee to Baal
(Rom. 11:4), the Old Testament, too, mentions the remnant of
"afflicted and poor people" who "shall take refuge in the name
of Jehovah" (Zeph. 3:12, 13).

It is not a matter here of a constitutive factor in election,[30]
as though the remnant were finding their salvation in their own
religious qualities, but of the recognition of this *sola gratia,*
this escape from the menacing judgment.[31]   Members of the
remnant are correlated to the election not because through works
or piety they already qualified for salvation,[32] but because they
know themselves to be the objects of unmerited, miraculous

---

30. See also Rom. 11:4, "I have left for myself seven thousand men."
31. For the relation between "remnant" and "judgment" see, for instance,
    Amos 5:15 and the article in Kittel (*op. cit.,* IV) on *leimma,* especially
    pp. 209ff.
32. Kittel, *op. cit.,* p. 207: the remnant has its origin "not in the quality of
    the saved but in the saving act of God."   See also p. 209.

mercy.[33] That is the reason Paul in Romans 9-11 can refer back
to the remnant according to the election of grace, when in his
days the unmerited mercy of God again becomes a point of dis-
sension.

This electing mercy is endangered by certain interpretations
of the "freedom" of God. Israel pursued righteousness but did
not obtain it, while the Gentiles, who did not pursue it, attained
to "the righteousness which is of faith" (Rom. 9:30, 31). There
is only one way that leads to salvation and that is the way of
God's election, which is at the same time the way of faith. When
one does not walk this way, he bases his expectations on his
fancied works (Rom. 9:32) and stumbles against the stone of
stumbling laid in Zion (Rom. 9:33). We are here close to the
profoundest reason for resisting any idea of "arbitrariness" in
God. Here we are confronted with the matter of stumbling, the
skandalon of election.

Man thinks to detect artbitrariness because he poses a point
of departure and applies a standard other than that of the justice of God. Thus, Pharisaically, he detects arbitrariness in
election "according to grace," because justification of the ungodly (Rom. 4:5), according to his moralistic standard, is utterly arbitrary. He then sees only the non-arbitrariness of the
Pharisee who fasts twice a week and tithes and then expects that
he shall go to his house, justified (Luke 18:11ff.). When
instead justification goes to the sinful publican, this is seen as
arbitrariness, because divine action does not correspond to the
works of the law. But this criticism of a fancied arbitrariness in
God unveils its own heretical irreligiosity, it is a stumbling over
the *skandalon*. It is reproached in the same way as are the
laborers in the vineyard (Matt. 20:1-16). When the laborers
hired at the eleventh hour received a denarius, those who have
worked a long and hard day criticize this equality in wages
(Matt. 20:12). This, too, is criticism leveled against "arbitrariness." But the answer nullifies the reproach. The master says,
"Is it not lawful for me to do what I will with mine own?"

---

33. See for the relation between "remnant" and "faith": Kittel, *op. cit.*,
p. 212, where it is correctly said: "He who belongs to the remnant, believes (Isa. 28:16, 17). That means, however, that faith is not the
condition for, but the sign of belonging to, the remnant. In this
relaton, therefore, the holiness of the remnant may be accentuated,
as, for instance, in Zeph. 3:13: the remnant "shall not do iniquity, nor
speak lies," etc.

(Matt. 20:15). This "freedom" may be seen as arbitrariness by sinful man. But the laborers in the vineyard are told specifically that there is no arbitrariness in the master's generosity in the closing words of the parable: "or is *thine* eye *evil,* because I am *good?*" (Matt. 20:15).

The evil eye sees arbitrariness in generosity, even in God's generosity, but this projection of arbitrariness only reveals the darkness of man's heart. This parable is followed by the words: "So the last shall be first, and the first last" (Matt. 20:16). Therein lies the warning for those who make accusations against God's goodness. The change (first-last — last-first) is not arbitrary but full of profound significance. It reminds us how deep the reasons for rejecting arbitrariness lie and how impressive an inroad is made into man's misunderstanding, as everywhere in the gospel God's election is seen, and protests arise against the so-called arbitrariness of grace.[34]

Thus we understand something of the origin of the problem of arbitrariness. The problem can only arise in the mind of the man who no longer knows his own place. It can be described as a stumbling over the rock of offense laid in Zion, where the law is in force: "He that believeth on him shall not be put to shame" (Rom. 9:33). If man thinks he can investigate the mind of God apart from this law, he dwells in the darkness of his own misjudgment of election. For justification of the unbeliever is not arbitrary. On the contrary, it is a revelation of the non-arbitrariness of God's grace without the works of the law. Not to recognize and travel this way of grace is nothing but resistance to the cross, the *skandalon* over which man stumbles (I Cor. 1:23). Grace, unmotivated by works, is truly

---

34. See Herman Ridderbos "Mattheus," in *Korte Verklaring,* II, 72. J. Ridderbos says that this parable has very much in common with the presentation of the elder son in Luke 15:25ff. Indeed, his evil eye, too, sees nothing but arbitrariness in the exuberant happiness of his father. The elder son hears music and dancing and then becomes angry. The words he speaks to his father show that he does not see any correlation but only the emptiness of arbitrariness without ethical implications. His reproach has no effect, for the father expresses his joy again. See also the allegations of arbitrariness in the face of the saving mercy of Christ, for instance, the healings on the Sabbath. See also Luke 15:2, "He receiveth sinners, and eateth with them." The protest that "Christ's practicing His *exousia* is arbitrariness finds its counterpart in the glorification of God (when the crippled man is cured) who had given such authority (*exousia*) to men (Matt. 9:8)."

different from an arbitrariness that cannot be squared with the standards of moralistic self-awareness. Not accepting God's grace was already condemned in connection with Israel's election, which also seemed incongruous (Deut. 7:7; see also 9:4, 5), but it was *the* struggle of Israel that culminated in the cross. Over against all this misjudgment and resistance the *wisdom* of God is revealed in that the election in grace in Christ corresponds not to man's morality and the works of the law, but to his guilt and unbelief.

That is the reason why in the light of Romans 9 the problem of arbitrariness can only arise in a mode of thinking that is estranged from revelation and that calls God's grace arbitrariness. It is not surprising that in the time of the Reformation the Roman Catholic Church often criticized the Reformed doctrine of justification and judged that it inevitably would lead to the concept of arbitrariness in God. Only in an analytic justification would the idea of arbitrariness be banished, because then God's judgment would be made according to the factual situation of our renewed existence. Forensic, declarative, imputative justification, however, would be "arbitrary" because God cannot call black white without becoming an arbitrary God. Hence, the contention about the arbitrariness in God touches upon the profoundest questions of salvation. But for Paul God's acts throughout the history of salvation eliminate every thought of arbitrariness; arbitrariness is ruled out by the sovereignty of His election. This is evident in the history of the patriarchs, which is one great and powerful illustration of the truth that God's Word has not been abandoned. It is not on the basis of works, but on the basis of that fact that He called. The law of faith has its foundation in the clearness of this non-arbitrariness: "He that believeth on him shall not be put to shame" (Rom. 9:33).

But it is possible that, while understanding something of this non-arbitrariness in election, one still finds a problem in the relationship between the potter and the clay referred to in Romans 9. Do we not here discern divine *exousia,* God's sovereign determination? And where lies the difference between this sovereign determination and arbitrariness? In order to find an answer to this question we want to remember that the example of the potter is often employed in Scripture. Paul does not use it arbitrarily when he wants to indicate God's unsearchable sovereignty and power; we meet this example already with Jeremiah who had to go down to the house of the potter who was working with a piece of clay. When the piece of work was marred, the potter used the clay to start another vessel "as seemed good to the potter to make it" (Jer. 18:2-4).

When that procedure is applied to Jehovah, does not His act acquire the trait of arbitrariness? The answer to this question is that precisely here any arbitrariness on God's part is completely ruled out. It is only necessary to notice further the application of the metaphor of the potter: "O house of Israel, cannot I do with you as this potter?" (Jer. 18:6) Special attention must be paid to this "cannot I," this ability of God, when He acts one moment this way, and another that way. Whoever thinks of arbitrariness here, has misunderstood the meaning of this message. For what is it that God is doing at one moment or the other? He is not engaged in fickle, arbitrary acts and whims, but in concrete acts inseparably connected with the actions of Israel. He says: "At what instant I shall speak concerning a nation, and concerning a kingdom, to pluck up and to break down and to destroy it; if that nation, concerning which I have spoken, turn from their evil, I will repent of the evil that I thought to do unto them. And at what instant I shall speak concerning a nation, and concerning a kingdom, to build and to plant it; if they do that which is evil in my sight, that they obey not my voice, then I will repent of the good, wherewith I said I would benefit them" (Jer. 18:7-10).

It is quite impossible to designate this as arbitrariness. On the contrary, all God's acts described here are undetachably linked up with the conversion or the inconvertibility of His people. God is the same at the moment He makes a pronouncement as in the following moment when He repents of His words. The exclusion of all arbitrariness is clear in relation to conversion and inconvertibility.

At each moment there is abundant majesty and sovereignty in all God's acts; but this is the sovereignty not of arbitrary acts, but of meaningful and comprehensible acts, truly transparent in the light of His revelation, trustworthy, and not to be feared. The variations and transitions in God's acts are not arbitrary, for man knows *how* and *why* God acts thus and not differently. Arbitrariness is only found with man. When God intends to bring Judah to disaster, and Jeremiah is still calling Judah to repentance (Jer. 18:11), he faces arbitrariness in the men who

say: "It is vain; for we will walk after our own devices, and we
will do everyone after the stubbornness of his evil heart" (Jer.
18:12).[35] It is striking that here mention is made of the stubbornness of the heart, a phrase so often used when thinking of
arbitrariness in God. It is good to remember that in Jeremiah
18 the stubbornness of men's hearts opposes the non-arbitrariness of God. In the arbitrariness of man's life lies the terror
of life, of a life that does not understand that the path of divine
acts is all clearly revealed beforehand, and therefore serves only
to call to true repentance.

Isaiah, too, speaks of the relation between the potter and the
clay. Because he speaks of the marvelous work of God there
seems to be good reason here to raise the question regarding
arbitrariness. But a closer reading shows that this passage is
concerned with God's judgement over the people who honor Him
only with their lips (Isa. 29:13). What marvelous work will
God do among these people? The answer does not point in the
direction of arbitrariness but opens up perspectives to the
riches of the mystery of the New Testament. We are confronted with the marvelous work of God in which He will destroy the wisdom of the wise and will obscure the understanding
of the discerning (Isa. 29:14). We approach the gospel of which
Paul speaks when he quotes these words of Isaiah and speaks of
the foolishness of the cross. The highest divine wisdom is revealed over against the wisdom of the discerning (I Cor. 1:20ff.).
Surely, one may be offended here on account of a fancied arbitrariness, but it is really the offense of the "foolishness" of the
cross, in which all the wisdom of the wise is obscured by the mystery of God's love. Counter to this fancied arbitrariness Isaiah
speaks of the perversity of the people (Isa. 29:16), and it is in
this connection that he uses the relation between the potter and
the clay. "Shall the potter be esteemed as clay; that the thing
made should say of him that made it, He made me not; or the
thing formed say of him that formed it, He hath no understanding?" (Isa. 29:16).

God's wisdom and sovereignty are directed against the pride and

---

35. Aalders, in *Korte Verklaring* on Jer. 18:12, points out that the people
cannot have spoken these words literally, but that through these words
(which are laid in their mouths is given the evaluation of their inner
being as God knows it.

sin of man who does not accept submission to Him.[36] For God's wisdom contradicts the arbitrariness of man. God's acts are not irrational or without reason, coherence, perspective, and constancy, but meaningful and comprehensible. The whole mystery of salvation is the opposite of arbitrariness. Only he who does not surrender to it in faith and repentance discovers, because of his own stubbornness and blindness, arbitrariness in God's acts. And he must listen to the word from on high, the word of the free and sovereign God, whom to oppose is the greatest irrationality and the worst arbitrariness — the clay against the potter!

As in Isaiah, so it is in Romans 9. Man who does not understand the depths of divine wisdom, nor the riches of election, who wants only to live in his belief in the non-arbitrariness of his own works and morality, can see only arbitrariness in the sovereign freedom of God. He asks concerning God: "Why doth he still find fault?" (Rom. 9:19). But Paul knows there is more to say. He knows that God's sovereign determination is teleologically oriented and that He by way of the *exousia* is preparing to reveal the riches of His glory (Rom. 9:23) in the fulfillment of Hosea's prophecy. Arbitrariness *seems* to be present here. Is there not a *lo-ammi* and then again an *ammi*, a *lo-ruchama* and then again a *ruchama?* But with both Paul and Hosea the grace of God is the light in these transitions which rules out all arbitrariness.

Thus it turns out that the origin of the concept of arbitrariness lies in the unrepenting heart that deviates from God's way and loses sight of Him in the literal sense of the word. It can be said that the problem of arbitrariness finds its source exclusively in the blindness and confusion of man regarding God's acts. It is understandable, therefore, that the believer who rediscovers his God is able to employ the image of the potter and the clay in a manner that rules out every thought of arbitrariness. When

36. It is their work that is done in darkness and it is they who hide their deep council from Jehovah (Isa. 29:15). In the relation potter-clay the author refers back to creation: Creator-creature (Isa. 29:16). See also Isa. 45:9 on the image of the axe and the saw with reference to the self-glory and boast of Assyria (Isa. 10:12, 15, 16), which portrays, as Rengstorf says, "the freedom and independence of God over against men as His creatures and over against their wishes and claims" (Kittel, *op. cit.,* VI. 118); cf. O. Michel, *op. cit.,* p. 211, on the image that is used "in order to make clear the resistance of the creature against the Creator."

man's heart is opened up for the gift of salvation, he can bend
before the superiority of God's acts and he can even take up
the image of the potter in his prayer "But now, O Jehovah, thou
art our Father; we are the clay, and thou our potter; and we all
are the work of thy hand. Be not wroth very sore, O Jehovah,
neither remember iniquity for ever" (Isa. 64:8, 9). Here the
use of the Father-name shows us that all thought of arbitrariness in God is completely excluded, and the tension between
sovereignty and fatherhood has disappeared.

That happens in connection with confession of guilt and with
prayer. The sovereignty of God is not diminished, yet nowhere
does it show traits of arbitrariness. Only apart from repentance can the problem of arbitrariness loom large. But that which
then seems arbitrariness is nothing but the realization of God's
lawful judgment against pride: "Woe unto him that striveth
with his Maker! a potsherd among the potsherds of the earth!"
(Isa. 45:9). The "woe" pronounced here is not an indication of
arbitrariness; it is criticism of the rebellion which — unjustifiedly — gave rise to the thought of arbitrariness. And he who gives
up his pride and discovers the graciousness of the Father will
continue to protest against the idea of arbitrariness in God, because any comparison with human arbitrariness must, also ter-
minologically, be rejected as casting a shadow over Him who is
Light, and in whom there is no darkness whatsoever (I John
1:5).

What we have seen so far finds its support in Scripture, which
speaks of the glory and wisdom in all the works of God's hands,
of the absolute trustworthiness of His Word, and of the stability
of His covenant that never will fail. It is never true that behind
all this there remains something threatening, a shadow that takes
away the light. It is in response to this stability and trustworthiness that frequent calls to adoration and praise are heard. The
song of praise disappears — and must disappear — wherever
the concept of arbitrariness begins to obscure man's outlook on
God. The subjective response to an arbitrary God is not
adoration but fear and fatalistic submission. Arbitrariness puts
an end to every song of praise. A song cannot be sung in the
face of the unapproachable *mysterium tremendum*. It gives
way to fear in the face of all-powerful arbitrariness, in the face
of the *deus absconditus* who is more *tremendum* than *fascinans*.
God's attitudes from one moment to the other are then no longer

those of Jeremiah 18, but are changes made in arbitrariness and incalculability and therefore unavoidable and terrifying.

The changes of attitude described in Jeremiah 18 provide a combination of threat and promise by which the heart of man might begin to listen again, but changes of mind in an arbitrary God would be reasons only for fear and terror in the face of the Unapproachable in His arbitrary acts, acts that would even threaten His own revelation. Such arbitrariness calls to mind the irony of Elijah when he supposes that Baal "peradventure" is musing, traveling, or sleeping, and that therefore the answer to the calls of the priests does not come (I Kings 18:27). But Israel knows of the redeeming constancy in the name "Hearer of prayers," and it is comforted with the promise: "Behold, he that keepeth Israel will neither slumber nor sleep" (Ps. 121:4).

It is not difficult to discover throughout Scripture the lines of the pattern of God's acts and to point out many passages in which the concept of arbitrariness is implicitly or explicitly contradicted. All God's acts reveal a divine order and pattern and are shown to us in such connections that we may discover regularity and order. With that we do not mean a rational transparency or a simplistic *theodicee* which attempts to justify God to human thinking. His acts are too elevated for that, too majestic and sovereign, His judgments too unsearchable, His ways past tracing out (Rom. 11:33). His ways are higher than ours and His thoughts higher than our thoughts (Isa. 55:9). Scripture can speak of God's unknown footsteps (Ps. 77:19), and it clearly indicates the limits of human insight: "Who is this that darkeneth counsel by words without knowledge?" (Job 38:2). "Hast thou entered into the springs of the sea, or hast thou walked in the recesses of the deep?" (Job 38:16). "Have the gates of death been revealed unto thee? Or hast thou seen the gates of the shadow of death? Hast thou comprehended the earth in its breadth? Declare, if thou knowest it all" (Job 38:17, 18).

Scripture often contrasts man with God. Everywhere it is understood that God is greater than man (Job 33:12), and that the breath of the Almighty makes us live (Job 33:4). The limit of our understanding is clear (Job 37:15ff.), for "touching the Almighty, we cannot find him out: He is excellent in power; and in justice . . ." (Job 37:23). "Shall he that cavilleth contend with the Almighty? He that argueth with God, let him answer it" (Job 40:2). And only one legitimate answer is possible; it is the answer Job gave: "Once have I spoken, and I will not answer; yea, twice, but I will proceed no further" (Job 40:5).

In the divine answer to Job (out of the whirlwind) the hippopotamus and crocodile are described in all their power. The hippopotamus, this symbol of strength for man, is called the chief of the ways of God (Job 40:19), and all standards by which man might measure the incomparable God in His acts are taken away from him. He who begins to understand this has to acknowledge: "I have uttered that which I understand not, things too wonderful for me, which I know not" (Job 42:3).

But this complete removal from human standards and criticism nowhere in Scripture implies arbitrariness in God. Rather, we are repeatedly struck by the marvelous fact that he who discards such critical standards sees the way opened for him to a knowledge of God whereby His majesty and sovereignty no longer terrify. It is *after* hearing the tremendous voice in the whirlwind that Job makes his confession: "I had heard of thee by the hearing of the ear; but now mine eye seeth thee" (Job 42:5); and it is *after* confessing that God's way was in the sea and His footsteps were unknown that Asaph speaks the comforting words: "Thou leddest thy people like a flock, by the hand of Moses and Aaron" (Ps. 77:20).

We see repeatedly that God's will and acts are not arbitrary. Certainly, there is God's freedom, but it is not the freedom or the whim of an unknown "highest power." It is the freedom of God. The point is always — as Bavinck puts it — "the will, not of blind fate, of an irresponsible chance, of an obscure natural power, but the will of an almighty God and of a merciful Father. His sovereignty is a sovereignty of unlimited power but also a sovereignty of wisdom and grace. He is God and Father at the same time."[37]

It is for this reason that in the accentuation of God's sovereignty and the simultaneous rejection of arbitrariness the wisdom of God is always referred to. Scripture itself teaches this wisdom. In Proverbs 8 God's wisdom is introduced speaking at the crossroads, where humanity passes, and it cries: "Hear, for I will speak excellent things; and the opening of my lips shall be right things. For my mouth shall utter truth; and wickedness is an abomination to my lips. All the words of my mouth

---

37. Bavinck, *op. cit.*, II, 210.

are in righteousness; there is nothing crooked or perverse in them" (Prov. 8:6-8).

Wisdom speaks here of its own excellence, righteousness, and truth, not as though they represent independent virtues by which divine wisdom can be measured and to which it has to correspond; rather, all that wisdom speaks of comes up out of the deep spring of divine wisdom itself in apriori mercy and justice. It is easy for him who has understanding to recognize wisdom's virtues (Prov. 8:9). This wisdom is the source of all human wisdom; it was present in the first of the works of God (Prov. 8:22); it was His daily delight, rejoicing always before Him (Prov. 8:30). It is of this wisdom that Job 28 also sings. It cannot be valued with the finest gold of Ophir, or with any precious stone (Job 28:16). And after the hymn on wisdom's great value follows the practical commendation: "Behold, the fear of the Lord, that is wisdom; and to depart from evil is understanding" (Job 28:28). Wisdom can never be compared with anything that lies outside itself. Its origins are in eternity, and man must not refuse it (Prov. 8:33). Happy is the man who listens to it (Prov. 8:34). "For whoso findeth me findeth life, and shall obtain favor of Jehovah" (Prov. 8:35).

We can make a meaningful transition from the objectivity of divine wisdom to the subjective response to it and sum up all that has been said of divine wisdom as "the fear of the Lord." It is a matter of insight into trustworthy and unassailable reality. We are not able to get beyond this wisdom to discover a foundation for it. On the other hand, it is unwarranted to make this divine wisdom, which leads to life, relative by setting it alongside of a formal *potentia absoluta* which offers another and still deeper wisdom. Such a *potentia absoluta* will only threaten to negate the divine wisdom revealed to us, which speaks to us in the crisis of life. The crucial issue of the controversy regarding the arbitrariness of God will always be the controversy concerning the trustworthiness of God in His *revelation*.

In connection with the concept of arbitrariness in God we want to remember the words of Hebrews 2:10: "For it became him, for whom are all things, and through whom are all things, in bringing many sons unto glory, to make the author of their salvation perfect through sufferings." In this text the word translated "became him" has attracted much attention. It has been interpreted as an attempt to rationalize the irrational of

God's acts of salvation in Jesus Christ, to include it in a transparent, rational system — what was reasonable to God, was therefore fitting for Him. Michel speaks of this as a "striking" word. It is indeed striking when we think of the difference between sovereignty and arbitrariness. Is it a word with which the author attempts to escape the tensions of the irrational to point to some authority to which God would be bound after all? Is it an attempt to avoid arbitrariness, the way we reject human arbitrariness by referring to a plan or law? Was it "fitting" to God? Michel sees in Hebews 2:10 a rational, dogmatic moment, that finally ends up in the *"cur deus homo?"* of Anselm.

We can understand how Michel comes to this thought for we read the same word spoken by Christ when He is about to be baptized by John the Baptist: "Thus it becometh us [is fitting for us] to fulfil all righteousness" (Matt. 3:15). It is used by Paul with respect to believing women, that they adorn themselves "which becometh women professing godliness" through good works (I Tim. 2:10), and with respect to separation from all impurity "as becometh saints" (Eph. 5:3). In all these cases the issue is subjection to a law, a norm, a seemliness, sometimes with respect to Christ who was born under the law (Gal. 4:4) and sometimes with respect to the faithful who may live, not in autonomy, but in theonomy. In connection with this it has been suggested that the author in Hebrews 2:10 did not intend to subject God to a certain law, but wanted to systematize God's acts within some framework in order to avoid the idea of arbitrariness. Especially Stählin has been thinking thus. He thinks that in this word, compared to the common Biblical concept of the *mysterion,* there is some loss of impact, especially with respect to the radical *skandalon*-character of the cross.[38] The author of Hebrews, Stählin thinks, is not of the stature of Christianity's first generation, and he substitutes "befitting" for the depth of the foolishness and offense of the cross.

The letter to the Hebrews sounds then much more logical than earlier letters because clear wisdom has taken the place of the original foolishness. Stählin sees the author of Hebrews on the way to a more or less logical *theodicee,* which here, as so often, has led to a diminishing of the offense of Christianity. It strikes our attention, however, that Stählin thought for a moment of another expression in the New Testament which deals with

38. G. Stählin, *Skandalon,* p. 281.

"must" (*dei*) and says that Paul and Jesus knew of reasons why Jesus had to be degraded and had to die, a connection also mentioned by Michel. But Stählin sees in this nothing important enough to change his viewpoint and he continues to think of Hebrews — *ad hoc* — as different from the rest of the New Testament. He finds in it an attempt to surmount the wholly staurocentric mode of thinking.

Stählin's position is untenable for us. The author of Hebrews certainly does not try to reach beyond the cross. The very word "befitting" is connected in Hebrews 2:10 with leading to glory through suffering. The reference to the New Testament *dei* should have made Stählin more careful. There is no reason to think here of a deviation from the testimony in the rest of the New Testament. The word "befitting" must not be interpreted to mean that there is a norm standing above God. It must be seen the way Calvin, Augustine, and Bavinck saw the struggle around the concept *exlex* and *sibi ipsi lex*. It deals with all that is most profound, with the fullness and harmony of the divine attributes, with God's wisdom which is revealed in all His works. The cross does not harm this wisdom; it reveals it. The foolishness of God is wiser than men: I Corinthians 1 even tells us that Jesus Christ has become our wisdom (I Cor. 1:30). Not an irrationality of God's arbitrariness but the harmony of His work is shown to us in His revelation.

It is striking that the same word is used in an altogether different context in Hebrews 7:26 where we read: "For such a high priest *became* us, holy, guiltless, undefiled." Here there is, no more than in Hebrews 2:10, mention of a formal and abstract *necessitas;* there is only the connection between our guilt and salvation granted to us in Christ. This High Priest who offered Himself (Heb. 7:27) is the same who according to Hebrews 2:10 is made perfect by God through suffering.

The correlation between guilt and the covering of guilt, between sin and reconciliation, is the meaningful and harmonious connection which cannot apriori be constructed in our thoughts; it can only be read in the revelation of God's virtues and the reality of granted salvation, and can thus only be fully understood. Here the mystery is not rationalized, but the revelation is respected by which confusion of God's act with arbitrariness is ruled out. This separation does not do away with the mystery; rather, it enables us to understand that the essence of the mystery does not lie in dark inscrutability. The point at issue is

not primarily a noetic problem of inscrutability as a mark of the
mystery. It is not an academic mystery, but the mystery of salvation and redemption. *Eprepen* as well as *dei* can have a place in
the word of the cross, and its meaning is revealed in the course
of the history of salvation. In *eprepen* and *dei* the mystery is
forever separated from arbitrariness.

It is better, therefore, rather than to speak of an attempt to
come to a rational *theodicee* in Hebrews 2, to speak with Win-
disch of the way of Christ which is "adapted to God's essence."
One can speak this way without speculating about the essence of
God in such a way as to separate the essence from the fullness
of all God's attributes and revelation. The very heart of the
speculation about arbitrariness was that it placed the sovereign
will (as the essence of God) in isolation. Nominalism wanted
to make that will as *free* as possible, and Feckes is correct when
he says that in nominalism "the divine will has no regulative in
God's intellect or in His other perfections because it is superior
to them all."[39] This absolute freedom of will was for nominalism
the background of all of the order of salvation; but it is precisely
that background that was the greatest danger to the order of
salvation, causing it to lose its essential connections and to become no more than the factuality of the result of God's contingent
will. Scripture protests against this arbitrariness.

There *is* a third way between the *potentia absoluta* and the
subjection of God to a law. That third way is the way of revelation. That revelation is not mere appearance but trustworthy
reality. When the ancient Church fought the modalistic concept of the Trinity, its profoundest motive was to prevent a devaluation of the revelation regarding God and its trustworthiness. The same protest will have to be raised against every concept which threatens the revelation by placing an absolute power
behind that revelation. In the controversy about arbitrariness,
the trustworthiness of revelation and the whole process of salvation are at stake.

The meaningful acts of God do not allow us to accept salvation in its factuality as strange, irrational reality. With all the
saints we are able to know the love of Christ which surpasses
all knowledge that we "may be filled unto all the fulness of God"
(Eph. 3:18, 19). The knowledge which surpasses knowledge —
that is no intellectual game, full of daring paradoxes; it is the

39. C. Feckes, *op. cit.,* p. 13

knowledge by way of which the breadth and length and height and depth are revealed. This knowledge is not the knowledge that puffs up, but the knowledge that edifies (I Cor. 8:1).

It must be clear how much all this is connected with the doctrine of election. It is not without reason that we discuss these questions about arbitrariness at the very beginning of our discussion of election, for election and arbitrariness are often identified. But Scripture urges repeatedly that there is no place in our feeling and thinking for any analogy between human arbitrariness and God's sovereign and gracious acts.[40]

If anywhere, then here the analogy means a fatal trespassing of the boundaries we are to observe. Such trespassing is a violation of the fullness and the attributes of God, which the Christian proclaims as the attributes of Him who has called him out of darkness into His marvelous light (I Pet. 2:9). The marvelousness of this light is as far removed from every shadow as the east is from the west.

We know that we shall not be able to discuss the election of God properly without continually reminding ourselves that there is no arbitrariness in God's acts. It will never be possible to find a solution for the questions of he doctrine of election indeterministically because such an approach would affect the freedom of God's election.[41] And we must remember that this freedom is sharply distinguished from all arbitrariness and dark irrationality. It is of great importance that in the revelation concerning election the light of non-arbitrariness shines forth. It is the light of God's election that becomes visible when we hear that God has elected the poor to be rich in faith and heirs of the Kingdom (James 2:5); that He has elected that which was foolish, weak, and despised, in order to put to shame the wise and strong; that He has elected the things that are not, in order to bring to nought the things that are, that no flesh

---

40. Sometimes Scriptural references have been pointed out which were thought to contain elements of arbitrariness in God, for instance, God's word in Isa. 66:3, 4. It is clear, however, that this is a very sharp word of judgment in which there is no arbitrariness at all. For this analogy indicates precisely the correlation between guilt and judgment.

41. See concerning this indeterminism: E. Weber, *Das Problem der Heilsgeschichte nach Römer* 9-11 (1911), pp. 11ff. Also W. Sanday and A. C. Headlam, "A History of the Interpretation of Romans 9:6-29," *Romans, International Critical Commentary,* pp. 269-275.

should glory before God (I Cor. 1:26-29). It is the light of election that shines in the gospel when Christ's coming is directed toward seeking those that are lost, and when He calls to repentance, not the righteous, but sinners. This is not arbitrariness; this does not convey that there is no longer any distinction between good and evil. When man stubbornly misinterprets God's command and holiness, then election may well become arbitrariness for him. We read in Scripture that God justifies the ungodly (Rom. 4:5), but it must be remembered that everyone who transposes this divine justification into a human judgment becomes guilty of the most serious arbitrariness. "Woe unto them that call evil good, and good evil; that put darkness for light, and light for darkness; that put bitter for sweet, and sweet for bitter!" (Isa. 5:20).

That is nothing but a morally arbitrary rejection of the law of the Lord and a contempt for the word of the Holy one of Israel (Isa. 5:24) and which can take on such proportions that the whole order of life is overthrown: "That justify the wicked for a bribe, and take away the righteousness of the righteous from him" (Isa. 5:23). "He that justifieth the wicked, and he that condemneth the righteous, both of them alike are an abomination to Jehovah" (Prov. 17:15). What a gulf there is between divine non-arbitrariness and human arbitrariness here! Whoever has understood this radical difference will be on his guard against participating in undermining the trustworthiness of God and the certainty of salvation, for such participation eventually leads one to think of arbitrariness in God.[42]

Before we end this chapter we want to point out that in our age various thoughts have been advanced which can hardly be distinguished from the concept of arbitrariness in God. We think especially of the ardent protest that arose against the humanized concept of God in which He was measured according

---

42. F. W. Schmidt correctly indicates how differently Luther and nominalism treat the sovereign majesty of God. For instance, in Luther's *Römerbrief Vorlesung* (1515), he does not rationalize the concept of God, but contrasts divine and human wisdom: "*aliter de deo sapientia est, quam de homine*" (F. W. Schmidt, ed., *Martin Luther, Vom freien Willen*, 1934, p. 325). Compare Luther's words: "We must honor God and the Sovereign as the most compassionate One, as He is to those whom He justifies and saves, without their merit, and we must therefore yield and honor His divine wisdom and believe that He is equally justified in rejecting us" (*ibid.*, p. 279).

to the human standards of love, benevolence, and tolerance.[43] In this anthropocentric humanization of the concept of God, not God, but man is of central importance, and the love of God is no longer understood as sovereign love. However — under the pressure of the catastrophic events of the twentieth century — other aspects of the concept of God have assumed importance; in reaction to this unbiblical humanization new motifs have appeared in twentieth-century theology, motifs that speak again of God's transcendence and His sovereignty. Aulen, for instance, refers to the holiness motif, and to the dualistic-dramatic, the eschatological, and the social motifs.[44] All of these reflect a radical change in the concept of God, for in them God is again seen in His divine independence.

It cannot be denied that in our century such shifts of emphasis have become apparent. An attempt has been made to think again theocentrically. In such a situation the anthropological, individualistic emphasis can no longer say anything of value about God. Instead, the irrationality of the idea of God has come to the fore as a concept supposedly more Biblical than the anthropocentric interpretation of Christianity which made God a projection of man's desires and value-judgments. It is understandable that this shift also affected the exegesis of Scripture, in order to show that this was not just a matter of the irrationalistic tendencies of the period, but of a new and closer approach to the old message of Scripture. Paul Volz's *Das Dämonische in Jahwe* (1924) reveals this. In the context of what has been said of Volz elsewhere,[45] we now want to focus our attention on only one point he makes — the connection between this demonic aspect in God and the idea of arbitrariness in Him.

According to Volz, especially the Old Testament presentation of God reveals unmistakable "demonic" features. Volz does not even hesitate to say "almost Satanic." We — as Christian

43. See G. Aulen, *Het Christelijk Godsbeeld* (1927). Aulen mentions in this connection, mild providence (Enlightenment), naturalized love (Schleiermacher), and ethical love (Ritschl). In his opposition the sovereignty of God becomes then the main motif. See his discussion on Kierkegaard, p. 325ff. and, in general, G. Brillenburg Wurth, *De Theologie van Gustav Aulen* (1931).
44. Aulen himself expresses this in his interpretation of sovereign love which cannot be confined to the boundaries of the order of justice — a trend of thought that pervades all of his concept of reconciliation. See for this his *De Christelijke Verzoeningsgedachte* (1931).
45. See my *Faith and Perseverance*, Chapter 6.

readers of the Old Testament — are unaware of that, Volz
thinks. We have been breathing in an altogether different climate
and find it difficult "to see and understand behind the presentation
of the just and wise God who is a merciful and loving Father,
the elementary power, the terror of the Old Testament concept of God."[46] We no longer see this Jahve of the Old
Testament who directs His "demonic wrath" against His enemies;
but "the effect is still more sinister and demonic when
Jahve thunders against His own chosen people."[47] In the
Old Testament we encounter instances "where Jahve appears as
a demonic being, and belief in Him is mixed with horror."[48]

To Volz this demonic concept of God is not the presentation
of an obscure, primitive past which has now lost all meaning.
It is something real and permanent, and real piety always confronts us with it. Not "if you seek me with all your heart,
you shall find me," but "I will have mercy on whom I have
mercy" is the Scripture's key to the original sources of religion.
He who does not understand *this,* does not know religion. "Only
when man's concept of God and man's piety incorporate the
idea of the powerful, the terrifying force and the cowering timidity,
when the righteous and gracious God has also become the Terrible One, only then do we stand before the vastness of the
Godhead and on the threshold that leads to the heights of
faith.[49]

This mode of thinking is unacceptable for more reasons than
for its terminology only. Even if Volz only meant to protest
against a humanized concept of God, it still would not be permissible to employ his terms. But their use implies more. Volz does
not mean to criticize this "demonic" God, no more than the concept of arbitrariness intends to be critical. Rather, in his view of
the demonic in Jahve, Volz means to accentuate the irrational in
God, His elevated position far above all human rationality — a
view which ranks Volz with Rudolf Otto. But it is striking
that in this irrationality the connection between guilt and the
wrath of God is weakened. This weakening exerts its influence
on the relationship between man and the salvation of God and
carries uncertainty into that relationship.

46. *Ibid.,* p. 4.
47. *Ibid.,* p. 10.
48. *Ibid.,* p. 25.
49. *Ibid.,* p. 40.

Certainly, in both the Old and New Testament we read of God's wrath — against His own people as well as against His enemies — but it is nowhere detached from the perfect holiness which reacts against guilt. That explains that His wrath may attain tremendous proportions,[50] and yet altogether lacks the traits of the demonic,[51] so that in repentance and faith there is always a way to turn from wrath to grace. But the alleged "demonic" aspects in the wrath and jealousy of the Lord block this way. They uphold the irrationality of the freedom of God and leave no room for a way by which the wrath of God may be turned away in repentance and prayer and acceptance of God's judgment. Nor is this turning arbitrary, but full of divine grace.[53] In this turning from wrath to grace God's sovereignty is recognized. This turning is never a matter of course, but is experienced and acknowledged as mercy, precisely because of its freedom.

That is why the preaching of God's wrath — no matter what proportions it assumes — never affects the basis of one's trust whenever this trust rediscovers the way to God's heart in experiencing His judgment and its righteousness. Arbitrariness is so far removed from God's wrath that we see repeatedly that He is wrathful against His people that they may return to Him. The Scripture gives abundant evidence of this. Jehovah is a God of surprises and His ways are higher than our ways, His thoughts deeper than our thoughts, but nothing can change what He has revealed about Himself. He "lets none of his words fall to the ground" (I Sam. 3:19).

This does not limit and humanize the greatness and glory and majesty of God. Rather, these become apparent precisely in the trustworthiness of His revelation. The correlation between faith

---

50. See Kittel, *op. cit.*, V, 397ff.
51. Although Fichtner says that this cannot be explained by an ancient belief in demons, he nevertheless sees with Volz "the demonic" as real in God (Kittel, *op. cit.*, V, 403), and at the same time speaks in other formulations of "irrational, in the final analysis not explainable, enigmatic, mysterious, primitive power, completely undependable (*ibid.*, pp. 402, 403). But Fichtner acknowledges: "To be sure, Jahve's acts were more and more removed from the atmosphere of the incalculable" (*ibid.*, p. 403), namely, in connection with the cause of God's wrath (man's turning away from Him).
52. See the numerous "returns" in the prophets. See especially Jer. 4:1-4.
53. See Isa. 51:17-23 and Ps. 77:10. Fichtner (in Kittel, *op. cit.*, V, 410) refers especially to Isa. 54, where we do not look "into the heart of a tyrant who dispatches wrath and love arbitrarily."

and salvation does not at times take on a different character
and become, for instance, a correlation between the horrible
and the awe-inspiring in God. Rather, all the aspects of God's attributes are revealed in the revelation of His covenant. When
Volz writes that the God of the Old Testament cannot be "a
super-marvelous God," but that we must regain precisely these
traits,[54] then one can say that he who misjudges the wrath and
holiness of God does not know what he does and humanizes the
concept of God, because the gripping and marvelous thing
of the Old Testament is that God is not demonic and arbitrary.
God's attributes are revealed throughout His entire revelation
and in all aspects of His holy covenant but they never detract
from His trustworthiness. That is the reason why God always
comes back to His own words in reminder and admonition, in
promise and in threat. His Word stands forever, and Israel's
feasts are a solid proof[55] that the history of salvation does not
consist of a series of contingent acts of God without coherence
and reason. Israel has been guilty in its response, not to the
contingent deeds of God, but to the trustworthiness of God's
Word. The menace of the idea of arbitrariness in God is nowhere
more evident than when Volz, to show what he thinks essential
in religion, quotes not the divine words about seeking and finding Him, but Paul's: "I will have mercy on whom I have mercy"
(Rom. 9:15).

Whoever — for the sake of finding the essential in religion
— begins making choices and shuffling the emphases, fails to
recognize that this problem is unreal for Paul. It is the same
Paul who speaks these words concerning God's sovereign grace
(Rom. 9:15), and who cites Isaiah's: "I was found of them that
sought me not; I became manifest unto them that asked not of me"
(Rom. 10:20; see v. 21). Both passages are essential. Whoever detaches God's sovereignty from these contexts may ve-
hemently protest against the humanization of the concept of God,
but he must pay the price of "demonizing" Him, which is not
less reprehensible, for it no longer distinguishes the sov-

54. *Op cit.*, p. 41.
55. See Lev. 23:2: "The set feasts of Jehovah, which ye shall proclaim
   to be holy convocations, even these are my set feasts." They accentuate the continuity in the historical acts of God toward His people. That
   this continuity is not at all identical to something self-evident is obvious. Rather, it is this very continuity that is full of ever new responsibility. See II Chron. 35:6; II Kings 23:22, 23; II Chron. 30:1ff.

ereignty of God from an "absolute power" which in its arbitrariness threatens the very order of salvation.

We find similar thoughts with Snethlage, who argues ardently for what we may call a "demonic" concept of predestination. He attacks the Church for being so infected with humanism that it can hardly believe in predestination any longer, let alone confess it in the modern world. He believes that whenever predestination does not stand in the foreground, moralism must bear the blame.[56]

To men like Aulen the love of God is central but it is characterized as a general love for mankind. It is no longer understood as Fatherly love, which is exclusive. The Father-concept, which automatically excludes those who are not the Father's children, implies the idea of predestination. Snethlage wants to plead for an anti-moralistic interpretation of Christianity as he finds it in Jesus, Paul, Augustine, the Reformers, and the Jansenists He does not want to accept the humanized concept of God of the Enlightenment from which all terror- and fear-inspiring aspects have been removed.[57]

Snethlage finds that the nucleus of authentic Christianity is everywhere neglected at the present time. "What happens to predestination then, the cornerstone of Christianity and the Reformation?"[58] Why, in the preaching of the gospel, do we hardly hear a single word said of predestination? Original, tragic-dramatic Christianity has vanished. There is no longer an understanding of the ardency with which the Synod of Dort once defended the particularistic nature of God's love and rejected as the *summum* of godlessness the position of the Arminians that Christ died for all people.[59] The "demonic" traits of the Old Testament concept of God have been forgotten, namely, that God is a terror-inspiring Majesty and that the Sinai volcano has never been extinguished. And as in the Old Testament, so also in the New Testament, love, according to Snethlage, is nothing but a "demonic love of a demonic God, who, without explaining why, throws out the wedding guest who has lent an ear to the invitation but is found without the sign of election.[60]

56. J. L. Snethlage, *De Anti-Ethicistische Godsidee en Haar Practische Conesquenties* (1930).
57. Snethlage refers particularly to the article by Paul Voltz.
58. Snethlage, *op. cit.*, p. 17.
59. *Ibid.*, p. 13.
60. *Ibid.*, p. 15.

In today's Christianity Snethlage finds that these demonic aspects have been replaced by a revolting familiarity which is revealed in the modern and cheap eschatology proclaimed at the graveside — the higher life on the other side — an eschatology behind which Snethlage places a big question mark because hope must be combined with fear when one remembers that the sovereign God elects *and* rejects.

Does this indicate a modern capitulation to the doctrine of predestination? Definitely not! Snethlage says emphatically that he has broken with the Christian world-view because it cannot be reconciled with modern scientific culture.[61] It belongs to mythical thinking and it is even impossible to separate therein the permanent from the transient.

Yet, Snethlage wants to speak of the principal motifs of Christianity[62] and he mentions by name the "number of tragic motifs: God, sin, death, which occur in religion." The issue for him is the philosophic criticism that defends the autonomy of the various problem fields, including that of religion. And in this field predestination is an important concept — "the embodiment of the magic-dramatic motif." In predestination the absolute sovereignty of the religious principle is carefully delineated.[63] One must not carry moral givens into the field of religion because in so doing sovereignty and autonomy would be violated.[64] Religion is not immoral, but amoral. That is the way in which the tragic-dramatic motifs that dominate religion become clear. There is also an ethical problem field but that must remain separate from tragic religion.

From this view of the tragic aspects in religion Snethlage can give an important place to Leninism, which also has incorporated the dramatic outlook.[65] But we are not interested here in the lines which Snethlage draws from Augustine and Calvin to Lenin,

61. Snethlage, "Christentum als Vorstellung und als Motiv," in *Zeitschrift für Theologie und Kirche* (1930). Cf. *De Anti-Ethicistische Godsidee,* p. 18.
62. Snethlage, *De Anti-Ethicistische Godsidee,* p. 18 and *Zeitschrift für Theologie und Kirche,* p. 279.
63. Snethlage, "Die Prädestination im Lichte des Kritizismus," *Zeitschrift für systematische Theologie* (1930), p. 35; *De Godsdienstige Filosophie van Immanuel Kant* (1931), pp. 243, 245.
64. See his criticism of Kant, who by absolutizing ethics does not maintain religion as an independent problem field (*De Godsdienstige Filosophie,* p. 238).
65. Snethlage, *Leninisme,* p. 8.

but in how he thinks of predestination. We find here the most extreme secularization of Paul's statement "not out of works but out of grace." The religious is separated from the moral — that is what predestination means. And in this secularization of election the demonic, tragic, and dramatic motifs find a place. Snethlage agrees with Wendt that predestination does not do justice to man's awareness of moral freedom and responsibility. However, that causes not its weakness but its power, because free will has no place in religion. The error lies in connecting concepts like "sin" with free will and then interpreting them morally, not tragically.

If one accepts the tragic interpretation he can honor the "demonic" traits completely, and Christianity would be able to protest emphatically against the humanized interpretation of Christianity. It is a terrible dilemma with which we are here confronted: humanization or demonization. It is good to know that we do not have to choose between them, that we may reject this dilemma completely. In humanization the image of God is measured by human standards, and this evokes reactions like those of Volz and Otto. But in demonization, arbitrariness is evoked with the "tragic" awareness of life as its subjective correlate.[66]

66. The three notions, demonic, tragic, and dramatic, are not well distinguished by Snethlage. One could ask, for instance, about the difference or the connection between the demonic and the tragic. In the literature on the tragic we often encounter the close relationship between arbitrariness and the tragic, for instance, with Miguel de Unamuno: "Das tragische Lebensgefühl" (in *Philosophische Werke*), originally printed in 1913 (Spanish), in which the rational concept of God (*summum esse*) is confronted with "the God of free arbitrariness" (p. 210) with a reference to "Kierkegaard's leap of desperation." Unamuno, whom Przywara called "the Spanish brother of Kierkegaard," also refers specifically to Pascal in *Die Agonie des Christentums* pp. 125ff.) with the question whether Pascal is not implicated by the Vatican Council (p. 132). There is a sharper attempt to distinguish in Max Scheler, "Zum Phänomen des Tragischen" (*Vom Umsturz der Werke*, 1919, I, 239-270). Especially with Scheler one can study the connections and interrelations with the problem of arbitrariness particularly where he connects the tragic with "the impossibility of localizing guilt" (p. 261) and applies that to Christ's cross — that Jesus' death was tragic because it was not a "judical murder" (p. 262). The conclusions at which Scheler arrives are very close to the concept of arbitrariness. It would be important to compare Scheler and Tillich (*Das Dämonische*). See also E. Przywara "Tragische Welt" (*Ringen der Gegenwart* I, 342ff.) and "Tragische Seele" (*ibid.*, II, 880ff.). Przywara rejects all these considerations and sees in Thomas

It should not be surprising that we discussed Snethlage's views rather extensively. For when humanization arouses a protest in favor of predestination, and liberal theology puts Paul on a pedestal, we must be careful not to fall from one error into the other. Even with an appeal to Paul and with a plea for predestination one can go far from the true message of Scripture. For here the eclogue becomes arbitrary, and Scripture is perverted so that the cast-out wedding guest is seen as *compendium praedestinationis,* because he did not carry the sign of election, even though he had accepted the invitation. In this accentuation of sovereignty, as well as in the preference for Paul's reference to sovereign grace ("I will have mercy on whom I have mercy"), the doctrine of election is affected to its very roots. This "demonic" interpretation of predestination is — although Snethlage's influence has not been very great — a warning example of the perversion of the essence of election.[67]

Divine election and moralism have often been set in opposition. Either from a critical-philosophical or from a theological perspective, men have seen in predestination — especially in its antimoralistic orientation — a connection with other important themes in the gospel, particularly with the phrase "not out of works" of Romans 9.

How important this strong light of the gospel is, is shown in man's repugnance to the light, which repugnance is precisely here revealed.[68] It is quite understandable, therefore, that

---

"the liberator of the tragic soul." (Here again we meet the well-known interpretation of Luther — arbitrariness and exclusive activity!)

67. Nowhere do I see this misjudgment more clearly than when we confront Snethlage with Luther. In Luther there is not a trace of humanization, but how different is his exegesis of Rom. 9:15 when he writes: "This sentence seems hard and horrible, but actually it is full of sweetness, because God has appropriated all help and all salvation for the sole purpose of granting salvation." See also his reference to Rom. 11:32. See Martin Luther's *Vorlesung über den Römerbrief,* 1515-16, (transcribed by E. Ellweien, 1928, p. 336). See Luther's discussion of Rom. 9 for an explanation of the eclogue.

68. Think also of HC, Q. 24 (a very relevant question when the Catechism was written — witness the criticism), concerning whether the doctrine of justification does not make men careless and profane. This question reflects an awareness of the existing criticism which accuses the Reformation of teaching that human arbitrariness is a result of divine arbitrariness.

theology repeatedly occupied itself with the danger of moralism as opposed to election even when predestination has not, as with Snethlage, become a vague idea.

It was especially Noordmans who, in "Praedestinatie" (*Geestelijke Perspectieven*, 1930), during the time of anti-humanistic and anti-moralistic reaction occupied himself with these important questions. No matter how far his viewpoint is removed from Snethlage's, the two authors' positions converge to some extent. That becomes evident when we see that Noordmans is concerned with the trans-moral character of predestination. "Predestination brings us above the normal moral sphere."[69]

It is not the Nietzschean position of "beyond good and evil," but there is something similar to Nietzsche in this reaching over and beyond morality.[70] God's predestination brings disorder in our moral world[71] and, says Noordmans, the best illustration of that may be found in some Russian novels in which "there is a glimmering of this preference for that which is lost and degenerate."[72] Predestination is thus the heart of the Church, although everywhere in the doctrine of the Church a certain accommodation to our moral sense can be found.[73] Noordmans apparently alludes to the New Testament eclogue and Christ's love for that which is lost. He automatically touches here upon the question of arbitrariness. Is God's election not arbitrary from the point of view of our morality? "The divine sovereign election lies as far removed as possible from our moral concepts. It is the most difficult one for us to understand. We are inclined to feel in it only arbitrariness and power."[74] This is the offense taken at Jesus, who loves publicans and sinners.[75]

But at the same time that Noordmans accentuates this radical trans-morality, he also understands the menace of arbitrariness. Since our moral judgment does not reach further, we may well speak of "power"; but "a more comprehensive, more penetrating judgment would discover the moral factors of predestination."[76]

---

69. *Op. cit.*, p. 4.
70. *Ibid.* For the rest, these two trends of thought are antipodal to each other.
71. *Ibid.*, p. 7.
72. *Ibid.*, p. 13.
73. *Ibid.*, p. 14.
74. *Ibid.*, p. 8.
75. *Ibid.*, p. 9.
76. *Ibid.*, p. 5.

Indeed, "the seeming arbitrariness would project itself in beautiful contours before an intellect of higher order."

This is a very remarkable position, in which Noordmans avoids Snethlage's reasoning and distinguishes predestination from arbitrariness by the act of faith. Nor is it simply a matter for an "intellect of higher order," for Noordmans implicates us in this prospect and says that, in spite of our limitations, surrender to God's good pleasure does open a way: "In the moments that we surrender we shall know that election is not arbitrariness but the highest morality,"[77] and "in the word 'grace' the Christian Church will hear the moral contents of God's sovereign election."[78] One may be of the opinion that the word *moral* is not at all clear in this connection, but it is certain that Noordman's intention is clear: he rejects arbitrariness in electing grace — as Paul in Romans 9 — and speaks therefore of the "mystical rapture" with which the chapters 9-11 of Romans close.[79]

While Noordmans was interested from the very beginning in the sovereignty of grace in the election of the Father of Jesus Christ,[80] the questions that repeatedly arise here occupied him later also. That was especially the case when in *Gestalte en Geest* (1955) he discussed life as action and as order.[81] In this connection Noordmans makes much use of the word "tragic." He chooses to use the words "drama" and "tragic," which are also used by Snethlage. But he qualifies them: human suffering can never be called tragic except in a figurative sense. If the harden-

77. *Ibid.*, p. 7.
78. *Ibid.*, p. 9.
79. *Ibid.*, p. 5. It seems to me that Noordmans is incorrect when he writes that Paul in the first part of Rom. 9 ("as long as he remains formal and considers things abstractly") cannot but push to the foreground the principal of power and then goes on to indicate the "moral beauty" of God's plan for the world. This contradicts Rom. 9-11 in its whole course of development, and also the reference to election in Rom. 9:11 that precedes the reference to Moses, Pharaoh, and the potter. See further for Noordmans' view, "De Betekenis van Kohlbrugge voor de Theologie van Onze Tijd" in *Geestelijke Perspectieven*, especially on predestinational Reformed theology and on the limitations of ethical religion (*ibid.*, p. 36).
80. Predestination "must in Christ be liberated from its abstractness," "Praedestinatie," p. 10). It is clear that Noordmans does not have any interest in a religious motif, but that his concern lies with the reality of the electing God. That is perfectly clear also when he speaks of the "idea of predestination" and when he calls it "the highest in the hierarchy of Christian ideas" (p. 14).
81. *Ibid.*, p. 51.

ing of the heart is called tragic by him, it is only tragic in a special way; and its tragic aspect is defined with many reservations.[82]

In what he calls tragic, Noordmans does not reach beyond the order of things into arbitrariness. Rather, he accentuates that in hardening of the heart sin becomes more and more man's own sin. According to him the Bible does not warrant the thought of any elements of fate, not even when it speaks of sin and guilt.[83] Noordmans does ask, however, where certainty may be found: "Is there not in the Bible something that goes beyond and above tragedy, above and beyond the clash between two or more superhuman powers?"[84] "Who will battle his way through the tragedy of fate?" But in all tensions, in "this tragedy of history" he finds a hymn, a gospel. "Above and beyond tragedy justice sometimes steps out of its tent. The one Name points out the way of escape out of the tragic confusion of our lives."[85]

It is clear how far Snethlage and Noordmans are removed from each other. The words they both use — tragedy and drama — are used in very different contexts. Snethlage deals with a philosophic concept, Noordmans with God's election, the gospel. That is the reason why Noordmans can speak with Otto of the *mysterium tremendum*.

Together with the rejection of a humanized concept of God, Noordmans with ever increasing emphasis rejects also the concept of arbitrariness. He protests against every interpretation of the divine acts that is based on the moral process within us. Such an interpretation would be the result of man's search for a reason "to turn his face, and man would want that reason present in the form of a moral condition."[86] Noordmans rejects here the so-called analytical justification. But at the same time he refuses to acknowledge the idea of arbitrariness in God. For the thoughts of God are not idle thoughts; it is only that they do not find support in the human ethical process. God's thoughts are not occupied with our virtues but with our sins and needs. "This characteristic of God's thinking bothers our ethical pride,

82. *Ibid.*, pp. 51, 52. See references to the most tragic night of Saul's life (*ibid.*, p. 33).
83. *Ibid.*, p. 52.
84. *Ibid.*, p. 24.
85. *Ibid.*, p. 35.
86. *Ibid.*, p. 60.

but we do not have the right to complain that it turns His thoughts into a vacuum."[87]

There is an ethics of God's heart, and this ethics is not affected by the rejection of analytical justification. Nor is this ethics threatened by absolute arbitrariness. For it is here that God's love and mercy are revealed, and in the way of confession of guilt and of faith arbitrariness is banished. It is, says Noordmans, the elder son of the parable, not the younger, who complains that the father is unpredictable and his thinking unethical.[88] This is the context in which arbitrariness is rejected — the context of sin. There is nothing arbitrary in God's turning away from sin. Nor is His the attitude of the pagan god who alternately nods or shakes his head. Our God is the Father of the New Testament.[89]

With Noordmans, and with many others, the rejection of arbitrariness concentrates on Christ and His cross. The rejection of analytical justification and the plea for synthetic, declaratory, imputative justification are not the result of playing a game with concepts; they find their foundation in the cross. When in the Reformation the righteousness of Christ was called the foreign righteousness (*justitia aliena*), this "foreignness" did not imply a reference to arbitrariness in God which remained foreign to human life. Rather, it was a reference to that other, that foreign, justice which does not arise in us but which grants grace out of mercy. Precisely for that reason arbitrariness and the doubts that come with it are banished by the certainty of salvation. "Therefore, when at times your heart trembles for your life and your lip quivers as you face destiny, do not take it too tragically. God does not do so. From eternity He determined your destiny in His Kingdom."[90] When God changes the shadow of death into the light of morning, that is not arbitrariness but the gospel.[91]

The thought of arbitrariness can only arise from unbelief and pride. It is a pure fabrication of man's heart, the last stand against the offense of the cross in which man fails to discover that the foolishness of God is wiser than men.

87. *Ibid.*, p. 61.
88. *Ibid.*, p. 62.
89. *Ibid.*, p. 64.
90. *Gestalte en Geest*, p. 95.
91. *Ibid.*, p. 97.

We have discussed in detail the idea of arbitrariness in God. We have seen that we may never take this road, for he who takes it will find that on it everything becomes obscured: faith and its certainty, revelation and the history of salvation, election in Christ, and the very nature of election. Diametrically opposed to the electing God are the arbitrariness of sin, anarchy, guilt, resistance, the arbitrariness of the time of the Judges when there was no king in Israel (Judg. 18:1, 19:1) and everyone did what was right in his own eyes (Judg. 17:6, 21:25), the arbitrariness of any age, whenever justice is disregarded and life is mutilated until the end of time.

In the arbitrariness of man life is no longer safe. There is a "strangeness" that encounters life, a strangeness from which arises the problem of senselessness and "the absurd" that makes life unbearable. This arbitrariness is not just the result of misrepresenting God's grace and justice; it is also the opposite of God's holiness and glory. That is the reason why we are warned not to project our arbitrariness into God and why we are called to conversion, which makes us find peace again in the covenant that never fails and in God whom we may hold true to His Word.

That God's acts are not arbitrary is nowhere more clearly shown than in Nehemiah 9. It is a story of tremendous scope, of grace and of judgment. Throughout the story shines the light of the pillar of cloud and the pillar of fire (Neh. 9:12), of God's righteous laws (Neh. 9:13), of His gifts of bread and water and, especially (in the face of man's guilt), of His mercy (Neh. 9:17-19). Not terror or fright but faith is the subjective correlate of this non-arbitrariness. For in the prayer of Nehemiah can in tsis connection be said, "and [thou] foundest his heart faithful before thee" (Neh. 9:8).[92]

Here God's election is not dependent on morality. Rather, man's heart is raised above arbitrariness when it finds rest in God's mercy. While the idea of arbitrariness casts man's life into arbitrariness, God's mercy liberates it unto certainty and trust. He who trusts this mercy — without the works of the law — will ever increasingly understand that this is precisely the way in which he comes into contact with divine election, election that is revealed in the way of faith.

---

92. Cf. this phrase about the faithfulness of Abraham's heart with the other phrase in the same verse: "and hast performed thy words; for thou art righteous."

CHAPTER FOUR

ELECTION AND THE HIDDENNESS OF GOD

AS a matter of course we encounter still other questions when we now shall discuss the relationship between election and hiddenness. We have discovered that the election of God is by no means arbitrary; but the situation is more complex with respect to the hiddenness of God. The hiddenness of God can be interpreted in various ways, some of which even come close to agnosticism. But even he who knows Scripture, knows that there, too, we read of the hiddenness of God. Hence it is quite natural that precisely in connection with God's election His hiddenness is repeatedly mentioned, and that the question whether God's election is not hidden plays various roles. Later we shall devote a separate discussion to the relationship between election and the certainty of salvation, but now we wish to consider that question which so often is the occasion of doubt and uncertainty: the question whether God's election does not belong to those aspects of faith which, because of their hiddenness, fall — and must fall — beyond the knowledge of faith. Is that perhaps the meaning of those statements which appear in the history of Church and theology regarding the hiddenness of election? And, if this is the case, of what use is it to dismiss election, which because it is related to faith, is always oriented toward God's *revelation?* Moreover, if God's election is indeed hidden, is it then still possible with confidence to adhere to and rely upon God's revelation, both for time and eternity? Can we then still speak of the *comfort* of election?

These questions confront us with the meaning and function of the doctrine of election in the life of the Church. Questions about election touch immediately upon the task of the ministry, which is continually asked to "compensate" for the so-called "hiddenness" of election. If election definitely belongs to the hidden things, in distinction to the revealed things that are for us and our children (Deut. 29:29), is it then possible that the confession of the doctrine of election still has a function in the realm of the Church, or does that doctrine unavoidably become "background," acknowledged as true but unknown to us in content and purpose? In other words, does God's election still belong to the *kerygma* of the Church, or must it remain in the background because of its nature? But how, in the latter case, can it avoid becoming a menace to the simplicity and certainty of man's faith, threatening his very assurance of eternal salvation?[1] It is not surprising that these were important questions at the time of the Reformation, and that they still are so today.

We can even refer to a confessional answer to these questions. CD, I, 14 says not only that the doctrine of divine election "according to God's wise counsel" was preached by the prophets, by Christ, and by the apostles, and after that was taught in Scripture, but it adds: "so it is still to be published in due time and place in the Church of God."[2]

---

1. The question about the relation between election and preaching has received ample discussion. See Augustine, who discusses the question whether the treatment of predestination does not decrease the benefit of preaching (*De dono perseverantiae*, XIV, 34). Augustine refers for his answer to Scripture, for instance, to Phil. 2:13 and 1:6. He treats this matter also with reference to the question whether the truth may be kept unmentioned after the example of Christ's statement: "I have yet many things to say unto you, but ye cannot bear them now," John 16:12 (*ibid*. p. 40). He then emphasizes the necessity of speaking the truth. It is striking that Augustine remarks here that the enemy of grace always refers to man's merit, and should we not oppose him by referring to the testimony of Scripture? Calvin refers to Augustine's considerations in the *Consensus Genevensis*. See also Chapter VII.

2. That this must be done "with reverence, in the spirit of discretion and piety . . . without vainly attempting to investigate the secret ways of the Most High" is an important and necessary warning but does not cancel the significance of the preceding statements. We point out that in numerous discussions of election the connection with preaching and with the practical implications of this doctrine is indicated. See also M. W. Nieuwenhuyze, "De verkiezing met het oog op de practijk des geloofs" (in *Enigheid des Geloofs*, Vol. III, Nos. 25-26; 16-23 Sept., 1949); E. G. van Teylingen, "De leer der verkiezing en de geloofspracktijk" (*ibid.*, Vol. IV, No. 1; Oct. 14, 1949); G. J. Steeder, (*ibid.*, Oct. 28, 1949); J. van Genderen, "Verkiezing en Prediking" (*ibid.*, Vol. VI, No. 1ff., beg. Oct. 5, 1951.); J G. Woelderink, "De waarheid der verkiezing en haar ontwikkeling" (*ibid.*, Sept. 16, 1949); Rudolf Grob, "Erwählung und Verkündigung" (*De l'élection éternelle de Dieu*, 1936, pp. 157-167). See also Chapter VII.

This accords completely with the spirit of the Reformation, which so emphatically opposed the isolation of election from the life of the Church. The Reformers were concerned to show that the confession of the doctrine of election did not menace the assurance of salvation. Calvin, for instance, continually refers to Christ, not as a compensation to the hiddenness of election, but as the mirror of election. In this he followed Augustine, who spoke of Christ as the *manifestatio electionis*.[3] Luther and the Lutheran confessions describe Christ as "the Book of Life." Such words prove that the Reformers, at any rate, did not view God's election as an obscure, inscrutable, and unapproachable background which could impair the message of salvation. Election was not seen as a cloud intercepting the sunlight. Rather, the Church's message could and was allowed to give a definite answer to all questions about election and its hiddenness, namely, the answer of the trustworthy revelation in Jesus Christ.

In the sixteenth century a radical critique arose against the Roman Catholic view of the hiddenness of election. The Council of Trent states emphatically that election is a hidden mystery into which no one can penetrate to determine with certainty "that he belongs to those that are destined to be saved." According to Trent, election is so hidden that it is impossible to know who has been elected by God, unless God reveals it in a special manner. Thus Trent posits a connection, not, as the Reformed Church, between the knowledge of salvation and the revelation in Christ, but between the knowledge of election and a special message from God. Apart from such a message the hiddenness of election remains.[4] Stakemeier has said that the point of Trent was "to describe the practical attitude of the Christian in the face of the hiddenness of election,"[5] and he refers to Romans 11:33-36. He reminds us of Seripando, who "asked for the mute adoration of this mystery which God wanted to keep hidden from us in order that our hearts remain humble before Him."[6] Trent teaches, then, the hiddenness of the mys-

---

3. See my *The Triumph of Grace in the Theology of Karl Barth* (1954), pp. 280ff.
4. Denzinger, *Enchiridion*, pp. 805, 825.
5. A. Stakemeier: *Das Konzil von Trient über die Heilsgewissheit* (1947), p. 185.
6. See on this humility: E. Stakemeier: *Der Kampf um Augustin auf dem Tridentinum*, (1937), pp. 218ff., who says that Seripando's view became victorious and officially accepted.

tery of election except for certain special messages from God.[7]
Stakemeier uses in this connection the words of Rudolf Otto:
"God is for us the *fascinosum* so that we place our lot in His
hands, but He is also the *tremendum* and that makes us
humble."[8]

Diametrically opposed to this mystery, this hidden election,
and this "mute reverence," the Reformation emphatically posited
God's revelation, the manifestation of the election in Christ which
rules out the necessity of a special message of election.[9]   Even
Calvin, who so often has been accused of teaching an obscure,
hidden election, spoke of the revelation of election.   No one, he
said, can avoid thinking at one time or another: What revelation
do I have of my election? (*Inst.* III, xxiv, 4).   If this thought
becomes pressing, it can torture and perplex a man continually.
He then begins to search into the "hiddenness" of election, and
that, says Calvin, is always disastrous.   He who searches the
eternal counsel of God apart from His Word in order to become
certain of his election, throws himself into a dangerous abyss.
On the contrary, says Calvin, it is possible to be no longer terrified by the hiddenness of election.

Inquiry into predestination may be compared to venturing upon a dangerous sea; however, it may be safe and calm and it is
possible to sail pleasantly when man does not attempt to go into
dangerous regions by his own will (*Inst.* III, xxvi, 9).[10]   But
the way of exceptional divine messages is not safe.   He
recommends, rather, the way in which the eye is turned to
Christ, in whom alone the Father is well pleased (*ibid.*, 5). And
then from Calvin comes that well-known word about the cer-

7. See Denzinger, *op. cit.*, p. 802.   See further my *Conflict with Rome*
(1955[3]), Chap. V; V. Heynck, *Zur Kontroverse über die Gnadengewissheit
auf dem Konzil von Trient*, who refers to the newly discovered fact
by Malafassa who "very emphatically opposed the possibility of man's
certainty of salvation" (*Fransz. Studien*, 1955).

8. E. Stakemeier, *Der Kampf um Augustin*, p. 219.   See also Gustaf
Ljunggren, *Zur Geschichte der Christliche Heilsgewissheit von
Augustin bis zur Hochscholastik* (1920), especially pp. 269ff.

9. This does not imply that medieval thinkers did not reflect on the
relationship between Christ and election.   See about Bonaventura:
Ljunggren, *op. cit.*, p. 276ff.

10. See also *Inst.* III, xxi, 1 for the possibility of predestination becoming
dangerous because of the curiosity of the people who cannot be restrained
from wandering into forbidden paths, and climbing to the clouds,
determined, if it can, that none of the secret things of God shall remain
unexplored.

tainty of election: "But if we are elected in him, we cannot find the certainty of our election in ourselves; and not even in God the Father, if we look at him apart from the Son" (*ibid.*).

Christ alone "is the mirror, in which we ought and in which without deception, we may contemplate our election" (*ibid.*). Calvin does not reject the investigation of predestination, but if we investigate it we must remember that we penetrate into the hiddenness of divine wisdom so that "he who rushes forward securely and confidently, instead of satisfying his curiosity will enter an inextricable labyrinth" (*Inst.* III, xxi, 1). If the question concerns the hiddenness of God's will we shall have to remember that He has made it knowable to us by His Word, and for that reason Calvin repeatedly indicates to us a way which we must and can walk. Never will man be able to find out anything by himself *in abstracto* as the result of his desire to penetrate into God's secrecy (*ibid.*).

There is only one way to view election without illusion or deceit. The hiddenness of election does not have to be compensated for by any extraordinary revelation, a message as to what has been decided before God's judgment throne, (*Inst.* III, xxiv, 4) ; rather, by walking the way of faith God's revelation in Christ is revealed. Calvin refers to Augustine, who calls Christ *"clarissimum lumen praedestinationis et gratiae"* (*Inst.* II, xvii, 1), and according to Calvin there is no greater temptation from Satan than when he disquiets the believers with doubt concerning their election and then tempts them with the desire to investigate it in a wrong way (*Inst.* III, xxiv, 4). Why should we soar above the clouds to obtain certainty about God's counsel, or continue to live in uncertainty if God Himself in His Word is sufficient witness? (*ibid.*, 3).

Apart from this Word man will certainly fall into an *exitialis abyssus*, but this *abyssus* is not a characteristic of God's real election. The image of the abyss can arise only when man travels "apart from the way." There is only one way. "Jesus Christ is the mirror to which we must lift our eyes if we want to gain knowledge regarding our election. For he who believes in Jesus Christ is the child of God" and for that reason "Christ is worth more than a thousand testimonies."[11]

---

11. H. Otten, *Calvins theologische Anschauung von der Praedestination* (1938), p. 37. Since I indicated in *Triumph of Grace* the important references I was struck by the clearness of this deciding aspect in Calvin's *Consensus Genevensis* (1552), (*"De aeterna Predestinatione"*),

That is the reason why Calvin can speak on the one hand of "hidden election" and on the other hand of "revelation," the proclamation of election.   Election is not hidden in the sense that there are no answers to our questions about it, but rather in the sense that apart from Christ we may not attempt to penetrate into the hiddenness of God's will.

It is not surprising that Calvin in an important discussion refers to Deuteronomy 30:14, a passage that has been quoted in many discussions.   He refers to it when he speaks of God who has made our election known unto us (*Inst.* III, xxiv, 3).[12] Deuteronomy speaks of God's commandment in a manner which is also interesting with respect to election.   For God says of that commandment: It is not too hard for thee, neither is it far off" (Deut. 30:11).   It is not in heaven, nor is it at the other side of the sea.   "But the word is very nigh unto thee, in thy mouth, and in thy heart, that thou mayest do it" (Deut. 30:14). Here the question concerns the distance or the proximity of God's commandment.   That it is distant, mysteriously hidden, is emphatically denied.   It is not unattainable and it does not belong to the hidden things mentioned in Deuteronomy 29:29, but rather to what is revealed to us and our children.   He who thinks he must apprehend it afar off misjudges the urgent proximity of the commandment and the responsibility which it entails. The connection between the proclamation of election, of which Calvin speaks, and the reference to Deuteronomy 30:14 is not far-fetched, for Paul also refers to this passage when he speaks in Romans 10:6ff. of the righteousness of faith.   What does the righteousness of faith say?   "Say not in thy heart, Who shall ascend into heaven? (that is, to bring Christ down): or Who shall descend into the abyss? (that is, to bring Christ up from

---

which is all the more significant because precisely this aspect is criticized and regarded as belonging to Calvin's most harsh formulations. See H. A. Niemeyer; *Collectio confessionum in ecclesiis reformatis* (1840), pp. 218ff.   Think of the polemics between Calvin and Bolsec and the hesitations on the part of the rest of the Swiss churches (especially Bullinger).   This *Consensus* has not become a generally accepted symbol (Schweizer, *Die Centraldogmen der reformierten Kirche*, 1854, I, 231ff.).   And now we find also in this *Consensus* numerous references to Christ as the mirror of salvation.

12. See also, about the hiddenness of His will which He decided to make known to us, *Inst.* III, xxi, 1.

the dead). But what saith it? The word is nigh thee, in thy mouth, and in thy heart: that is, the word of faith which we preach" (Rom. 10:6-8). Paul speaks here of God's gift, which is not so far away that man must first exert himself before he can obtain it. Salvation is preached in Christ; it is not necessary for one to travel a long way to overcome its hiddenness; he should simply accept this gift in faith.

And as Paul refers to Deuteronomy and discovers relationships with the structure of revelation, so Calvin refers to the "closeness" in Deuteronomy when he speaks of the proclamation of election. This proclamation is not at all a theoretical communication which can be understood apart from faith, but it is a proclamation concerning the way that leads to Christ. Election is not an epistemological mystery which always remains hidden to us, but it is a revelation in Christ and thus is close to us.

It was undoubtedly Calvin's intention, when he referred to Deuteronomy 30, to underline with those words "It is not far away" (Deut. 30:11), and "Say not in thy heart" (Rom. 10:6) that profound argument for the knowledge of election in his *Institutes* where he emphasizes the closeness, the proximity — in contrast to the hidden abyss and the obscure danger — of which Scripture often speaks with reference to salvation.

This proximity he does not limit simply to the historical level of God's Word and promise and Kingdom in order to draw a contrast between the hiddenness of God and the historical closeness of God's salvation. Rather, he rejects this differentiation as a temptation, and even discovers in it Satan's most powerful temptation. We should consider what Scripture teaches concerning the approaching Kingdom (Matt. 3:2) and God's eschatological Day (Rom. 13:12), and in connection with that concerning man's coming nearer, like the heathen who were at first far off but now have come close through the blood of Christ (Eph. 2:13, 17), and like the believers who are called upon to "draw nigh to God, and he will draw night to you" (Jas. 4:8).[13] When Calvin reads this being nigh in Paul's reference to Deuteronomy 30, (Rom. 10:8), he does not hesitate to call us to the assurance of salvation by way of faith in Christ. Do not say in your heart. . . .

For here we need not descend into the abyss (Rom. 10:7). It

13. See Heb. 7:19, and Kittel, *T.W.N.T.*, II, 329ff.

cannot be done and it may not be done, and he who thinks that
the "hidden" election is remote and then attempts to solve
the problem of election for and by himself must experience that
then election becomes an abyss and a labyrinth in which he can
only lose his way.

It is clear that Calvin goes an altogether different way than
Rome. For Calvin election is only then a threatening shadow,
a menacing fact, when it is approached apart from "the way."
For Rome election remains the background, the mystery which
rules out any certainty of salvation. Here humility becomes the
subjective correlate of the *tremendum,* and although in exceptional cases the certainty of salvation is conveyed by means of
an extraordinary revelation, the exceptional aspect of it indicates
how much this mystery is and remains hidden in the way of
the Church. The exceptional has lost its connection with the revelation in Christ. It is a different sort of mirror from the one
taught by Calvin.

We must remember this contrast clearly in order to understand that the questions and worries of many people, especially
in connection with God's election, are based upon a view far
different from that which influenced the Reformation so profoundly. For many people election is that doctrine which unavoidably evokes the same problems that overschadows Trent:
whether we can know with certainty that we belong to the
numerus praedestinatorum.

This *numerus* problem casts its deep shadow over the assurance of salvation and returns as a burning problem after
each pastoral admonition. Man wants to solve it, even though
he cannot solve it as a problem standing by itself, detached
from the way of salvation. It then makes its influence felt in
many distractions which continually disturb the depths of his
soul. The reference to the revelation in Christ is understood as a well-meant attempt to still the storm of questions and
doubts, but at bottom it is thought to be nothing but an impotent
pastoral device, an effort to compensate for the "high tension" of
the hidden election. And so long as the reference to Christ as
"mirror of election" continues to be regarded as such a compensation, and its depth remains undiscovered, the question
will arise again and again whether this *speculum* is truly capable
of such reflection and whether it really is so simple that the
depths of election are understood and experienced when one
flees to Jesus Christ. The *numerous* problem as an abstract prob-

lem continues, then, to cast its shadow over all the concreteness of the gospel; and the hiddenness of election, rather than
its revelation in Christ, fills the heart.[14]

The question that engages us can be illustrated more precisely
in connection with an expression which Luther often used:
Jesus Christ is the Book of Life. This expression, as well as
Calvin's *speculum electionis,* was meant to indicate the knowability of election, not *in abstracto* but concretely. Christ is the
Book of Life which man can and must read. It cannot be said
that Luther's expression was the serious result of an exegesis
of those words in Scripture which speak of the Book of Life.
It is more a bold pastoral intuition which at this point confirms
again the close connection between Lutheran and Reformed
theologians on central questions.

In the Formula of Concord we find the expression *liber
vitae* in the chapter on election. There, too, we find an aversion similar to Calvin's against an illegitimate penetration into
the secrets of God's will. Of predestination it is said: "It cannot
be searched and found in the secret counsel of God, but it must
be sought in the Word in which it has been revealed"; and this
Word of God "leads us to Christ, who is the Book of Life, in
which are contained all the names of those who shall have life
eternal, as it is written: 'He has elected us in Christ before
the foundation of the world'." Further, it is emphasized that,
if one wants to consider predestination correctly and fruitfully,
"one must cultivate the habit not to speculate about the unsearchable and hidden predestination of God, but think and reflect how
the counsel and ordinance of God in Jesus Christ — who is the
true Book of Life — is revealed to us in His Word."[15]

Thus Calvin, by pointing to Christ as the mirror of election,
and Luther, by referring to Christ as the Book of Life, have
shown us in similar manner the same pastoral and theological
thesis regarding the knowability, the revelation, of election. And
the burning question here is whether Trent has not reached too
far, above and beyond the humility which would suit man in
the face of this *mysterium tremendum.*

It is difficult to deny that to many the expression Book of

---

14. Think in this connection of the "number question" in Luke 13:23,
    "Lord, are they few that are saved?" The answer is straightforward
    and hides nothing: "Strive to enter in."
15. Müller, *op. cit.,* pp. 554 and 707.

Life offers less solace than evidently is possible in Lutheran theology. We are confronted with the fact that for many believers precisely that expression, Book of Life, is felt to be an indication of the hiddenness, the non-revealedness of election. Is it not true that for many this book is a book of hiddenness which we cannot and may not read, a book in which names are written before the eye of God, but unknown to us? And cannot much of this doubt be described as uncertainty about the question whether *our* names are written in that book?

The Lutheran designation of Christ as the Book of Life may be a remarkable pastoral discovery, but it may also be no more than an intuition. Does its rather loose connection with the words of Scripture about the Book of Life perhaps indicate an illegitimate use of this expression, by which not sound exegesis but intuition leads us to certainty?

The person who mutely resists this Lutheran intuition and continues to think of the Book of Life as a hidden record of unknown names — a thought which can terrify the heart — must be very surprised when he notices in Scripture the manner in which it speaks of the Book of Life. We may remind ourselves of the word which Christ once spoke to His disciples: "Nevertheless in this rejoice not, that the spirits are subject unto you; but rejoice that your names are written in heaven" (Luke 10:20). When the seventy returned from their triumphal mission in which the evil spirits were subject to them there was joy in their hearts. They had acted in Christ's name, and Christ Himself attached the vertical perspective to their horizontal triumph: "I beheld Satan fall as lightning from heaven" (Luke 10:18). Christ did not at all minimize the profound meaning of what had happened, but suddenly He spoke a warning. They must not lose themselves in what was to be seen in the horizontal happening as such, but they must pay especially close attention to the background of this powerful incident which occurred through them.

Those deeds of the disciples — regarded in themselves — were still open to further interpretation; and, furthermore, the danger threatened that they might lose themselves in the earthly aspect of their spiritual battle. For that reason they must remember that the way they traveled could be joyful to them only if they understood and continued to understand that behind their work and activity stood God's gift: their names were written in heaven. This must be their deep joy: not their deeds in them-

selves, as though their work found its origin in them, but God's
authorization and His grace. We are struck here by the profound relation between their names being written in heaven and
their joy. That is a strange connection, which is far removed
from the usual one which correlates the Book of Life (the hidden book) with the uncertainty and hesitation of the believer.

This contrast is very strong and furnishes a fundamental correction of the wrong interpretation of the Book of Life, the
more so since it does not concern just an isolated passage of the
Bible. If we think that the Book of Life is a mysterious entity,
a hiddenness, and that the names written therein are unknown
to us and must remain unknown — perhaps for reasons which
Trent calls our humility — then we are struck by Paul's testimony when he writes clearly of Clemens and his fellow workers
that their names are written in the Book of Life (Phil. 4:3).
It seems that the Book of Life to Paul is not a mysterious entity: he speaks freely of it and "reads" in it, with the result that
he mentions names that are written in it.

It is also striking, however, that such passages are nevertheless infrequent in Scripture and that the Book of Life is mentioned in certain other connections, especially the dynamic connection: "He that overcometh shall thus be arrayed in white
garments; and I will in no wise blot his name out of the book
of life" (Rev. 3:5). The Book of Life appears here in the
context of admonishment and perseverance. It lacks the traits
which it often displays in dogmatic theology and in the
consciousness of many believers. In the terminology of the latter one would hesitate to speak so emphatically of the possibility
of "blotting out," and one would perhaps see in it a weakening of
the doctrine of the perseverance of the saints. But Scripture
speaks thus freely, the more so, since we already hear of the
Book of Life in the Old Testament. Moses prays for forgiveness for the people and says "if not, blot me, I pray thee, out
of thy book that thou hast written" (Ex. 32:32).

And not only in the consideration of Moses, who supposes that
he is written in the Book of Life, but also in the divine answer
this "blotting out" is mentioned: "Whosoever hath sinned against
me, him will I blot out of my book" (Ex. 32:33). Blotting out
is correlated with guilt, and the question may therefore be
asked — in the exegesis — whether Gispen is correct when
he writes: "The Lord does not say whether He always does
that, or ever does that." That probably is related to the fact

that Gispen continues: "Later on more about this book is re-vealed, about the electing counsel of God. This verse must be understood in the light of Scripture."[16]

Is this connection between the Book of Life and the decision of election correct? It is understandable how this interrelation has come about, for the New Testament speaks so concretely about the Book of Life that it is impossible in this non-dogmatic terminology to explain one passage systematically without the aid of others. It is very remarkable that the Book of Life is also mentioned as having a steady, specific content in the sense that the aspects of stability and certainty are clearly attached to it. We hear of the assembly of the firstborn "whose names are written in heaven" (Heb. 12:33), and in Revelation we hear that all those "who dwell on earth will worship it [the beast], everyone whose name has not been written before the foundation of the world in the book of life of the Lamb that was slain" (Rev. 13:8). We even read of those "whose name hath not been written from the foundation of the world in the book of life of the Lamb" (Rev. 17:8), while being cast into the pool of fire is connected with those whose names are not written in the Book of Life (Rev. 20:15), and finally it is said of the new Jerusalem that only those will enter it whose names are written in the Book of Life of the Lamb (Rev. 21:27).

These passages clearly indicate the depth aspect of salvation. It is not a matter of hiddenness which goes beyond the knowl-edge of faith, and consciousness of which is only a menace and un-certainty (the silent threat), but there is a profound connection indicated between the election in Christ of Ephesians 1:4 and the passages in Scripture about the Book of Life. It is not accidental that the Book of Life is mentioned in connection with the Lamb. Greijdanus writes that the Book of Life is also called the Book of the Lamb "because it was given to Him, and because those names were written in it for His sake."[17] The unassail-ability of salvation in Christ lies expressed in it.

Passages about the Book of Life are abundant in Revelation, the book in which safety and solace are promised in the face of all apocalyptic dangers and threats. But these passages do not imply passivity (Rev. 3:5); they convey, instead, a word of promise to those who persevere in the way of faith. That is

16. Gispen, *Korte Verklaring*, II, 196.
17. In his commentary on Revelation, p. 274.

the reason why in really Scriptural thought no correlation can be maintained between the Book of Life and a hidden threat to the certainty of salvation. The Book of Life does not stand as a hidden thing over against the revelation of God in the world. He who believes that it does interprets the Book of Life out of its Biblical context. It becomes the "unknown" and as such it can no longer bring joy. But in the Bible it is not something far distant, not a vague, threatening reality, but the foundation of salvation, which is understood and experienced in the way of faith. He who refers to the Book of Life to "prove" the hiddenness of election has not understood the joy which Scripture clearly associates with it. It is the Book of Life and of the Lamb.

The Book of Life is connected with deep joy (Luke 10:20), with service of the gospel (Phil. 4:3), and with solace amidst great terror. "In the New Testament the Book of Life becomes free of fatalism, it becomes the expression of the certainty of salvation for God's children who know themselves chosen for eternity because they have their eternal foundation in God's counsel of grace."[18]

Truly, the presence of one's name in the Book does not depend on one's faith and perseverance, but it is correlated with it. When Kittel writes: "Here we find the idea of predestination but not without the emphasis on the motif of willing obedience,"[19] he is perfectly correct; but that correlation we find meaningfully manifest throughout Scripture, most unmistakably in II Timothy 2:19: "Howbeit the firm foundation of God standeth, having this seal, The Lord knoweth them that are his: and, Let every one that nameth the name of the Lord depart from unrighteousness."

With respect to this Book of Life no speculation is therefore permissible. Only in the way of faith and perseverance does the foundation of salvation become visible. The Lutheran typification (Book of Life) and Calvin's mirror of election conform exactly to the structure of the Book of Life and the Lamb. Just here we see that an incursion is made into all fatalism, and that there is a way in which certainty can grow. We learn not to speculate about hidden things, but to adhere to the revelation given for us and our children.

In Revelation 20:12 we hear of the books that are opened "and another book was opened, which is the book of life." The

18. Kittel, *T. W. N. T.*, I, 619.
19. *Ibid.*

dead are judged on the basis of what was written in the books, on the basis of their works. Here is mention of open books *and* of the Book of Life. Greijdanus mentions only that the books stand side-by-side of the Book of Life and does not say more about it. But it is strange that they stand there beside each other, the more so since judgment is made according to what is written in the books, according to man's works. The light of the Book of Life falls here unexpectedly on the concreteness of the life of faith and of its works. It is clear that this side-by-side arrangement is not meant as a contrast. That would be the case if the books contained only the aspect of meritorious good works, and if the Book of Life contained only the aspect of election and *sola gratia*. But the Book of Life is the Book of the Lamb, and he who has his name written in it reveals his election in the concreteness of his life of faith on earth. That is why judgment can be made on the basis of man's works, as Paul also says that we shall be judged according to our works. Finally, the depth aspect of the "opened books" is also revealed in the passage: "And he that is athirst, let him come: he that will, let him take the water of life freely" (Rev. 22:17; see also 22:21).

Thus those Scriptural passages in which the Book of Life serves as a basis for admonition and comfort do not allow it to be interpreted as a threat to certainty because of its hiddenness. It is still possible, however, that we might encounter such a shadow somewhere else in Scripture. For is there no reason at all to reflect on that expression which has played such an important role in the history of dogma, the *deus absconditus*? Does not the Word of God teach clearly and explicitly that God hides Himself (Isa. 45:15)? Is this, perhaps, where we are confronted with the hiddenness of election?

Before we seek an answer to this question we want to point out that in dogmatics we meet with a well-known distinction that is very similar to hiddenness: the distinction between the hidden will of God and the revealed will of God.[20] This distinction, says Bavinck, was worked out thoroughly by Scholasticism, taken over

20. Latin: *voluntas arcana — revelata;*
   voluntas decernens — praecipiens;
   voluntas beneplaciti — signi.

by Roman Catholic theology, and treated with great respect in Reformed theology.[21]

The fact that in this context the terms *voluntas decernens* and *voluntas beneplaciti* are also used proves how complex is this distinction between hiddenness and revealedness. Bavinck points out that the Reformed Church kept only the former distinction and rejected the one between *voluntas antecedens* and *consequens,* which elsewhere became very popular but which was seen by the Reformed Church to be a violation of the *simplicitas Dei.* The question is why they have not felt this objection with reference to the distinction between hidden will and revealed will, the more so since the *voluntas arcana* (*decernens, beneplaciti*) was regarded "as the really essential will of God," that is to say, the will that always moves on and reaches God's goal. Precisely for that reason the question can arise whether we then can know the actual will of God. We know the *voluntas revelata;* but this will, this seal, this precept of God, this direction for our conduct, is described by Bavinck as "actually not the will of God but only His command and precept."[22]

The actual will of God is, then, not that which He gives us as a precept, but that which He in Himself wills to do and fulfills. That is why we must now attend to this distinction. For, on the one hand, if the revealed will of God is not indeed His actual will, we do not know God's will; on the other hand, if the revealed will of God is also His actual will, we are confronted with a contradiction. The answer has always been that the *voluntas signi* (*revelata*) nevertheless receives its name from its relation to God's will, that it is a *signum voluntatis in Deo* and "consequently must correspond with His *voluntas beneplaciti.*" We are confronted with a profound dilemma: the hiddenness of God's will (one with God's essence, unchangeable and always fulfilled) *versus* the unactual will (God's ordinance),[23] or a contradiction in the will of God, or at least a tension between hiddenness and revelation with respect to His will.

In all Reformed discussions of this distinction the contradiction is emphatically denied. According to Bavinck it is ruled out because the will of the ordinance "is precisely the way in which

21. *Gereformeerde Dogmatiek*, II, 211.
22. *Ibid.,* pp. 213-214.
23. *Ibid.,* p. 214. Bavinck also says that the *voluntas signi* is God's will in the methaphorical sense.

the *voluntas beneplaciti* is fulfilled" (cf. *Inst.* I, xviii, 3).
He means that God fulfills His counsel and that man also in
his sin "becomes an instrument, although unwilling, of His
glory."[24]

It is clear that the point at issue here is the nature of God's
acts, especially in connection with sin, and we can see clearly
that Augustine as well as Calvin and Bavinck are occupied with
the same Scriptural problem: the unfathomable connection between God's counsel on the one hand, and man's transgression
of His ordinance on the other hand. But it seems that we are
not permitted to conclude that the will of the ordinance is
not God's actual will, but only His precept, His norm or
rule. We object against this "only," and it seems that Bavinck
himself confirms this when he says that he who denies the will
of God — as *voluntas signi* — in law and gospel, disparages not
only the majesty of the moral law but also God's holiness.[25] For
that means that in God's revealed will we do not deal with an
unactual will and not with an arbitrary precept which in its contingency does not bring us into contact with God Himself, but
with God Himself in His holiness. And that is the reason why
we may not let Augustine's valuable view (*contra voluntatem
Dei,* but not *praeter voluntatem Dei*) end in the distinction between an actual and unactual will of God. For when doing so
one cannot escape the danger that the will of God in law and
gospel is overshadowed and even threatened by that "actual"
will of God.

The will of God threatens, then, to become "background"
which remains unknown to us in God's revelation. We realize
that it is impossible to give a rational solution to the expression
contra, non praeter, but precisely for that reason we want to
avoid speaking of the unactual will of God.[26] Futhermore,
we face the undeniable fact that the will of the ordinance is in
no way an arbitrary command of God, but precisely that will
of God which becomes visible in Jesus Christ (Eph. 1:9).

The "will of the ordinance" is not foreign to what is called
the "will of the decision"; nor is the "sign" (*signum*) unrelated

---

24. *Ibid.*
25. *Ibid.,* p. 215.
26. The inadequacy of such a mode of speaking can be seen with Braun
    (Heppe, *Dogmatik,* 1861, p. 69). See also the critique of Barth, *K. D.,*
    II, 1, 667.

to His pleasure (*beneplacitum.*)[27] And only if we do not distinguish between actual and unactual will of God can we acknowledge the relative value of the distinction between the hidden
will of God and the revealed will of God. For then the intention of Augustine, Calvin, and Bavinck can become clear (*contra, non praeter*) without the element of shadow over the revealed will becoming visible in the hidden will. And in this way
we shall not go astray from that mode of speech in Scripture
which forbids identification of the will of the ordinance with un-
actuality.[28]

We shall now discuss in what sense the Bible allows us to
speak of the *deus absconditus,* the hidden God. It is important
that we first realize the content of the concept *absconditus*. Practically speaking, this hiddenness may mean no more than the
ignorance of which the altar at Athens gave testimony: the altar to the unknown God (Acts 17:23). In this way the *absconditus* is contrasted with the revelation which is so clearly
revealed by Paul's word in Athens: "What therefore ye worship
in ignorance, this I set forth unto you" (Acts 17:23; see also
v. 27).

Here revelation stands over against ignorance and hiddenness, and the question arises whether this contrast is not so clear
that the revelation rules out the hiddenness and the hiddenness
rules out the revelation — a question which can also be put this
way: Does not God's revelation make any discussion of the hiddenness of God impossible? This question leads us automatically
to the testimony of Scripture because we cannot, apart from
Scripture, speak of the concepts "revelation" and "hiddenness,"
but only of the God who reveals Himself.

It cannot be denied that Scripture often speaks of God in such
a manner that we are naturally inclined to use the word "hiddenness." Our aversion to all forms of atheism and agnosticism
may not make us blind to that fact. It is not merely an inci-

---

27. If the word *signum* really is to have meaning in the distinction, then
    only in *signum voluntatis Dei*.
28. It struck me that the distinction between revealed and hidden will is
    mentioned in the exegesis of the Lord's Prayer (F. W. Grosheide,
    H. N. Ridderbos) and not in the exegesis of Gethsemane. This is
    quite understandable but indicates at the same time that the two wills
    cannot be separated from each other. Cf. Paul's apostolate through
    the will of God (I Cor. 1:1) and the will of God with respect to suf-
    fering (I Peter 3:17, 4:19).

dental word which Paul speaks when he says that God dwells in an unapproachable light (I Tim. 6:16).

This passage stands in close connection with numerous testimonies of Scripture which speak emphatically of God's hiddenness. We think not only of "the secret things" that "belong unto Jehovah our God" (Deut. 29:29), but also of God's emphatic word to Solomon that He chose to "dwell in the thick darkness" (I Kings 8:12). In the history of salvation that darkness is often mentioned.

When Israel stood afar off, Moses approached the darkness wherein God dwelt (Ex. 20:21). He said to the people: "And ye came near and stood under the mountain; and the mountain burned with fire unto the heart of heaven, with darkness, clouds, and thick darkness. And Jehovah spake unto you out of the midst of the fire; ye heard the voice of words, but ye saw no form; only ye heard a voice" (Deut. 4:11). "Clouds and darkness are round about him" (Ps. 97:2).

God Himself "made darkness pavilions round about him, gathering of waters, thick clouds of the skies" (II Sam. 22:12) while "thick darkness was under his feet" (II Sam. 22:10; see also Ps. 18:10). We hear continually of this mode of revelation, even when He appears: "I will appear in the cloud upon the mercy-seat" (Lev. 16:2).

In all these passages we are struck by the unmistakable fact that God never contrasts His hiddenness with His revelation. All the clouds and darkness do not make the reality of God's revelation dubious for one moment (see Ps. 97). From the midst of this hiddenness comes the voice of God.

Moreover, the revelation comes to man clearly, not obscurely. This is shown in a passage which contains both aspects: "Lo, I come unto thee in a thick cloud, that the people may hear when I speak with thee, and may also believe thee for ever" (Ex. 19:9). That is to say, God chooses to *reveal* Himself precisely by means of the cloud of hiddenness.

There is no contradiction here between revelation and hiddenness, between a *deus absconditus* and a *deus revelatus*. Rather, we see that God comes this way in His revelation to make clear the way in which man shall approach Him. God's glory and holiness become visible in this mode of His revelation. Man cannot penetrate to God through the cloud and the darkness, but must listen in humility, respect, and faith.

There are boundaries here, and warnings are given: "Draw

not nigh hither: put off thy shoes from off they feet, for the place
whereon thou standest is holy ground" (Ex. 3:5). The revelation of God leads to communion and friendship (Jas. 2:23), but
this friendship must be distinguished from any form of familiarity (Gen. 18:27, 30-32). And it must be remembered that God's
will to dwell in darkness does not imply a dark revelation. Precisely in that connection we hear of a place to dwell for ever
(I Kings 8:13). To this God, who chooses to dwell in darkness, prayers are sent when the temple is dedicated, prayers full
of faith, trust, and adoration. Here, rest is given (I Kings 8:56),
and the Lord is praised for all that He has promised: "There
hath not failed one word of all his good promise, which he promised by Moses his servant" (I Kings 8:56; see also 9:3). Good
words are coming from Him who chooses to dwell in darkness!
This darkness is an awe-inspiring reality, but it is not a menace
to the reality of revelation. It only makes revelation marvelous
and majestic, free and gracious. It is impossible that man
should approach God if God did not approach him.

It is clear that in this light the expression *deus absconditus*
does not say much in itself, and that it needs closer study. It
cannot be applied to God as a simple description of Him. He
who speaks of God's hiddenness can only do so correctly by observing the interrelations of Scripture when it speaks of the
darkness and the voice, the cloud and the Word, the hiddenness
and God's appearance. From the riches of Old Testament revelation we learn that no altar may ever be erected to an "unknown Jehovah." Not revelation, but a heedless approach to God
is condemned and excluded by His darkness.

We meet the same conditions also in Isaiah 45:15, a passage
often connected with the concept *deus absconditus*: "Verily thou
art a God that hidest thyself, O God of Israel, the Saviour." It
strikes our attention that the same chapter also mentions the
revelation of God: "I have not spoken in secret, in a place of the
land of darkness; I said not unto the seed of Jacob, Seek me in
vain" (Isa. 45:19; see also v. 23). Isaiah apparently does not
believe that this accentuation of God's revelation contradicts the
statement in verse 15.

According to Ridderbos this hiddenness implies that God and
His acts are shrouded in a veil of mystery which cannot be pen-
etrated by human thinking.[29] Revelation does not do away with

29. J. Ridderbos, *Isaiah*, II, *ad loc.*; see Isa. 40:28, 55:9, Rom. 11:33.
See also Isa. 45:15, which contains a prayer.

this hiddenness but presupposes it and makes it felt.   The hiddenness does not affect salvation granted in revelation; it protects it against misunderstanding.   The God who hides Himself is contrasted with the idols, and all those who make them will be ashamed; but Israel is delivered by an eternal salvation (Isa. 45:16, 17).   Throughout the Old Testament we encounter these connections.   God's ways was in the sea, His paths in the great waters; but His footsteps were not known (Ps. 77:19).   But this song of holy and inscrutable ways does not end in mute submission to a distant, hidden God, but in thanksgiving and joy in Him who is near: "Thou leddest thy people like a flock, by the hand of Moses and Aaron" (Ps. 77:20).   It appears that the hiddenness of Jehovah's acts does not blot out His characteristics as the Shepherd of Israel.   Scripture says that it is the glory of God to conceal a thing whereas it is the glory of kings to search out a matter (Prov. 25:2).   Gispen speaks of the respect that God inspires "because of the hiddenness of His rule."[30]

It is clear that these are not human secrecies, but rather manifestations of the divine inscrutability and the unsearchableness of God's ways (Rom. 11:33; see Eccl. 8:12, 11:7-9, 26:14, 28:21).

All this makes clear that one cannot speak of the hiddenness of God *in abstracto* (*deus absconditus*) but of God in His works as Creator and Redeemer, and of God in the historic relation to His people.   His hiddenness is not a "metaphysical" property; rather He *wills* to dwell in darkness (I Kings 8:12) and He *keeps* Himself hidden (Isa. 45:15).   And we see Him in His hiddenness when His people, unreceptive to Him, travel their way independently of Him (Gen. 18:17).   He can sovereignly reveal something, but He can also hide it (II Kings 4:27).   But this hiding becomes frightening when it is the hiddenness of judgment.   Then it can happen that the word of the Lord becomes scarce and that the visions are not numerous (I Sam. 3:1).[31]   In history this scarcity is then, again, alternated with God's voice speaking to Samuel, and it is a voice that speaks in trustworthiness, for none of God's words fall to the ground (I Sam. 3:19).   It is hiddenness, but only to be seen in the connections and interrelations of life, in the development of God's acts in history,

30. H. Gispen, *Korte Verklaring* on Proverbs, II, 217.
31. See K. Schilder, *Licht in de Rook,* 1951, pp. 69ff.

in the revelation of His faithfulness: "His anger is but for a
moment, his favor is for a lifetime: weeping may tarry for the
night, but joy cometh in the morning" (Ps. 30:5). "For a
small moment have I forsaken thee; but with great mercies will
I gather thee. In overflowing wrath I hid my face from thee
for a moment; but with everlasting lovingkindness will I have
mercy on thee, saith Jehovah thy Redeemer" (Isa. 54:7, 8).

Many times Israel had to feel and learn to understand the
seriousness of God's hiddenness. It had to find the way in which
the light broke through the darkness. Meyer, summarizing his
investigation of God's hiddenness in the Old Testament, writes:
"So flees the man who prays, from the hidden God to the revealed God."[32] This can be truly applied to Israel, but not only
to Israel. And in this statement every dualistic concept of God
is impossible. For this hiddenness, in Meyer's judgment, is a kind
of judicial hiding correlated with guilt, unreceptivity, and stubbornness.[33] So "hiding Himself" and "leaving His people" cannot be made into an attribute of *deus absconditus,* but can be
understood only as an occasion for Israel to pray: "Hide not
thy face from me; put not thy servant away in anger" (Ps. 27:9;
see Ps. 69:18, 102:3, 143:7) and to receive assurance that her
way is not hidden from the Lord (Isa. 40:27). And if it is true
what Oepke says: "The hiddenness of Jehovah can become
utterly unbearable for man" — here he refers to the book of
Lamentations (3:6) — then we see precisely here also the way
that leads back to the new and renewed mercy of God (Lam.
3:22-24).[34]

It has been pointed out that sometimes the Jews, because they
felt they were without any present revelation, took refuge in
the apocalyptical as a compensation for this hiddenness. However this may be, the "compensation-concept" is not constitutive for this fleeing from *deus absconditus* to *deus revelatus.*
For the way out of God's threatening and righteous judicial hiddenness to His revelation and new mercy is found only when
man is prepared to confess his guilt and to have faith.[35] Then,
having found God again as *deus revelatus,* he will acknowledge
the righteousness of His hiding.

The way back cannot be better described than in the words

32. Kittel, *T. W. N. T.,* III, 970.
33. *Ibid.*
34. *Ibid.*
35. *Ibid.,* p. 971.

of the Canons of Dort, when they speak of the fall into sin and of the guilt unto death. Then darkness comes over man's soul "until when they change their course by serious repentance, the light of God's fatherly countenance again shines upon them (CD, V, 5).

What the Old Testament makes so very clear — that in the way of faith God's revelation is not threatened by His hiddenness and His unapproachable light — is confirmed throughout the New Testament.

Here, too, we are confronted with the same motifs. The Old Testament motif of the inscrutability of God's ways does not simply disappear in the clear light of revelation; rather, we hear the New Testament speak with great emphasis of the revelation of the mystery, "kept in silence through times eternal, but now is manifested, and by the scriptures of the prophets . . . made known unto all the nations" (Rom. 16:25, 26; see Eph. 3:9, I Cor. 2:6ff.). But this revelation of the mystery continues to show the same characteristics of the Old Testament relation between revelation and hiddenness in the sense that it can be understood and approached only in faith. Here again hiddenness comes to the fore: "I thank thee, O Father, Lord of heaven and earth, that thou didst hide these things from the wise and understanding, and didst reveal them unto babes" (Matt. 11:25). This does not at all detract from the riches of the fulfillment in Christ. In Christ treasures of wisdom are hidden (Col. 2:3). He who would identify this hiddenness with obscurity does not understand that this identification appears nowhere in the New Testament. This revelation is not to be compared with something discoverable, to which one can approach apart from faith. Apart from faith the entrance is closed, as the prediction of Christ's approaching suffering remained hidden and obscure to His disciples (Luke 18:34). "But now they are hid from thine eyes" (Luke 19:42).

The New Testament, furthermore, leaves no room for the idea that hiddenness is a threat to revelation. This is ruled out by its testimony regarding the reality and trustworthiness of revelation, a testimony also given in the Old Testament. There is no modality here according to which, behind the mode of revelation, a new problem could arise in connection with God's "actual" will. This modality, which in the early Church attacked the doctrine of the Trinity, serves us as a warning, also regarding our reflection on the relationship between revelation and hiddenness. To be sure, in the Old Testament as well as in the New we are told that no one can see God because He is the invisible God (I Tim. 1:17; see Col. 1:15) and dwells in an impenetrable light, "whom no man hath seen, nor can see" (I Tim. 6:16),[36] but by this revelation of His own invisibility God means to reject every attempt to approach Him independently.   At the same time we are reminded, as a warning and a solace, of His self-revelation, so that His invisibility does not affect His riches and trustworthiness but indicates that this revelation is the only way (see Heb. 11:27), as it is written in John 1:18 after the passage about the invisible God: "The only begotten Son, who is in the bosom of the Father, he hath declared him." (See Christ's saying in John 5:19 and 6:46.)

This does not mean that Christ is simply a compensation over against the threat of God's invisibility, but that He is the revelation Himself.   The Old Testament does not portray a terrified retreat from God's unapproachable transcendence,[37] but provides a prelude to the revelation in Christ alone, in whom the fullness of God dwells bodily (Col. 1:19).   This makes us understand something of the word of Christ to Philip, who asks Him: "Show us the Father, and it sufficeth us" (John 14:8). It is as if Philip, after all he had heard from Christ, still missed something, something of the deepest and most real: "Show us the Father." Christ answers: "Have I been so long time with you, and dost thou not know me, Philip? he that hath seen me hath seen the Father; how sayest thou, Show us the Father?" (John 14:9).   Christ is not a compensation for a lack of revelation, but He is revelation itself, and that makes Philip's question strange, incomprehensible, and superfluous.[38]

All that has been discussed so far is of decisive significance for the relationship between election and hiddenness.   For the

36. See Heb. 11:27, John 1:18, 4·12.   See in the Old Testament: Gen. 32:30, Judg. 6:22, 13:22, Isa. 6:5, Ex. 33:20.
37. That is the reason why we think that Fascher is incorrect when he discovers all sorts of disharmony in the Old Testament and, for instance, interprets Gen. 18 as "naive realism," while it is clear that these variations are connected with the fact that invisibility does not exclude revelation. See especially Ex. 33:23. Cf. also I John 3:6 and John 3:11.
38. Cf. Fascher, *Deus Invisibilis,* pp. 74-75.   On John 14, see F. W. Grosheide, *Commentaar op Johannes,* II, 300ff.   See also his reference to Ex. 33:18ff.

question that occupied us at the beginning of this chapter was
this: Do we not encounter the shadow of the *deus absconditus*
over the *deus revelatus* when we discuss the doctrine of election?
Is there not a silent threat to the whole order of salvation,
to all that comes to us in the historical plane of revelation?
Is it perhaps only logical that this shadow, this threat, obtained form in the nominalistic *potentia absoluta* of which we
already spoke, and can we escape the tension between the *dues
absconditus* and the *deus revelatus?*

The answer to these questions must be that this would be
the case only against a background of bi-theism, a dualistic concept of God in which hiddenness and revelation are opposed
to each other. With such a concept we might know about the
deus absconditus, but we should not know who this God is,
what His will contains, and what His deepest intentions are.
Such a completely unbiblical concept of God separates the
God of revelation from our lives, and mitigates the absolute
trustworthiness and sufficiency of that revelation. We should
still not come in contact with God's holy plan, His holy counsel,
His deepest intentions, and all emphasis on the *deus revelatus*
would still not be able to eliminate forever the question: "Show
us the Father and it sufficeth us." The pastor could no longer
enjoin adherence to the *deus revelatus,* for this adherence
would then inevitably acquire the nature of a compensation. The
traits of the *deus absconditus* would shimmer through those of
the *deus revelatus,* and dualism would continue to affect the believers. But such a relativistic view makes Paul's words of revelation unexplainable when he says that he has not neglected "to
declare the whole counsel of God" (Acts 27:27; see also 4:28),
a passage echoed clearly in the Heidelberg Catechism in which
Christ is honored as our chief Prophet and Teacher, "who has
fully revealed to us the secret counsel and will of God concerning our redemption" (HC, Q. 31).

There is no doubt that the crisis which often arose with respect
to the doctrine of election — the crisis of certainties — can be
described as a crisis with respect to the reality and the trustworthiness of God's revelation.

In our discussion of the relationship between election and
hiddenness we come naturally to the words of Rudolph Otto, who
in times of crises and catastrophe (1917) began to point to the

"wholly other."[39] The expression in itself is not very clear, since it is also used to indicate the incomparability of Jehovah, as in Isaiah 40: "To whom then will ye liken God? or what likeness will ye compare unto him?" (Isa. 40:18; cf. Micah 7:18). But it is clear that Otto gives this "wholly other" a more specific meaning when he associates it with such names as "the numinous" and "the simply marvelous that contrasts with all that is here and now, the totally other, the heavenly."[40] Otto discovers this concept of God everywhere in Scripture and especially in Jesus' teachings, in which we hear "of that curious fear and trembling for the secrecies of the otherworldly."[41] It is a matter of the *mysterium,* but then as *mysterium tremendum,* which is also *mysterium fascinans.* It is more than the marvelous. It evokes stupor, terror, absolute astonishment. It not only goes above and beyond our knowledge; the wholly other by virtue of its character and essence is incommensurable to man, so that he recoils from it in utter astonishment."[42]

The great influence of Otto's book can easily be explained. By his protest against the humanization of the concept of God he focuses our attention on God's holiness and transcendence (Isa. 6), and on the *trishagion* (HC, Q. 121). All his considerations are based on the wording of the Lord's Prayer: "Our Father who art in heaven." It often happened when praying the Lord's Prayer that the aspect "in heaven" was neglected in favor of the concept of friendship, the child-Father relation and the *communio.* But the converse is also possible. The idea of God being "in heaven" may cast shadows over the communion and assurance of believers. And although Otto tries to transcend this dilemma (*tremendum* and *fascinans*), his emphasis becomes clear in his discussion of predestination.[43]

He calls predestination "nothing but a heightened feeling of dependence on the part of man as creature.[44] Volz, too, follows this line of thinking which emphasizes the irrational (see Chap. 3). Otto believes that that religion which is most strongly determined by irrational motifs and elements — Islam — is also the religion in which predestination is most strongly emphasized.

39. R. Otte, *Das Heilige.*
40. *Ibid.,* p. 96
41. *Ibid.,* in connection with Matt. 10:28, 21:41, Heb. 10:31, 12:29.
42. *Ibid.,* p. 27.
43. Cf. *ibid.,* p. 38 on the contrast and harmony between the two.
44. *Ibid.,* p. 105.

He associates this irrationality with the transcendence of God, with God's hiddenness. Man can only stammer here, and his attempt to speak of God can be understood only as "an attempt to find comprehensible expression for a concept that cannot be explained," as an "appellation full of secrecies."[45]

This experience of the "numinous," in which various elements play an essential role, is the core of religion as such. It is the "prime element of the soul."[46] Otto discovers it in the whole field of religion: in Goethe's emphasis on the "demonic,"[47] in "the numinous in Buddhistic sculpture,"[48] and in "the emptiness in the architecture of Islam."[49] But he points especially to the numinous in Christianity, first in the Old and New Testament, where it finds, so to speak, its sublimation, but then also in the history of the Church and theology. He reminds us of the *theologia negativa* (the nameless God), and of Chrysostom and Augustine, and of many other instances when something was said to be understood of that which transcends all categories of thought.[50] This understanding was often rationalized in the "schools" when tensions had to be relieved, but the motifs returned everywhere and made their influence felt.[51] Here the dominant note is not that of sin in the face of God's majesty, but of profanity, the lostness which is nothing but "the natural profanity of all that is created."[52] The *mysteriosum* is correlated with the *desperatio*.[53]

It is interesting that Otto refers especially to Luther as his main witness for this understanding of the numinous. Was he not the Reformer who over against the "schools" and the balanced concept of God knew again how to speak of the *deus absconditus?*[54] We touch here upon a frequently discussed point in the history of doctrine, where especially the Roman Catholic Church strongly charges that precisely Luther — and with him

45. *Ibid.*, p. 106.
46. *Ibid.*, p. 143.
47. *Ibid.*, p. 170.
48. Otto, *Das Ganz Andere, Aufs. das Numinöse betreffend* (1929), I, 114ff.
49. *Ibid.*, p. 108; cf. the "parallels" in the Islam: *Das Heilige*, p. 106.
50. Otto, *Das Ganz Andere*, pp. 21ff.
51. Otto, *Das Heilige*, p. 122.
52. Otto, "Die Christliche Idee der Verlorenheit," in *Aufsätze* (1929), II, 206, and "Die religiöse Idee der Urschuld" (*ibid.*, pp. 208ff.) on the truth element in the doctrine of fall and original sin.
53. Otto, *Das Heilige*, pp. 117-119.
54. *Ibid.*, p. 113.

the Reformation — so emphasized the transcendence and hiddenness of God that it affected the reality of man's communion with
Him, and caused his view of God's proximity to fade.[55]

Did Luther, who, against Erasmus, taught so emphatically the
predestination of the sovereign God, really construct a connection between election and hiddenness which obscures the manifestation of God's salvation? *Deus absconditus?* Although it
is impossible here to discuss at length Luther's view of the *deus
absconditus*,[56] it should be stated that he did not intend to picture
a dualistic or bi-theistic God. More than once Luther's thoughts
have been interpreted from the point of view of nominalism, and
hence an element of arbitrariness as well as of hiddenness has
been deduced from them.[57] This interpretation has been abandoned of late, because it has become clear that precisely this element
of threat to salvation is in flagrant contradiction to Luther's intentions. Luther's basic motif is not the contrast between the *deus
absconditus* and the *dues revelatus,* but concerns the *manner* in
which God reveals Himself to man, by which every *theologia gloriae*
is judged, and by which the necessity of the *theologia crucis* is indicated. The great emphasis which Luther and also Calvin put on
the revelation in Christ — *in cruce* — already indicates clearly that
in the concept of the *deus absconditus* they do not intend to make
revelation relative.[58] Only the *theologiae gloriae,* which thinks it
can know God directly apart from Christ and the cross, faces the
hidden *deus absconditus.* Kooiman has discussed this motif in
Luther's thought at length, as has also Von Loewenich, and he
has shown that the concept of the *deus absconditus* is not intended
to cast a shadow over revelation, but rather to clarify revelation
in its specific mode.[59]

55. Cf., e.g., Erich Przywara's interpretation of Luther.
56. For literature on this, see among many others: Kattenbusch, *Deus ab-
    sconditus bei Luther. Festgabe für J. Kaftan,* 1920, pp. 177-81; W.
    v. Loewenich, *Luthers theologie crucis,* 1929; G. Aulen, *Het Chr.
    Godsbeeld,* 1929, pp. 218ff.; J. Dillenberger, *God Hidden and Revealed.
    The Interpretation of Luther's Deus Absconditus and Its Significance
    for Religious Thought,* 1953.
57. See especially A. Ritschl: *Geschichtliche Studien zur Christlichen
    Lehre von Gott, Jahrbuch für deutsche Theologie,* 1868, pp. 68ff.
58. See P. Bühler, *Die Anfechtung bei Martin Luther,* 1942, p. 188;
    Regen Prenter, *Spiritus Creator. Studien zur Luthers Theologie,*
    1954, pp. 30, 309.
59. Kooiman, *Gods Maskerspel in de Theologie van Luther,* pp. 69ff.
    W. v. Loewenich, *Luthers theologia crucis,* p. 25.

Students of Luther's thought have directed their discussion of Luther's concept of the *deus absconditus* not only to his abundant treatment of the *theologia crucis*[60] — the mode of revelation — but also to his *de servo arbitrio*. In *The Bondage of the Will*, written against Erasmus, the idea of *deus absconditus* occurs in a peculiar form and various interpretations of it have been given. Von Loewenich, who sees Luther's idea of the *deus absconditus* as essential and abiding, has written these words about some particular statement in *The Bondage of the Will*: "Thus the *deus absconditus* and the *deus revelatus* diverge widely." He then poses the question: "But is it then still possible to adhere to the concept of the indivisibility of God?"[61]

We do not intend to analyze Luther's profoundest intentions with the *de servo arbitrio,* whereby in any case his polemics with Erasmus must be taken into account, but it must be maintained that Luther did not intend to establish a contradiction in the concept of God; he wanted, rather, to emphasize the hiddenness of God over against Erasmus' humanization of the concept of God. Thus it can be explained that Luther later — in his full emphasis on the *deus revelatus* — does not at all disown the statement *"de servo arbitrio."*[62] Much attention is paid to what Luther in his exegesis of Genesis said to his students in order to fortify them against misunderstanding. He had feared that after his death his thoughts on the *deus absconditus* might receive too much emphasis. And he adds that one must not investigate the predestination of the hidden God, but that one must find rest in what God has revealed in His Word.[63] Perhaps the matter may be summarized in these words: What at first — in *de servo arbitrio* — seems to be a contrast, becomes later the way of revelation of the one God whose hiddenness never is intended to be a menace to His trustworthiness. And therein lies the unity of Luther's doctrine of election. One may discuss the question whether Luther was altogether successful in avoiding the idea of

---

60. See already in the Heidelberg disputation of 1518. Cf. H. Fahsel, *D. Martin Luther.   Der Reformator im Kampf um Evangelium und Kirche.   Sein Werden und Werken im Spiegel eigener Zeugnisse,* 1955, pp. 88ff. See also Ph. S. Watson: *Let God Be God. An Interpretation of the Theology of Martin Luther,* 1954.
61. *Op. cit.,* pp. 31, 32.
62. *"Justum meum librum"* (1537).
63. The passage is supplied by Von Loewenich, *op. cit.,* p. 43.

contrasts in God,[64] but it is evident that he, as opposed to Erasmus, wished to acknowledge completely and fully the sovereignty of God's grace, the grace of the electing God,[65] and that for the certainty of salvation he refers to the absolute trustworthiness of the *deus praedicatus.*

In principle, the compensation-idea in the doctrine of election is overcome in these Reformed (that is, Luther's and Calvin's) views which allow a place for faith and trust, but not for the silent adherence to a *mysterium tremendum* or for gnawing uncertainty. The Christian message finds its solid foundation in the fact that Paul's testimony, that the Word is trustworthy (II Tim. 2:11), holds also for the doctrine of election. The Reformation testifies that the grace of God has appeared "bringing salvation to all men, instructing us" (Titus 2:11), and one sees in the preaching of this grace the legitimate duty of the Church, also in the greatest temptation (HC, Q. 44). Such a manner of speaking sounds strange to him who individualistically and apart from the Way desires to penetrate into divine election. But such an abstract *numerus*-problem is seen as illicit by the Reformation, and is rejected as a heresy of Trent.

Karl Barth has posed the question whether the Reformed reference to the *liber vitae* and the *speculum electionis* can truly withstand the doubts that may arise in man's heart. He asserts that the valuable noetic reference to Christ as the revelation of election, as it was made in Reformed theology, especially by Calvin, missed the ontic element, and that for that reason this well-

---

64. Kooiman (*Maskerspel,* p. 67) is correct when he says that Luther, by the term *deus absconditus,* did not mean the unknown God. When he adds "not even God in his unapproachable, unsearchable majesty," then the question may be asked whether Kooiman wants to maintain this also with respect to the *de servo arbitrio.* It seems impossible to interpret *de servo arbitrio* exclusively in connection with the mode of revelation.

65. F. W. Schmidt speaks of an ethical-religious determination in *de servo arbitrio* (*Vom unfreien Willen,* 1934, p. 293) which means to give expression to the Pauline doctrine of grace, but he acknowledges the dangers of Luther's interpretation. It is clear that with the term "religious determinism" these dangers have not been eliminated, for Luther speaks, against Erasmus, of the *necessitas* such as it is generally recognized (p. 25). This does not mean that we may conclude that Luther is a fatalist, but there are problems here that are linked up with the *deus absconditus* (at least in *de servo arbitrio*).

intended pastoral device repeatedly — in the question regarding the assurance of salvation — clashed with doubts and ever recurring questions.[66]

We touch here directly upon the question that has occupied us: revelation and hiddenness. We have seen that with Luther and Calvin precisely at that point the greatest clarity is found. In this clarity lies the antithesis with Rome. Therefore, the question arises whether after all a defect lay at the basis of their theology which made it difficult to calm the storm of questions. It is the question whether the reference to Christ is more than a pastoral-practical way of mitigating the "high tension" of the election of God. If that were the case the Church's message could still be threatened by a remaining hiddenness. Then the *mysterium tremendum* in the background would become the threat by which everything would again become problematic — everything, and certainly the controversy between Rome and the Reformation regarding the certainty of salvation.

With this question which almost seems to become the focal point in the doctrine of election, we are immediately confronted with that Biblical passage which played such a decisive role in the doctrine of election, and which is also decisive with regard to Reformed faith and practical teaching, namely the passage about the election *in Christ* (Eph. 1:4).

---

66. See *Kirchliche Dogmatik*, II, 2 and my *The Triumph of Grace in the Theology of Karl Barth* (1956).

CHAPTER FIVE

ELECTION IN CHRIST

IT was not unintentional that the previous chapter ended
with those important words: election in Christ. Reflection
on election and hiddenness can take no other direction when we
believe that no hiddenness can make the revelation of God merely
relative, for it is Christ who has made God known unto us
(John 1:18), and it is therefore impossible to detach the election of God from the revelation in Christ. Both Luther and
Calvin have indicated the grave danger of reflecting on election
without thinking of Christ. He who has recognized this danger
and who understands that the revelation in Christ is not a
"compensation" for the hiddenness of God, will therefore automatically come into contact with those words that again and
again have been the cause of reflection on the election of God:
election in Christ.

It cannot be denied that in the history of the doctrine of election especially these words have always been the cause of much
polemics. How is Jesus Christ, the Redeemer of the world, the
content of God's gospel, connected with election? We know
that the formulation of this question could be criticized. This
wording could give the impression that Christ and election are
two entities that somehow must be brought into a certain relation to each other.

And yet, in view of the polemics regarding Christ and election, the question cannot be worded differently if we want to
confront ourselves with the depth and the mystery of this connection, for the point at issue is not merely a theoretical speculation or a constructed connection, but the very meaning of the
Bible. Indeed, the pastor, when dealing with the knowledge of
election, points necessarily and exclusively at Jesus Christ with
that absoluteness with which John the Baptist testified, "Behold
the Lamb of God, that taketh away the sin of the world!"
(John 1:29). The all-important question is whether reflection
on the election of God may indeed legitimately begin and end

with the election in Christ, and point at it as the basis for a truly consoling pastoral message.

If there is any problem that brings disquiet to many, it is whether the joyful gospel of God does not lose much of its true gladness in the world because of the fact of election. Although John writes about communion with the Father and the Son so that our joy may be complete (I John 1:4), it cannot be denied that this "completeness" is often lacking. And although the lack of this joy can be variously explained, we must face the fact that it has often been associated with the doctrine of election.

To be sure, trustworthiness of the gospel of Christ is not being denied, but the question is raised whether this gospel is really for us, and whether the promises of the gospel are directed at us, or whether we must first be assured regarding our election in a different way before we can appropriate them. It is clear that under these circumstances the preaching of the gospel loses its power, and man is in continuous uncertainty. For his certainty must then come from a different source, and then it is difficult to understand Paul's statement regarding the veracity of the promise: "For the Son of God, Jesus Christ, who was preached among you by us . . . was not yea and nay, but in him it is yea. For how many soever be the promises of God, in him is the yea: wherefore also through him is the Amen, unto the glory of God through us" (II Cor. 1:19-20).

Is this perhaps a "kerygmatic" trend in Paul's thinking, running parallel to a "predestinational" trend, or is there a harmony in which the one is not limited by or ruled out by the other, but in which yea is truly yea, and the Amen of certainty is spoken to the glory of God?[1] It is clear that this harmony is essential for all of the gospel. It is the foundation for the entire gospel message and it penetrates into the depths of temptation and doubt. If we distrust the yea of God we are not thereby entitled to discredit His revelation, saying that it gives us a simultaneous yea and nay; we must rather look to our own smallness of faith and our unbelief in the face of the Amen of God, the faithful Witness (cf. Rev. 3:14, 1:5).

---

1. See the connection in II Cor. 1. The occasion is given by the question whether Paul is, or is not, dependable (II Cor. 1:17). In order to overcome that distrust (which harms the interest of the gospel) he points to the faithfulness of God.

All vagueness is impossible in this witnessing. It is the witness of Him who has seen and heard and "he that hath received his witness hath set his seal to this, that God is true" (John 3:33). He speaks the words of God (John 3:34), and on the Son the Father has set His seal (John 6:27). "If I bear witness of myself, my witness is not true" (John 5:31). But also, on the other hand, "even if I bear witness of myself, my witness is true; for I know whence I came, and whither I go" (John 8:14). There is not one testimony of Christ to which a testimony of God must be added because then it would lack validity and trustworthiness. For it is a testimony of Christ in conjunction with God's testimony, without any uncertainty (cf. John 5:32, 37; 8:18), so that he who does not believe in God, makes Him a liar, "because he hath not believed in the witness that God has borne concerning his Son (see I John 5:9, 10). When we think of all this, we understand the power of the pastoral message which in all circumstances refers to Christ.

It is clear, however, that the danger is not imaginary that man in his reflection on the election of God may reach a place in which the light of absolute trustworthiness no longer shines out in all directions, because it is caught up and obscured by false presuppositions about the doctrine of election. And that is the reason why it is so important to observe how in Scripture we find not tension and contradiction, but harmony: election in Christ.

In reflecting on these words, our attention has been drawn repeatedly to the question whether Christ could and should be called the foundation, the origin, of man's salvation, or whether one should say that He is the executor of election. Barth concentrates his criticism of the Reformed doctrine of election especially on this point. The Synod of Dort was correct, he says, when it rejected the view of the Remonstrants according to which Christ was the foundation of election, because of the connection in which this view was brought forward by the Remonstrants.[2] At the same time, however, the Synod of Dort

---

2. Karl Barth, *Kirchliche Dogmatik*, II, 2, 76. For the connection and the context in which the thesis of the Remonstrants is placed, see Muller, *Reformierte Bekenntnisschrifte* (1903), p. lix. According to Barth, this connection and context is that for the Remonstrant the grace of God in Christ is offered to all men (II, 2, 73), making belief or unbelief the decisive factor.

left the problem itself unsolved, although it was really actual. This point of controversy is indeed interesting, because the issue is certainly not a desire to penetrate speculatively into the salvation in Christ, but to intercept the light which Scripture itself sheds forth.

Hence the question whether Christ must be regarded as foundation or as executor of the election of God was raised long before Barth thought of making it a critical point of Reformed doctrine. It had to be that way, for the questions concerning Christ and election stood from the very beginning in the light of clear and concrete Scriptural testimony. We think of Paul's words in which he praises the riches of election: "even as he chose us in him before the foundation of the world" (Eph. 1:4), a passage related to his other statement that in God was the good pleasure "which he purposed in him [Christ]" (Eph. 1:9). Paul elsewhere speaks of the power of God "who saved us, and called us with a holy calling, not according to our works, but according to his own purpose and grace, which was given us in Christ Jesus before times eternal" (II Tim. 1:9).

In all these words we see an immediate and explicit relation between election and Christ. The history of the doctrine of election may be interpreted as an effort to understand the meaning of these words. We must not lose our way in the labyrinth of speculation, but we must listen to the testimony of Scripture.

In our struggle to understand the meaning of these words, we are repeatedly confronted with the question whether we have apprehended that meaning correctly when we unhestitatingly call Christ the foundation of election. That the Remonstrants have also done that is no reason to change our position. For in itself it is possible to use the expression without making the interpretation of the Remonstrants our own.

However, we are confronted with the fact that especially from the Reformed side sharp criticism has arisen against the idea that Christ is the foundation of election, although these men certainly did not want to disparage the Scriptural testimonies regarding God's election in Jesus Christ. The motivation for this criticism is clear. The concern of the Reformed view is that Christ should not be called the "foundation" and the "cause" of election as if divine election were motivated by Christ's act. This criticism is similar to that which has been directed against

the concept of "persuasion," according to which Christ is the
causa salutis in the sense that He persuaded the Father — who
at first was not thus inclined — with His suffering and His
death to a forgiving attitude and to an actual granting of salvation.   Thus, a tension was construed between the inclination of Christ and the inclination of the Father; the inclination
of Christ supposedly led to the Father's great turnabout. This
view flagrantly contradicts Scripture, which teaches that God in
Christ was reconciling the world unto Himself (II Cor. 5:19),
and that it is precisely the coming of Christ, sent by the Father,
which is the revelation of God's love (I John 4:9).

These same objections that were — correctly — brought
against the concept of "persuasion" we also encounter in the
criticism of the idea that Christ is the foundation and cause of
election. Bavinck says: "But that does not yet mean that Christ
as Mediator is the *causa impulsiva, movens, meritoria* of the
decree of election.   In that sense, Christ was called the cause of
election by many Roman Catholics, the Remonstrants, the Lutherans, and many of the more recent theologians.   But the Reformed theologians have rejected this, and correctly so."[3] Why
have they rejected this? Because, says Bavinck, "Christ is a
gift of love from the Father and that love precedes the sending
of the Son.   The Son did not move the Father to forgiveness,
but electing love originated with the Father Himself."[4]

This does not imply a different interpretation of Ephesians
1:4 and other passages in Scripture. On the contrary, they are
interpreted to mean that the Divine, merciful initiative was not
an answer to what happened in time, but that this initiative was
established in all its depth and profoundness before the foundation of the world, in Christ.   In all these passages concerning

---

3. Bavinck, *Gereformeerde Dogmatiek*, II, 365.
4. *Ibid.* In connection with the rather general criticism on the part of
   the new theology against the concept of persuasion, more appreciation
   could have been expected for the Reformed criticism of the term *fun-*
   damentum electionis. Cf. also, regarding the *causa impulsiva*
   (Heidegger and Bucanus) Heppe's *Dogmatik*, (1861), p. 124,
   with reference to God's *eudokia,* and especially Polanus, who mentions
   what is not *causa efficiens impulsiva,* to wit: *voluntas hominis, praevisa*
   fides nostra, praescita hominum merita, preces nostrae aliorumve, per-
   severantia nostra and *meritum Christi* (p. 125). Heppe seems to be
   deprecating, but his intention is the same as we find elsewhere (cf.
   Bavinck), namely, to reject the concept of persuasion, and to point
   to the love of God.

the election in Christ — manifest at the end of the times for our sake (I Pet. 1:20) — the concept of persuasion and of the *fundamentum electionis,* if by such is meant a persuasion, is completely ruled out.

After rejecting this interpretation of the foundation and the cause, the question arises whether in rejecting this view we have automatically chosen for that other view, according to which Christ is no more than the executor of the election of God. Is Christ, then, nothing but a means to realize a decree that was established apart from Him? Scriptural testimony tells us differently; it speaks not of mere execution but of election in Christ, and the expression that Christ is a means to execute the decree of election does not do justice to the profoundness of Scripture.

We may now understand that, when Reformed scholars criticized the term "foundation" and "cause" in the sense of "persuasion," they did not thereby mean to imply that Christ was only an "executor." They felt correctly that this word would not do justice to the Biblical perspective of the words "in Christ." For the reasons mentioned above, the term "foundation" was usually rejected, though not without further clarifications: sometimes, if further clarified, that term was even defended.[5] Van der Zanden, for instance, writes: "In order to give expression to that interrelation between our election and election in Christ, we could call Christ the foundation of our election, but this term could be misunderstood," and he adds, "Christ is the cornerstone of election and in that sense the foundation of the election of His Church."[6] This shows that the interrelations in the history of the Reformed doctrine of election are less simple than much of the criticism against it indicates. For a correct analysis, one must avoid the dilemma between saying that Christ is either the foundation of election or only the executor of a decree established apart from Him. Much criticism of the Reformed view has failed to recognize precisely why and how it rejected the concept of persuasion. Only from such a lack of appreciation is it possible to conclude that the Reformed doctrine of election is characterized by a preference for an abstract decree of election, so that in the exegesis of Ephesians 1:4 it comes close

5. Cf. Barth *K. D.,* II, 2, 73.
6. L. Van der Zanden, *Praedestinatie in Christus,* p. 36.

to the Remonstrant view which interprets it as a decree of the order of salvation, detached from the election in Christ.[7]

This reproach implies that Reformed theology leaves no room for the election in Christ. A strange interest in the eternal, pre-temporal, independent decree of God has supposedly replaced it. Reformed theology is said to have followed the analogy of the man who made a plan and after making it, looked for someone to carry it out. The executor is still important but the actual decisions had already been made by the designer. That, then, is the reason why in the Reformed doctrine of election an unavoidable and necessary mutation took place in the interest of the believers, which had detrimental effects on their belief and life.

A. H. Haentjes, for instance, accuses Calvinistic dogmatics of emphasizing only that eternal, pre-temporal decree of election, so that it actually dissolved the historical aspect of reconciliation in election. For the essential part had already taken place in election, so that Christ could only interpret and mirror it. Christ was supposedly the great *interpres electionis,* as is evident, according to Haentjes, in Calvin's term "mirror of election." Christ mirrors and reveals the (eternal) election. "He is the interpreter of the eternal counsel of God with respect to the salvation of the elect."[8] A specific relation of Christ to election was no longer necessary because all emphasis was placed "on that eternal counsel which actually makes Christ's work superfluous, so that it only serves as a mirror, while His mediatorship and his mediatory work become unimportant."[9] Haentjes then speaks in violent denunciation of the "Jewish deism" which supposedly is evident in a God who in His decree stands eternally above

7. Barth (*K. D.*, II, 2, 74) discovers everywhere a duality, namely, of a prior decree that actually is independent of Christ and the decree of salvation that has Christ as its content. This form of criticism does not do justice to the composition of the formulations, and it is definitely incorrect when Barth says that it became unavoidable "to seek the actual divine decree outside of the Redeemer Jesus Christ." We wish to remark that what Barth says of the Bremen school (p. 73) does not imply that they render the correct solution. Barth thinks that they have not succeeded either to get to the point from which "their interpretation could have acquired the traits of a real correction of the Calvinistic doctrine while avoiding the fundamental Arminian error" (p. 74).

8. A. H. Haentjes: *Remonstrantse en Calvinistische Dogmatiek* (1913), p. 179.

9. *Ibid.,* p. 180.

time, thus making temporal events of no consequence whatever. Haentjes says that it was precisely the Remonstrants who wanted to honor Christ as *instrumentum redemptionis*. They wanted to restore the decisive significance of time and history, which in the Reformed doctrine of election, in spite of assertions to the contrary, had been neglected.

One can say that according to Haentjes there is no room in Calvinistic dogmatics for a decisive occurrence in time, but only for a mirroring of what once — in eternity — happened and was decreed. And this, he thinks, explains the Reformed resistance against the term "foundation" or "cause" of election. History has vanished between the walls of the doctrine of election.

As a matter of course this criticism did not remain unanswered. For we are dealing here with an interpretation which touches a decisive point, namely, whether the mirror of election should be interpreted as a devaluation of the history of salvation. G. Oorthuys is correct when he wonders in surprise whether that had been Calvin's intention. He thinks this explanation to be in flagrant contradiction to Calvin's teachings: "Indeed, Calvin has beforehand contradicted it emphatically and repeatedly."[10] Haentjes has misunderstood especially the concept of *speculum*. Calvin never meant by that term that nothing important can happen in history, or that Christ only mirrors and reveals what was in God's counsel from eternity. Rather, Calvin wanted to indicate with the *speculum* the way to the certainty of salvation. This way can be traveled and leads toward a goal, because in Christ there was a decisive happening in history, an act of God in which Christ "has earned for us the grace of God and salvation (*Inst.* II, xvii)." Although Calvin did not accept the concept of persuasion, and although he indicates that God the Father with His love precedes the historical reconciliation which He founded in Jesus Christ (*ibid.*, II, xvi, 3), this preceding does not imply a devaluation of the historical work of Christ, as if eternity would make any occurrence in time meaningless. It implies, rather, that God (as Calvin paradoxically puts it) reconciles Himself with us because He has loved us beforehand.

The riches of election and reconciliation cannot be stated in terms of a dilemma between the persuasion theory and a mere

10. G. Oorthuys, "De Praedestinatie in de Calvinistische Dogmatiek" in *Onder Eigen Vaandel,* p. 201.

reflection of that which already had happened and already was decreed; or, for that matter, in terms of a dilemma between the historical and the eternal. Calvin consciously reaches past such dilemmas in reaction against those "who are more subtle than orthodox" (*ibid.*, II, xvii, 1), who do not want to use the word "merit" with respect to Christ, because that would mean obscuring the grace of God. They maintain that "Christ is only an instrument or minister, not, as He is called by Peter, the author or leader or prince of life" (*ibid.*). Over against this devaluation of history and its decisive value, Calvin states that the love of God is the first cause of our salvation (*ibid.*, 2), but that Christ is not merely a *causa formalis*. For since we obtain justification by faith, the groundwork for our salvation must be sought in Him. Precisely in order that nothing should obstruct His love, God has established in Christ the means for reconciliation.

In spite of his rejection of the persuasion-concept, Calvin recognized that the historical fact of salvation is supremely important. Note his striking words: "There is great force in this word *propitiation;* for in a manner which cannot be expressed, God, at the very time when He loved us, was hostile to us until reconciled in Christ" (*ibid.*, 2, 3). This formulation shows clearly that we deal here with the unspeakable mystery of God's love in time, which is also His eternal love. But in spite of all these halting words — "unexpressible," "yet hostile," "until" — it is not accidental that Calvin refers precisely here to Ephesians 1:4. There is no indication at all that he is interested solely in the decisive decree of God, upon which nothing of historical consequence could follow. Calvin did not humanize God's counsel, and thereby render unintelligible the Scriptural declaration that Herod and Pilate with the Gentiles and the people of Israel did "whatever thy hand and thy counsel foreordained to come to pass" (Acts 4:28).

So far, it is impossible to become impressed by all the criticism. We think of K. Dijk's remark, who denies that the Reformed forefathers taught that Christ stood outside of God's counsel.[11] But then, how is it possible that the yea still stands over against the nay, and that the reproach of the abstract sovereign counsel of election cannot be silenced? The question concerns not only the history of dogma, but the very foundation

11. K. Dijk, *Van Eeuwigheid Verkoren*, p. 90.

of the whole doctrine of election. For such as abstract and isolated divine counsel immediately implies a determinism regarding election, with fixed and immutable decrees of God in which there is no mention of His love and grace.

Especially since Barth concentrated his criticism of the orthodox doctrine of election on this point has this reproach often been repeated. Nor is it a trivial objection; the history of this doctrine shows that an abstract doctrine of election is not at all an imaginary danger. It is still possible that Paul's words in Ephesians 1:4 and elsewhere do not receive their due attention in certain modes of thinking. At least one should not ignore this possibility, since Reformed theology in particular has often been accused of an abstract doctrine of election.

Apart from Barth's criticism of Calvin, it has recently been suggested that Calvin undeniably and without camouflage gave expression to this abstract concept of election. We are thinking here of the sharp criticism of J. K. S. Reid, who bases his discussion on a specific expression in which Calvin allegedly revealed his deepest intentions regarding the doctrine of election. Reid summarizes that concept in these supposed words of Calvin: *ratiam praecedit electio* (election precedes grace). Here, according to Reid, election is separated from grace, and "if this is true, one's worst forebodings are fulfilled. The God and Father of Christ is a God of grace. Who, then, is this God, who determines men's election before grace becomes operative?"[12] And Reid adds: "The first necessity is to abandon once for all the disastrous concept which finds expression in Calvin's words: *gratiam praecedit electio.*"[13]

A closer look reveals that Reid bases his criticism on a very incorrect presentation of Calvin's thinking. For Calvin does not say in a general way "election precedes grace," but he says: "If election precedes that divine grace by which we are made fit to obtain immortal life, what can God find in us to induce him to elect us?" (*Inst.* III, xxii, 1).

This is quite different from the fatal *gratiam praecedit electio,* for here Calvin is busy taking all dignity away from man, as he thinks especially of Ephesians 1:4. "Elected in Christ,"

---

12. J. K. S. Reid, "The Office of Christ in Predestination," *Scottish Journal of Theology,* I, 12.
13. *Ibid.,* p. 173.

Paul says, and with that he takes away all our self-esteem. When God found nothing worthy of election, He turned to Christ (*ibid.*). In Him we are adopted to the heavenly inheritance "because in ourselves we are incapable of such exellence." It is God who makes the faithful suitable to be partakers of the inheritance of the saints. And then follows the sentence which we quoted and out of which Reid took his words. Calvin did not at all intend to say that election precedes grace, and therefore is without grace. Calvin is concerned here with the question of *merit,* and simply points out that God by His grace makes us suitable to be partakers of the future life, and that grace is preceded by God's election which opposes "our merits of every description" (*ibid.,* III, xxii, 1). Calvin quotes Paul to show that God has elected us before the foundation of the world in order that we should be holy, and without blame before Him. This "in order that" is the core of Calvin's demonstration (*ibid.,* 3). Calvin's word, mutilated by Reid, can be employed against any form of analytical doctrine of self-justification, but it cannot be interpreted in the sense of an election without grace, apart from and outside of Christ. For election does not oppose grace, but it is the cause also of the grace of sanctification, which for precisely that reason is protected against the self-exaltation of the believer.[14]

In spite of this oft-repeated criticism, it must be acknowledged

---

14. Although it would be worth while to analyse all of Reid's article, we wish to point out only a few things here. Irresponsible, for instance, is the following. When Calvin writes that Christ is "the Eternal Wisdom, the Immutable Truth, the Determinate Counsel of the Father" and that we do not need to fear "that anything which he tells us will vary in the minutest degree from that will of the Father after which we inquire" (*Inst.* III, xxiv, 5), that, according to Reid, is a proof of "a certain nervousness"! He discovers everywhere the *"haereditas damnosa"* "taken over from Calvin himself," namely, "decree is prior to grace." With a complete misconception of the *fundamentum*-problematics in Reformed theology (over against "persuasion") he concludes with the reproach that "the will of God has been petrified in the decree" (p. 177). And when Calvin speaks of Christ and election in such a manner that it is clear that he does not mean that "*the* election precedes *the* grace," he speaks of a "remarkable statement" as "the flicker of a flame which promises more light, but whose promise is never fulfilled" (p. 9). Compare Hyperius' statement regarding the election and Christ, of which Reid says: "But this type of definition is regarded by orthodox Calvinists as defective" (p. 13). All of Reid's dogmatic-historical remarks are very debatable and show bias by way of his own view at the end of the article (p. 179ff.).

that Reformed theology has always wanted to take into account
the Biblical message with respect to the election in Christ. This
consideration never fell away because of an acceptance of a
mere act of sovereignty which had nothing to do with the
love and grace of God. Even though the exegesis of Ephesians
1:4 emphasizes the exclusion of all merit by mentioning the
name of Christ,[15] that certainly does not mean that His name
is mentioned only to illustrate and accentuate the merciful election of God. Rather, election in Christ rules out all merit
because it is election in Christ, so that also this passage confronts us with the electing counsel of God which is not based
on works (cf. Rom. 9:11). It is quite understandable that Ephesians 1:4 is always encountered when one reflects on the counsel of God, for that text praises the election of God — not as
an abstract act, as the counsel of a *potentia absoluta* — in such
a manner that it can be immediately followed by these words:
"having foreordained us unto adoption as sons through Jesus
Christ" (Eph. 1:5).

This makes impossible the idea of an abstract, merciless, and
loveless sovereign decree. The Biblical passages are so clear
that they can never be disregarded without serious results. This
does not mean that they are always easily understood; for
precisely when the freedom and sovereignty of God are emphasized to oppose synergism, the danger is acute that sovereignty becomes an empty concept. Here, too, the testimony of
Ephesians 1:4 may cause difficulties.[16] Gomarus, the well-known
supralapsarian, when he reflected on Ephesians 1:4 came to
the conclusion that "in Christ" should be understood as "through
Christ," but he did not intend that to mean that Christ was only
the means and executor of God's decree. He found a solution
by saying that "Christ in accordance with His divine nature also
participated in the work of election."

Even one who hesitates to call this view accurate (does "in
accordance with His divine nature" conform to the trend of
thought in Eph. 1?) must agree that a serious attempt has
been made to reflect on the meaning of this passage in Scripture, a reflection which is possible only when one removes
himself intuitively from the abstract concept of sovereignty.

---

15. See Calvin, for instance, *Inst.* III, xxii, 1, 2, 3 and his commentary
    on Ephesians 1:4.
16. See L. Van der Zanden, *op. cit.,* p. 38: "From the supralapsarian point
    of view it becomes difficult to maintain election in Christ."

It must also be remembered that Gomarus was arguing here
against the Arminians. They, too, had appealed to Ephesians
1:4 when they declared that the elect were chosen in Christ and
therefore were considered to be believers, because no one is
chosen without faith in Christ. That is, they interpreted Ephesians 1:4 as saying that we were elected as *in Christo insiti,*
in our quality as believers. The fundamental Arminian approach
is clearly revealed in this exegesis, which is so strongly rejected by Gomarus. Paul, he says, does not say that God elects
us as existing in Christ, as if the condition of faith should
precede, but *in* Him, that is to say, *through* Him.[17] Gomarus
means to say that we are not elected because we (by virtue
of faith: *praevisa fides*) are in Christ, but in order that we
should be holy (cf. Eph. 1:4). In election we do not stand
as saints, but as sinners. And that is the reason why Gomarus
(correctly) rejects the Arminian exegesis, and then understands
the words "in Christ" as His being one with the Father, and
this leads him to say that Christ, too, elects us.

Not only Gomarus, but also others have reflected on the
election in Christ. It is striking that in spite of the criticism
against the concept of persuasion and in spite of the danger of
misunderstanding, the expression *fundamentum electionis* recurs
many times. The idea, apparently, was not to isolate the sovereign decree of election from Jesus Christ, but to stress that
all of Christ's saving work is related to God's good pleasure so
uniquely that it is no longer possible to describe the relation between the divine plan and its execution by means of an analogy
to a human plan, in which the planner seeks the means to execute his design. We repeatedly get the impression that the
profoundest motif of the Reformed doctrine of election was not
the abstract sovereign decree, but the rejection of the theory
that Christ's work was a *causa impulsiva* of God's election, and
of every interpretation of the election in Christ in which faith
would become the condition of election.[18]

---

17. "In" and "through." Gomarus' intention becomes apparent from his
    reference to Col. 1:16.
18. We find the sharpest reproofs in Reid. He appreciates Bucanus'
    view, but also discusses the idea that Christ was elected *"post nostram
    electionem"* (cited and rejected by Walaeus), and then remarks: "The
    main body of thought lies nearer that cited by Walaeus than that repre-
    sented by the simple statement of Bucanus." Usually, Christ was

It is of great importance to mention that also the Canons of Dort contain a refutation of this sharp criticism. Referring to Ephesians 1:4 they speak of the election in Christ "whom He from eternity appointed the Mediator and Head of the elect and the foundation to salvation" (CD, I, 7). Clearly there is no thought here of an abstract decree of election, for in these words our eyes are simultaneously directed to the election of God and to the Mediator, while elsewhere there is mention of "the gracious election" (CD, I, 10), of the "eternal and unmerited grace of election" (CD, I, 15), and of the "grace of unmerited election."

The terminology of the Canons is varied and does not pretend to be scientifically exact, but precisely in that variation of terminology the meaning is unmistakable. Think, for instance, of the formulation in the Canons where there is mention of the "sovereign council and most gracious will and purpose of God the Father" (II, 8) while the Canons say that this counsel originates in the eternal love of God for the elect (II, 9). The Canons do speak of God's good pleasure, but this *beneplacitum Dei* is not detached from the grace of God. When, in opposition to the Remonstrants, they mention what is "merely and solely the good pleasure of God," there occurs a reminder of Deuteronomy 10 to explain that Israel did not receive the gospel because it was more worthy or better than other nations, but because God delighted to love them. Thus the Canons also reject the criticism that election is "merely and solely the good pleasure of God."

None of this may be omitted when the Canons are discussed. It is therefore difficult to understand that in Woelderink's analysis of them these points are hardly mentioned. He calls the relation of the decree of election to Christ unclear. But when he himself speaks of the love of God according to which He elects and preserves the saints, Woelderink neglects to refer

---

isolated from the degree of God: "Christ is merely the exhibitor of a decision already made in an eternity in which He has himself been, even if existent, at least inoperative. On the other hand, His role is to give effect to a decree, in whose formation He has apparently had no hand." It is difficult to make this representation agree with the reflection on Eph. 1:4 in Reformed theology. How seriously Reid's reproach is meant is shown by his words: "As one passes in review the various roles assigned to Christ in election, it is difficult not to despair" (p. 16).

to the Canons (II, 9). This is a curious omission because precisely in this connection the eternal love of God is emphasized.[19]

This shows how careful one must be if he wishes to accuse orthodoxy of overemphasizing the sovereign power of God in election. Precisely because the concept of the *potentia absoluta* —against which Calvin warned (see Chap. 3) and which he called an invention — is so dangerous, the orthodox doctrine of election has always contained a warning against it. Therefore, it is simply irresponsible to brush aside Reformed attempts to show the harmony of election with the grace and the love of God in Jesus Christ, and to suggest that this "arbitrary power" actually underlies the Reformed view.

After this obviously necessary defense, we now come to the important question about the meaning and intent of those often discussed words regarding the election in Christ. He who thinks here — as Gomarus does — of Christ's participation in election in accordance with His divine nature, would think it possible that we should also read of an election in the Holy Spirit, since He, too, is the electing God. It is now generally agreed that Paul had a specific intent when he used the expression "in Christ." Van der Zanden says that according to Paul the election is "centralized and founded"[20] in Christ, and that for that reason we speak correctly of election only "when we see it from where Christ stands. The election in Christ is therefore not just a chapter in the teaching of Paul, but it governs all of this doctrine."[21] From that he concludes that we must not contemplate what God decreed before the foundation of the world, for . . .

---

19. J. G. Woelderink, *De Uitverkiezing* (1951), p. 21. Since Woelderink sees at this point a deviation from the direction taken by the first articles, which begin with the gospel, he should have taken more seriously the formulations we mentioned. It is peculiar that Woelderink mentions the expression in CD, I 10: "gracious election," but he does not care for this "gracious." He says instead that election acquires "a certain independence" here, as though it were an entity with its own characteristics. This criticism is not fair; it does away with the emphasis of the Canons on the gracious aspect of election. Compare Woelderink's incorrect definition: "In 'gracious election,' election is the main thing and 'gracious' is just a descriptive adjective." Woelderink's criticism of the wording in the Canons of "the election" and not of "the electing love of God" is also unfair. Besides, Woelderink's book itself bears the title *Election*!

20. Van der Zanden, *op. cit.*, p. 15. Cf. Dijk, *op. cit.*, p. 68.

21. Van der Zanden, *loc. cit.*, or Dijk, *op. cit.*, pp. 111ff.

that decision is revealed in Christ. "We do not know another decree than the one revealed unto us, and there is no other decree."[22] All salvation lies anchored in Christ. There is not a separate, sovereign decree followed by the love of God as the way of its realization because one cannot say anything regarding this decree without speaking of Jesus Christ.

We violate this maxim when we contrast an abstract eternity to an abstract time. But Scripture teaches us not to do this. It shows us the interrelation between God's sovereign electing act and His only-begotten Son. Paul says elsewhere that God has set forth Christ to be a propitiation (Rom. 3:25), and Peter speaks of the Lamb foreknown indeed before the foundation of the world (I Pet. 1:20). From the very beginning the reference to Christ is implied in the depth-aspect of God's salvation, and any separation between sovereign decree and realization is simply condemned. He has predestined us in love (Eph. 1:5). The blessing of Christ is one with the election in Christ (Eph. 1:3-4), and Paul's hymn of praise is truly one continuous doxology.

It is understandable that much attention has been paid to the expression "in Christ." According to Grosheide, "in" means "anchored in, resting upon."[23] We encounter the word more than once in the New Testament when we hear of being alive unto God in Christ Jesus (Rom. 6:11), the eternal life that God grants in Christ (Rom. 6:23), the release from the condemnation of those who are in Christ, and of the Spirit which has liberated us in Christ from the law of sin and of death (Rom. 8:1). These words indicate a profound interrelation. In addition, we read the expression "through," which is more indicative of the working cause, and as such is distinct from "in" as "resting in Him." Bavinck has presented the meaning of "in Christ" in such a manner that the *Christus mysticus* is actually the object of predestination,[24] and that for that reason the expression *causa electionis* may well be used.[25]

Christus mysticus — by that Bavinck does not mean the Arminian exegesis of Ephesians 1:4, against which Gomarus correctly

---

22. Van der Zanden, *op. cit.*, p. 25. Cf. Calvin on Eph. 1:4: "That love with which God has loved us before the foundation of the world, was established in Christ as a foundation."
23. F. W. Grosheide, *Christus de Heiland*, p. 85.
24. Bavinck, *Gereformeerde Dogmatiek*, II, 368.
25. *Ibid.*, p. 364.

protested, but that man's merit is ruled out and that all believers
are contained in Him. In Him — he who attempts to define
this more clearly will easily employ more words than Paul
needed for his song of praise to God's election in Christ. The
Confessio Helvetica Posterior of 1562 says, for instance, that
God elects us in Christ and because of Christ (Art. 10). That
expression is not meant to improve on Paul's words, for Paul,
too, often speaks of "through Christ." "In" and "through"
are not meant as two different aspects of one and the same
situation. They both indicate the one electing act of God which
in history becomes revealed as His act in Christ.

Oepke refers to Ephesians 1:4 as a passage where "in" must
be taken comprehensively, "taking together a multiplicity into
a unity."[26] The notion of "comprehending" is yet another way
to indicate the mystery of the election in Christ. It does not
necessarily shed new light, but it does make clear that Paul
wants to emphasize the decisive significance of Christ in the
election of God. We read that God elected us in Christ, that
He has carried out this eternal decree in Christ, and that in
the fullness of time He will unite all things in Him (Eph. 1:10).
The absolute significance of Christ's work of salvation stands
here in the center: from eternity, in time, and in the *eschaton,*
when all things in Him "are taken together in their total."[27]
Paul speaks of this *eschaton* in the same chapter in which he
speaks of the election in Christ (Eph. 1:4), of "before the foundation of the world," and of the bestowing of grace in the
Beloved (Eph. 1:6). Paul exhibits this mystery with all
its perspectives when he speaks of the believers who know of
this plan in Christ, of this riches which in all its unspeak-
ableness is clear and revealed in the fact that from eternity
and until the fullness of time the issue at stake is this "gracious
economy in Christ."[28] In this economy — in Christ — there
is no human merit, but only redemption through the blood of
Christ, forgiveness of our sins, and the riches of His grace
(Eph. 1:7).

It is clear that for Paul there is no discrepancy to be bridged
between what happened in eternity and what happened in time.
And he finds it impossible to think of the plan of God without

26. Kittel, *T.W.N.T.,* II, 538.
27. *Ibid.,* III, 628.
28. S. F. H. J. Berkelbach van der Sprenkel, *De Kerk. De Brief aan de
    Efeziërs* (1941), p. 17.

thinking of Jesus Christ, as Van Leeuwen remarks, with reference to Ephesians 1:4, "the counsel of God is not an immutable and fixed decree." This fixedness and immutability are foreign to Paul's hymn on the love of God. The power and evidence of Paul's testimony have safeguarded the Church and theology at decisive moments against a devaluation of God's election to such a fixedness of decree, which is only later realized in the work of Christ. Scripture does says "through Christ" with respect to salvation, and there is no need at all to balk at the word "instrumental" — as when Paul writes that we are reconciled with God through (*dia*) the death of His Son (Rom. 5:10) — provided that the word "instrumental" is stripped of all impersonal connotations, and that we think of God's act as being in Christ who is the author of our salvation (Heb. 2:10). That is what Paul wants: Christ as the central point of the act of God; and it is beyond all doubt "that God through His act in Christ has opened the way, and with that has dispensed with all human merit, and has done away with every intermediary instance."[29] There is no discrepancy for Paul between "in Christ" and "through Christ." The instrumental and the comprehensive are one in Christ. They touch upon each other in the exclusion of all human merit.

The election of God is an election of mercy, precisely because it is election in Christ. That is why the Bible shows us the way of belief, and why "in Christ" can become the foundation of a pastoral message that points at Christ as *speculum electionis*. This is not meant as an escape, a rock to which we must cling in the face of the tremendous fact of election; no, the very structure of that election is revealed in Christ. There is election only in Christ, and for that reason we may look up to Him. The ontic foundation is not wanting in the noetic and consoling message; it is found in election, "elected in Christ."[30]

Since election is in Christ, Paul can write that God has carried out His eternal plan in Christ, and that in Him "we have boldness and access in confidence through our faith in him" (Eph. 3:12) This call to boldness and confidence is not a last pastoral escape from the menace of a "hidden" election,

29. Kittel *op. cit.*, II, 66.
30. There is a profound connection between Calvin's reference to the *speculum electionis* and his exegesis of Eph. 1:4.

but it is *the* way of the glad tidings. The boldness *corresponds*
to the merciful election. This faith in Him makes no mistakes;
it is in harmony with God's choice. That is why faith cannot
be frightened from a different direction (eternity) than the one
from which the gospel came to us. Nor do the sovereignty of
God and His inscrutable majesty affect this boldness. Because
we have this High Priest, we may with boldness draw near to
the throne of grace (Heb. 4:16). The throne should not be
forgotten because of grace, neither should grace be forgotten
because of the throne. This boldness penetrates to where God
reveals Himself most gloriously. Nothing can go deeper and
farther than this boldness.

For many people the divine foreknowledge, the idea of
"before the foundation of the world," and His good pleasure have an element of threat and uncertainty rather than
of comfort. They see in it the depth, distance, and unknown
by which nothing that comes to us in this dispensation is completely free from threat and uncertainty. And once they are on
this way, they read into it a sort of metaphysics, an objective
state of affairs regarding the relation between eternity and time
whereby time represents the known and eternity the unknown,
the uncertain, and therefore the threat.

Such presentations are the most serious threat to the comfort
of election. The more they become dominant in heart and life,
the more one's receptivity to the hymns of praise in which
these Scriptural words have been placed disappears, and man's
cunning heart can employ the doctrine of election as an excuse,
or find in it an explanation, or even justification, for his uncertainty. Precisely for that reason it is necessary to understand again how the words "time" and "eternity" function in
the gospel.

These words do not occur in Scripture as a threat, but in
the decisive depth-aspect of salvation. They are not placed in
a context in which they make us dizzy in the face of an unapproachable "eternity," or make us step back from an unfathomable abyss, but they are intended to show us the source
of our eternal salvation. That is shown already in the words:
"before the foundation of the world." The issue here is not a
metaphysical contrast between time and eternity, but the foundation of salvation in God's plan as immutable reality. "Before"
indicates that this divine act of salvation, preached to us by

the gospel, is free from what we know in the world to be arbitrary and precarious. To be sure, in this depth-aspect of God's salvation it becomes at the same time evident that this salvation did not originate in our flesh and blood, and that it is by no means of human merit or creation. But precisely this fact does not obscure the way; on the contrary, it illumines it. "Before the foundation of the world" means to direct our attention to what can be called the opposite of chance and contingence. History and the gospel are not minimized, but the riches and fullness of salvation in history are shown to be anchored in God.

This is the same depth to which Paul refers in Romans 8 by the words "before," "purpose" (Rom. 8:28), "foreknew" and "foreordained" (Rom. 8:29), which imply not a threat but the foundation of certainty. When Paul speaks of God's plan of salvation which is carried out and realized (Eph. 3:11) because it rests in the love of God, this "beforehand" leads to a song of certainty and victory. Therein is testified that nothing can separate us from the love of God in Christ (Rom. 8:35), and in that same song the love of God is glorified which is in Christ (Rom. 8:39). The immutability of God's work is based on this plan, which will reach its goal in spite of dangers and weaknesses (cf. Rom. 8:26). The origin and the goal are correlated in the one act of God (Rom. 8:28-30), as it realizes itself in time from predestination to calling and justification, and finally to glorification.

This is not only the case with those passages in which "before" is of great significance; it also is the case with respect to God's good pleasure. This pleasure does not stand in contrast to the historical gospel which comes to us. The word *eudokia* can in the gospel be connected with "fear not" (Luke 12:32), but also with the good news itself (*euaggelion-eudokia*). To be sure, this divine good pleasure as God's powerful sovereignty stands in contrast to man's power and wisdom (cf. I Cor. 1:21), but precisely so does the *eudokia* become revealed in its most profound significance, and so is it preached in its saving power. There is no threat involved here. It is the divine pleasure which is discernible only to those who believe. That is the rationale of the harmony of Scripture wherever it speaks of the election of God. In all the multiplicity of the Biblical testimony there is always a relation to that one focal point: *God's* salvation.

These close and unbreakable connections are exhibited no less in that doxological beginning of Ephesians 1 — elected in Christ before the foundation of the world. Mittring was correct when he summarized this book of the Bible as "the mystery of Christ,"[31] and the place which this mystery takes in the whole of God's works makes it forever impossible to speak of the decree of God as merely a formal framework in which salvation is placed later. The word "decree" causes this misunderstanding whenever it is interpreted out of its context in Scripture. It is then interpreted as a decree which was pronounced in our absence, in which we were not really involved, and which, therefore, does not come forth out of divine love for us. Bavinck has protested against this interpretation according to which the counsel of God "is as a design which lies ready and waits only to be executed,"[32] He denies that God's counsel can be described as "an act of God in the past," and he calls that counsel "an eternal act of God, finished from eternity and continuing from eternity, apart from and beyond time."[33]

It is clear that he who speaks of God's counsel in terms of human categories will have to be aware of the inadequacy of his words. So Bavinck, and many others with him, try to avoid portraying the decrees abstractly by saying that this is not a matter of a *decretum absolutum,* but of the *Deus decernens,* and that one cannot speak of before and after with respect to God.[34] The counsel of God is said to be "the will of God that works from eternity; the willing, deciding God Himself.[35] These statements occur in a passage defending the doctrine of the decree of God against criticism.

In the same passage Bavinck also opposes those who make God dependent on historical occurrences, and who view His work as merely part of the course of events in history, thus denying the priority of His initiative, His plan, His counsel, and His decree.[36] But although the sovereign character of God's

---

31. Karl Mittring, *Das Christusgeheimnis. Eine Einführung in den Epheserbrief* (1936[2]).
32. Bavinck, *op. cit.,* II, 334.
33. *Ibid.*
34. *Ibid.,* p. 303-4.
35. *Ibid.,* p. 334.
36. Cf. O. Weber, *Grundlagen der Dogmatik* (1955), p. 510, about the motif in the doctrine of the decrees as the will "to describe God's work as His very own, based exclusively in Himself."

counsel would thus be affected, we should not be tempted to take Bavinck's rejection of an abstract act less seriously.[37] It is, of course, possible to avoid this sovereign and loving priority by pointing to the anthropomorphic character of the word "decree," and then forgetting that these anthropomorphic expressions have a truly explanatory purpose. It is therefore incorrect to see one of the fundamental errors of the doctrine of election in the term "decree." It all depends on how one speaks of the decrees of God. Is it done in the sense of a purely formal decree, followed by salvation in Christ?[38]

The answer to this question is of great importance to a correct understanding of the doctrine of election.[39] One may not limit the divine sovereignty or violate the immutability of the counsel of God, but neither may one detach the counsel of God from those connections which Scripture repeatedly points out to us, and which find their point of concentration in the love of God. That is why in the history of the doctrine of election the most important decisions have always been made with re-

37. Kuyper has opposed in this connection the intermediary theologians who, with respect to the eternity of God, rejected all mention of earlier and later. Kuyper points at our human way of thinking of God's work, without which we cannot imagine anything, and he reminds us of the term "before the foundation of the world."

38. K. Dijk, *Van Eeuwigheid Verkoren* (1952), p. 68, says correctly that it is better "not to speak of another decree lying behind and beyond the gracious election in Christ" because that would too much detach election from Jesus Christ.

39. The matter has been discussed, e.g., in connection with the Westminster Confession. Chapter III contains a statement on "God's Eternal Decrees" (see Muller, *op. cit.*, p. 549) between the chapters on the Trinity and the Creation. This very point has been the topic of many discussions dealing with the relation of election to Christ, evidently starting from the concept that WC, III, detaches God's decrees from Christ. See on the later "Declaratory Act," Muller, *op. cit.*, and *The Confession of Faith of the Presbyterian Church in the U.S.A.* (1945), p. 140. The Declaratory Statement reads: With reference to Chapter III of the confession of faith: that concerning those who are saved in Christ, the doctrine of God's eternal decrees is held in harmony with the doctrine of His love to all mankind." For criticism of the Westminster Confession, see J. G. Riddell, "God's Eternal Decrees" (*Scott. Journal of Theology,* 1949, pp. 353ff.) who places it at this point over against the Scotch Confession, Article VII, which begins with the election in Christ. Riddell's criticism does not mention that also in the Westminster Confession "in Christ" is mentioned in connection with election (in Chap. III): "hath chosen in Christ unto everlasting glory, out of his mere free grace and love" (Müller, *op. cit.*, p. 551).

gard to Ephesians 1:4, which has provided the basis for strong
resistance against any form of abstractionism and determinism
in which the traits of the living God, the Father of Jesus Christ,
are obscured by the hiddenness and the menace of inscrutable
fate.[40]

We must face the fact that Barth has concentrated his
criticism on the doctrine of the *decretum absolutum* at precisely
this point. He asks whether the pastoral reference to the mirror
of election is not seriously threatened because of the "absolute
decree." Apparently he takes it for granted that an abstract
decretum absolutum lies at the base of the orthodox doctrine
of election. We ourselves have pointed out the abstraction
and rejected it because it is contrary to Scripture, especially to
Ephesians 1:4. If Barth had intended to warn exclusively
against that abstraction, we could have no objection whatsoever. Pointing at the mirror of election cannot be a pastoral
escape; it must be founded in the revelation of God's election.
Furthermore, we want to acknowledge that this abstraction has
often threatened the solace and comfort of election, so that a
serious warning is quite valid. To isolate election from the love
of God in Christ is dangerous also because it is impossible afterwards to connect the two. The gospel can be preached with real
urgency and challenge only when the mirror of election is a
clearly reflecting mirror. This clearness we see in the light
of the revelation of Scripture with regard to the election in
Christ.

Evidently, therefore, the discussion of Barth's doctrine of
election cannot be concerned with a defense of the abstract over
against the concrete, of the sovereignty of God over against His
love; rather, we suggest that classical Reformed theology has

40. Especially in our time, tremendous and often one-sided reaction can
be observed against "abstraction" in the doctrine of election. While
recognizing the legality of this defense it is important always to investigate whether this does not harm the doctrine of election in some
other way. Cf. H. Cunliffe-Jones, "Is the Use of the Word 'Predestination' Really Necessary?" (*Scott. Journal of Theol.*, 1950, pp. 409ff.).
The one-sidedness of this reaction comes from a reference to Eph. 1:4
and the identification, based on that, of predestination with grace without
considering the concept of predestination more closely in connection
with Rom. 8, even though in this connection there was good reason to do
so, the more so since every thought of abstraction over against grace is
excluded here. Cf. J. Nelson, "Predestination," *Scott. Journal of
Theol.* (1953), pp. 244ff.

been aware that this interpretation of election depreciates Biblical testimony. To be sure, in the historical situation the sovereignty of election was repeatedly — and correctly — emphasized. But these emphases (Luther against Erasmus, Calvin against Pighius and Rome, Dort against the Remonstrants) were not meant to propagate the concept of an abstract sovereign decree by a *potentia absoluta*, but were directed precisely against the disregard of the sovereignty of grace. That the doctrine of election was defended against the doctrine of free will may not be interpreted as determinism; nor may election be lifted out of its historical context. In polemics, the emphasis on sovereignty has sometimes given the impression that concern lay with sovereignty as such. However, the actual intent came repeatedly to the fore, and it is a testimony to the power of Scripture that here the dangers of abstraction (sovereign election without the love of God) were seen and repeatedly conquered.

It is clear that Barth thinks differently of the history of the doctrine of election. Apparently he has interpreted the doctrine of the decree of God in the sense of a *decretum absolutum* as such. Against that notion he affirms that "in the place of this empty spot" (the *decretum absolutum* as such) the name of Christ must be mentioned.[41] For if that were not done, if Christ did not participate in the election of God, we should not be able to find shelter and rest in Christ in the face of election, and in that case "we should have to ask for God, or perhaps for the Holy Spirit, while passing by the Christ." Barth's protest is sharply revealed when he writes: "We then should be compelled to reflect on a *decretum absolutum*, instead of reaching for and affirming in God's election the revealed grace of God."[42] Barth's intention is perfectly clear; we see that precisely here he finds his greatest objection against Calvin's doctrine of predestination. He is of the opinion that Calvin "not only does not answer but evidently never experienced or saw" the question which occupies him (Barth), that is, the question regarding Christ and election.[43]

We want to indicate here that this dogmatic-historical judgment

41. *K. D.,* II, 2, 111.
42. *Ibid.,* p. 113.
43. *Ibid.,* p. 119. For that reason he calls Calvin's "electing God" a *Deus nudus absconditus.* He calls it the fundamental error of Calvin's doctrine of predestination that Calvin ultimately "detached God from Jesus Christ" and "looked past the grace of God which became manifest in Christ."

does not conform to Calvin's reflections on the *speculum electionis* and on Ephesians 1:4. There must be another factor involved here. It certainly is not correct to say that Calvin did not see the question, although it may be asked whether Calvin always answered that question clearly and adequately. At a decisive point he rejected precisely the penetration into *deus nudus* (the Father alone, as Calvin puts it) by saying that the heart of the Father rests in Christ.

The situation, then, is quite different from that presented by Barth, and we must conclude that his objection stems from his own opinion regarding Christ as "the basis for the realization of election."[44] Therefore we ought not to conclude our discussion of Barth's view with a defense of an abstract sovereignty-decree — without the divine love — but with a closer reflection on the relation between Christ and the election of God.

The actual point at issue is not the contrast between abstract (classical Reformed doctrine) and concrete (Barth), but it is Barth's thesis that Christ Himself is the subject of election. This is the root of Barth's criticism and protest. If Christ Himself is not the subject of election, then in preaching one can no longer point meaningfully to Him. Hereby Barth does not direct our attention to Christ Jesus in His divine nature, as participating *vere Deus* in the Trinity to perform the election of God, but he directs us to the references in Scripure that discuss Christ's election. Especially the words of John are meaningful to Barth: "I know whom I have chosen" (John 13:18); "Ye did not choose me, but I chose you, and appointed you" (John 15:16); "But I chose you out of the world" (John 15:19). These words lead Barth to the conclusion that Christ is not only the object of God's pleasure but that He himself is this pleasure in action. He is not just the instrument of divine freedom, but Freedom itself. "And thus He is not only the chosen, but Himself the Elective one; His election must first be actively understood.[45] He elects together with the Father and the Holy Spirit. In God, He is no less original subject "of that choice than that He is its original object." As man He confirms the choice of God, because He originally participates in that election. It is His own election.

44. *K. D.,* II, 2, 129.
45. *Ibid.,* p. 112

Jesus Christ is precisely the subject of election. Election is revealed in Him. If He were only the elected, how could we know anything about our election? No, He is the concrete presentation of the Divine decree of the Father, the Son, and the Holy Spirit. The words of the Gospel of John must be understood as referring to the true election of God. This election of Christ (as subject) is not a taking upon Himself of a certain function, but an act of divine sovereignty[46] in which God's eternal decree is transparent, nay, stands before us, revealed in Christ. That is the reason why Barth turns against Thomas, who limits the election of Christ to His passive relationship to the Father, and to Christ's human nature. That, he thinks, is a forbidden limitation in the light of John's Gospel. Christ as man can "at first do no more than undergo, experience, and accept divine election," but He is also subject of the election, "the electing God."[47] Otherwise the election of God would become a separate mystery, detached from Christ, and man would remain in the shadow of a *decretum absolutum*. Christ is not "one of the works of God that make up for predestination," but there is a passive and an active election in Christ. And this way only — since Christ is the electing God Himself — our election becomes revealed in Him, not as a symbol or illustration, but as historical reality, in which the message of comfort can find its supporting basis.

It has been remarked already that Barth's appeal to Scripture for his doctrine of Christ as subject of election is limited almost wholly to a few passages in the Gospel of John which speak of Christ's calling and election to the apostolate. The question arises therefore whether Barth is justified in drawing his far-flung conclusions. In order to answer this question, it must first be pointed out that this electing of Christ — as done historically during His human life — is undoubtedly very closely connected with the whole process of salvation. It is understandable, therefore, that its connection with the eternal election of God has often been discussed, the more so, since the word that Christ uses for the election of God is the same as is used elsewhere in Scripture. Calvin pondered this problem and, although he does not see in John 15:16 the *communis electio piorum*, he thinks it refers to an *electio particularis* of the dis-

46. *Ibid.*, p. 114.
47. *Ibid.*, p. 115.

ciples. But he does see a direct connection: the election of the disciples is also without any merit on their part. "Ye have not chosen me, but I have chosen you!" In this call to discipleship there is a clear similarity to the structure of the election of God, namely, in the emphasis on Christ's full initiative,[48] so that their choice did not issue from their own lives but from Him. This is not surprising, says Calvin, for the Father acts through Christ and Christ with the Father.

It is generally felt that this election of the apostles reflects the pattern of God's whole work of salvation. The apostles, who represent the believers of the New Testament, are elected through Christ's act, not theirs. The origin of their service is put clearly: Christ appoints the twelve (Mark 3:13), He chooses them (Luke 6:13), and He sends them out (Matt. 10:5). To be sure, Christ speaks thus of their election to special service[49] but this service is not merely a contingent historical occurrence without relation to the work of God in Jesus Christ. Christ's choosing, which is connected with a "knowing" (John 15:16), may therefore not be isolated from the knowledge and the will of God.[50] We do not answer Barth's appeal to the words of John by isolating Christ's choosing from God's election.

Another question is whether Barth is correct in concluding from these words that Scripture wants to present Christ as the subject of election, and to portray Him here as the electing God. To be sure, we may never apply a quantitative measure to Scripture in order to separate the important from the unimportant, but we must insist that these passages in John which stress election *by* Christ are precisely those which present His unique call to the apostolate. Without minimizing at all the

---

48. See also Calvin on John 15:18, where he says that this election cannot be detached from eternal election.

49. According to Grosheide, John 15:16 does not speak of the office of the apostles (*Commentary*, II, 352) but speaks of what is valid for all Christians. Bouma (*Korte Verklaring*, II, 108) interprets this as dealing with the "election to the apostolate." This is connected with the fact that Grosheide, with respect to John 15:18, thinks it best not to think of election to salvation, but nevertheless indicates "that precisely in John the doctrine of predestination comes repeatedly to the fore" (p. 262), and says of John 15:16 that this reference has something to do with what we call "election" in dogmatics. In connection with the election of the apostles, see also John 6:70.

50. C. H. Dodd, *The Interpretation of the Fourth Gospel* (1953), p. 162, speaks of Christ as "the divine knower" and refers to Num. 16:5: the knowing of God in the schism at the time of Moses.

unique significance of this act of Christ, we ought to note that the Bible also directs our attention to Christ as the Chosen One of God.

This does not at all rule out the trinitarian character of election, but we are confronted here with such an inscrutable mystery that we must fully respect all the emphases in Scripture. And we see then that Christ is presented to us, not only in His activity, but also in His passivity, as the Chosen One of God, in whom God has His good pleasure. We hear of the Messiah, the Anointed One, about whom it is said: "This is my Son, my chosen" (Luke 9:35), a word which finds its echo in the mockery at the cross: "He saved others; let him save himself, if this is the Christ of God, his chosen" (Luke 23:35). This relationship to the Father is the focal point of the New Testament message, when the prophecy of God's Chosen Servant (Isaiah 42:1) is fulfilled. In the New Testament we hear of the counsel of God that is fulfilled in and through Christ, all that the counsel and hand of God had foreordained beforehand to come to pass (Acts 4:28).

He is the foreknown Lamb (I Peter 1:20), the object of God's love before the foundation of the world (John 17:24), delivered according to the determinate counsel and foreknowledge of God (Acts 2:23), called and given as a covenant to the people, a light unto the nations (Isa. 42:6). All this does not at all imply mere passivity. He is given to be a Light and to open the eyes of the blind and bring out the prisoners from their dungeons (Isa. 42:7), to suffer actively as the Man of Sorrows, but in all this it stands in the foreground that Christ is the Chosen One in the humiliation and fulfillment of His Messianic calling. Precisely the same Gospel, which gives such a clear account of Christ's calling the apostles, gives us also the testimony of Christ's submissiveness to the Father. "For I spake not from myself; but the Father that sent me, he hath given me commandment, what I should say and what I should speak" (John 12:49). Here all our attention is directed to that relationship and hence to the Messiah, to the Servant of the Lord, to the Mediator between God and man.

It would be easy, at this point, to fall into the Nestorian heresy by over-emphasizing Christ's role as the Chosen One and underestimate the trinitarian mystery. It would be easy to see Christ only as the man chosen to fulfill God's will on earth. But that view detracts from the trinitarian character of the election of

God, for thus the man Jesus Christ is only seen as object of election.[51]

At the same time, however, it must be fully understood that precisely in this subordination of the Son to the Father is the trinitarian character of the election and reconciliation revealed, and that therein lies the foundation for our salvation. That is why Scripture repeatedly speaks of this mystery of the man Jesus Christ. It speaks of Jesus of Nazareth, "how God anointed him with the Holy Spirit and with power; who went about doing good, and healing all that were oppressed of the devil; for God was with him" (Acts 10:38). This "was with him" is not at all a violation of the trinitarian mystery, or of the confession *vere Deus*, nor is it a violation when Christ Himself says that the Father was with Him (John 16:32). Peter confessed Him, with whom God was, as the Son of the living God (Matt. 16). But Scripture takes the incarnation, the choosing, and the sending so seriously that it can speak that way: God was with Him. We want to emphasize this in order to show how impossible it is to think of "God in Christ" in such a manner as to forget that Scripture presents Jesus Christ to us as the One sent by the Father, as the Mediator between God and man. When Barth poses as main thesis for his doctrine of election that Christ Himself is the electing God, the question must be asked whether his appeal to John's words indeed warrants this thesis.[52]

---

51. In spite of all difference, the thought is related to what Kuyper discusses in his *De Vleeswording des Woords* (1887), Chap. XXI, about election "of the Man Jesus Christ." Cf. A. G. Honig, *Alexander Comrie*, p. 246, and K. Dijk, *Van Eeuwigheid Verkoren*, p. 113.

52. E. Buess, "Zur Praedestinationslehre Karl Barths" (*Theol. Studien*, 1955, Vol. 43), says: "The N. T. displays some hesitancy in mentioning Christ as the Subject of eternal election" (p. 48) and: "While Barth immediately comes up with the statement: 'Jesus Christ is the electing God,' he lets go of the possibility to do justice to this direction of divine election as coming from on high. In the New Testament, the difficulties which our knowledge encounters because of the hiddenness of election, are more sharply revealed." Buess correctly refers to Eph. 1:4, where the election is mentioned as a deed of the Father and "it is not immediately the act of Christ Himself" (p. 49). "The New Testament makes a sharp distinction between the divine subject and the divine-human object of election" (p. 52; cf. p. 63). The manner in which Barth speaks of Christ as the electing God is, I think, closely connected with all of his Christology and with what I elsewhere called the problem of "theopaschitism," (*The Triumph of Grace in the Theology of Karl Barth*, 1956, Chap. XI). This is also linked up with Miskotte's opinion (in connection with my considerations on theopaschitism) that the word

It is perfectly clear what motivates Barth to this line of thinking. He wants to solve the problem connected with preaching Christ — the *speculum electionis* — in a manner that will banish all uncertainty. He wants to anchor our election in the factuality of Christ, whom he presents as the electing God, who is gracious to man and wants to live in communion with him.

But the question must again be asked whether God's coming to us in Jesus Christ is not a reality which can be known only in the way of faith. The confession that Christ is *speculum electionis* is a glorious and inviolable objective reality, but it is a confession which does not render the way of belief superfluous; rather it points at that way so that we can follow it. If Barth's argument is that the consoling pastoral message misses its ontic foundation, we must reply that it is rather Barth's doctrine of election with its universality that evokes the problem which Barth thinks the Reformation left unanswered. For with Barth Christ is not so much the mirror of election as the manifestation of the election of God, a universal manifestation which may be disregarded in unbelief, but which cannot be undone.

We feel that Barth ought to reconsider his criticism of the Reformed teachings. We can and must listen to his warning not to separate God's sovereignty from His love, and His election from Jesus Christ, for in view of the many dangers and misunderstandings that have become evident in the course of history this warning remains necessary. But Barth misses the point, historically as well as dogmatically, when he disregards Reformed reflections on the words "in Christ" and instead finds a foundation for man's certainty of salvation in an electing Christ. He cannot in this way escape the objectification and fixedness which he thinks he discerns in the Reformed doctrine of election. We can only escape this fixedness and rigidity if it becomes clear that insight into the mirror of election is possible only in the way of faith. No theological reflection can by itself lead to this insight. It can only serve the preaching of the gospel by indicating the way of faith. This way can now be traveled because the inscrutability of election no longer poses a threat. Since elec-

---

"Mediator" in the N. T. is not at all central, and that by working with "the Biblical categories of Christ's Mediatorship, one comes to deal with difficulties of representation and transparency which could be avoided" (K. H. Miskotte, "De Triomf der Genade," *Kerk en Theologie*, Vol. IV, 1955, p. 111).

tion is election in Christ, the light of the message shines clearly. Because this light shines, the gospel may be preached, not as
a proclamation regarding an accomplished state of affairs, but
as a call and summons. He who travels the way of faith and
puts his trust in Jesus Christ alone, will understand that beyond
Him there arises no new, ultimate problem, but that in Him this
problem is solved. God's election is election in Christ. "Not
because of works, but because of grace." In this way the tension
between sovereignty and grace, which so often became manifest
in the thinking of many people, will disappear. For this grace is
truly sovereign, and this sovereignty is no longer a hidden menace (the arbitrariness!) which obscures grace. The election of
God in Christ is not a violation of the way of salvation, but its
proclamation.

When we discuss Christ and the election of God, the *propter*
and the *per,* and the trinitarian character of all of God's acts, we
need not be surprised that in this way we encounter all the questions which are concentrated in the doctrine of the so-called
pactum salutis. We all know that this doctrine has been regarded
as speculation and scholasticism. Precisely in the context of this
chapter it is desirable to investigate this criticism and to ask
whether this doctrine indeed trespasses the boundaries of the
Biblical message.

It is clear why the *pactum salutis* is discussed here, for in
this doctrine the matter at stake is the place and function of
Christ in the divine process of salvation. And this doctrine is
employed especially to oppose the idea that election was decreed
completely apart from Christ, and that He was nothing but the
executor of that decree. What does the *pactum salutis* signify?
Is it possible to furnish Biblical evidence for such a *pactum* as
a real "covenant"? Does not a pact always presuppose an "over
against," as in the covenant between God and man? And are we
perhaps dealing here with a speculative mode of thinking which,
impressed by the importance of the covenant-concept, also begins
to apply this concept to the trinitarian relation in the divine
being? Is it incidental that Bavinck in his *Dogmatiek* remarks
that the development of the *pactum salutis* is not free from
scholastic subtleness?[53]

53. Bavinck, *op., cit.,* III, 193.

According to Bavinck, many irrelevant references have been quoted to support this doctrine; in spite of that, however, it is based, he says, on a Scriptural concept,[54] while also Kuyper is of the opinion that we "are fully justified to carry the concept of the *foedus,* the *pactum,* into the inter-divine life."[55] He thinks that the point at issue is not the question whether the covenant relationship in the divine being is revealed to us "in complete terminology," but only "whether the relationship between Father, Son and Holy Spirit occurs in Scripture by itself and *quod ad opus salutis* in such a manner that it finds its correct expression only in the covenant-concept."[56]

What is the meaning of speaking of a *pactum salutis* between the three Persons? Bavinck thinks the basic motive lies in the submissiveness of the Son to the Father. This relationship between the Father and the Son is most clearly revealed during Christ's life on earth, but it does not begin with the incarnation. Already with the incarnation we deal with the execution of the work assigned to the Son. The relationship "falls in eternity and existed already during the time of the Old Covenant"[57] when Christ was already in office. The work of salvation, according to the *pactum salutis,* does not derive from history but from the depth of the trinitarian being of God. Bavinck says that the covenant between the Father, the Son, and the Holy Spirit is revealed in all its glory in the doctrine of the *pactum salutis.* Kuyper, however, has asked an important question with respect to the *pactum salutis*: "Now we are faced with the question how — if from eternity there was indeed a *constitutio mediatoris* — that could have happened without ending up in tritheism. If that *pactum salutis* existed in eternity, would not then the equality be a fiction, and is it then still possible to speak of the equality of being between Father and Son? Does that not compel us — willy-nilly — to give up the idea of the Trinity?"[58] Kuyper wants to indicate the problem which seems unavoidable in the *pactum salutis*: does not a federal relationship involve such an independence of the Persons with respect to each other that tritheism can no longer be avoided,[59] especially when in a

54. *Ibid.,* p. 194.
55. Kuyper, *Locus* III, p. 90.
56. *Ibid.,* p. 81.
57. Bavinck, *op. cit.,* p. 194.
58. Kuyper, *op. cit.,* p. 89.
59. *Ibid.,* p. 80.

pactum there is a *constitutio mediatoris,* and a subordination
of the Son to the Father, and when these seem to be based
on an agreement which gives the *pactum* its power and validity?
Is it acceptable to speak of such a *pactum* with all the implications
it carries? All these questions are by no means irrelevant. This
appears already from the fact that Barth has rejected the doctrine of the *pactum salutis* while Woelderink has ardently defended it in connection with his criticism of Barth's doctrine of
election.

That the danger of the tritheistic formulation is not at all
imaginary appears from many discussions of the *pactum salutis,*
for instance, when Vos says that we may not confuse the *pactum
salutis* with predestination, because in predestination the divine
Persons act in unison while in the *pactum salutis* the Persons
enter into judicial terms with each other. "In predestination
there is the one undivided will; in the counsel of peace this will
appears as having its own manner of existence in the Persons."[60]
And Vos adds: "The unity of the being of God cannot give rise
to any objection here. To emphasize that unity so strongly that
the Persons can no longer enter into judicial terms with each
other would lead to Sabellianism and would undermine the
reality of the work of salvation with its relations between Person
and Person."[61] One could ask here whether it is permissible
to juxtapose the "undivided" will of God with this entering into
judicial relations. We are again confronted by a great mystery
when we consider the *pactum salutis,* and with it the danger of
a tritheistic formulation of the nature of God.[62]

It cannot be denied, however, that in the doctrine of the *pactum
salutis* a deeply religious motif lies embedded. According to
Heppe, the matter at issue in this doctrine is not a concept reminiscent of Coccejus[63] which originally was lacking in the doc-

60. G. Vos, *De Verbondsleer in de Gereformeerde Theologie,* p. 25ff.
61. *Ibid.,* p. 27.
62. Great care befits us when we see that the formulations and definitions
    are in constant need of closer scrutiny. See K. Schilder, *Heidelbergse
    Catechismus,* I, 383 "[it is] a coming together different from ours
    because it is without beginning and therefore at the same time a being
    together from and for eternity." See Schilder's warning against the
    easy ascription to God of forms of human agreements (p. 384).
63. Heppe opposes Gass, who was of the opinion that "the application of
    the concept of union to the Persons in the Trinity was the actual new
    contribution of Coccejus to federal theology" (H. Heppe, *Geschichte*

trine of the covenant; rather, the concept that the *foedus gratia* was based on the eternal *sponsio* of the Son and the *pactum salutis* which it implies are found already with Olevianus. This is all the more reason for us to be interested in the actual, religious motif of this doctrine. Vos speaks of the Reformed view being in harmony with the doctrine of the *pactum salutis* since both emphasize that redemption is the work of God.[64] Even though it often is too humanly presented and not always skillfully defended, the core lies in the principles of Reformed theology and has endured all attacks.[65] In this doctrine there is no special preoccupation with eternity as abstractly contrasted with time, as if eternity would be more valuable than time. The doctrine of the *pactum salutis* does not origniate "from an inclination to bring back the covenant into the decree, but to concentrate it in the Mediator." Vos adds that its transcendent eternity is far less emphasized than is usually thought. "Eternal" has here a unique meaning: "It is eternal in so far as it falls within the Trinity, which exists eternally, but not eternal in the sense that it is above all historical reality."[66]

The motifs of immutability, faithfulness, unshakable foundation, inviolable certainty, and lasting comfort come repeatedly to the fore in the reflection on the *pactum salutis*. They are concentrated in the word *pactum*.[67]

---

des Pietismus und der Mystik, 1879, pp. 205ff.). Cf. J. van Genderen, *Herman Witsius* (1953), pp. 142ff.; cf. also Comrie's view: J. J. van der Schuit, *Het Verbond der Verlossing* (1952), p. 10.

64. G. Vos, *op. cit.,* p. 32. Cf. Van der Schuit, *op. cit.,* p. 13, who emphasizes the religious importance and rejects (on the basis of the *pactum salutis*) that the Reformed doctrine of election was cold and Stoic. Rather, it is concerned with "the sweet secrecy of God's being moved" (p. 13). For the confessions, Van der Schuit refers to HC, Q. 21 (Christ as the Anointed One ordained by the Father) and to CD, II, 9. Cf. A. Kuyper, who speaks of putting predestination into the foreground and who describes the "motive" in these words: "Because Calvinism wanted God to remain God, it confessed the origin of all grace to lie only in God's inscrutable mercy" (*Calvinisme en Revisie,* 1891, p. 23).

65. Vos, *op. cit.,* p. 32. He mentions the fact that the doctrine of the *pactum salutis* has often been used against the Remonstrants.

66. *Ibid.,* p. 35.

67. See on the variations in the relation between Father and Son, and between Father, Son and Holy Spirit: K. Schilder, *Heidelbergse Catechismus,* I, 382. The fact that often there is no specific mention of the Holy Spirit is due to the central idea in the *pactum salutis,* namely, the *constitutio mediatoris.*

It may be asked, however, whether this religious motif —
that all of salvation is the work of God — is correctly expressed
by means of the term *pactum*. Especially Barth, in his *Kirchliche
Dogmatik,* has criticized the use of this word. He discusses
Coccejus' treatment of the *foedus*-concept which indicates a pre-
temporal trinitarian concurrence between Father and Son, of
which then the *foedus gratia* is the outcome.[68] Barth then poses
many questions concerning this "inter-divine decree"[69] Is there
first a decree, a special inter-divine agreement and obligation
that must be distinguished "from the being of God"? And can
a *pactum* exist between Father, Son, and Holy Spirit, as if one
could represent the first and second Persons of the triune Divin-
ity as two divine subjects and then have them enter into nego-
tiations with each other and engage in mutual obligations?"[70]
That, says Barth, is nothing but mythology, for which there is
no place in the doctrine of the Trinity. God is one, and only man
can function as "partner." To entertain the concept of an intra-
trinitarian *pactum* is to court the dangers of dualism and the
judicial uncertainty of the *foedus gratia,* for then one is speaking
of different subjects who do not unite until "differences have
been straightened out." On the contrary, says Barth, a special
decree or *pactum* is not necessary to unite God over against man
and with Himself, for otherwise God would not be God. But in
the covenant with man something new does enter in, namely,
the content of a special act of will which is based not in God's
being, but in His freedom. That is a decree, a decision, an act
of grace; but no special decree is necessary between Father,
Son, and Holy Spirit, because they are one.

Barth evidently interprets the *pactum salutis* as something that
has the function of constituting the unity of God; he carries the
analogy so far that the closing of the *pactum* must then be preceded by a state in which Father, Son, and Holy Spirit were
not yet one. It is clear, however, that this analogy can never
be the intention of the *pactum salutis*. We are confronted here
with the peculiar fact that Barth discerns a source of uncertainty
in this doctrine, which is precisely contrary to its original intent. The doctrine of the *pactum salutis* points to the eternal and
solid foundation of salvation in the trinitarian love of God for
man. The concept of the *pactum salutis* indicates an analogy

68. *K.D.,* IV, 1, 67.
69. *Ibid.,* p. 68.
70. *Ibid.,* p. 69.

which underlies the absolutely harmonious economy of salvation.

Woelderink wrote in 1951 that Barth in his doctrine of election borrowed from the doctrine of the *pactum salutis*. He sees a connection here with Barth's preference for supralapsarianism and describes his doctrine in these words: "The main themes of Barth's construction are the election of the triune God, in which the Son of God is chosen and chooses Himself also, and the readiness of the Chosen One to fulfill the purpose of His election; they are the beginning and the end of all God's decrees."[71]

Woelderink wrote this when Barth's criticism of the doctrine of the *pactum salutis* had not yet been published. Is it possible that Woelderink made an incorrect deduction here? It seems to us that this question must be answered negatively. For Barth's criticism is especially directed against the tritheistic interpretation of the *pactum,* but since this is not necessarily connected with the doctrine of the *pactum salutis,* one can say that his criticism does not affect what at bottom is meant with this doctrine. Therefore Woelderink's presentation of Barth's views is not necessarily incorrect. If the analogy does not lie in the transition from dividedness to unity, and if *pactum* and *conventio* refer not to uncertainty and disparity but rather to stability and unity (and therein to comfort and solace), then one may be alerted by Barth's criticism against threatening dangers, but that does not mean that the real meaning and significance of the *pactum salutis* is in danger. Rather, precisely here we are confronted with the question which was attempted to be solved in the doctrine of the *pactum salutis,* namely, how we must understand that testimony of Scripture which speaks of the submissiveness of the Son to the Father, the Servant of the Lord.[72]

It is beyond doubt that the doctrine of the *pactum salutis* has been meant to indicate the depth- and stability-aspects of sal-

---

71. J. G. Woelderink, *op. cit.,* p. 33.
72. In connection with Barth's criticism of the doctrine of the *pactum salutis* we note that Barth in his doctrine of reconciliation (*K.D,* IV, 1, [1953]) has indicated as the actual mystery of reconciliation the obedience in God Himself. He gives there a transformation of the doctrine of the *pactum salutis,* but it is clear that he is confronted with the same questions. See my *The Triumph of Grace in the Theology of Karl Barth* (1956).

vation in Christ. When we speak of depth-aspect, we mean that eternity does not stand in contrast to what in time becomes historical reality, but rather that the salvation accomplished by Christ's death of reconciliation cannot be merely historical, but that it has its eternal foundation in the love of God. If we speak of *pactum salutis* to indicate this aspect, we do not thereby attempt to humanize the counsel of God. We wish, on the contrary, to indicate an analogy with what is called a "covenant" or "pact" on earth. Much, then, depends on the *tertium comparationis,* since we do not wish to transpose what cannot be transposed without violating the honor of the triune God. It is clear that we may not humanize the reality with which we are here confronted. When Kuyper discussed the doctrine of the covenant, he warned against humanizing, saying that the analogy is not simply a manner of presentation, a mode of expression to convey the idea of God's faithfulness.[73] This warning is also appropriate with respect to the *pactum salutis,* for here we have not a mere human concept, but a reality which confronts us at once as the *constitutio mediatoris* and as the *sponsio* of the Son of God.

It is certainly not incidental that the doctrine of the *pactum salutis* originated from reflection on the submissiveness of the Son to the Father. In connection with that, Kuyper tried to formulate more closely the covenant-concept in the *pactum salutis.*[74] He investigated the constituent elements of a covenant on earth, and then attempted to develop step by step the significance and meaning of the Divine *pactum.* Kuyper said that a covenant is possible only "if there is no higher power present which can enforce the practice of justice,"[75] and if the purpose is to prevent evil. These two aspects Kuyper applies not only to the relationship between God and man, but also to the *pactum salutis.* Because Father, Son, and Holy Spirit are each other's equal, "and there is nothing that can be imagined to stand above them," it follows that also the mutual relation between the three Persons must be based on a mutual word, on a mutual declaration

73. Kuyper, *De Leer der Verbonden,* p. 10.
74. Kuyper says that the entering into a covenant belongs "to the necessary manifestations of God's essence," and endeavors to undo it from all contingency (*ibid.,* p. 18). It is "directly and absolutely based in the essence and the attributes of God" (p. 19).
75. *Ibid.,* p. 21.

of will, and therefore must have the characteristic of a covenant.[76]

It seems clear that this line of thought is unsatisfactory as a basis for the doctrine of the *pactum salutis*. In earthly relationships Kuyper sees the covenant as a necessity against some threatening evil, because there is no higher power that can intervene authoritatively. In analogy to that, the *pactum salutis* also acquires these traits of a human pact.[77] This is unsatisfactory because it is impossible ever to speak of any sort of *dubium* in the trinitarian unity and alliance necessitating a mutual declaration of will. Futhermore, the *pactum salutis* originates in the riches and fullness of God's love. The motif of the absence of a higher power (as necessitating the closing of a pact) as well as the necessity to unity against threatening danger must be eliminated. For this presentation is burdened by carrying into the pactum *salutis* an element of threat and uncertainty.

We must insist that Reformed theology did not arrive at the doctrine of the *pactum salutis* in this way, but rather from the message of Scripture regarding the inscrutable relationship between the Father and the Son in the truly unfathomable humiliation of the Servant of the Lord.[78] Man will always lose himself in analogies. He must keep a constant and watchful eye on this mystery, for only then will the doctrine of the *pactum salutis* truly touch upon the profoundest mystery of the gospel, and not be merely a construction of man's thought. Speaking dogmatically, we must delimit the boundaries of the anal-

---

76. *Ibid.,* p. 24.
77. Kuyper says also that all federal relations "are determined by the occurrence of the non-divine in angels and men" (*ibid.,* p. 80) and that the three Persons federally wish to overcome that which as non-divine is opposing the divine (p. 81). The questions that arise here are obvious when one considers that the relation between Father, Son and Holy Spirit from eternity must have been based on agreement.
78. It seems to me that there is nothing clarifying in Schilder's trend of thought: "Actually, every decision can be reduced to a pact and represented as convention: There is a *pactum salutis,* but also a *pactum damni,* a counsel of peace, but also a counsel of condemnation, a *pactum creationis,* a counsel of creation, but also a *pactum restaurationis,* a counsel of redemption. Thus we can continue *ad infinitum*." (*Heidelbergse Catechismus,* I, 383). This latter term, *ad infinitum,* is not critically intended. It is a reason for joy that theology did not take this course, but strictly adhered to those aspects as are clearly stated in Scripture.

ogy[79] in order to indicate in the concept of the *pactum* that reality of the work of redemption which has its foundation in the union of Father, Son, and Holy Spirit: the mystery of the Servant of the Lord.[80]

The foregoing has sufficiently indicated why the questions regarding the election in Christ and the *pactum salutis* continually touch upon each other. They do this regarding the sovereign love of God, which forms the foundation of the salvation in Christ. For precisely in the *pactum salutis* we see the immutability and stability which find expression in the song of praise of Ephesians 1. Thus we can appreciate why the Canons speak in the same connection of God's election in Christ, whom God appointed from eternity the Mediator and Head of the elect and the foundation of salvation (CD, I, 7).

He who makes a separation here, and — mark the danger of analogy! — places divine election and counsel beside each other, and then sees the *pactum salutis* as an agreement on the manner of execution of the decree of election,[81] has misjudged the significance of the *pactum salutis* and can no longer resist Barth's criticism of this form of the *pactum salutis*.

79. Kuyper has indicated these boundaries sharply when he speaks of "the actual concept of this *pactum*" and when he eliminates all the human aspects which accompany the closing of a pact on the human level (*Locus* I, Part V, 3, p. 44).

80. The variation in the di- or tri-pleuric interpretation of the *pactum salutis* does not imply a contention between the Christological and the pneumatological interpretation. Even where considerations are based on the concept of subordination of the Son to the Father, the sending of the Holy Spirit is always mentioned, but always in undetachable connection with the incarnation. At any rate, there has been no attempt to parallelism by placing the *inhabitatio Spiritus Sancti* alongside of the incarnation as a humiliation.

81. We think of the considerations of R. H. Bremmer on "election" and "counsel of peace" which were opposed by C. Trimp in *Tot een Levendige Troost Zijns Volks* (1954), pp. 46ff. Bremmer refers to election as the "act of the undivided" triune God. The word "individual" (as designation) is very informative here. J. J. Van der Schuit writes that election in Christ "logically" precedes the covenant of redemption (*Het Verbond der Verlossing*, 1952, p. 19). It seems better to adhere to the confession of CD, 1, 7, where the eye of faith at one glance obtains insight in the salvation in Christ. Trimp points out that CD, I, 8, says that He also has decreed "to give them to Him" but that this does not imply a separate decree regarding the manner of salvation. Besides, it is difficult to say what Van der Schuit means with the word "logically."

From the foregoing it is evident that our reflection on the election in Christ and in connection with that on the *pactum salutis* does not yield an abstract doctrine of election. But such abstraction is a continuous danger to the doctrine — as is evidenced by its history — and must be guarded against continually. The testimony of Scripture to the message of God's decree "before the foundation of the world" does not separate man from the gospel, but brings him closer to it. To say that God's counsel is eternal is not to make it remote, but to guarantee the inviolable reality of what is near. Hiddenness is not placed in contrast to revelation here, but the mystery of the will of God is forever made free from all contingence and arbitrariness. And it becomes clear how impossible it is to abstract the election of God from Jesus Christ, the Word that became flesh. Because of this impossibility, Jesus Christ is truly the mirror of election and for this reason the pastoral message finds in Him an immovable foundation.

When it thus becomes evident that the way of salvation is not made problematical because of the "depth" of eternity, light falls also on the many questions which sometimes threaten the peace of man's heart. The seriousness with which he torments himself concerning these questions seems, then, the necessary correlate to this feeling of depth, and the long duration of this crisis is indicative of the fact that he travels a way which cannot be traveled. It is the way in which man seeks a solution *praeter consilium Dei,* apart from the counsel of God, which, according to Scripture and confession, is only revealed to us in Christ (cf. Acts 20:27).

In spite of the message of salvation, the problem of the first, and therefore the last, decree remains knocking at the door of man's heart until the compelling call is heard: "Behold, I stand at the door and knock: if any man hear my voice and open the door, I will come in to him, and will sup with him, and he with me" (Rev. 3:20).

If anywhere, then here the words apply: "He that hath an ear, let him hear what the Spirit saith to the churches" (Rev. 3:22). *Veni, Creator Spiritus!*

CHAPTER SIX

ELECTION AND REJECTION

WE have discussed the meaning and implication of the words "election in Christ." Scripture showed us that in the doctrine of God's election the issue is not a *decretum absolutum,* abstracted from Jesus Christ, neither a *necessitas rerum* which cannot be changed under any cirucmstances, nor a dark and irrational power of the *potentia absoluta.* Rather, Scripture points in its doxologies and songs in praise of the free election of God to the deep, unfathomable source of salvation in Jesus Christ. "He chose us in him before the foundation of the world . . . having foreordained us unto adoption as sons through Jesus Christ" (Eph. 1:4-5).

Many tensions in the history of the doctrine of election are centered around that little word "us," and many feel that there is something irritating, something provocative, in it because it implies a delimitation, a distinction. It has been pointed out that this "us" has often acquired strange overtones which can hardly be distinguished from high-minded self-esteem. And the question is asked whether this self-esteem is not inevitably implied in the doctrine of election, in this word "us." Should we not automatically, with this "us," think of "the others"?

We shall ask these questions again (in the last Chapter), but now we wish to focus our attention upon them in relation to the dispute about election and rejection.

Is it still necessary to speak of rejection after discussing the election in Christ? Or is it possible and therefore also legitimate and necessary to be silent about rejection, and to discuss the task of the Church implied in election: the *eu-aggelion,* the glad tidings?

These questions automatically remind us of the fact that the Canons of Dort speak of election and rejection when opposing the Remonstrants (CD, I). When in the Canons and other confessions, and also in reflection upon dogmatics, we repeatedly meet with these two words beside one another, we could get the impression that we are confronted with an obvious duality of two symmetrical "decrees" of the divine predestination, decrees of the same structure as a Yes and No, side by side as *predestinatio ad vitam* and *ad mortem*.

What does this conjunction "and" mean between these words? Is election always conjoined with the word "rejection," which we also encounter so often in Scripture? Does the confessional manner of speaking of rejection find its origin in the logical conclusion that election implies rejection?[1] Or does it find its origin in the testimony of Scripture itself? We cannot ignore the urgency of these penetrating questions.

According to the "logical" paradigm, the doctrine of double predestination would then be described as a reference to God's absolute apriori sovereignty before which man can only bow and keep silent. Predestination would then be the general concept, and the two decrees of election and rejection would stand side by side as subordinates of the one denominator (predestination) of the divine *prae* in two different directions.

Frequently the Church's doctrine of election was interpreted as such a transparent double predestination, and for that very reason people left her forever. And often fervent contention arose around this very point. It seemed as if it was no longer possible to interpret the content of double predestination in more than one way. It became a traditional characterization which embodied everything that criticism wanted to bring up against the Church's doctrine of election.[2]

1. This has often been said, especially in connection with Calvin's statement: "There could be no election without its opposite reprobation" (*Inst.* III, xxiii, 1). It is clear, however, that Calvin does not speak that way in *abstracto* (on the basis of the concept of election) but in connection with the words of Scripture regarding the nature of God's election. In this light Jacobs' remark on *Inst.* III, xxiii, 1 (that Calvin thought rejection to be systematically necessary) must be interpreted (P. Jacobs, *Praedestination und Verantwortlichkeit bei Calvin,* 1937, p. 55).
2. As examples I cite: Julius Kaftan, *Dogmatik* (1920[8]), p. 505, about the *decretum electionis et reprobationis,* where reprobation is called the "logical" complement of the election-concept" as a result of an incorrect approach of interpretation; H. Stephen, *Glaubenslehre* (1928[2]), pp. 248ff., who refers to double predestination as "one-sided emphasis of the irrationality of the history of salvation" and as more Old Testamentish than New Testamentish, the result sometimes being a "reveling in the absolute denial of human solidarity and the tenderness of man's heart" (p. 248); P. Althaus, who says that the doctrine of

The basic thought thereby was that the doctrine of election was presented as a parallel, a symmetry between election and rejection. And the question was asked whether against this background it still was possible to speak of a gospel addressed to everyone, and whether preaching did not come to stand in the light (or shadow!) of this double predestination. And sometimes it was even asked whether rejection, as election, could and should be preached as the truth of God, as part of the gospel, and whether in that case it would not be better to bring a dual message instead of the *eu-aggelion,* namely, an *eu-aggelion* and a *dys-aggelion.* Is there, besides the Book of Life, a Book of Death, and is that the meaning of double predestination?

It is obvious that these questions need an answer. It will not do merely to say that this is all a matter of caricaturization. Criticism has been, and still is, too frequent to put aside these problems without reflecting on them. That is all the more impossible since these theological questions return in the life of the Church, making people wonder whether the gospel is not devaluated because of the unassailability of the fact of double predestination. In the history of the Church this question has repeatedly confronted the ministry, and it did not arise from the certainty of theological criticism but from uncertainty and despair.

Is it true that the doctrine of predestination shows us that the mirror of election cannot help us, because in that mirror we can discover nothing but the quality of a *mysterium tremendum?* "Lo, these are but the outskirts of his ways: and how small a whisper do we hear of him! But the thunder of his power who can understand?" (Job 26:14). We remember that Calvin once spoke of the *decretum horribile* (*Inst.* III, xxiii, 7). What does this "horrible" mean, and what must this "horror" signify in our lives?[3] Do we, via Calvin, end up after

double predestination "is shipwrecked on the gospel word regarding God's all-embracing will of grace" (*Die Christliche Wahrheit,* 1948, II, 430) ; W. Elert remarks that it has logic as its point of departure (*Glaubenslehre der Christliche Glaube, Grundlinien der lutherischen Dogmatik,* 1940, pp. 555ff.) ; and finally, E. Brunner, *Dogmatik,* I, 1946, who speaks about "the problem of double predestination" (pp. 347ff.), and about "the terrible *Theologumenon*" (p. 347).

3. A. Sizoo translates: "horrifying decree." Schilder rejects the idea of "terror-inspiring" as representation of *horribile* and reminds of the

all with Volz and Otto, with the horror and the stupor and
the feeling of being nothing but earth and ashes, and is that the
meaning of the doctrine of predestination? Is the "horrible"
a *lapsus* in the history of the doctrine of election or an echo
of the gospel of God?

When we reflect for a moment on the impact and seriousness
of all these questions — in theology and life — then it must
first of all be remarked that the situation is more complicated
than these simple questions suggest.[4]
This becomes evident from the fact that the Reformed doctrine of election repeatedly discusses this parallel and always rejects it. A serious warning is constantly given here, but critics always neglect this warning and thereby attack a mere caricature.
This warning is met not only in dogmatical discussion but also in
the Confessions of the Church; it is even explicitly mentioned in
the Canons of Dort, that is to say, in the "defense and warning"
supplied to the Canons; for there, where the doctrine of election
is defended against misunderstanding and caricatures, it is denied
"that in the same manner in which the election is the fountain
and the cause of faith and good works, reprobation is the cause
of unbelief and impiety (Conclusion of the Canons). Then it
is emphatically stated that the Reformed churches "not only
do not acknowledge, but even detest with their whole soul"
such teaching.
It is important to investigate why this "in the same manner"
is rejected in Reformed theology. In the light of the epilogue
which offers a defense against false accusations in connection
with the doctrine of election, one can say that this phrase means

---

Biblical translation which was known in Calvin's days (Vulgate) where
the word occurs as "terrifying, appalling and great, for instance, of the
day of the Lord" (*Heidelbergse Catechismus*, IV, 92). At any
rate, the criticism that nothing of God may be called "horrible" is
simplistic because that view is based on the present-day interpretation
of the meaning of the word, and because the word must also be
compared with what Calvin often says of predestination against those
who investigate and inquire outside of the Word of God. For then
predestination is a labyrinth (cf. *Inst.* III, xxi, 1). Elert, who speaks of
the *decretum horribile* as terrible phantasy" (*Der Christliche Glaube*,
p. 559), displays thereby something of an old-Lutheran effect.
4. That this question is far more complicated is evident from the fact
that S. U. Zuidema says that he does not find with Kuyper a *gemina
praedestinatio* and discerns a difference between Kuyper and Calvin
on the one hand, and Gottschalk en Schilder on the other.

to reject the deterministic interpretation of the doctrine of election. We are especially interested to know why this is here concentrated in a formulation which touches upon the relationship between election and reprobation.

Criticism against a faulty juxtaposition of election and rejection is not found in the Canons only. We take Bavinck as first example. According to him, there is no objection against speaking of double predestination, but that does not mean "that predestination in the one case is of the same nature as in the other."[5] He points out that Scripture uses words like *prothesis, prognoosis* and *proorismos* almost exclusively for the predestination unto salvation, and for that reason, says he, it is not correct to co-ordinate the predestination *ad mortem* with the predestination *ad vitam,* and then to consider death as well as life as final goal. Election and rejection do not run alongside each other as two parallel lines, and each simplified deduction from the starting point of double predestination errs at a certain point. That appears already from the fact that election and rejection are often placed beside each other as the twofold revelation of God's attributes, that is, God's mercy and His justice. Bavinck then remarks that also from this point of view the parallel cannot be established, because all of God's attributes (also His justice) are already revealed in Christ so that one cannot say — in the parallel — that eternal destruction was necessary for the revelation of God's justice).[6] Furthermore, Bavinck continues, no one in the Reformed Church has dared to speak of a *praedestinatio ad peccatum.* Not only is God not the author of sin, but neither is man created for destruction.

It is clear that Bavinck touches here on the problem of the origin and reality of sin and the counsel of God over all things. He obviously does not want to draw two lines from the counsel to the order of causality, two lines to our temporal reality, which then could and would have to be completely "explained" and "deduced" from the one, twofold causality of double predestination into transparent causal monism. The structure of the decrees of God would then have become logical and transparent

5. *Gereformeerde Dogmatiek,* II, 352-53.
6. Bavinck must be thinking of passages like Isa. 1:27 and Rom. 3:25. According to Bavinck "it cannot be said that God could not have revealed His glory in the salvation of everyone if that had been according to His will," and "it cannot be proven that with this final purpose of God's glory this double state would have to be necessary" (*ibid.,* p. 348).

and a metaphysics of cosmology could then form the copestone
of the doctrine of election: from the twofold decree to the
realization and via this realization to the goal, set, apriori, by
God. His decrees would then be transparent over the whole line,
as the all-comprising causality of God which would also com-
prise sin and unbelief. Election and rejection would then
have the same structure, in spite of the great difference in content. When Bavinck rejects these parallels, it does not follow
that he intends to explain sin as an autonomous human deed,
which is only known by God in a *nuda praescientia* and therefore
would find its explanation in the concept of "allowance"; for
Bavinck accepts that fall, sin, and punishment are "incorporated"
in the counsel of God and "in a sense, are willed by God. But
then only in a certain sense, and certainly not in the same manner as grace and salvation."[7]

It strikes us that we meet here with the same words as in
the Canons: "not in the same manner." That shows Bavinck's
deep conviction that in the description of the relation between
God's counsel and sin the concept of causality does not apply.
From a deterministic point of view one could without any hesitation come to a mere parallel (*eodem modo*), and draw without any difficulty the consequence of a twofold causality. Why
should one hesitate in that case? Determinism does not for a
moment! But it is one of the most important facts in the
history of the doctrine of election that precisely at this point we
notice a definite hesitation and a consciousness of the important
fact which already in the Canons came to expression in the rejection of the simplistic parallelism.[8]

We encounter a similar sort of criticism of the parallel in Dijk's
writings. He calls election "primary" and adds: "These two

7. Bavinck, *op. cit.,* p. 350.
8. About the Canons, see: J. Daane, "The Principle of the Equal
    Ultimacy of Election and Reprobation" (*The Reformed Journal,* Nov.
    1953). The "equal ultimacy" is defended by C. Van Til in his work
    The Defense of the Faith, 1955, pp. 413ff.: "Since I take my point of
    departure in God and his plan, I think of this plan as back of
    reprobation as well as back of election" (p. 413), and "reprobation
    is surely equal with election" (p. 416). Van Til is reminded of
    Kierkegaard, who speaks of human existence "without reference to
    that counsel" (p. 412), as though in the rejection of equal ultimacy the
    issue at stake were a denial of God's counsel. The real issue, however,
    is whether one takes one's "starting point in the counsel of God"
    (p. 417). Van Til does not see a single (legitimate) question arise
    here, and therein he stands on the side of Hoeksema.

parts of God's predestination may not be placed beside each
other as co-ordinates, for rejection is subordinated to election
but, at the same time, rejection is the necessary result of election."[9] Dijk continues by calling rejection "non-election" and
he describes it as "the dark, negative side of election." He deems
the problem of co-ordination so important that he discusses it
separately as the problem of the order wherein election and rejection occur in God's counsel. He thinks it incorrect to say
that "in the same manner and in the same meaning both are
contents of God's decree."[10] He asserts, rather, that in predestination election "is the first and the highest," while rejection is the "other side" of election.[11] With Bavinck, Dijk clearly
indicates here the connection that rejection has with sin. Sin
and destruction are not willed by God the way grace and salvation are. Sin takes a different place in God's counsel than does
belief, and that is the very reason why according to Dijk there
is "dissimilarity between election and rejection." Election and
rejection do not result from the one "causality" as two parallels
in the ways of belief and unbelief. They are not "equivalent-par-
allel," as is already shown in the fact that belief is from God,
while unbelief is not. Dijk goes on to say, "In election, belief
as gift of God is the fruit of the decree to life eternal (Eph. 2:8),
but with regard to rejection, sin and unbelief are not a result
of God's decree, nor His gift; they originate within us; they are
the means to destruction in a manner altogether different from
the one in which belief is the means to salvation."[12]

Thus, at a decisive point, we see attempts made to avoid *the*
danger of the doctrine of election, namely, the break-through of a
metaphysical determinism which leaves no room for variations and
differences but which subsumes everything under the one causality of God. Even though these men had no desire to undermine
the doctrine of sovereign election, they did not hesitate concerning the *eodem modo,* and this fact is of great importance and
leads to significant consequences.[13]

9. K. Dijk, *Van Eeuwigheid Verkoren,* p. 130.
10. *Ibid.,* p. 141.
11. *Ibid.,* p. 142.
12. *Ibid.,* p. 143.
13. Already in his *Om 't Eenwig Welbehagen* (1942), in which he
   called the doctrine of reprobation the most difficult part of the doctrine
   of election (p. 368), Dijk refuted the concept of co-ordination and
   spoke of reprobation as being subordinated to election (p. 391).

Criticism of the parallel is not meant to imply minimization of the sovereignty and absoluteness of God's good pleasure. Dijk says, in fact, that just as election is not based merely on foreseen faith, rejection does not rest merely on "foreseen unbelief."[14] But even though the solution of the *praescientia* or *praevisio* is not accepted, the parallel is nevertheless rejected. And the most important question — both for theology and ministry — is whether in view of the majesty and apriority of God's counsel it is truly possible to reject the *eodem modo*. Or is it perhaps true that criticism of the parallel reveals nothing but a last-minute retreat from the consequence of one's own doctrine of election?

It cannot seriously be denied that the Canons' denial of "in the same manner" is full of significance, for when we reflect on God's election, it is immediately seen in the light of Scripture that our salvation finds its sole origin in the electing love of God, in the absolute apriority of God's election. Faith itself will always speak here with the Canons of the "fountain and source," and it will never want to place itself beside election as the second source and cause of our salvation. On the contrary, the essential thing in faith as a gift of God is that it is based on this truly monopleuristic act in the election of God. Faith in its "instrumental" character knows only of this one and sufficient, this absolute and merciful, "causality." The confession of this causality is the same as the confession of our sins and helplessness and the knowledge that it is not a product of our flesh and blood. With respect to the *causa,* the source of our salvation, the believer knows: "Herein is love, not that we loved God, but that he loved us and sent his Son to be the propitiation for our sins" (I John 4:10). Faith and election are not co-ordinate factors, resulting in our salvation. That is why the Counter Remonstrants were so fervently opposed to and rejected the doctrine of election on the basis of a *praevisio fides,* in which faith changed its character and obtained a meritorial function. Faith was no longer seen in its orientation to salvation but became a quality in man which was foreseen by God and as such became operative in His election. But the election of God is known and understood through and because of faith, and the confession of belief in this sovereign election permits us to glory only in the Lord (cf. I Cor. 1:26-31).

14. *Om 't Eeuwig Welbehagen,* p. 395.

However, that which is clear concerning faith evokes many questions with respect to rejection. He who would continue his logical deductions in the line of "fountain and cause" and would want to speak here with the same ease of causality, would fall into determinism, thereby giving a metaphysical explanation of sin and unbelief which would contradict the epilogue of the Canons. Determinism cannot hesitate here; if it did, it would abandon its own logic. Determinism, irrespective of its form, would think a difference in structure as indicated in the epilogue to be contradictory to the one causality of double predestination. For determinism deduces everything from the one determining causality of God's election, and all difference within the predetermination becomes automatically relative and unimportant. This particular concept of *causa* becomes the central, all-embracing concept in the doctrine of election; it is the all-explaining principle. In the Canons it has been clearly recognized that this simple explanation of "everything" from the causality of God cannot be maintained, and that it carries very serious dangers with it for a correct understanding of the gospel. It is important that the Canons reinforce the point of view of the epilogue in the body of the text when they say: "The cause or guilt of this unbelief, as well as of all other sins, is in no wise in God, but in man himself; whereas faith in Jesus Christ and salvation through Him is the free gift of God" (CD, I, 5). The Canons do not show any hesitation when the relation between faith and the divine origin of salvation is discussed.

Election is the fountain of all saving good, and out of it flow the fruits of faith, holiness, and other gifts, and finally also life eternal (CD, I, 9). This line of thinking is not followed when sin and unbelief are discussed. Rather, man is then indicated as the cause and reason of unbelief (CD, I, 5; cf. also II, 6).

But there is one passage that seems to contradict this, namely, where the Canons say: "That some receive the gift of faith, and others do not receive it, proceeds from God's eternal decree" (CD, I, 6). The question arises how we must reconcile this "non-granting" with the statement of I, 5, where it is said that God is not the cause of sin and guilt. One's first impression is that this is a simplistic way of explaining causality. But when we read I, 6, we see that it directs our attention to the acts of God in the life of man. He softens man's heart and bends it to faith, but other hearts He leaves in their sin and stubbornness. Unless we want to interpret the Canons in a supralapsarian manner — which is impossible[15] — we shall have to interpret this as a connection which is laid between sinfulness and stubbornness on the one hand, and the judicial acts of God on the other hand, not in the sense that either belief or unbelief become an independent and autonomous power over against the counsel of God, but in the sense that the non-granting is evidently meant as the judicial act of God toward man in sin. And when all the acts of God are regarded in the light of His counsel and decree, then this does not imply a deterministic explanation but a reference to the sovereignty of God, who in a lost world does not elect on the basis of merit because all men are in the same state of damnation (CD, I, 6).

It is possible, of course, that misunderstanding might occur when granting and non-granting occur side by side in such a seemingly formal manner, but although it could be wished that also in I, 6 the light of the epilogue had been shining more clearly and that therefore the criticism of the *eodem modo* had been more explicit, it nevertheless is not permissible to infer from I, 6 that God may be called, if not the reason, then at any rate the *causa* of unbelief. The latter is emphatically denied in I, 6.

Although it may be difficult to indicate completely and clearly the harmony between I, 6 and I, 5, we should remember that it is inherently difficult to give any answer that in itself would be transparent to reflective and reasonable thinking. On the one hand, we want to maintain the freedom of God in election, and on the other hand, we want to avoid any conclusion which would make God the cause of sin and unbelief.

It is certainly not accidental that the same opaqueness is noticed wherever these things are discussed. It is not the opaqueness of paradoxical irrationality, but the opaqueness which is due to unbelief and which can be described from two sides: from the side of God's judgment and from the side of man's sin. He who here allows his thinking to become one-sided falls into the abyss of either violating God's freedom or accusing God of causing sin, which at the same time implies his own excuse. The imbalance in the *causa*-concept which we observe in Calvin and in the Canons is, on the level of human insight, a proof of the inexplicability of sin and unbelief. We prefer this imbalance rather than any synthesis from the point of view of the *praescientia* of determinism.

15. Compare T. Bos, *De Dordtse Leerregelen* (1915), p. 32. Compare Art. 16 of BC.

In this connection we note that the Canons in their defense against the Remonstrants confess that the exclusive origin of all salvation lies in God, and that they never shrink from using the word *causa*. The word "fountain" is even added, and that word, which is richer and more meaningful, at the same time protects the word *causa* against scientific criticism which does not understand the language of the Church. But this causality is rejected with respect to unbelief. Man is seen as the *causa,* and we may not explain man's unbelief in the light of the counsel of God. The Canons are dealing with man, with real and sinful man before God. It had to be indicated here — precisely in the confession of free election — how illegitimate it is for sinful man to think that he could use the counsel of God as a principle of explanation. We are reminded of another defense which the epilogue offers. The thought is rejected "that God by a mere arbitrary act of his will, without the least respect or view to any sin, has predestinated the greatest part of the world to eternal damnation and has created them for this very purpose." That is an emphatic denial of what many critics conceive to be an essential part of the orthodox doctrine of election.

It can, therefore, be said that the Canons provide no more than an imperfect, human expression of the mystery of election, but in a time which requires that we try to understand the motifs of theological thinking, we may demand that this sharp defense be honored as an essential motif. For thus, very seriously, do the Canons mean to make clear that God is not the author of sin and unbelief.

It is certainly not Reformed theology that feels called upon to protest against the "essential asymmetry."[16] It is, rather, one of its most important characteristics that it emphatically affirms this asymmetry without falling into the doctrine of *praescientia*. In doing so, it reaches beyond the dilemma between determinism and indeterminism.[17]

16. This term comes from G. Philips, who sees in it a mark of Roman Catholic theology. Others, too, have indicated the problem of symmetry and parallelism; for instance, P. Althaus, *Die Christliche Wahrheit,* II, 436; K. Barth, *K. D.,* II, 2, 15, 18, 144, ("symmetry"); 191 ("equilibrium"). Barth sharply criticizes the orthodox doctrine of election, which he sees caught in this fatal misunderstanding of symmetry.

17. See on determinism also: H. Groos, *Die Konzequenzen und Inkonzequenzen des Determinismus,* 1931; A. H. Roose, *Het Determinisme in de Praedestinatieleer,* 1886; G. C. Berkouwer, *The Providence of God,* 1952.

In the rejection of the parallel there lies a deeply religious concern. Resistance is offered here against deterministically viewing the relation between election and belief and the relation between rejection and unbelief as a symmetrical relation, with as point of departure the one predestination which is seen as sovereignly functioning in two parallel lines.[18]   When it is asked wherein the reason lies for the Reformed criticism of the symmetry, it can certainly not be found in an attempt to deny the counsel of God over all things, or even to limit it.[19] Rather, one will have to say that this criticism comes from a conviction that the Word of God does not warrant this idea of symmetry. And that explains why the criticism of symmetry has focused attention on the Scriptural testimonies regarding rejection.

Most prominent in this connection is the fact that Scripture repeatedly speaks of God's rejection as a divine answer in history, as a reaction to man's sin and disobedience, not as its cause. We think of the relationship which becomes evident when Samuel says to Saul that "because thou hast rejected the word of Jehovah, he hath also rejected thee from being king" (I Sam. 15:23). Because Judah did not keep God's commandments, it is said: "Jehovah rejected all the seed of Israel" (cf. II Kings 17:20). The rejection here is obvious; it is not an arbitrary, obscure act of Jehovah; it is clearly His holy reaction against sin. Whenever rejection is mentioned in the relationship between God and His people, not a static but a dynamic relationship is evident. The rejection and the curse are mentioned in connection with the warning "if thou wilt not . . ." (cf. Deut. 28:15ff.). There is a clear connection between sin and curse, sin and rejection. The "therefore!" of divine rejection is an answer to the causality which is at work here, the actual and only *causa* of sin, which can be denied but is nevertheless real. Israel — when it took the way back — knew of this causality when it prayed not to be rejected, a prayer that was also a plea for forgiveness: "Thou hast utterly rejected us; thou art very

18. That such a schematism does not prevail in the Canons appears also from other parts, not in the least from CD, V, where the confession of faith pervades the development of the argument, for instance, when there is mention of the "fountain" which can be indicated in "God's free mercy" (V, 8) and in His mercy and faithfulness. CD, V refutes the Lutheran accusation according to which the Reformed doctrine is deterministic-causal. Cf. my *Faith and Perseverance*, 1958.
19. Cf. C. Van Til, *The Defense of the Faith* (1955), p. 415.

wroth against us" (Lam. 5:22). "Cast me not away!" is David's
prayer when he becomes aware of all his sins (Ps. 51:11). That
divine rejection may occur here — legitimately — is recognized
in a prayer which asks for forgiveness and a new beginning with
God. And God in His love is always willing to grant this plea,
not as a matter of course, but because He testifies that He does
not give His people a bill of divorcement (Isa. 50:1ff.), and
that He will not forsake His people for the sake of His great
name (I Sam. 12:22). But when rejection comes into view as
threat and warning, then there is the answer to the *causa* question. It is the causality of sin; it is its terrible result.[20] God
does not turn away from rejection as a mere matter of course;
but in His mercy He severs the bond between sin and rejection.

Thus the act of God's rejection is presented to us as an "act of
God in history,"[21] as a reactive deed, a holy, divine answer to
the sin of man. He refused the tent of Joseph and did not choose
Ephraim (Ps. 78:67), but only because of sin and faithlessness
(Ps. 78:42, 56, 57). God heard what Israel did, He saw the way
it walked and then greatly abhored Israel (Ps. 78:59). That
is why the riches of God's mercy become revealed in history
when He says: "Thou art my servant. I have chosen thee and
not cast thee away; fear thou not, for I am with thee" (Isa.
41:9).

Rejection is mentioned many times in the Old Testament.
Th. C. Vriezen has pointed out[22] that, although it is often mentioned, it is as often emphatically repudiated; for instance: in
Samuel 12:22: "For Jehovah will not forsake his people for his
great name's sake, because it hath pleased Jehovah to make
you a people unto himself." This text is not contradictory; rather,
it shows a relationship between God and His people which
cannot be described in static categories, a relationship wherein
the solace of non-rejection falls like a light through the cloud of
threatened rejection. It is not fate to which Israel is bound, and
he who would speak here of the changeability of Jehovah has not
understood the dynamics of Israel's history under the eyes of
its Covenant God.

When we reflect on all this and consider that Scripture speaks
so concretely and transparently of the act of divine rejection as

20. Cf. the "causality" in Rom. 2:5.
21. Bavinck, *op. cit.*, II, 355.
22. Th. C. Vriezen, *Die Erwählung Israels im A. T.* (1953), p. 99.

God's answer to sin, we could ask whether there is reason to add anything to this Scriptural testimony. Must we not humbly stop at this point and accept the sin-causality of which Scripture speaks? In this question the whole struggle about rejection can be summarized. Is this perhaps the "essential asymmetry" between election and rejection, according to which we think on the one hand of the cause and fountain of our salvation (election), and on the other of the cause of God's rejection (man's sin)?

The latter question has been very often discussed in the history of theology. It has been mentioned in connection with the word of Hosea 13:9: "It is thy destruction, O Israel, that thou art against me, against thy helper." We find Hosea 13:9 quoted in the Formula of Concord when it speaks of election and says that the beginning and cause of evil is not in God's foreseeing "but in the wicked will of Satan and man" and then adds, "as it is written: 'Israel, you bring yourself to destruction, but your salvation is with me alone.' "[23] In this connection the *causa mali* is placed over against the other *causa* of our salvation in God. We touch here — leaving aside the correctness of the exegesis of Hosea 13:9 — upon an attempt to go deeper into the problem of causality by denying that it is possible to operate with the one principle of *causa* in a twofold manner. It is striking that a very general Christian agreement prevails at precisely this point. Not only is the passage quoted which states that godlessness does not please God (Ps. 5:4), but also John's testimony that all that is in the world is not of the Father but of the world (I John 2:16), and James' word that every good gift and every perfect gift come down from the Father (Jas. 1:17).

Wherever the question regarding the *causa* arises, Scripture speaks clearly: "Whosoever doeth not righteousness is not of God" (I John 3:10), while it is said of sin that God hates it (cf. Zech. 8:17). This clearness with regard to the causality-question led to the apriori principle that God is not the author of evil. The history of the Church — and also its reflection on election and rejection — shows the deep awareness of John's word: "This is the message which we have heard from him and announce unto you, that God is light, and in him is no darkness at all" (I John 1:5).

23. Vriezen (*ibid.*, p. 101) also refers to Ps. 94:4 and Judg. 6:13, where God speaks of salvation after Gideon's complaint, "Now Jehovah hath cast us off."

24. Müller, *Bekenntnisschriften der lutherische Kirche*, p. 704.

This problem of causality with respect to sin and unbelief has repeatedly come to the fore. Calvin, who was particularly preoccupied with the nature of predestination, reflected on it at length — especially when he had to answer objections to his doctrine of election. He spoke of the reproach against what I shall call the "apriority" of rejection as he interpreted it. Is it understandable, he asks, that God from eternity has destined some to death, who, because they were not yet born, had not yet been able to earn the judgment to death? (*Inst.* III, xxiii, 3). We recognize the causality problem here. Is there a predestination apart from guilt? In this connection Calvin stresses two points: eternal death through God's judgment, and man's own nature that leads him to this judgment. Men charge God with being the cause of their destruction, Calvin says, but disregard the cause of condemnation, which they are compelled to recognize in themselves.

It is striking that Calvin repeatedly points to the actual situation of sinful man before God. All that must be said of God's predestination can never serve to take away man's sin, "which engraven on their own consciences, is ever and anon presenting itself to their view" (*Inst.* III, xxiii, 3). On the one hand, Calvin recognizes God's absolute predestination, and on the other, he looks for another cause: "Moreover, though their perdition depends on the predestination of God, the cause and matter of it is in themselves" (*Inst.* III, xxiii, 8).

According to Jacobs, Calvin often uses a twofold *causa* concept: *causa* as decree of God's will (the actual, most profound foundation), and *causa* as *causa* in man himself, that is, synonymous with the *materia* that is found in man. There are, says Jacobs, occasions where Calvin "declares the cause of reprobation to lie with man and yet at the same time with God."[25] It is clear, however, that Calvin does not operate with two equivalent metaphysical *causae*. He struggles with the problem of the relation between God's counsel and man's sin. On the one hand, he does not want to withdraw man's lot and destination from God's counsel, from his predestination, but at the same time he points concretely and existentially at man and at the cause that is found in him. Man in opposition to God is man at fault, and it is impossible — also in one's thinking about God's

25. P. Jacobs, *Praedestination und Verantwortlichkeit bei Calvin* (1937), p. 155.

counsel — ever to take a stand outside of that profound fact in order to judge God's predestination (cf. *Inst.* III, xxiii, 3). Judgment always corresponds to man's sin. Calvin's words regarding rejection always imply that rejection in God's judgment is unthinkable without preceding sin.

It is nevertheless clear that Calvin has seen the actual *causa* in predestination, as he also writes, for example, in his commentary on Romans 11:7: "For what Paul means with regard to the reprobate is, — that the beginning of their ruin and condemnation is from this — that they are forsaken by God." Paul refers many times to man's blindness and stubbornness as scourges of God with which He punishes crimes already committed. Calvin understands these passages to teach that Paul does not here indicate a connection between crime and punishment.[26] According to Calvin, Paul really wants to prove "that not those were blinded who so deserved by their wickedness, but who were rejected by God before the foundation of the world." The difficulty is then solved by Calvin when he says that the *causa* of godlessness is situated in the wickedness of man's nature which is abandoned by God. The godless are punished with blindness because of their wickedness, "but if we seek for the source of their ruin we must come to this that being accursed by God, they cannot by all their deeds, sayings, and purposes, get and obtain any thing but a curse." It is clear that Calvin does not put the two *causae* on a level. He often speaks of the first cause when he rejects the proximate causes, sin and unbelief; man makes a pretext "to cover the first [cause], which is hid from our view."[27] The first and real cause for Calvin is and remains God's predestination, also as rejection, while the cause in man is subordinated in the sense that sinful man is condemned by God. There is causality in man but we must look further than that. There is a deeper, a deepest, *causa*. When Paul says that God gives a spirit of bitterness, says Calvin, that means that Paul penetrates to the real cause.[28] Sinners are robbed of their intelligence by the hidden judgment of God. The relation between sin and judgment is always present, but behind this causal connection lies another *causa,* another origin: the one of rejection!

26. According to Calvin one gets the impression that the references Paul makes "do seem, all of them, to be foreign to his purpose."
27. Commentary on Rom. 11:7.
28. Commentary on Rom. 11:8.

One could ask whether Calvin's view of a prime cause does
not lie on a par with the *eodem modo* which is rejected by the
Canons. We saw that the epilogue speaks of a difference in the
connection between election and belief on the one hand, and
rejection and unbelief on the other. It is nevertheless clear that
Calvin — judging by his writings — would have agreed with
the criticism of the Canons against the *eodem modo,* because
man through his sin "merits" judgment, and he does not
merit salvation in the way of belief. Everything depends on
the meaning which one attaches to the concept of *causa.*

But does Calvin simplistically deduce sin and unbelief causally
from God's predestination? It is a fact that he uses many
formulations which must be understood as causal (*causa, fons,
principium*) and which may give the impression that in spite
of his protestations, he does, after all, point to God as the
prime cause of unbelief. It is understandable, therefore, that
Calvin was often challenged to show that he held to the contrary.
When Calvin remarks that one cannot remain with the proximate
causes but must go back to the prime cause to which those
other causes are subordinate, one could get the impression that
God is the prime cause of the proximate causes.

All this shows that one can never come to an acceptable
solution by means of the concept of cause. It will always be
impossible to escape from the thought of a causal determination,
and the divine cause and the human cause are ultimately placed
beside each other as entities that are, after all is said and done,
equivalent, even in the subordination of the human cause to the
divine cause. And that explains why men repeatedly flee from
this causality to indeterminism, in which man's freedom is
placed over against the omnipotent act of God — and then, in
reaction, a movement is launched against this indeterminism
in which causal necessity is re-emphasized.[29] Although the notion
that the divine decree is a cause of judgment, parallel to the
human cause, has been repeatedly denied in Christian theology,
it has not always been made sufficiently clear on what basis
this fatalism could be legitimately rejected.

In that situation it is always a joy to observe that Calvin
earnestly and emphatically rejects fatalism and insists repeatedly
that the human cause, sin, is the real cause of judgment. When

29. See the important remarks regarding the use of causality by Heinrich
Barth, *Die Freiheit der Entscheiding im Denken Augustins* (1935), pp.
189ff.

Calvin emphasizes that nothing occurs apart from God's counsel
and sovereign act, he begins immediately thereafter to speak so
seriously and existentially of sin as the real cause that —
happily! — the transition becomes obscure when he suddenly
writes that the real cause of sin is not the counsel of God but
man's sin. This latter fact is so real and concrete for Calvin
that he asks: "Why should man still seek that cause in
heaven?"[30] Suddenly, Calvin can no longer get his point across
by simply subordinating the human cause to the divine cause.
Man at fault has really no reason to look further and deeper,
as into a labyrinth, while the real cause of his destruction is
so very, very near. Calvin does not want to deny here the
inscrutable connection between God's counsel and sin[31], but he
points out that sin is unhidden and affirms that God hates
it. With great emphasis he resists the objections of Pighius,
who by implication accuses him of all sorts of "inferences,"
and he resists especially the accusation that in his point of
departure he can no longer maintain that the human *causa* (sin)
has any significance.[32] Calvin does not allow himself to be
diverted from the existential character of his view — man
coram Deo — and he points again at sin which is not obscured
by the counsel of God but which definitely acts as a cause of
judgment.

That is why there is no place in Calvin's teachings for the
eodem modo which is also rejected in the Canons. Because
of election there is no reason why man — before God — should
not be allowed to penetrate to the deepest *causa,* the origin
and fountain of salvation. Rather, the gospel calls and admonishes
us to do that. But the presence of sin and unbelief may not
be excused by a reference to the divine causality. "Why should
he still seek the reason in heaven?"

30. See in the *Consensus Genevensis* the comparison with Medea, who
    speaks of proximate causes. That is ridiculous, says Calvin, because she
    herself was at fault. C. Van Til (*Defense of the Faith,* 1955, p. 415)
    refers to Calvin's struggle with Pighius and his distinction between *causa
    remota* and *proxima.* However, the point at issue Van Til leaves un-
    touched (the *causa* concept) and thus he remains far beneath the level of
    Calvin's discussion.
31. Van Til's accusation that he who rejects equal ultimacy can no
    longer escape Arminianism is quite unjust and is based on Van Til's
    starting point in God's counsel.
32. Calvin wrote: *"nego iniuriam fieri reprobis, quia digni sunt qui
    pereant"* (*Consensus Genevensis,* ed. Niemeyer, p. 266).

It is not our intention to defend every one of Calvin's utterances regarding the doctrine of election. On some occasions he speaks of the relation between divine and human causes in such a manner that other expressions make us feel relieved. But those words are not less serious, for he fervently rejects the idea that God is the author of the fall, and says that horror overcomes him when someone begins to think in this direction. He even writes that Pighius would have been right if he, Calvin, had said that the estrangement of man from God issued from the inspiration of the Holy Spirit and that — as Pighius intimidated — the fall was one of the works of God. Here he resists the idea of a transparent causality by which sin and death as a punishment of sin could be explained "in God." Even though Calvin confesses that God's counsel also rules over sin, and that it is impossible ever to give a solution here by means of the concept of the *praescientia* or permission, it repeatedly becomes evident that Calvin does not wish to offer any solution and hence he confesses *ignorantia nostra*. The only thing he then can do is to refer again to the word of Augustine that that which happens against God's will does not occur apart from His will. But there is no *ignorantia* — *coram Deo* — regarding sin and the judgment of God. Calvin indicates here the boundary at which Asaph stood in Psalm 73:22. And if the depth of God's riches is to be sung, shall we not investigate the depth of the fall?

Dort's criticism of the *eodem modo* finds its *preludium* in Calvin. Every discussion of causality fails, must fail. "Sin does not stand in any such continuous relation with reprobation. It does not originate from reprobation, and it is not in the same way an outward sign of reprobation as salvation is of election."[33]

God may be called — in our human language — the author and cause of our salvation (cf. *Inst.* III, xxi, 5), but every attempt will fail to construct here a parallel with rejection,[34] and every instance that this impossibility is understood is a new joy in the history of this dogma. This joy is not based on the understanding of sin in its relation to God's counsel, but it originates because of the recognition that boundaries are respected and no ways are followed which allow us to place God

33. P. Jacobs, *op. cit.,* p. 156.
34. When Calvin speaks of the *causa* in connection with sin, he mentions man and Satan in one breath with respect to man's fall.

in the shadows in order to excuse ourselves. It is the joy of
Article 13 of the Belgic Confession, where the goodness of God
is praised and where it is confessed that nothing happens without God's ordinance.

Indeed, this ordinance is not limited or made relative, but
it is at once protected against misunderstanding: "nevertheless,
God neither is the author of nor can be charged with the sins
which are committed." It certainly is not accidental that we
meet here — as so often happens in the history of the Church —
with two words. Not only is the idea rejected that God is "guilty" of our sins, but also the idea of His being the "author." It
is not surprising that in Article 13 the superiority of God's counsel is so clearly indicated. That superiority is an act which super-
sedes human intelligence, and we cannot curiously investigate it.
And there is nothing contradictory in speaking of God's ordinance
and at the same time of His "allowing" sin. Precisely after
speaking of God's ordinance concerning all things one can also
speak of allowing, not as an independent solution over against the
ordinance but in reference to the foundation laid in this very
same Article: neither author nor guilty of sin.[35]

We saw in Calvin[36] that the relation between election and
reprobation was a prominent question. This is also evident in
other Reformed theologians, especially Bullinger. At various
occasions Bullinger has been described as the originator of a specific type of Protestantism which, especially because of its approach
to election, could be characterized as similar to that of the
Heidelberg Catechism.[37] This type of Protestantism was sup-

---

35. Compare the discussion of Article 13 by A. D. R. Polman in *Onze
Nederlandse Geloofsbelijdenis*, II, especially about God's Providence
and evil (pp. 88ff.) and Thomas' "sound reason" with respect to God's
goodness (p. 88). This chapter is important also on the doctrine
of predestination, especially over against Roman Catholic theology,
which is very strongly inclined to reveal the reasonable aspect in
God's providential acts with respect to evil in contrast with Augustine,
Luther, and Calvin (p. 89).

36. We do not intend to give an extensive discussion of Calvin's doctrine of
election, for in that case mention should be made of his exegesis of
Romans 9-11. It seems to me that Calvin at various occasions made
an unjustified appeal to Romans, for example, to Rom. 11:7 and 17.

37. Defended in the 19th century by Ebrard, Heppe, and Gooszen. See
especially Gooszen, *De Heidelbergse Catechismus*, 1890.

posedly more soteriological-Biblical than the speculative-intellectual type of Calvin.

In one of his letters to Bullinger, Calvin objected to the manner in which Zwingli had spoken of God's election in his *De Providentia*.[38] But Bullinger was not quite at ease about the consequences of Calvin's doctrine of election. That was especially revealed in the conflict between Calvin and Bolsec. For Bolsec had appealed to Bullinger with the result that Calvin wrote to the latter. From Zwingli (in Zurich) came the answer that he believed the elect to be chosen without any personal merit, but that the reprobates were lost because of their sin. Bullinger himself, too, wrote to Calvin. In answer, Calvin wrote the well-known *Consensus Genevensis,* which was not accepted in Zurich.

Bullinger did not reject reprobation, but he saw much unsolved here and he had difficulty establishing his position. Although he wanted to accentuate the comfort and solace of election, he wondered about this question: If God "ordained" Adam's fall, how is it then possible to escape the inference that He is the author of sin? No matter how he tried to understand Calvin's most basic motives, he continued to warn against dangers, and in the *Confessio Helvetica Posterior* of 1562, written by him, he taught emphatically the solace and sovereignty of election. In Article 8 he emphasized that God is not the author of sin. Hardness and blindness are acts of God as Judge and Avenger, while the question whether He willed that Adam should fall, and caused him to fall, is reckoned to belong to the *curiosae quaestiones*. In Article 10, election in Christ and *propter Christum* is discussed. The reprobates are only casually mentioned as those who are beyond Christ, and the decree of rejection is not further mentioned. The question whether few are elected is answered with a reference to Luke 13: strive to enter in! All emphasis falls on the question of personal assurance. All searching for stability and certainty apart from Christ is rejected and all emphasis is placed on the solace and comfort of election.

Since Bullinger conceived this election to be free and sovereign, the Remonstrants certainly are not justified in appealing to him, for his adherence to the sovereignty of grace caused

38. A. Schweizer, *Centraldogmen,* I, 120.

him to stand in opposition to the *praevisa fides*.[39] It is not true, for example, that Bullinger minimized the freedom of God's election because of man's free will, and thus weakened the *sola gratia*. But he did hesitate to say anything concrete about the relation between the counsel of God and sin, and in connection with that about rejection (reprobation). It is this hesitancy about the causality and the transparency of sin that is also seen in Myconius' answer from Basel to Calvin's question regarding Bolsec. Myconius confessed fully the election of the world and stated that God "sends this gospel through the entire world." The Father does not compel all, but those who do not believe are themselves the cause of their damnation.[40]

Many have professed to see a sharp difference between Calvin and Bullinger,[41] but this is questionable. We see in Calvin the same emphasis on the *speculum electionis* as we find in Bullinger (especially in the *Confessio Helvetica Posterior*) and we see also that Bullinger certainly did not want to deny that sin does not stand as an autonomous power over against God and His counsel. It is striking that the *Confessio Helvetica* also appeals to Augustine's statement in the *Enchiridion*: "*Contra,* but not *praeter voluntatem Dei* (against, but not in spite of the will of God)," the same thought which Calvin advanced at a decisive point in his discussions.

It is clear that there is a point of common ground in these questions which, according to Calvin, belong to the great and diffcult problems (*Inst.* III, xxi, 1). Calvin as well as Bullinger sought for a different connection than the one of simple causality in which something is deduced from something else. Rather than causality, one could call it *finality* in connection with the goal which God reaches when he "allows" evil and then through His *omnipotentissima bonitas* makes good come out of evil, more than when He would not permit evil.[42]

Calvin relates Bullinger's hesitation to a lack of consistency in regard to faith and unbelief, but when Calvin then continues,

39. A. J. van 't Hooft, *De Theologie van H. Bullinger in Betrekking tot de Nederlandse Reformatie* (1888): "It was not without reason that the Remonstrants appealed to the latter [Bullinger] although Trigland was correct when he pointed out that Bullinger was not a Remonstrant" (p. 91).

40. Schweizer, *op. cit.*, I, 219.

41. Van 't Hooft, *op. cit.*, p. 91.

42. Calvin declared that he agreed with Augustine (*Consensus Genevensis*, p. 269).

he himself immediately eliminates the idea that God is equally the cause of unbelief as of faith. Precisely in that elimination he touches again upon Bullinger's hesitation, a clear proof of how profoundly reflection about the *causa* problem determines all reflection on reprobation.

Kolfhaus was therefore quite correct when he pointed out the basic agreement between Calvin and Bullinger.[43] Bullinger certainly did not search for a form of synergism in the line of Melanchthon, nor for free will as a factor cooperating with predestination, but for that boundary which Calvin also repeatedly indicates when he says that sinful man has no reason to look for further and deeper causes than the cause found in his own sinfulness. And for that reason it is understandable that for both the pastoral message had the same intent and seriousness, a message in which the *eodem modo* is overcome by the gospel without diminishing the sovereignty of God's election.

We are confronted with the same questions when we consider that in the Confessions of the Reformed churches by far the greatest attention is paid to the election of God. There is not a trace of possibility that here election and rejection are placed parallel to each other as a twofoldedness of the one divine causality. What Jacobs says of Calvin (that in his preaching and commentaries the election of God is repeatedly discussed, while rejection is not mentioned),[44] can be said with as much validity of the Reformed Confessions.

When B. B. Warfield speaks of a "soteriological interest, in which the Confessions were composed,"[45] he adds that "the doctrine of sovereign preterition" is not always explicitly defined, and he speaks of a sometimes "merely incidental treatment," even without any allusions, which can also be said of some Confessions by Zwingli and Calvin. According to Warfield, this striking fact may not be interpreted as criticism, as an unwillingness to accept, and therefore as a refusal to discuss. He gives a different explanation: "It may rather be supposed to be omitted just because it is so fully presupposed." But this explanation, it seems to me, is unsatisfactory, for it is much more

---

43. "The dogmatic foundation on which the doctrine of election is based was the same with both of them" (W. Kolfhaus, "Der Verkehr Calvins mit Bullinger" in *Calvinstudien,* 1909, p. 884).
44. Jacobs, *loc. cit.*
45. *Predestination in the Reformed Confessions* (1901), pp. 119-122.

likely that we approach here the essential structure of the doctrine of election. From a deterministic point of view one would have to speak simultaneously of election and rejection. The *necessitas* of determinism does not permit a single preference or variation or emphasis or a "more or less", and it does not allow to speak of election being primary.[46] But in the light of Scripture, the "disturbed" balance in the Confessions is not only understandable but completely legitimate. For the Confessions did not mean to give an explanation of how everything, in the same causal manner, is derived from God. When they spoke of the light of election they spoke also of the shadow, but never with any trace of parallelism.

Warfield is correct when he does not want to read criticism in the content of the Confessions, not even with respect to that "shadow." But it is incorrect to say that its composers lived "in such confidence in the implication of preterition in the very idea of election as seemed to render its separate statement unnecessary."[47] One should rather say that when these men spoke of election and non-election, they wanted in the first place to speak with Scripture of the election of God in Jesus Christ.[48] By saying that the omissions do not imply negation, the significance and meaning of this confessional manner of speaking is not yet clarified.

But Warfield offers a second explanation, namely, that the complete or partial "omission" was connected with the practical aspects of the doctrine of election. The Confessions passed "lightly over all that is not immediately utilizable by the simplest Christian consciousness." But this explanation does not satisfy either, because it suggests that there are aspects of the doctrine of election that cannot, or can only with difficulty, be made useful for the common believers.

These explanations are therefore unsatisfactory. Rather, one must understand that in the Reformed Confessions there is an intuitive and reflexive understanding of the Scriptural message of election.

---

46. K. Dijk, *Van Eenwigheid Verkoren*, p. 142.
47. The unsatisfactory aspect of this explanation becomes clear when we consider that elsewhere Warfield says that the Biblical authors did not make the doctrine of preterition a part of their *explicit* teaching ("Predestination," in *Biblical Doctrines*, 1929, p. 64).
48. Cf. HC, Lord's Day 21; CD, I, VII, where all emphasis is placed on the election in Christ, with reference to Eph. 1 and Rom. 8. Cf. also the whole discourse of CD, I, 16, which deals with "passing by."

There are other Confessions in which questions about the nature of election are prominent. As an example we cite the Brandenburg Confessions, composed after Brandenburg changed from Lutheranism to Calvinism. To these Confessions belong, for example, the *Confessio Sigismundi,* of which Warfield writes that therein is found "an attempt to soften the statement of the doctrine [of preterition]."[49] Wherein lies the problem? In the first place, it is clear that the election of God is confessed as the foundation of salvation out of mere mercy and grace without any merit. In this connection it is said that "God in His severe justice has from eternity disregarded all those who do not believe in Christ, and has prepared them to eternal damnation as it is emphatically written that he who does not believe in the Son, is already judged, and will not have life eternal," while it is declared that God is not the cause of man's damnation and that He does not find joy in man's death,[50] for that would be contradictory to Scripture. "The cause of sin and preterition can only be found in Satan and the unbelievers who, because of their unbelief and disobedience, are cursed by God."

Antithetically, this Confession is further directed against "blasphemies." These blasphemies include on the one hand the doctrine of an election *propter praevisam fidem* and also the teaching "that He does not grant salvation to the majority which He, without any reason, and not because of their sinfulness, has condemned, for the righteous God has not decreed anybody to damnation unless it be because of sinfulness, and for that reason the rejection to damnation cannot be thought of as an absolute decree or an arbitrary ordinance." These words do not touch merely upon the fact that judgment always corresponds to sin, but the confession is directed against an absolute decree which in itself has no bearing on sin.

That in these Brandenburg churches the problem of rejection and sin became very acute is also shown in the Leipzig *Colloquium* of 1631, which also speaks of rejection but in such a manner that it does not occur "out of such an absolute de-

---

49. Warfield, *op. cit.,* p. 123. De Klerk, *Gereformeerde Simboliek,* p. 70, says that here the Reformed doctrine of predestination is confessed. Bavick says of the *Confessio Sigismundi* and the *Colloquium Lipsiense* that they "do not represent the Reformed doctrine faithfully" (*Gereformeerde Dogmatiek.* II, 320).

50. Müller, *Bekenntnisschriften,* p. 841.

cree or naked will, as if God either from eternity ordains or in time creates the greater part of the world or any men, without regard to their sins and unbelief to eternal damnation or to the cause thereof; but the reprobation as well as the damnation takes place out of His just judgment, the cause of which is in man himself, to wit, his sin, impenitence and unbelief,"[51] so that "the entire fault and cause of the reprobation and damnation of "the unbelieving is in themselves." It is especially striking that here not only damnation but also reprobation is mentioned. And finally, we meet with the same thought in the *Colloquium Thoruniense* of 1645. Here, too, election on the basis of *praevisa fides* is rejected, but it is said besides that it is "foreign" to their belief "as if we held that eternal election and reprobation are made absolutely, without any respect to faith or unbelief or to good or evil works." What does this mean? For election, that faith and obedience are not "cause or reason of election" but "means of salvation, foreordained in them by God"; but reprobation, on the other hand, not only original sin but also, "so far as adults are concerned, unbelief and contumacious impenitence are not, properly speaking, foreordained by God, but foreseen and permitted in the reprobates themselves as the meritorious cause of desertion and damnation and reprobated by the justest of judgments."[52]

Warfield speaks of "the peculiarities of the Brandenburg Confessions,"[53] and indeed there are particular emphases in these Confessions which stress that rejection cannot occur apart from man's sin. But it is too simple to speak with Warfield of "Lutheranizers and Anglicanizers" among "the teachers of the Reformed Churches" and to mention in that connection the Brandenburg Confessions. It must be said, rather, that the composers wished especially to reject what is also rejected in the epilogue of the Canons, "that God, by a mere arbitrary act of His will, without the least respect or view to any sin, has predestinated the greatest part of the world to eternal damnation, and has created them for this very purpose."

And precisely at this point there is the danger that the solution is sought in the direction of the *praescientia*. We saw that danger already in the development of Lutheran theology, and the Brandenburg Confessions, too, incline in this direction. The

51. Warfield, *op. cit.*, p. 83.
52. *Ibid.*, p. 87.
53. *Ibid.*, p. 125.

result of this could be that the *praescientia* is first brought in as
a central concept regarding rejection, and then also with respect to
election, and finally also with regard to the *praevisa fides*. Thus
the balance, the parallel, has then — *mirabile dictu* — returned
again to the *praevisio*!

But this danger which appears everywhere may never lead
to a reaction in which determinism finally effaces every asymmetry. The hesitation which Bavinck displayed was not merely
psychological, but it was connected with the essence of the
matter. This hesitation can become a thesis — a temptation
to make the *praescientia* and *permissio* a solution! — but it
can also develop into the fear which is not without reason
called the fear of the Lord, and which in the Confessions is
repeatedly and clearly mirrored in the rejection of the parallel.

From various sides we have considered what Philips calls
the "essential asymmetry" of election and rejection. This problem is so many-sided that we may be certain that it is not a
false problem. We are reminded of that when we consider that
the criticism of the *eodem modo* in the Canons also has its
parallel in the Roman Catholic doctrine of election. This doctrine opposes the so-called "predestinationalists" who teach
a double predestination in the sense that God from eternity
has foreordained one group to salvation and another as decidedly
to preterition, and that Christ did not die for the reprobates.[54]
The defenders of this view appeal to the Council of Orange
(529), which rejected a *praedestinatio ad malum*. Rome confessed with Valence (855), with reference to Romans 9:21, a
praedestinatio ad vitum (*electorum*) and a *praedestinatio ad
mortem,* but the latter is understood to be indissolubly connected
with the divine *praescientia,* so that she scornfully rejects the
notion that *"aliquos ad malum praedestinatos esse divina potestate, videlicet ut quasi aliud esse non possint,"* while Trent again
rejects the *praedestinatio ad malum*.[55] The Reformed view also
rejects the *praedestinatio ad peccatum*[56] and in the distinction of
the Roman Catholic Church between *ad malum* and *ad poenam*
one clearly discerns an anti-deterministic defense. But when this
hesitation turns into a thesis, we are suddenly confronted with

54. Diekamp, *Dogmatik,* I, 237.
55. Sessio VI, Can. 17 (Denz.).
56. Bavinck, *op. cit.,* II, 350.

the *praescientia,* as it appears in the well-known Roman Catholic distinction between negative and positive reprobation.

In this subtle distinction regarding the rejection of God we stand face to face with the core of the Roman Catholic doctrine of rejection. In the positive reprobation — via the *praescientia* — sin is taken into account. It is always conditional.[57] Positive reprobation is apriori, but not in such a way that sin — in the *praescientia* — is discounted. A reprobation which would not indicate this connection would be contrary to God's general will to salvation, so that positive reprobation is placed over against what is seen as essential in the Reformation: absolute apriority. Positive reprobation corresponds to sin, to the *praevisio demerita.*

Besides this positive reprobation Roman Catholicism speaks also of a negative reprobation. It consists in the decree of God to permit some of His moral creatures to sin and thus lose salvation. It is called negative because God does not work something, but lets something happen, on our part. Man excludes himself, and God wishes to reveal His perfection by letting man do so. This is the way in which the Roman Catholic doctrine of rejection is constructed by means of the two concepts: *praescientia* and *permissio.*[58] We see here clearly that the "essential asymmetry" is clarified with these two concepts.

The full power of Reformed criticism became active against this solution when it urged that the relation between the counsel of God and man's sinful acts could not possibly be comprised in these categories (negative and positive; *praescientia* and *permissio*) which were taken from human life and applied to the electing God. Again we are confronted with the fact that indeed there was some realization of the problem which occupied the Canons (no *eodem modo*) but that it was impossible to give

57. According to Roman Catholic doctrine, positive reprobation is provisional: J. de Groot, *De Katholieke Encyclopedie* (1954), XX. 394.
58. The Molinists, too, thought of negative reprobation as provisional (strong accent on the freedom of will!), this in contrast to the Thomists who did not want to call sin the motive of negative reprobation. That is impossible, for this negative reprobation is no other than the divine permission to these demerits and thus it logically precedes rather than follows their being foreseen. The thought of negative reprobation is different: "God has wanted to make manifest His goodness, not only in the form of His mercy, but also in that of His justice." That is why there is an "allowing." After this allowing *praescientia* is seen, to which positive reprobation corresponds.

a solution to this real problem other than the one of the *praescientia*. This implies a warning for anyone who wishes to take the essential asymmetry seriously, namely, that the connection between asymmetry and *praescientia* is nothing but a false solution.

The danger is not imaginary that, because of the multiple connections of asymmetry with *praescientia,* asymmetry is given up, and hesitation regarding the parallel between election and rejection is suppressed and abandoned. When we, moreover, see that the *praescientia,* connected with reprobation, repeatedly extends its influence over the sovereignty of election,[59] we can understand the inclination to prefer the symmetry above the dangers of the doctrine of *praescientia.* Nevertheless, this temptation will have to be suppressed because the issue is not at all a subtle theological question but a decisive interpretation of the doctrine of election as a whole. Where all hesitation with respect to the symmetry has been overcome, we see the advancement of a doctrine of election which proceeds from one central concept, namely, causality, and this irrevocably ends up in determinism.

It is clear that the reserve, the shrinking back from this view, has repeatedly been of great importance in the history of Church and theology. This hesitation was not known in Reformed theology with respect to the election of God. It spoke with emphasis and without hesitation of sovereign, merciful election. It placed election over against merit, and every connection between the two was rejected. Hesitation occurred where rejection was concerned. It did not originate from a lack of logical thinking or from a lack of courage to draw consequences. It was religious in character. It suddenly became evident that man — *coram Deo* — could not and was not allowed to decide that there was a profounder cause than his own sins. That is the nature of that remarkable hesitation which we observe everywhere, a legitimate hesitation because here two causes are connected with each other: the human cause is linked up and "traced back" to the divine cause, and with that the concreteness and seriousness of the human cause is minimized. What is possible and necessary for man in the face of the electing God, namely, the confession of salvation from God, the *sola gratia,* cannot be taken over with

59. I think of this phenomenon especially in connection with Roman Catholicism, Remonstrantism, and orthodox Lutheran theology.

respect to rejection because, if one does, one makes irreligious excuses for himself.

From the first and profoundest cause, a shadow will always fall over the second and human cause, namely, the shadow of sin. That is the reason for Bullinger's apprehension, and for Calvin's resistance against the paradoxes of Zwingli and his fervent defense against Pighius, as if Calvin had taught the fall to be one of the acts of God. In this hesitation about the symmetry of election and rejection, the issue is not the autonomy of morality, neither a delimitation of God's counsel, nor an absolute freedom to decide on the part of man on which God's decree is made dependent. Nothing can be made independent of the counsel of God. Against, but not in spite of, the will of God, says Augustine, and Calvin agrees with him. This counsel overcomes man's sinful acts; and who is able to maintain concepts like *praescientia* and *permissio* at the cross of Christ?

But he who seeks to avoid man's autonomy will still have to be on his guard against causality. That is where the symmetry originates which obscures the gospel. It is then still possible to say — because of the evidence in Scripture — that God is "of course" not the author of sin, but this opinion can then no longer be justified in the light of the aforementioned causality. And in the light of this causality, the only thing one can do is to accept without hesitation the symmetry, the parallelism between election and reprobation. It may seem as if faith is ultimately based on the supreme sovereignty with its twofold causality. But actually, the holy, electing and rejecting God has been interposed into a scheme of human causality, and thus there is no longer room for that fervent pathos with which Calvin and Bullinger rejected the reproach of determinism. For this twofold causality becomes then a principle of explanation, and rejection of the *eodem modo* is no longer fully understood in its profound significance. Life then is understood in the light of election and reprobation, in the light of the "deduction" of belief and unbelief from this causality.

It is a great temptation not to take with full seriousness the criticism of the Canons, because the closed system of determinism seems to explain everything. But *coram Deo* no longer plays a role here, and all of the gospel is pressed into this system in such a manner that many of the simple words of the gospel can no longer be comprehended. It can then no longer be understood that the question is not one of a mere symmetry, but that

God has loved the world (John 3:16). It is then no longer understood that God did not send the Son to condemn the world
(John 3:17) but that the world should be saved through Him.
This is the profoundest reason for rejecting parallelism. This
rejection does not imply the triumph of a simple sort of universalism. Immediately after John speaks of the purpose of Christ's
coming, he adds: "He that believeth on him is not judged: he
that believeth not has been judged already, because he hath not
believed on the name of the only begotten Son of God" (John
3:18). He who contemplates and approaches the gospel from the
point of view of symmetry can no longer understand that Christ
has come to be a crisis in the world, but he can only see in Him
the execution of the symmetrical decree. He still may point at
Simeon's word that Jesus Christ is set for the fall and rising of
many in Israel (Luke 2:34), but this can hardly be counted as
evidence since the same Simeon testifies: "Mine eyes have seen
thy salvation, which thou hast prepared before the face of all
peoples; a light for revelation to the Gentiles, and the glory of
thy people Israel" (Luke 2:30-32). The gospel can be understood and preached only if balance, symmetry, and parallelism
are excluded. And by that gospel, the Holy Spirit will "convict
the world in respect of sin, and of righteousness, and of judgment: of sin, because they believe not on me" (John 16:8).

With that, we touch upon the most serious question which
must have our attention in this chapter. It is the question whether
God's rejection belongs, and can belong, to the *kerygma* of the
Church. Is it possible to see God's rejection differently than as
God's holy answer to human sin?

We have indicated that Scripture repeatedly directs our attention to the rejection of God as reaction. And it is understandable that much reflection on rejection has been concerned with
that particular aspect. Bavinck remarks that Scripture makes
little mention of rejection as eternal decree,[60] while Dijk formulates it still more sharply when he says that we must admit "that
Scripture speaks of rejection solely as an act of God in time and
history," and he adds that we must be very careful in quoting
certain Scriptural references to "prove" the doctrine of rejection. Nevertheless, Dijk continues, although the Biblical references mention the acts of God but are silent on the counsel of

60. Bavinck, *op. cit.*, II, 355.

God, that does not yet mean that behind the act the counsel of God is not at work, "and that the sovereign God in His actual rejection does not execute an eternal decree." He thinks it dangerous "to condemn or reject the relevance of the revelation of God's acts to His decrees."[61]

It is clear which question we encounter here. At this crossroads, a last denial of human autonomy and independence is truly necessary. Dijk is correct when he rejects at this point the solution of the *praescientia,* as if that would make the relation between God's counsel and man's sin obvious. Dijk also — with Calvin's example — points to Christ's suffering, in which God's counsel becomes revealed. All human speech falters here. Dijk says, for instance, that sin and unbelief "are connected with" God's will,[62] and Bavinck says, when he deals with rejection, that God's reign is over all things and that He also has His hands in the sins of men. Indeed, it is not permitted ever to minimize this majestic, loving, superior act of God. Bavinck — quite relevantly — points to the will of Him "who some day will shed the full light over all the riddles of life."[63]

He who wants to understand these things by himself — concerning either the doctrine of God's providence or of His election — will become lost immediately. That is a lesson which the history of Church and theology teaches us. For in man's explanation of these riddles, errors are made either in one direction or the other. One either breaks through the Augustinian *non praeter voluntatem Dei* into the making of man's life autonomous, or one weakens the grave seriousness of the *contra voluntatem Dei.* All this results from an effort to "explain" God's ordinances and to scrutinize His inscrutable ways (cf. Rom. 11:33). In this scrutinizing and investigating, the song of praise is no longer heard and the *coram Deo* is replaced by that attitude which either denies and delimits God's counsel over all things or which tries to force that counsel into a scheme of transparent causality issuing in evil and corruption. It is possible — precisely, because we do not want to scrutinize the inscrutability of God's ordinances — to see clearly which way we may not and cannot walk, whether we are considering the doctrine of providence or the doctrine of the election of God.

61. K. Dijk, *op. cit.,* pp. 129-130.
62. *Ibid.,* p. 130.
63. Bavinck, *op. cit.,* II, 356-357.

If anywhere, then certainly here it must be clear that theology cannot for a moment remove itself from that light which shines for every believer from the Word of God. In this light we know that what the Church confesses regarding God's election and rejection and His inscrutable decree, His counsel and His plan, does not give us a key apart from faith to establish a system of cosmology from which we draw conclusions regarding our eternal destination. Instead, the roads we must walk are pointed out to us. When the Church, in the Canons, for example, speaks of God's decree, it does not mean that we are confronted with an impersonal, iron law, a *fatum* of causal determination. We may never minimize the sovereignty of God's election by the rash use of human expressions such as "decree," "plan," or "destination"; at the same time we must be on our guard not to speak of this electing and rejecting of God in a manner which is described by the Canons as a caricature. Dangers threaten here from both sides; on the one side, the serious danger of lack of appreciation of that real dimension of the divine "before" to which Scripture so emphatically testifies; and on the other side, the danger of humanizing the decreeing, electing, and rejecting God. It is not without reason that the Reformers have repeatedly spoken of the decrees of God as the *Deus decernens*. That did not imply any speculation, but rather a protest against the depersonalization and petrification of God's decrees. It implied an urgent warning against abstracting God's decree from Himself.

Even though the theologian's language may fail him, he must abide by this warning. K. Schilder provides another example when he rejects the concept of the "immovable petrefact." He adds that God's decree "occurs every moment anew," but he does not distinguish between decree and execution of that decree.[64] It is not difficult to point at unevenness and even contradictions in such formulations,[65] but we must discern the intention in such faltering words to counter all abstraction and to make it understood that the point at issue is the living, electing God, the *Deus decernens,* who reveals to us His sovereignty and freedom in the

---

64. *Heidelbergse Catechismus,* III, 135-136. Compare his rejection of the analogy of the plan of an architect, whereby the architect may die without the plan losing its merit. See also A. Kuyper, *E Voto,* II, on Lord's Day 21.

65. Striking is his "radically different" and "no essential difference," (*op. cit.,* pp. 434 and 474).

powerful "before" of His revelation, but who does that as the God who came to us precisely in His revelation. That is why Bavinck can say on the one hand that there is no before and after in God and at the same time warn against the historization of God's counsel in the identification of God's decrees with the facts of history.[66]

And the decree of God may never be presented in order to make God recognizable in His revelation. It must be just the other way around: only in and from His revelation will man learn to know Him, not in the petrification of a constructed concept of God but in the depth and riches of His majesty and grace. "I know that, whatsoever God doeth, it shall be for ever; nothing can be put to it, nor anything taken from it; and God hath done it, that men should fear before him" (Eccl. 3:14). That is not a passage which fits only into a deterministic viewpoint. It returns in the New Testament as an "in fear and trembling." But one knows the Bible poorly if he does not understand how this fear and trembling before His face is not the terror before a *mysterium tremendum,* but the finding of rest in Him who is faithful and does not forsake the works of His hands (cf. Eccl. 3:14 with Ps. 138:8).

Bavinck has emphatically denied that a different insight regarding rejection can be explained by differences in personality, as though Pelagius, Castellio and Arminius were kinder and more pitying men than Augustine, Calvin, and Gomarus. He opposes this view by saying that the latter faced reality squarely and "recognized also in these moving facts of life the will and the hand of the Lord." The well-balanced Bavinck uses words such as "twaddle and trifling" when he contrasts Pelagianism with Calvinism. Then follow these words: "It [Calvinism] refuses to be blinded, it does not wish to entertain imaginations, it accepts the seriousness of life in all its depths, it defends the rights of the Lord of lords, and it bows humbly and in adoration before the uncomprehended sovereign will of God Almighty."[67]

It is clear what Bavinck wants to convey. He denies that man can as a matter of course deny divine rejection, and he then speaks of the terrible reality of sin. He does not intend to give a solution but comfort, because in all what happens we can rec-

66. Bavinck, *op. cit.,* II, 303, 331.
67. *Ibid.,* p. 357.

ognize the will and hand of an almighty God who is also a merciful Father. Thus he wants, with Calvin, to wait for the day
on which we shall be shown the solution of all riddles and mysteries.[68]

When he comes to this point, however, Bavinck poses other
questions which touch immediately upon rejection. He reflects
on the sovereignty of God and quotes a "harsh statement" by
Augustine, to wit, that God could not be accused even if He
had wanted to condemn some innocent ones, a statement of which
it can be said that "some theologians, also among the Reformed"
have spoken in the same spirit. According to Bavinck, "this
manner of speech can be employed momentarily with someone
who thinks he can accuse God of injustice," but "almost all the
Reformed theologians, following Calvin, have emphatically rejected such a *dominium absolutum*."[69]

Bavinck wishes to establish and urge recognition of the right
and honor of God as God in the face of all human pride. As
long as that honor and right were protected "all those of the
Reformed persuasion advised the most careful and tender treatment of the doctrine of predestination and warned against idle
and curious investigation." The decree of God is not a *fatum*,
not a "sword of Damocles." And when Bavinck describes the
"decree" of rejection, he says that this terrible decree "says
nothing more than that all of sinful reality, all of world history
in the interrelations of its events, does not have its primary cause
in itself — how would that be possible? — but beyond itself in
the mind and will of God."[70]

One who reads this might think for a moment that Bavinck,
too, wishes to explain everything (also evil) causally in God.
But it is clear that he wants to take fully into account what he
writes repeatedly when he indicates the connection between the
will of God and sin. He always adds, "in a sense," and with that
he eschews every causality-explanation. He does not want to
reach beyond Augustine's *non praeter voluntatem Dei*. And that
explains why he speaks in this connection of the "great difference" between election and rejection.

God rejoices in His work of election and all His attributes
shine forth, "but that which He does in accordance with the decree of rejection is not directly and in itself the object and reason

68. *Ibid.*, p. 358.
69. *Ibid.*, p. 359.
70. *Ibid.*, p. 362.

of His rejoicing. Sin is not a good in itself; it is such only indirectly, because it is subjected and conquered, and reveals God's majesty, power and justice." We stand here at the center of Bavinck's doctrine of election and of his view on the origin of sin. He speaks of the divine origin of all things and of all reality, and the decree of election as "the source of all that is." But this is by no means intended to be a causal explanation analogous to human causes.

Bavinck, besides rejecting all human *hybris,* does not hesitate to say that predestination reaches its end and complete reality in election. And in this connection it can be understood how the doctrine of election does not rule out the real and serious preaching of the gospel, or only admits it as a "foreign element" in the Church of God. This is such a profound matter that it is necessary to pay special attention to it (Chapter VII.)

Symmetry and parallelism of election and rejection are so easy to understand that we need no longer be surprised that the question is asked: Why does God reject?[71] The answer, "To His glory," is, says Hoeksema, correct. "Is the Lord more glorified, now that some are rejected by Him, than if He had granted salvation to everyone?" He thinks he can answer this question. "Rejection exists to realize election; rejection was necessary to bring the elect to the glory which God had ordained for them in His infinite love." He does not hesitate to say that God "had to." He had to — Hoeksema wants to speak reverently — reject some. The cause of rejection, with which Calvin was so intensely occupied, retreats into the background. Hoeksema is concerned with the eternal decree as such.

The way to further speculation is now completely open. The "must" is worked out in such a manner that those who are rejected "must temporarily cooperate to the salvation of the elect, albeit in an antithetical manner." The rejected "are in a sense the price, the ransom, which God pays for the higher glory of His children."[72] He could not do otherwise for there was no other possibility for Him. The price had to be paid. . . .

---

71. H. Hoeksema, *De Plaats der Verwerping in de Verkondiging des Evangelies* (1927), p. 16. We shall speak of Hoeksema's view on preaching in connection with the Canons in Chapter VII.
72. Hoeksema, *op. cit.,* p. 17. I hesitated to cite these words because they contain something frightening and alarming, and they could — in reaction — cast a shadow on the doctrine of election, but for the sake of objectivity I include them.

I do not know of any attempt to penetrate more deeply into the counsel of God than this consideration in which sovereign election is placed under the pressure of this divine "must." Here a divine necessity is constructed, while concerning predestination the issue is precisely God's holy and sovereign freedom, in which He elects not according to man's works. When the question is asked on what considerations this opinion is based, Hoeksema tells us that he can prove his point of view. In the first place, he presents a proof from God's general revelation in nature and history. Hoeksema thinks that his view regarding election and rejection is verified in the lives of nations and individuals. He cites an inscription on a monument erected in memory of soldiers who died in battle: "They gave their lives that we might live," and sees it as a mirror "of election and rejection."[73]

Analogia electionis et reprobationis! Or differently: "The mother often gives birth to her child while she herself dies, and the one generation lives and dies in order to give life to the following." In other words, Hoeksema sees election and rejection as meaningful and transparent cosmological laws! We are presented here with a "natural" theology of predestination as illustration of God's election and rejection, to which is further added the world of flora: when the grain grows out of the soil, the laborer pulls out the superfluous plants to give more room to those that are chosen to ripen. "Here, too, we find election and rejection, albeit in an image."[74]

But, according to Hoeksema, we find this idea especially in Scripture. He cites Isaiah 43:4, God's word to Israel: "Since thou hast been precious in my sight, and honorable, and I have loved thee; therefore I will give men in thy stead, and peoples instead of thy life." Hoeksema thinks that this points to the eternal counsel of God. And he attributes the same motif to Proverbs 11:8: "The righteous is delivered out of trouble, and the wicked cometh in his stead," and in Proverbs 21:18: "The wicked is a ransom for the righteous!" This, according to Hoeksema, is the price which God pays in His eternal predestination to glorify and honor the just. Election and reprobation now become clear and transparent, even apart from Jesus Christ. Thus it becomes clear, and it cannot be different: "Rejection is the

---

73. Hoeksema, *op. cit.,* p. 18.
74. We are of the opinion that this kind of "service of images" is strictly forbidden in the second commandment.

necessary antithetical side of election."[75]   It seems for a moment
as though the symmetry is removed after all when we read:
"Election and reprobation do not merely stand beside each other,"
and "reprobation is subordinate to election."[76]   God's love remains the important thing.   But this light is not able to afford
comfort at this point because the transparency of election and
reprobation precedes this comfort as a natural theology of predestination, which only at the last is linked up with Jesus
Christ.

This "natural" theology of election with its Scriptural "proofs"
shows its weaknesses everywhere.   The *analogia electionis et
reprobationis* is discovered at the expense of the free and merciful
election in Christ, while the unsearchableness of God's ways
dissolves and disappears.   All discussion proceeds apart from
human sin, and every subsequent connection is nothing but a construction.   How can Hoeksema still defend himself against Pighius?

It is hardly necessary to pay much attention to Hoeksema's
Scriptural "proofs."   They have the typical marks of loose exegesis.   Who would want to conclude the necessity — for God —
of His predestination, especially of His rejection, from His superior acts in which He works for His people and gives lands as a
ransom for Cyrus?   And who would see a proof of "necessary"
reprobation when God interferes in the lives of the just and the
godless, as He sometimes suddenly changes the scenes?   Does
this change of circumstance reveal how the situation appears
to God?   We can only see in this kind of Scriptural "proof" how
dangerous it is to make concepts of election and rejection which
are each other's correlate, in order to make a necessity out of
God's freedom, which is the opposite of God's election.

There remains one question to be discussed in this chapter.
Although it cannot be denied that the Canons' criticism of the
eodem modo, of symmetry and parallelism, finds powerful support in Scripture, and that this criticism has made its influence
felt throughout the history of the doctrine of election, the question
has nevertheless been asked repeatedly whether some Scriptural
statements do not point to symmetry. It is generally agreed that
Scripture does not teach symmetry, but has not Paul in his letter
to the Romans given the material on which the concept of sym-

75. *Ibid.,* p. 21.
76. *Ibid.,* p. 23.

metry can be based with some seeming justification? Do we not
hear in this epistle the word of the living God: "I will have
mercy on whom I have mercy, and I will have compassion on
whom I have compassion" (Rom. 9:15), as well as that other
word: "So then he hath mercy upon whom he will, and whom he
will he hardeneth" (Rom. 9:18)? It has often been said
that Paul is here developing a *locus de praedestinatione,* that
he wants to describe the background of the election and rejection
of individual men in terms of a twofold predestination. In this
way, many passages from Romans 9 to 11 have been taken out
of their context and used in dogmatics to "prove" that Paul himself submits to symmetry and bases his considerations on a *dominium absolutum.*

There has been much discussion about the meaning of Romans 9 to 11. It is being accepted more and more that this passage is not concerned primarily with establishing a *locus de praedestinatione* as an analysis of individual election or rejection, but
rather with certain problems which arise in the history of salvation. In chapters which place such strong emphasis on the
sovereignty of God and the freedom of grace, we must always
take into account the danger that man in his exegesis may seek to
escape from the urging power of such testimony. Indeed, we see
repeatedly that for fear of determinism Romans 9 to 11 is interpreted "indeterministically," in the sense of a conditional predestination. Sometimes, for instance, the *praevisa fides* is carried into the exegesis. But E. Weber was correct when he
spoke of "the complete untenability of the indeterministic explanation."[77] He explained that this interpretation was meant
as a defense of man's freedom, but to the extent that this freedom
was emphasized, to the same extent the sovereign freedom of
God was minimized. Divine election was made dependent on
man's decision, resulting in "a complete re-interpretation and
mutation of the decisive concepts because all concepts were
changed in the direction of the *praevisio,* the *praescientia,* and the
permissio.[78]

Since the indeterministic exegesis is so clearly contrary to
the evidence in the Word of God, many have repudiated it. A.
Nygren, for instance, believes that Paul does not give a doctrine

77. E. Weber, *Das Problem der Heilsgeschichte* (1911), p. 19.
78. *Ibid.,* p. 18. Cf. Erasmus' exegesis in *Vom freien Willen* of Romans 9, especially on the "difficult question how God's *prae-scientia*
must be reconciled with man's free will."

of predestination here because he spoke of that subject previously in Romans 8:28-30. The interrelation of Romans appears in the harmony which Paul indicates between justification by faith and the promise of God, which in turn is bound indissolubly to the absolute sovereignty and freedom of God.[79] It is clear that the redemptive-historical point of view is of decisive significance for the exegesis of Romans 9 to 11, and that it is not at all necessary to believe that herein the sovereign freedom of God is minimized.

It is clear that Paul points to this sovereign freedom in the history of salvation. In the indeterministic exegesis, this history of salvation is robbed of its meaning and content, and the course of this history can no longer be seen and understood, for then the issue is a mutual delimitation of the freedom of God and of man, whereas Paul is referring to something entirely different. He sees no limitation at all of the sovereignty of God in His granting salvation, and that is precisely why the inscrutable mystery of God remains a mystery which in indeterminism would be completely robbed of its significance.

But the meaning of Romans 9-11 is no less misjudged when one explains these chapters deterministically, reading into them a system of cosmology in which everything is deduced from God as prime cause, making human activity of no significance. Such a concept of God is certainly not what Paul tries to give us. When he points emphatically to the sovereignty and freedom of God, he means thereby to reject all human *hybris*. Although the freedom of God is neither a pure arbitrariness (Chapter III) nor a formal *dominium absolutum,* it does rule out the possibility that man can stand in a position of critical autonomy over against God.

For that reason it is not permissible to minimize the sovereignty and freedom of God. God's mercy is not the result of human moral endeavor. "I will have mercy on whom I have mercy." We men, full of arbitrariness, often have difficulty in finding anything else but arbitrariness in this passage. But Paul wants to show here the essence of divine mercy, which is not an irrational *dominium absolutum,* but only mercy, commiseration, which issues forth from God's Father heart. His mercy is not an answer to our attempt to please Him; it originates with Him (cf. II Cor. 1:3). God's freedom is not ab-

---

79. A. Nygren, *Der Römerbrief* (1951), pp. 255-258.

stract; its nature is indicated rather by God's word to Moses "that God's grace is never based on any merit and that God is completely free in His mercy."[80]

This is not a terrorizing testimony, but it does carry a threat to those who seek mercy as the result of their own strivings. Apart from showing this particular error, the passage also indicates the profound richness of the word "mercy." Paul does not show us a closed door (*dominium absolutum!*) when he adds that it does not depend on man's will or his exertion but upon God's mercy (cf. Rom. 9:16). How clear it is that the dilemma between determinism and indeterminism has nothing to do with Paul's words about the freedom of God over against man, who calls God's election unjust and who would speak of righteousness only if it were distributed according to merit!

After Paul has drawn our attention to God's free mercy and grace he speaks of God's acts against Pharaoh. And especially in this connection it has often been thought that Paul comes close to symmetry, for here he speaks not only of commiseration (with the people of Israel) but also of stubbornness (on the part of Pharaoh). For God says to Pharaoh, "For this very purpose did I raise thee up, that I might show in thee my power, and that my name might be published in all the earth" (Rom. 9:17). Paul shows that according to Genesis Pharaoh himself hardened his heart (Ex. 8:15), and he certainly does not want to deny that. He does not rule out Pharaoh's voluntary, free activity, but he knows that Pharaoh in his activity does not constitute an independent power over against God, but that he is in God's hand and that God executes His counsel while overcoming Pharaoh's activity, to the salvation of His people. Paul follows the Septuagint (*exegeira*) here, while Genesis reports only that God allowed Pharaoh's continued existence. Paul, so to speak, interprets God's allowing Pharaoh to continue his existence as a "placing in an office." Even more strongly than in Genesis, the superior act of God is set in the context of the history of salvation. It is an act that does not destroy man's free will and activity, but that comprises everything. It precedes man's deeds, because God acts within those deeds of man — in Pharaoh's hardening of heart — and thus proceeds triumphantly and purposefully. It is clear that Paul does not want to direct our attention to the individual

80. R. Schippers, *Romeinen*, p. 41.

fate of Pharaoh, but that he speaks of him in order to show his place in the history of salvation, and it is certainly not permissible — as Calvin did — to draw conclusions here regarding the "example" of stubbornness because of God's eternal decree, and regarding the rejection of the wicked.

Calvin sees in Pharaoh an example which God wanted to set forth: "The predestination of Pharaoh to ruin, which is to be referred to the past and yet hidden counsel of God."[81] Calvin does mention, correctly, that Pharaoh's stubbornness cannot prevent God from delivering His people, and that God precisely by means of Pharaoh gives an example of His power. But although Calvin does not deny that Paul emphasizes this, he nevertheless reads here the revelation of eternal damnation, as in verse 18 of which he says: "That our mind may be satisfied with the difference which exists between the elect and the reprobate, and may not inquire for any cause higher than the divine will, his purpose was to convince us of this — that it seems good to God to illuminate some that they may be saved, and to blind others that they may perish."[82]

It seems clear that what Calvin indicates as Paul's essential point represents only a partial insight. We can agree with Calvin — over against every form of indeterministic exegesis — when he contends against those who interpret the "hardening" in verse 18 as "allowing to harden," or when he argues against the scholastic *praescientia*. But Paul is not concerned primarily to expound on the "ruin of the wicked" which "is ordained by His counsel and His will," but rather to point to God's power and freedom in the history of salvation as He proceeds to manifest His mercy.

In this connection we also wish to consider Paul's words in Romans 9:22, which are so closely related to the remarks made above. After he has criticized man who opposes God's sovereignty and who excuses himself (Rom. 9:19-20), and after he has spoken of God's *exousia*, he says: "What if God, willing to show his wrath, and to make his power known, endured with much longsuffering vessels of wrath fitted unto destruction. . . ." Especially the words "fitted unto destruction" are often mentioned in connection with the problem of symmetry and parallelism. Calvin has spoken without any hes-

---

81. Calvin, *Commentary on Romans, loc. cit.*
82. *Ibid.*

itation of the reprobates as the vessels of wrath, made for
destruction, as they were already thus predestined before their
births. To be sure, in Romans 9:22 we are not told why they
are such vessels, but this is because the reason is hidden in the
counsel of God.[83]

It must be said, however, that many no longer agree with
Calvin's exegesis of this passage, not because they wish to
minimize the sovereignty of God, but because they recognize
that Paul's words cannot legitimately bear this interpretation.
No doubt Paul is thinking of the holy and powerful wrath of
God. But everything depends on what is meant by the vessels
of wrath destined for destruction. It must be that Paul refers
here to Israel. Just as God wanted to reveal His wrath against
Pharaoh, so also against Israel but, simultaneously and through
that, He shows His majesty and glory. Again, this is not an
independent analysis of the destiny of individual man; it shows,
rather, the acts of the electing God through the course of history.
Paul does not want to indicate two separate lines, to wit, the
vessels of wrath (fact of reprobation) and the objects of God's
longsuffering (fact of election) ; Paul wants to show that in the
way of God's wrath against Israel the riches of His glory are
made known — concerning us "whom He also called, not from
the Jews only, but also from the Gentiles" (Rom. 9:24).

Nygren is correct when precisely at Romans 9:22 he points
out Paul's correlating the rejection of Israel with the salvation of the world, which is so eminently characteristic of
Paul."[84]   Israel has become the object of God's wrath, but
others have become the object of His mercy. Israel does not
understand that, but now Hosea's prophecy is fulfilled: *lo ammi*
becomes *ammi* and *lo-ruchama* becomes *ruchama*. God's wrath
against the objects of wrath does not mean that for Israel the
way to God's mercy is forever closed off, for that mercy will
reveal itself in "us," who are of the Jews and of the Gentiles.
Thus there is a turning of wrath into mercy, which is not the
way of good works, but the way of God's merciful election.
There is no symmetry or parallel between the elect and the
reprobates, but a free act of God which issues in the revelation
of His mercy.

But now Paul says of these objects of wrath that they are
fitted unto destruction. Van Leeuwen is quite correct when he

83. *Ibid.*
84. Nygren, *op. cit.*, p. 266.   Cf. Rom. 11:12, 15, 19, 30.

remarks that with regard to the vessels of wrath the passage does not say "prepared beforehand," while it does say so of the objects of mercy.[85] If Paul were thinking here in terms of parallelism between election and reprobation, we should expect that he would use the same terms for both. But when Otto Kuss says: "It does not say anything here, in contrast to verse 23, about the fact that God has prepared them; the passive mood leaves the reason for this significantly in the dark,"[86] that does not mean that God can be left out here, and that one could introduce an indeterministic exegesis of verse 22! The wrath of God on the objects of wrath, too, stands in connection with the teleological acts of God. But it does become clear that Paul is not thinking here in terms of a causality problem, nor is he trying to soften a harsh statement.

When Paul speaks of cause, he emphatically points to Israel's sin. But he does not see this sin as an independent cause that overrides God's counsel. In an inscrutable manner even this sin — in spite of the definite fact that it cannot be attributed to God — is not *praeter voluntatem Dei,* although it is against the will of God. That is why Paul nowhere sees a symmetry or parallel,[87] but a teleology in God's acts: the issue of the riches of God's glory. In this way we see also that the objects of wrath — against their will and in the wrath of God — are subject to God's majestic and merciful acts.[88] Pharaoh's disobedience and stubbornness run parallel to that of Israel, but in both cases they have not become independent of God; rather, they have been incorporated in the purposeful historical and eschatological acts of God.

This revelation of God's sovereign dealings with Israel, in and through its unbelief, carries a solemn warning. Not a warning against a *dominium absolutum,* but an urgent warning to fear unbelief! Now that the Gentiles have taken the place of Israel they must observe the mercy of God in order to enjoy the blessing of election.

Thus Romans 9:22, which seems to carry such a strong suggestion of parallelism, actually negates this parallelism and points out to us the freedom of God's acts, opening windows in all

85. Van Leeuwen, "Romeinen," in *Korte Verklaring,* p. 209.
86. Kuss, in his Commentary on Romans, p. 83.
87. Cf. also O. Michel, *Der Römerbrief,* p. 214.
88. Cf. A. Schlatter, *Gottes Gerechtigkeit* (1935), p. 306, who rejects speculation.

directions so that the outlook on God's free election is not obscured but becomes a great and ever-present blessing.

Every hesitation about or hidden resistance against the sovereign freedom of God, every form of indeterminism which defends man's cooperation against the divine act, will suffer ship-
wreck on Romans 9. But also every attempt to press the divine
act into a deterministic framework and thus to make it the
powerful competitor of man's acts will ever be doomed. For
every form of competition is made impossible. There are relations here which have no human analogies.

The struggle between determinism and indeterminism in the
doctrine of election is a futile one, and he who has discerned the
dangers of indeterminism may not go over to determinism as
though the explanation of God's freedom were to be found in
the concept of causality.

When man faces God — and he always does — in sin and
under the preaching of the gospel, he must be careful with the
concept of causality. He need not hesitate to speak of the cause,
the fountain of salvation, in all its richness of meaning. It is
that causality of which the psalms and hymns of praise sing.
Here man is allowed to think as deeply as he wants, in order
thus to understand the breadth and length and height and depth,
and to know the love of Christ which passeth knowledge (Eph.
3:18-19).

But this category of cause and fountain cannot be handled
abstractly and used by man to explain personal sin and unbelief.
To use it for that purpose would reveal the *hybris* of man's
heart. And such an explanation is condemned not only on this
personal and individual plane, but also in all reflection. Theology does not afford a separate dogmatic *gnosis* with which it
can proceed further than the average believer in understanding
salvation, or in comprehending better the acts of God with man.
The dogmatician may not live secretly with a theory of parallelism or symmetry, as if he were allowed to work with other and
deeper causes than those given to us in prayer, faith, and confession of sins. He who would turn God's rejection into an
explanatory device reaches beyond the immediate, religious simplicity of faith and falls into the abyss which is indicated by Dort
and all Confessions, the abyss where the God of salvation is the
author of sin.

But it is not sufficient merely to follow the Confessions. If
anywhere, then here religious experience must become man's

very own, if he would be kept from this abominable self-excuse. And in this experience, in this knowledge of God, in this defense against the great temptation, one will not limit God's freedom and counsel in electing and rejecting. Only with humbleness and veneration we may say after Augustine: what was *contra voluntatem Dei* was not *praeter voluntatem Dei*. This is not a theoretical play with words or concepts, but an insight which, although it does not help us to comprehend the cross, nor the course of history, indicates a way to walk in the presence of the electing God. As the Canons put it, this way cannot be trod by those who speak lightly of election (CD, I, 13), but those who do walk upon it will understand why Paul concludes by giving praise. That praise is not that of the *visio Dei*. The ordinances of God are inscrutable and His way cannot be comprehended (Rom. 11:23). In a mirror we still see darkly (I Cor. 13:12), but those riddles are spoken of in a song of love. There is no other and higher point of view. It is precisely faith and love that know of God's freedom, His election and mercy.

To this mercy — in freedom over against all human pretentiousness — the Church testifies in the world. It speaks of this divine free mercy as the comfort — according to Bavinck (see Chapter VII) — for the greatest sinner. For it is the content of election which is not of works but of Him who called.

CHAPTER SEVEN

ELECTION AND THE PREACHING OF THE GOSPEL

IN the previous chapter we dealt at length with the question whether historically the confession of a sovereign, free election of God did not put a restraint on the preaching of the gospel. We have seen that where election is confessed, there is also place for the preaching of the gospel. But the question remains whether there is any essential connection between the two, or whether perhaps the gospel is preached merely out of obedience to the command of the resurrected Lord without much thought being given to the connection between election and preaching. Furthermore, the doctrine of election, if understood in a certain manner, seems to make difficult or even quite impossible the task of ascertaining this connection. If in predestination "everything has been decided beforehand," has not the preacher lost his power to beckon and persuade? And is it not inevitable that the passivity of election covers the ways traveled by the heralds of the Kingdom?

But the question does not arise only where the Church's doctrine of election is understood in a certain way. It arises with various interpretations. If God predestinates, can the gospel really be meaningful? It is clear that this is a very important matter, for if uncertainty concerning this matter enters the hearts of the messengers, their zeal and appealing power become weak and eventually completely crippled. There is less and less of the fire and fervency that are so clearly evident in Paul's word: "Woe is unto me, if I preach not the gospel" (I Cor. 9:16). Paul uses here the word *anagke,* a very strong word which carries the idea of the absolutely necessary, the unavoidable.[1]

For Paul this *anagke* is not a divine force, not a cosmological principle or an abstract necessity; it is a very peculiar "must," which characterizes the essence of his apostolate, and from which he cannot and does not want to withdraw. This "must"

---

1. Kittel, *T.W.N.T.,* I, 351.

is the complete opposite of any arbitrary, private whim. It is full of the earnestness "from which he, if he does not want to incur the woe of damnation, cannot withdraw himself." It is not a painful burden but an order which he fulfills with gladness because he understands the meaning of his commission from the perspective of the Kingdom of God. We see this meaningfulness, this purposeful order, everywhere in the New Testament. There is not the slightest possibility that — because of the election of God — it "actually" would be superfluous. And the apostolic practice clearly indicates that the significance of the preaching of the gospel is beyond any doubt. The issue is the necessity of testifying of the crucified and resurrected Lord, and this necessity can be described in the words of Peter: "We cannot but speak the things which we saw and heard" (Acts 4:20). The revelation of God in Jesus Christ is not merely a fact from the past, but a message to be preached now, and always, to all nations.

There is a general recognition that there is no contradiction between the message of election and this apostolic *élan,* but in general there is less confidence regarding the connection between the Church's doctrine of election and her *élan,* her calling in the world to bear witness. It is clear that we may not disregard the seriousness of this question, especially not because, in the light of the history of Church and theology, we meet with definite dangers. Frequently a certain interpretation of the election of God has put a restraint on the preaching of the gospel. Just as some individuals may become passive and negligent because of the way they interpret election, so may the Church, which is commanded to carry the gospel into the world. The perspective of Paul, who traveled around the world and even wanted to go as far as Spain (Rom. 15:24, 28), may become vaguer and vaguer and the Ascension commission "unto the uttermost part of the earth" (Acts 1:8) lose its dynamic power.

There is also the question whether the clearness of the New Testament connections is mirrored in the history of the Church and in dogmatic reflection. Have the meaning and the power of the gospel been understood? Is it realized how it is possible that Paul, precisely in those often-discussed chapters, Romans 9 to 11, can speak of that calling, that necessity? "How then shall they call on him in whom they have not believed? and how shall they believe in him whom they have not heard? and

how shall they hear without a preacher?" (Rom. 10:14). And
is it understood that Paul's word about the *anagke* does not
prevent his citing the Old Testament word: "How beautiful are
the feet of them that bring glad tidings" (Rom. 10:15)?

There is indeed an interpretation of the doctrine of election
in which it is difficult to see the significance of preaching the
gospel. It is the deterministic interpretation, which usurps all
room for preaching because of its causal symmetry between
election and rejection. In so far as the preaching of the gospel
still is granted a place here, it is nothing but a "foreign body";
there is no room left for real preaching, for a serious testimony,
for a calling and admonishing appeal. Preaching labors under the
pressure of causality. The superiority of causality is too strong,
and ultimately invades all traditional ways in which the preaching of the gospel is still continued. Determinism has always
crowded out the *kerygma* from one direction or the other.

The preaching of the gospel is undermined not only because
the absoluteness of Christianity has been abandoned, but also
because the doctrine of election has been deterministically infected. Both the *anagke* and the "sweetness" are suppressed.
Paul's "woe unto me" is no longer understood, nor the message
that brings peace (Isa. 52:7).

He who reflects on these things will be interested to hear that
the Canons. which maintained the doctrine of election over
against the Remonstrants, also pay much attention to the preaching of the gospel. We first of all wish to point to what the
Canons say regarding the promise of the gospel: "Whosoever
believes in Christ crucified shall not perish, but have eternal life.
This promise . . . ought to be declared and published to all
nations, and to all persons promiscuously and without distinction,
to whom God out of His good pleasure sends his gospel" (CD,
II, 5). Furthermore, the call given by the gospel is mentioned
(CD, II, 6), and it is said that "As many as are called by the
gospel are unfeignedly called. For God has most earnestly and
truly declared in His Word what is acceptable to Him, namely,
that those who are called should come unto Him" (CD, III,
and IV, 8), while also Christ is said to be "offered by the
gospel" (CD, III, and IV, 9).

Central to the emphasis of the Canons is its discussion of the seriousness of this preaching of the gospel.[2] It has struck the attention of many that the Canons, more than any other Confession, have emphatically spoken of the preaching of the gospel; and many have wondered how it was possible to emphasize this seriousness and whether it was not endangered because of the presupposition of the Canons. It seems, however, that for the Canons themselves there is nothing strange in this correlation, and that is a proof that the background of the Canons is not to be found in a deterministic doctrine of election. There is undoubtedly a profound connection between the way in which the Canons criticize the parallel, and the clearness with which they discuss the preaching of the gospel.

There has been much disagreement regarding the remarks of the Canons about the preaching of the gospel. This disagreement has centered especially on the so-called general offer of grace. A case in point is especially the controversy within the Christian Reformed Church in America. And although it is not necessary to discuss fully this problem, which deals also with the matter of common grace,[3] we still wish to draw attention to some cardinal points because here, as we see it, the whole structure of the doctrine of election is at stake.

This is clearly shown in the case of Hoeksema,[4] who was not willing to criticize the Canons but instead gave his own interpretation of them. According to him, the promise mentioned in II, 5 is not general but particular because it is the promise of life eternal to everyone "who believes in Christ crucified."[5] To be sure, Hoeksema accepts the *call* of the gospel to all; God demands in the calling of the gospel faith and conversion, but this call is not an offer of grace. A sharp distinction must be made between the particular promise and the general demand.[6]

2. A. C. De Jong in *The Well-Meant Gospel Offer. The Views of H. Hoeksema and K. Schilder* (1954), p. 131, points out that the word "serious" occurs seven times in the Canons, not only in connection with preaching, but also with respect to repentance and conversion (CD, I, 1; V, 5). Quite correctly De Jong calls this *serio* "essential to a proper understanding of III-IV."
3. See the dissertation of A. C. De Jong.
4. Hoeksema, *Een Kracht Gods tot Zaligheid, of Genade Geen Aanbod,* 1931; *Het Evangelie, of De Jongste Aanval op de Waarheid der Souvereine Genade,* 1933; *The Prot. Ref. Churches in America. Their Origin, Early History and Doctrine,* 1936, *especially* pp. 322ff; *De Plaats der Verwerping in de Verkondiging des Evangelies,* 1927.
5. Hoeksema, *Een Kracht Gods,* p. 102.
6. *Ibid.,* p. 106.

Because Hoeksema makes this distinction, he had to enlarge
further upon the Canons.   For there is a passage which is
central to his argument, namely, that Christ is offered by the
gospel (CD, III and IV, 9).   To begin with, Hoeksema says
that, according to the Canons, not grace, but Christ is offered.
And in order to separate these two sharply, he points out that
we encounter a word in the Latin text which means "present"
or "show."[7]   Christ is presented, displayed to us in the gospel,
in the riches of His significance, but that does not imply an
offer of grace.

In this exegesis of the Canons we touch upon the core of
Hoeksema's doctrine of election as it becomes visible in his
interpretation of the preaching of the gospel.   According to
Hoeksema, Christ is presented to us, but this presentation is
objective and merely descriptive in character.   It does not imply
an appeal or invitation or offer.   It cannot imply this because
God gives a true invitation only to the elect, not to others, and
for that very reason one cannot speak of a general offer of grace.
The command to believe and be converted is general.   God's
demand comes to all, but He does not offer salvation to all.   For
in that demand God does not bend so deep and so low that man
could get the impression that it is His intention really to save.
God only demands, and that is all!

By this Hoeksema does not mean to rule out the missionary
mandate, but he wants to re-interpret the nature of preaching.[8]
This preaching is dominated structurally by the contrast between
the elect and the reprobate.   The act of preaching has a twofold
aspect.   The counsel of God sheds both a stream of light and an
obscuring shadow, and preaching must correspond to it.   Therefore it is impossible to bring the gospel (the light!) to all.   The
unity of the message is thus broken by the distinction between
light and darkness.   The requirement to believe comes to all.
But believe *what,* since grace is not offered to all?   The answer
is that man must believe what is shown to him.   There is a gulf
between the command to believe, and that which is never offered
but only objectively displayed without an invitation being attached.   Thus the invitation is completely lost in preaching which
only displays and pictures the facts.

It now no longer surprises us that Hoeksema sees no mystery

---

7. The Latin text is: *"nec in Christo, per evangelium oblato."* This shows
   that the meaning of the word *offerre* is at stake.
8. *Ibid.,* p. 201.

in the doctrine "that God has His gospel preached to all without exception, with the intention of saving the elect, and of hardening the hearts of the others."[9]   God's intention is, on the bases of the counsel of God and of election and reprobation, perfectly clear; and it is impossible that the rejected godless man "ever could get the impression that God offers or presents something to him."[10]   There is no mystery.   It is precisely God's intention to harden the rejected by means of the gospel and thus to worsen their judgment.

Why must the gospel be preached to all?   "For the simple reason that nobody knows who are the elect, head for head, soul for soul."[11]   And herein, and in the purpose of hardening the rejected, lies the significance of the preaching to all.   And that, says Hoeksema, is the framework in which the Canons are constructed when they say that God shows seriously and truthfully in His Word what pleases Him, namely, that those who are called come to Him (CD, III-IV, 8).

If anywhere, it is here that Hoeksema's exegesis of the Canons goes awry, because now the symmetry between election and reprobation becomes a scheme in which the gospel can no longer be truly preached.   The missionary mandate, "Make disciples of all the nations" (Matt. 28:19), can no longer function properly, according to its undeniable emphasis on the purpose of the gospel.   Neither is it possible to understand how Paul, knowing himself to be a servant of Christ, now that God was reconciling the world to Himself in Christ, could write: "We are ambassadors therefore on behalf of Christ, as though God were entreating by us: we beseech you on behalf of Christ, be ye reconciled to God" (II Cor. 5:20) ; or how Paul, presenting the Kingdom of God to the Jews in Rome, tried to convince them respecting Jesus from early morning till late at night (Acts 28:23).   We can no longer speak of glad tidings that go out into the world, except where the gospel reaches the elect.   We do not know who they are, but, the purpose of the gospel is twofold: salvation and hardening.   The symmetry casts its shadow over the *kerygma*.[12]

9. *Ibid.*, p. 208
10. H. Hoeksema, *Het Evangelie*, p. 212.
11. Hoeksema, *Een Kracht Gods*, p. 209.
12. Hoeksema seeks to maintain his distinction by all means. For instance, with respect to the words "If any man thirst, let him come to me and drink" (John 7:37), he says that this cannot be used as a proof, for not all are thirsty.   Consequently, says Hoeksema, the offer is not general (*Het Evangelie*, p. 237).   Cf. Hoeksema with A. C. De Jong,

He who does not accept this consequence, according to Hoeksema, has already fallen into the abyss of un-Biblical universalism.

It is quite evident that Hoeksema's systematizing of the counsel of God is closely related to his fervent rejection of the first point of the Synod of the Christian Reformed Church held in Kalamazoo in 1924.[13] In connection with the general preaching of the gospel, the Synod affirmed the "favorable attitude of God toward mankind in general and not only toward the elect." But Hoeksema emphatically rejected this favorable attitude on the basis of reprobation,[14] because apart from God's election there is possible only the eternal "sovereign hatred of God's good pleasure"[15] and because God has from eternity had before and with Him what takes place in time.[16]

Now the Synod did not intend to give a solution which satisfies the human mind; it is not without reason that in Point I it speaks of "a certain favor of grace of God, which He shows to all His creatures." But this hesitation could not convince Hoeksema because all hesitation regarding the "eternal hatred" in God is precluded and must be precluded.

We have mentioned this controversy because we cannot simply ignore it. The existential proportions which this struggle

---

op. cit., p. 49: "God, however, uses also that preaching to realize his counsel of predestination both of election and reprobation, so that he, without nullifying the ethical nature and responsibility of man, calls the one unto salvation and hardens the other. The preaching of the Gospel is therefore never grace for the reprobate, neither is it ever intended to be such by God."

13. This point quotes CD, III and IV, 8 and 9, and II, 5 in favor of the "general offer of the gospel." Hoeksema detects only Arminianism here because thus the decision depends on man. He decides in favor of the clear transparency of the preaching. The only void in this transparency is that we do not know the elect and reprobate.

14. Hoeksema says that Scripture "speaks everywhere of election and reprobation" (*Een Kracht Gods,* p. 169), that this is not hidden, and that he in no wise speaks "seemingly logically, hyperlogically, or rationalistically" (p. 171) against A. Kuyper Jr.'s criticism about which Hoeksema — without reason — was very much disappointed (p. 162). It must further be remarked that Hoeksema draws numerous conclusions from Scripture regarding election and reprobation even though he must sometimes admit that "there is no mention here of elect and reprobate as such" (note this "as such" in *Het Evangelie,* p. 211 and elsewhere).

15. Hoeksema, *Het Evangelie,* p. 243.

16. *Ibid.,* p. 293, with reference to Jacob and Esau (Mal. 1:11).

assumed, especially on the part of Hoeksema, with his call to repentance and his accusation that God as God was assaulted,[17] and also the many appeals to Scripture made by both sides, may convince us of the seriousness of the problem under discussion.

Many questions arise when, in contrast to Hoeksema, we listen to what Bavinck has to say regarding election. Without detracting anything from the Biblical teaching regarding the counsel of God, His foreknowledge and the "before the foundation of the world," Bavinck first denies the symmetry and emphasizes the election of God. In that connection he writes: "Election does not serve, as is so often taught, to repel many, but to invite all to the riches of God's grace in Christ." Precisely because the election of God is free and does not take place according to human justice and merits, "the doctrine of election is of such great comfort, both to the believer and the unbeliever." In this remarkable passage, Bavinck apparently does not proceed from an abstract concept of election, but from God's free election as it is taught in Scripture. He sees the nature of the *ekloge* to be not a matter of merit but of grace, and from that he draws the conclusion that there is now hope for the most miserable sinner![18]

If Pelagius and the Pharisees were right, the publicans would be excluded! "Pelagianism is cruel and hard." What Bavinck says here about election is in my opinion the profoundest part of his dogmatics. The gate to the *kerygma* is thrown wide open, not in spite of, but because of the freedom of election, which is not the freedom of a *dominium absolutum* or *potentia absoluta,* but of the living God of salvation. "No one may believe that he is rejected, for everyone is seriously and urgently called and is compelled to believe in Christ for his salvation."[19]

One might think for a moment that we meet here again the "demand" of Hoeksema, without offer and without invitation. But Bavinck uses the words "calling" and "duty" in an altogether different context, namely, in the context of the general message of the gospel.

That Bavinck and Hoeksema entertain two different views regarding the nature of preaching is very clearly shown in

17. *Ibid.,* p. 244.
18. *Gereformeerde Dogmatiek,* II, 365-366.
19. *Ibid.*

Hoeksema's criticism of Bavinck on this important point. Bavinck speaks extensively of the general offer of grace and advances no less than eight grounds for it. The seriousness with which Bavinck brings this matter to the foreground is due to the fact that the doctrine of election and individual satisfaction seems to exclude tne general offer of grace.[20] While Hoeksema, by virtue of his view on election and reprobation, attacks every offer and invitation, Bavinck speaks of a call of the gospel "which invites to faith in God's grace," and which may and must be brought to all without discrimination. He then poses the question whether the general offer of grace can be seriously intended, a question which returns us to the topic of this chapter: election and preaching.

It is striking that Bavinck proceeds from the command of Christ as the end of all controversy, but at the same time he adds to it a word that could have been directed at Hoeksema (Bavinck's dogmatics preceded the struggle in America), namely, that the gospel is preached to people "not as to elect or reprobate but to sinners who are all in need of salvation." And this offer of salvation is seriously intended. It is a proof — for all without exception — of God's infinite love, and it demonstrates that God does not rejoice in the destruction of sinners but therein that they repent and live. It tells to all "that the sacrifice of Christ is sufficient for the forgiveness of all sins."[21]

It is clear that it is not Bavinck's intention to give a rational solution of God's election and the preaching of the gospel. He refuses to accept a way in which it is no longer possible to do justice to the clarity of Scripture and the command given in it. He points out that the general preaching of the gospel is not something that bypasses God; on the contrary, he leaves the outcome in the hand of God while fully maintaining the preaching of the gospel.

That is why we must not look for a solution apart from faith. Bavinck realizes that the issue is not an antinomy in the work and Word of God, but a meaningful commission which is given along with salvation.

Even though Bavinck's formulations may not be sufficient to

20. *Ibid.*, IV, 709.
21. *Ibid.*, IV, 7.

answer all of Hoeksema's criticism,[22] that does not alter the fact that in Bavinck's defense of the general offer of salvation we stand closer to the gospel than in the seemingly systematic and smooth criticism of Hoeksema. For in Hoeksema dogmatic exegesis governs his criticism and the notions of "sinner" and "godless" become vague because of the concepts of "elected and rejected."

It could be asked whether the struggle is perhaps concentrated around the word "offer," with all the different values and interpretations which can be attached to this word. Beyond any doubt this word has played an important role in the discussions. Hoeksema interpreted the "offer" of grace as analogous to many human offers without urgency or appeal: take it or leave it. And when Dr. K. Schilder attempted to shed some light on the American struggle, he warned sharply against the Arminian concept of "offer" whereby God gives in Christ the possibility of salvation and then offers that salvation and leaves the decision with man.[23] Schilder was correct when he pointed out that in this manner justice was done neither to Scripture nor to the Canons. But, as is usually the case when a doctrinal conflict seems to be based on an interpretation of words, later on deeper motifs come to the fore. Schilder's criticism did not relax the tension. Besides, it had already become evident that those who maintained the offer of salvation did not have in mind the kind of "offer" criticized by Hoeksema and Schilder. We must remember here that in the Canons the word "offer" occurs in a special context: "Christ offered in the gospel" (CD, III and IV, 9).

This confronts us immediately with the power and emphasis of the preaching of the gospel, which is something altogether different from an "offer" that can be accepted or declined at will. Schilder pointed out correctly that when this offer is rejected in unbelief it makes a man morally reprehensible. And this fact, though it is in constant danger of becoming obscured, contributed considerable light to the discussion.

But even after some of the ambiguity of "offer" was removed, the controversy was not ended. The conflict was more than a matter of language, and it has significance far beyond the Amer-

22. I should mention that according to Bavinck God in His offer does not say what He Himself will do, only declares "what He wills that we shall do" (IV, 6).
23. K. Schilder, *Heidelbergse Catechismus*, II, 237ff.

ican situation. The background of the conflict is, we think, in the doctrine of election itself, from which issued Hoeksema's fervent rejection of the general offer of salvation. Because he proceeded from the sharp light and black shadow, God's eternal love and hatred, Hoeksema could not possibly understand the first point of the statement made by the 1924 Synod of the Christian Reformed Church regarding the "general love toward man," except as a step toward humanizing the concept of God. We saw elsewhere that from various sides protests have been raised against such a humanization, but it would be unfair to place Hoeksema on a par here with Volz, Otto, and Snethlage. There is, however, a point of contact between them when, for instance, the aspects of sovereignty are overemphasized at the cost of the harmony of Scripture. But unlike Volz, Otto, and Snethlage, Hoeksema sees everything in the light of his severe concept of predestination which limits the *kerygma* to the elect and withholds it from the reprobate. The *kerygma* is altered completely by this principle of explanation, and although the elect and reprobate are unknown, this distinction interferes from the very beginning with the preaching of the gospel.[24]

The crisis in this manner of thinking concerning the gospel becomes evident in the tension which is evoked between subject and object. The demand to believe and repent goes out to everybody, but what a man who is considered to be rejected must believe becomes completely uncertain. For this man, standing in the glaring searchlight of the preaching, is not confronted with an invitation but with the reality of rejection. He can — in the light of this supposition — no longer be called upon to believe in Christ and salvation. There is no room left for the perspective of the Canons, which relate the call to what is good in the sight of God, namely, that those who are called may come to Him.[25]

The seriousness of the struggle concerning the nature of the preaching of the gospel becomes still more evident when we

24. Cf. the last chapter of A. C. De Jong, *op. cit.*
25. It is understandable that this passage of the Canons played a role in the American discussion. There was for Hoeksema only one possible interpretation, namely, that it concerns only the elect. That *they* come to God, pleases Him. And they do come (here Ps. 135:6 is cited). See this interpretation by S. van de Kooy concerning "What Pleases Him" in *The Standard Bearer* of Feb. 15, 1940.

consider that an altogether different opinion regarding the preaching of the gospel has exerted a tremendous influence, namely, so-called universalism.   Precisely because the opponents of the general offer of salvation are sharply against universalism, it is impossible to disregard it.

Universalism should not simply be indentified with the doctrine of general reconciliation.   There is also a universalism which takes into account the rejection of the gospel on the part of man, so that the universal offer does not become realized and effective in every individual. This universalism leads to the conclusion that the decision lies with man.   The opponents of the general offer of salvation strongly resist it, and argue that in this universalism God's broad and wide intentions are ignored. God becomes a waiting God who in His powerlessness has actually been humanized. Thus the question naturally arises whether this universalism is true to the Scriptural testimony regarding God's free election.

Questions about universalism, especially in recent times, are concentrated on Barth's doctrine of election, for with him there occurs a peculiar mutation. In original universalism, the issue is a universal offer because Christ died for all, and election remains in the background for the moment. But with Barth, Christ's death touches precisely upon the election of all, which election has become manifest in Christ's death.   The universality of the message is no longer at odds with the fact of election, for it is based on the universality of election.   The message which is carried into the world forms the transition from those who already know (the believers) to those who do not yet know, but who are nevertheless comprised in the election. Rejection is now no longer an independent shadow and menace, but the accepted and therefore withstood rejection, namely, in and through Christ. This rejection is thus transmitted — as the rejection of Christ — into the kerygma and there becomes the essence of the glad tidings.

All tension between election and preaching is here dissolved, for precisely election (and rejection) are fully incorporated in the preaching. The pro omnibus of Christ's death and resurrection, in which election is manifested (God for us), is the all-important fact for the kerygma.   The sovereignty of God in election and rejection is summarized in Christ's election and rejection and comes thus to us as gospel, the gospel of the double predestination, as the absolute light of God in our darkness.[26]

It becomes clear that, although Barth's doctrine may not be identified with that of the Remonstrants, there is a point of contact, in that "Christ died for all." For Barth this view is immediately linked up with divine election, or rather it coincides with it. He does not simply pose the old universalistic thesis with its scheme of possibility and realization, but confesses a universal election. The offer, the *kerygma,* is universal because it testifies of this election, this divine light.

It becomes quite clear that there is no greater contrast imaginable than that between the rejection of the general offer of salvation and Barth's doctrine of election, and the question arises whether we are not forced to make a choice here. Is not this difference, this contrast, to be characterized as the dilemma between particularity and universality? Is not this dilemma and all its clear consequences unavoidable? We are convinced that this question must be answered negatively and that with that negation we touch upon the core of the doctrine of election, the *cor ecclesiae.*

We shall take our point of departure in the Canons, for there the problem of particularity and universality is specifically mentioned. On the one hand, we find a reference to a universal preaching of the gospel to all without exception and, on the other, we are confronted with an unmistakable particularity. We must now ask whether we have here an antinomy, an inner discrepancy within the Canons.

In the Canons the particularity appears in the statement that "... it was the will of God that Christ by the blood of the cross should effectually redeem out of every people, tribe, nation, and language all those, and those only, who were from eternity chosen to salvation and given to Him by the Father; that He should confer upon them faith, which, together with all the other saving gifts of the Holy Spirit, He purchased for them, by His death" (CD, II, 8; cf. I, 7).

In order to understand these words, further attention must be paid to the Rejection of Errors in the Canons. The Remonstrants are attacked in their doctrine of Christ's objective — "acquiring" salvation for all. The *pro omnibus* of the Remonstrants

---

26. Cf. *The Triumph of Grace in the Theology of Karl Barth,* Chaps. IV and X; H. Vogel, *Praedestinatio gemina. Theol. Aufs. für K. Barth.*

is an objective reality, a new situation, in which nothing is as yet implied regarding the obtaining of salvation. It teaches that God the Father had ordained His Son to the death of the cross without a certain and definite decree to save any, so that the necessity, profitableness, and worth of what Christ merited by His death might have existed, and might remain in all its parts complete, perfect, and intact, even if the merited redemption had never in fact been applied to any person (CD, II, 1, Rejection of Errors). Christ had acquired the mere right to establish a covenant with man, (CD, II, 2), and the authority of the perfect will "to deal again with man" (CD, II, 3). The Remonstrants wanted to distinguish sharply between the subjectivity and objectivity in man's salvation. Hence the Canons attack this scheme — possibility-realization — not only because in it man's free will must decide whether the benefits gained by Christ's death indeed become realized (CD, II, 6), but also because it implies contempt for Christ's death (CD, II, 3).

According to the Canons, the significance of Christ's death cannot be approached from the point of view of "possibility." His death was not so ineffective that it can only receive its direction and effect by man's acceptance. If that were the case, everything would come to depend on his free will, belief, and the obedience of faith.

It is striking that again in the Rejection of Errors the "offer" is mentioned. But that is not contrary to what was said at first about Christ being offered in the gospel. That kind of "offer" according to which the right obtained by Christ is to be left to man's decision is here condemned. The Canons cannot accept this because in that way salvation is no longer based on the mercy of God. This is the old error of Pelagius.

The main theme of the Canons appears also at this juncture, namely, the theme of free and sovereign grace over against a synthesis in which there is no room for this freedom and sovereignty. That is why the Canons would never rob preaching of its seriousness and truthfulness. Rather, in the center of the conflict, they emphatically maintain the freedom of divine mercy, the *sola gratia*.

In the light of what has been said above, it becomes clear that it is possible for the Canons to defend the general offer of salvation, not as a concession, but as an essential and integral part of Christian doctrine. The Canons do not aim at minimizing

the significance of Christ's death from the point of view of
election and reprobation, or at making relative the power of
His death, thus making dubious the serious preaching of salvation in Christ. Rather, precisely in their rejection of man's
freedom to decide, they retain the correct conception of the mercy
of God. And for that reason it is more correct to speak of
broadness than of minimization.[27] The Canons emphasize the
freedom of grace.[28]

In this connection it is important to remember that the Canons
speak of the death of Christ as a sufficient sacrifice. If the call
of the gospel is not accepted, and many do not repent, this is
not owing to any defect or insufficiency in Christ's sacrifice, but
to man himself (CD, II, 6, Rejection of Errors). Christ's death
is the only and most perfect sacrifice which is "of infinite worth
and value, abundantly sufficient to expiate the sins of the whole
world" (CD, II, 3). On the basis of this confession it is possible
to assure all men "that in this sacrifice lies an infinite power and
worthiness, so that in all the world no person could be sunk so
deep that Christ's sacrifice would not be abundantly sufficient for
the expiation of his sins."[29]

In this way we reject the dilemma which says that there is
either no general offer of salvation or universal election. We do
so by repudiating the schema of objectivity-subjectivity on which
it rests. According to that presupposition, one must either
accept an objective universal election whereby an eternal decision for all has already been made, or a subjective offer of
salvation whereby man can freely decide for himself.

We do not reject this dilemma because of its implicit attempt
to understand and comprehend the reality of the salvation of
God and the acceptance of that offer by man, but because making

27. Bavinck has repeatedly pointed out that universalism is only seemingly
    broader. He calls the Reformed confession "ampler of heart and broader
    of view than any other Christian confession. It finds the last, pro-
    foundest cause of salvation only in God's good pleasure, in His eternal
    compassion, in His inscrutable mercy, in the unsearchable riches of
    His omnipotent and free grace. What firmer and broader foundation
    could be found for the salvation of a sinful and lost humanity?"
    (Gereformeerde Dogmatiek, IV, 709).
28. Bavinck writes correctly: "This difference is incorrectly or incom-
    pletely represented, if it is exclusively defined in terms of whether Christ
    died for all people or for the elect only. That is not the way the Canons
    in the second chapter deal with and solve the problems of the differ-
    ences" (ibid., III, 463).
29. T. Bos, De Dordtse Leerregels (1915), p. 105.

the offer subjective is a clear violation of the freedom of election, and also because making election objective harbors unacceptable consequences. Thereby the gospel message is transformed into a mere communication regarding a new state of affairs, a new state of common reconciliation. The character of the gospel message — in appeal and admonishment, in promise and demand — can no longer be recognized.

Over against that stands the clear structure of the *kerygma* in its man-directed, appealing power. It does not make God's work, His acts in Christ, dependent on man's decision, nor does it state that God's acts acquire validity only through and in man's decision. Such a subjectivism is rejected by the Canons.

But it is true that the message of salvation does not consist in the communication of an occurrence which must then be accepted by man in faith. For the salvation of God concerns a historical act of God which itself gives direction, and which has an appealing, inviting, promising, and commanding force. Apart from faith man cannot discover it or know of the reality of reconciliation for all, to which he must respond with a decision.

This is no doubt what Bavinck meant when he said that the acts of God may not be presented as an objective reality "for all" apart from the *kerygma* and faith. He expressed this thought in his extensive defense of the general offer of salvation when he asserted that the preaching of the gospel does not say: "Christ died in your place, all your sins are reconciled and forgiven."[30] Rather, the gospel comes to man as a true *message* of salvation. It contains a call to faith, which call is implied in God's act in Christ. The *kerygma* is inseparably connected with Christ. It is filled with the coming of Christ into the world. Jesus Christ is the Light of the world, and in Him God loved the world and was reconciling it to Him. The grace of God hath appeared, bringing salvation to all men (Titus 2:11). The divine act is likened to the rising of the sun (Luke 1:78). Thus the gospel concerns all. God's will is revealed in Jesus Christ. His good pleasure and His coming have universal significance, so universal that He is a crisis in the world.

The mistake of universalism is not its fascination with the universal aspect of the New Testament. It must even be said that many "universalistic" texts, as Bavinck calls them, have frequently been partially robbed of their power by exegetes who were

---

30. Bavinck, *op. cit.*, IV, 709.

so opposed to universalism that they failed to appreciate the
full significance of such texts. So Hoeksema, for instance, interprets them in the light of a distinction between elect and reprobate and says that they concern only the elect. The universal
aspect, which is directly connected with the universal and cosmic
significance of Christ, is thereby neglected. The *Christus pro
omnibus* is attacked in such a manner that it no longer is
possible to realize fully that Christ's coming has meaning for all
of the world, and that the world in Him is confronted with a
new decision of crucial significance in the history of salvation.
This forced exegesis naturally evoked a reaction, so that ultimately universalism is strengthened instead of weakened. He
who studies the history of doctrine repeatedly discovers the power
of the dilemma between universalism and the denial of a general
offer of salvation. And even though this dilemma is solved
by the Canons, it nevertheless continues to play a role because
it creates the impression that at this point we are confronted
with two logical possibilities, apart from which there is no third,
nor indeed can be.

We are convinced that in the light of the Word of God there
is no such dilemma, because of the universal, cosmic significance
of Christ. Only by a full appreciation of that fact can we ever
transcend the dilemma. And this is ultimately confirmed by the
fact that both the rejection of the general offer of salvation and
universalism meet with great difficulties in Scripture. We have
already shown the former by citing the forced exegesis which
accompanies it.

As we have seen, universalism is not as broad as its appears
because it is limited by man's free decision. When Barth
opposes the universalistic scheme of possibility — realization and,
instead, proposes the irrevocably non-conditional and definite
universal election, then the problem still remains in other ways.
For Barth there is nothing left but the impossible possibility of
unbelief and the necessity of faith. Now the question automatically arises as to the actual meaning, power, and validity
of this universal election, especially when the reality of unbelief
becomes evident in the connection between universal election
and rejection of the *apokatastasis*.[31]

31. J. M. Hasselaar in "Twee Boeken over Barth" (*In de Waagschaal,*
    July 9 and 16, 1955), has attempted to show that there is harmony and
    that universal election does not relativize the *kerygma* by saying that
    the fact of our election "becomes clear only in the category of preaching
    (p. 975).

It is, however, impossible to construct our own solution from the problematics and unevenness of universalism and the rejection of the general offer of salvation. And, therefore, it is necessary to reflect on an other way in which the dilemma disappears. This way may be indicated as the way of the message, but at the same time as the way of faith.

It is, at any rate, necessary to do full justice to the universality of the gospel with which we are continually confronted in Scripture. We see already in the Old Testament that the particularity of the election of Israel has nothing to do with particularism but is precisely and fully directed at the universality of the acts of God in the Messiah for all peoples. The blessing of Abraham is closely connected with the call to be a blessing to others: "In thee shall all the families of the earth be blessed" (Gen. 12:3), which is "the program beyond the secluded position of Israel."[32]

This universality of salvation for the world must not be minimized, certainly not because of a fear of universalism, which objectifies this universality and does not take into account that the point of universality in the Old Testament is the act of God in the Messiah toward the nations of the world. This act of God is not presented to us as a deed which as a matter of course comes to all, but as a calling of God in grace and justice. The Old Testament does not give us a scheme of self-evident universalism, even where the universal perspectives are the clearest. Universalism is neither the theme of Israel's history nor of the other peoples' history. On Mt. Zion a feast will be prepared for all nations and Jehovah "will destroy the face of the covering that covereth all peoples, and the veil that is spread over all nations" (Isa. 25:6-7), but the way that leads toward this goal is the way of God in grace and justice, and when the time of salvation has come, universality has been caught up in the message of the Kingdom at hand, the message of repentance. But universality is not eliminated in the message. Again the light goes up over the nations in the way of grace and justice, and after Israel's rejection of the Messiah salvation goes to the nations and the message now seeks all.

Here lies the foundation for the preaching of salvation, and only he who is motivated by a reactionary distrust of universalism can be blind to that.

32. H. A. Wiersinga, *Zendingsperspectief in het Oude Testament*, p. 20.

He who has seen that universalism has abstracted universality from the acts of God can comprehend the anticipation and eagerness with which the apostles of the resurrected Lord went into the world. Their labor was directed to all nations and tongues. That does not imply a depreciation of the *ecclesia* — that of Christ — but it means precisely that the *ecclesia* is of the Lord and thus it testifies in the world.

Pentecost can be understood only in the light of Messiah's salvation, and only in that light can one speak of the fact that the gospel is directed to all. This impressed Bavinck when, with regard to the offer of salvation, he called attention to the passage in Ezekiel that God has no pleasure in the death of the wicked but rather that he should return from his way, and live (Ezek. 18:23),[33] without denying the Biblical distinction between elect and reprobate. He does not, like Hoeksema, make distinctions between the wicked who repent and those who do not, and he does not exclude the latter from the first part of the Ezekiel text.[34] It is a matter of course that the first and the second parts of God's word are inseparable (i.e., His not having pleasure in the death of the wicked, and having pleasure in man's repentance), and the text is completely misunderstood when one carries the scheme of election-reprobation into it. Bavinck did not for a moment intend to do that. The point of the text for him lies in "having pleasure" and "having no pleasure," the divine act of grace and salvation which also is the core of the most critical preaching. When God says to the wicked, "Thou shalt surely die" (Ezek. 33:14, 15), and when this wicked man repents and "shall surely live and not die," God is not changeable in this twofold "surely." He remains exactly the same. He is the same because He always acts for the sake of human life. The God of Israel really has no pleasure in the death of the wicked. What must we think of the statement: "This does not at all imply an offer of grace?"[35] Of course, this is not the offer of a humanized God who pleads for recognition, but it is an offer that truly points out the way, promising, admonishing, and threatening; it is an invitation, a call to conversion.

33. Bavinck, *op. cit.*, IV, 7 and III, 461 (Ezek. 18:23, 33:11).
34. Hoeksema, *Het Evangelie*, pp. 210-211. Hoeksema presents an exegesis which actually amounts to an anlytical doctrine of justification. When God says that He rejoices in the conversion of the wicked, it is precisely the wicked who are mentioned in the beginning.
35. Hoeksema, *Een Kracht Gods*, p. 79.

He who thinks he can contrast the message of the living God with a series of conclusions taken from an individual and personal doctrine of election, devaluates in a deterministic manner the concrete Word of God regarding the harmony between that which pleases Him and that which does not please Him. He who says that God has pleasure only in the repentance of the wicked who have been elected destroys that harmony.

But the controversy concerns many more passages, especially in the New Testament. These are the passages which speak so universally of "all" that universalism derived its easy conclusions from them. We are reminded of what Paul said: "This is good and acceptable in the sight of God our Saviour; who would have all men to be saved, and come to the knowledge of the truth" (I Tim. 2:3-4), and of Peter's words: "not wishing that any should perish, but that all should come to repentance" (II Pet. 3:9), and of John's: "He is the propitiation for our sins, and not for ours only, but also for the whole world" (I John 2:2), and of many other passages.[36]

In the course of history there has been much contention over these texts, especially over I Timothy 2:4. The explanation has often been given that this concerns the will of God as *voluntas antecedens,* the general will to salvation, which is then followed by His *voluntas consequens,* as the result of man's free decision. That was already the question which occupied Augustine when he, considering I Timothy 2:4, remarked that there the will of God seems to be frustrated by the will of man. In this connection Augustine also cites Matthew 23:37: "How often would I have gathered thy children . . . and ye would not!" Is God's will frustrated by man's? Where, he asks, is His omnipotence by which He does everything. in heaven as well as on earth? Though he believed previously that "all" meant *omnes praedestinati,* he later affirmed that it meant the human race in its diversity (see I Tim. 2:1-2). This exegesis has exerted great influence, and since Paul speaks here of intercession for all people, one cannot possibly say that this exegesis is apriorily dogmatic.[37]

Of course, the danger of such exegesis is always present. We get the strong impression that such texts, containing the word "all," became lost in a general approach to Scripture. Take,

36. Cf. W. Elert, *Der Christliche Glaube* (1940), p. 560.
37. Augustine is often discussed in connection with the Roman Catholic exegesis of this text. It is pointed out that Augustine at first understood I Tim. 2:4 as God's general will to salvation.

for instance, II Peter 3:9, where the apostle speaks of the day of the Lord and says that God is not slack concerning His promise but that the continuity in the development of history is connected with God's longsuffering, and then follow those words that God does not wish that any should perish, but that all should come to repentance. What does this "all" mean? Greijdanus correctly rejects universalism of the Remonstrant brand; but then he speaks of "all elect," although the text does not mention the word "elect" at all. Over against that view, universalism interprets this as dealing with God's general will to salvation, saying, however, that this will is not effective in all respects since man delimits this universality of divine will. But Scripture never speaks of God's will as such, and in the universal passages — Peter, Ezekiel, and perhaps also I Timothy — the issue is that will of God which is presented to us in the dynamic and living context of the calling to repentance and to the knowledge of the truth.

We must first understand the Biblical mode of speaking of the will of God (I Tim. 2:4). The attempt has repeatedly been made to escape the difficulty — God's will and its efficacy — by presupposing a certain duality in the will of God. But this unsatisfactory solution is soon put aside, the more so since it affects the urgent power of all these passages. Then again the conclusion has been drawn that behind this "will" is hidden a real will which actually desires something else, or that it is a provisional will (universal and *antecedens*) which ultimately is delimited again by man's free decision. Scholasticism pondered this problem at length, but it never came out of the impasse. What shall we think of this paraphrasing of Scripture: "The persons for whom God *antecedenter* wills salvation, are *all* people"?[39] Even though Thomas Aquinas does not mean here persons *in abstracto*, but concrete persons, the *antecedenter* nevertheless dominates the whole exegesis, and the question is whether it is therefore still useful to describe God's *voluntas* in this manner: "His will has a real point of landing where He lets the good descend," for it is precisely this point of landing which is in question if God's will (salvation for all) is only a *voluntas antecedens*.

One wonders whether the gospel is not overshadowed here by theology, and whether such passages can really be understood

38. Greijdanus, *Kommentaar*, p. 341, on I Tim. 2:4.
39. Cf. Dr. Sebastianus, *Gods Heilswil* (1952), pp. 32ff.

only in the light of a distinction which does nothing but undermine the power of these very passages. Why not, we might
ask, understand this will as *consequens,* and why not make a
choice for absolute universalism with the consideration that
God's will will always be effective anyway?[40]   At any rate, the
comprising of "all" by the *voluntas antecedens* (by virtue of the
nature of the distinction itself) is a very dubious matter. This
will may in a sense be effective and be fulfilled, namely, as "the
will of means to salvation," according to Sebastianus, but it is
far from absolute in its effectiveness where actual salvation is
concerned. And the difficulties are not solved when that "will
of means to salvation" continues to be called "will to salvation."
For if those whom God wants to bring to salvation with His
voluntas consequens are the predestinated, the question arises
about the seriousness of the *voluntas antecedens* which comes
to the fore in such urgent references in Scripture. It is no
longer convincing when at this point reference is made to the
mystery with these words: "This seems to be a mystery concerning which God does not want us to apply a theological
scalpel."[41]   This mystery, it seems to us, is not the mystery
of Scripture, certainly not when it is said that "with regard to
predestination, that which belongs to the free will is not distinguished from that which belongs to predestination proper." It
is impossible to recognize in this mystery the characteristics of
the free and sovereign election of God.[42]

Nor is it possible to comprehend the universal-sounding
Scriptural references by means of the distinction between the
revealed and the hidden will of God. For precisely in what is
then called the revealed will of God, the good pleasure of God
in Jesus Christ is the central point, the pleasure of God in the
one Mediator between God and men (I Tim. 2:5). Paul, an
apostle and teacher of the Gentiles (I Tim. 2:7), testifies to this
salvation and proclaims it. This *kerygma,* as the message of
God's saving act, has an essentially universal quality, and only
that explains the universality of the New Testament. "The whole

---

40. Cf. W. Michaelis, *Versöhnung des Alls* (1950), p. 133. "It is not
   a powerless will which makes God will that all men are saved . . . . God
   wants to save and He does."
41. Sebastianus, *op. cit.,* p. 43.
42. In the discussion Sebastianus admits that the suggested difference is
   not illuminating and that Thomas would not have gone so far if he
   had not found this "humanization" in the Fathers.

New Testament testimony is pervaded by a tremendous joy:
the universality of Christ."[43]   This cannot be denied because
of reactionary feelings against relative and absolute universalism.
But this universality is nowhere made into an objective state of
affairs to be merely announced, whereupon it may or may not
be observed.   For this universality of the gospel is like an arrow
directed at a target, and no one is excluded, not even the worst
of sinners (I Tim. 1:16).

Behind the message in all these universal references one does
not need to fear the real, hidden will which in the end might
prove to be a shadow will, or a limited *voluntas consequens* which
ultimately replaces the *voluntas antecedens*.   Rather, in the message of salvation — according to the will of God made known
to the nations (Rom. 16:26) — the way of repentance and of
the knowledge of truth is pointed out to us.   That is the appeal,
the invitation, the calling voice, and the admonition in this
will of God.   Kerygmatic universality does not preclude but
include the call to belief and repentance.   One cannot speak of
that universality apart from faith and repentance, and one certainly cannot be casual about it.   The apostolic epistles and the
missionary practice of the apostles are in agreement in that
respect.

When Paul preaches God's act of salvation to the nations,
it is announced to "all" that they must repent.   The universality
of the gospel comprises essentially this universal call (Acts 17:
30; cf. 16:31).   In this universal *kerygma,* mention is also
made of the judgment, to that day on which God will justly
judge the earth in Jesus Christ (Acts 17:31; cf. 24:25).

He who seeks to solve the problem by bringing objectivity
and subjectivity into a state of equilibrium does not appreciate
the essence of this message which is God's message and which
cannot be objectified. The mystery is not solved by an equilibrium
constructed and comprehended by us, but in the way of faith,
which accepts the good tidings of the gospel and also the significance of that one act of God wherein He has loved the world.
That is why the Canons are correct in rejecting the Remonstrant
universalism, and at the same time opening the gates wide to
the *kerygma*.   It is not given to us to see through God's work,
not even where His love in Jesus Christ meets us in majestic
greatness.   But that which evaporates as soon as we attempt

43. Kittel, *T.W.N.T.,* V, 895.

to comprehend it is understood and accepted in the way of faith. God's will in Jesus Christ is not like a power which can be described only in deterministic language, but it finds its goal and effect in the way of the message of salvation. This message derives not a single threatening element from the fact of election. The message itself is the testimony to God's election, but it can be understood and accepted only in faith. The universalistic thesis cannot be confronted with a particularistic thesis.

The contrast is not one between universalism and particularism, for it is logically impossible to reach beyond this dilemma. But with the Canons we confess the freedom of God's election and the general preaching of the gospel. In this combination we do not see an antinomy or an irrational paradox. Rather, we understand something of the profound interrelations in the nature of election. He who would understand election as a formal *dominium absolutum,* as the arbitrariness of God, must consider the Canons to be very illogical indeed.

But he who, with Bavinck, dares to accentuate the solace of election for both believer and unbeliever, and does not do so on the basis of a universalistic denial of the freedom of God, but on the basis of "not out of works but out of grace," will understand in the practice of the Church the unity between its confession of election and the offer of salvation. This confession of election is not a menace to preaching but its tremendous divine stimulus. And when in the history of the Church some interpretation of the doctrine of election seems to make all preaching superfluous or senseless, that can be explained only on the basis of a serious misunderstanding and a fatal caricature. It is to the praise of the much critized Canons that they have rejected this caricature and have reminded the Church of the universality of the message which is no other than the mirroring of God's love for the world.[44]

In the light of the foregoing it can no longer be doubted that the election of God has a place in preaching. He who thinks that God's free election should not be discussed, and who wants to keep it a latent doctrine, is not only opposed by the teachings

---

44. In his discussion of "Erwählung und Verkündigung" (*De l' élection éternelle de Dieu. Actes du congrès international de théol. Calviniste,* 1936, p. 164) R. Grob has said: "There is tension but no contradiction between the task of the preacher with respect to election and the task of doctrine with respect to predestination."

of the New Testament but leaves room for the notion that the doctrine of election casts a shadow over the preaching of salvation. That the idea of a latent doctrine has all too often been entertained can be explained only in terms of a wrong doctrine of election, namely, of a deterministic deformation of it. Such an idea of election had better be abandoned, because it means the undermining of man's calling and responsibility. This way cannot be followed by him who sees election as a gift of God, not based on our works but on grace. If such election is no longer preached, the gospel is no longer a gospel of free and sovereign grace for the Church. The gospel of *free* election is a radical exclusion of all self-exaltation. With Paul it was such an essential point that Augustine and Calvin have repeatedly admonished the Church not to be silent about election! Therefore, the solution to all the problems cannot be given by a latent doctrine, but by the Biblical message which delivers us from all determinism and formalism and which admonishes us faithfully to walk the "ways of the elect" (CD, I, 13).

The question is only natural whether rejection must also be mentioned in the message of the Church. It is clear that rejection can also be made into a latent doctrine which will exert its influence in a hidden way.

He who rejects this position as an inner contradiction faces the question of how we in preaching must speak of rejection. The problem of parallelism or symmetry is of decisive significance here. When this parallelism is accepted it is only logical that it forces itself into the structure and content of the preaching of the gospel. But this creates a special problem. Election must be preached because it makes preaching legitimate. There is truly no tension or contrast between the election of God and the gospel. But is there also a relationship between the gospel and rejection? When Hoeksema posed this question, he stated that it did not have to be defended that rejection ought to have a place in preaching; it should be taken for granted. The question was only which function rejection had in preaching.

In the first place, he says, election appears more gloriously by preaching rejection. Rejection must be preached as "the antithetical shadow-side of election." Although Hoeksema says that election and rejection are not on the same level, and that rejection is "subservient" to election, he nevertheless only formally mentions the preaching of rejection. When Hoeksema becomes more exact, he says that in preaching it must become

clear that the Lord God is sovereign. But it is clear that thereby
he has not yet touched upon the essential problem of the
preaching of rejection, because his conception of rejection is that
of "eternal hatred," and it is striking that in his discussion on
the preaching of rejection he repeatedly mentions the sovereignty
of God.[45] But in spite of a certain restraint here, he nevertheless
retains a scheme of formal parallelism between election and
rejection.

Even though he says that God's love remains the main thing,
that statement can be seen only in the light of his entire conception: "He has elected in eternal love and in, or if you wish, because
of, that love, he has also rejected."[46] It is instructive to note that
when he discusses the role of rejection in preaching the judgment of God, there is not the slightest mention of unbelief in
connection with this judgment, or of the rejection of God by
man. From this it follows that according to Hoeksema the
preaching of rejection is an independent theme, along with the
preaching of the judgment of God. In spite of an attempt to
avoid the parallel, the force of symmetry remains in the preaching
of rejection as the opposite side of election, completely abstracted
from Jesus Christ and God's salvation in the world. This is
not to be identified with the teaching of the Heidelberg Catechism
in Lord's Day 31, which mentions the preaching of salvation
in connection with the preaching of the judgment since these
belong together in the testimony of the gospel.

Behind this judgment-preaching is not symmetry but involvement with the one point of view: "as long as they do not repent."
The preaching of the judgment of God is so closely linked up with
the message of Christ that Lord's Day 31 closes with the words:
"according to this witness of the gospel God will judge, both in
this life and in that which is to come," a statement that is a clear
echo of the testimony in Scripture (Acts 17:31), and is based
on the convicting work of the Holy Spirit — "of sin, because
they believe not on me" (John 16:9). The *kerygma* does not
require the preaching of rejection alongside that of judgment.

45. Hoeksema, *De Plaats der Verwerping in de Verkondiging des
    Evangelies* (1927), pp. 5, 21ff. It is striking in this connection that
    rejection, from the point of view of the elect, must be presented to
    the Church because the Church must understand that "it is not of him
    that willeth, nor of him that runneth, but of God that hath mercy" (p.
    22). It is not very clear why Hoeksema relates this to rejection.
46. *Ibid.*, p. 22.

Lord's Day 31 with its penetrating declaration of God's judgment
is not an incomplete, but truly a complete description of the
keys of the Kingdom.[47]

Only in a deterministic view of election can this be seen as a
delimitation of the sovereign counsel of God. Actually, the description of Lord's Day 31 (in its completeness) conforms to the
teaching of the New Testament. There is not the slightest
possibility that this judgment-preaching could be deepened and
strengthened by means of a fancied symmetry. This judgment-
preaching has its own depth and power by virtue of the gospel.

Hence, preaching testifies of Him who is the revelation of the
love of God and who, because of that love, could say: "For
judgment came I into this world, that they that see not may see;
and that they that see may become blind" (John 9:39). The
preaching of grace and judgment do not run parallel: they form
a unity. That unity expresses everything because it is the whole
counsel of God (Acts 20:27).

One more question needs our attention. What is the meaning
and import of what Scripture calls the "hardening of the heart"?
It is clear that this question is closely connected with the
relationship between election and hardening, as is shown, for
instance, when determinism can hardly distinguish it from
fatalism.

Hardening finds a place in the shadow of symmetry, and is
seen as the essential meaning and purpose of the preaching in
so far as it is addressed to those who, although unknown, are
supposedly rejected by God. The Scriptural references regarding
hardening are further understood in this light. Hardening is seen
as having the function to reveal the causal relation between
God's rejection and man's unbelief and subsequent judgment.
We are of the opinion that this confronts us with a complete
distortion and over-simplification of many Scriptural references.

By way of illustration we cite the view of Hoeksema, who has
spoken of hardening in the above-mentioned manner. When he
attacks the general offer of salvation and thinks that the offer
comes to the reprobate only as command, because God in His
"eternal hatred" means nothing more than that, Hoeksema defines

---

47. See especially K. Dijk, *Het Gericht Gods in de Prediking des Woords*
    (1952), p. 25, on Lord's Day 31. Here, too, the opposite side is men-
    tioned, but it lacks all abstractness (p. 27). The wrath of God may
    not be ignored (pp. 28, 31).

the purpose of preaching more closely. God has His gospel preached to everyone without exception, "with the intent to save the elect, and to harden the others."[48] The result corresponds completely to God's intentions. Hoeksema does not doubt for a moment that we find this doctrine of the hardening of hearts in Scripture. He reminds us of Isaiah 6 (the commission to Isaiah), of Mark 4 (concerning the purpose of the parables), and also — as could be expected — Paul's statement regarding a savor from death unto death and a savor from life unto life.[49] It is not necessary to investigate in detail how he understands these passages. There is great uniformity in the exegesis. All these words are seen as clearly indicating a hardening of heart which is the immediate effect of the eternal rejection of God. And all this is then applied to the purpose of preaching which, for the supposed reprobate, can not mean anything but hardening of the heart.[50]

He who reflects on what Scripture teaches about hardening of the heart will certainly not be able to find the solution by speaking only of the self-hardening of man's heart in sin and unbelief. To do that, the testimony in Scripture would have to be drastically reduced, for it speaks often of God Himself who does the hardening. It is typical of the testimony in Scripture that it speaks of both man's self-hardening and God's hardening of the heart.

First of all we point out how much emphasis Scripture places on man as the cause of hardening. Pharaoh is one of the first to be mentioned in this connection; he hardened his heart again and again after each plague that was sent upon Egypt. But this self-hardening occurred also in Israel. "Harden not your heart" (Ps. 95:8) is the admonishment, with a reminder of Meribah and Massah in the desert. And the seriousness of hardening is clearly manifest in this, that if Israel continues in its hardness of heart, then God in His wrath will not allow it to enter

48. Hoeksema, *Een Kracht Gods*, p. 208; cf. p. 61.
49. *Ibid.*, pp. 84ff.
50. There is much literature about hardening of the heart: F. Hesse. "Das Verstockungsproblem im A. Testament (*Beihefte Z. A. W.*, No. 74.) 1955; K. L. Schmidt, "Die Verstockung des Menschen durch Gott" (*Theol. Zeitschr.*, 1945, pp. 1-17; P. Althaus, *Die Christliche Wahrheit*, II, 436ff; W. Eichrodt, *Theologie des A. Testaments*; K. L. Schmidt in Kittel, *T.W.N.T.*, V, 1027, and many articles in Kittel regarding the parables.

into His rest (Ps. 95:11). Self-hardening is man's doing which leads ever deeper into darkness; "he that hardeneth his heart shall fall into mischief" (Prov. 28:14). It can be described as traveling a road of less and less receptivity, as no longer listening or seeing: "But they refused to hearken, and pulled away the shoulder, and stopped their ears, that they might not hear. Yea, they made their hearts as an adamant stone, lest they should hear the law, and the words which Jehovah of hosts had sent" (Zech. 7:11).

A heart as an adamant stone is the ultimate result of self-hardening. It is a heart of stone which can be affected only by God (Ezek. 11:9, 36:26), but then truly only by a miracle, because the dynamic process of self-hardening results in ever more severe petrification (cf. Deut. 5:7).

Not only in the Old Testament, but also in the New Testament we meet with hardening of the heart. We read of the reaction of disobedience and hardening against the preaching of the apostles (Acts 19:9). The Gentiles are described in the hardening of their hearts (Eph. 4:18). As in Psalm 95 Israel is warned, so the Church is admonished not to harden its heart (Heb. 3:13). And — not to mention more — in the encounter between Christ and His disciples there is mention of their hardening their hearts.[51] When they do not recognize Christ walking on the sea, the reason is not simply inadequate sense perception but the result of the fact that in the previous miracle they had not truly seen Jesus in His miraculous power, "for they understood not concerning the loaves, but their heart was hardened" (Mark 6:52).

This shows the undeniable danger and seriousness of hardening the heart. One thing is clear, however: we may not bring hardening into a direct and causal relation with eternal rejection. Such a relationship must definitely be rejected as simplistic, for it does not recognize how varied are the instances of hardening in Scripture. Scripture does not warrant a division into elect and reprobate as those who are, and who are not, hardened. It presents hardening as a fact of life, deep down in man's heart which is subject to all kinds of changes. It is impossible to draw conclusions regarding the background of eternal hardening. And Scripture teaches what God can do with a heart of stone. It

---

51. We think also of the threefold denial by Peter, a process of hardening, although the word as such is not mentioned. Evidently, in denial, too, there is a progressive process (Matt. 26:70).

warns against hardening (II Chron. 30:8) and calls man to turn from his hardness (Jer. 3:12). When the disciples of the Lord have hardened their hearts, He does not reject them but He teaches them so that they may repent of their hardness. This Scriptural testimony does not make hardness less serious, but it shows that it is not absolute; it can be changed. Evidently there is for the disciples a way which leads from hardness of heart to love and apostleship. It is not a way which man can walk in his own strength. In man himself there always lies something of the irrevocability of hardening. But this human absoluteness is not absolute in the eyes of God.

That is why it is not permissible to say that hardening of the heart is the correlate of reprobation and to interpret all Scriptural texts in that light. He who thus petrifies everything which in Scripture is fluid — under divine admonishing — can no longer see how it is possible that the irrevocability of hardening of the heart can be limited and taken away by God (cf. Jer. 7:21-28).

But Scripture mentions also that God hardens man's heart. Think, for instance, of Pharaoh's refusal to let Israel leave Egypt. We read not only of Pharaoh's self-hardening but also of God's sovereign deed. He announces that He will harden Pharaoh's heart (see Ex. 4:21; 7:3; 9:12; 10:1, 20, 27; 11:10; 14:4), while Paul in Romans 9 points at precisely this act of God as an act of His sovereignty. It is not an arbitrary sovereignty, but an act in which God makes Pharaoh a tool in the revelation of His power and glory in Israel. Likewise we read of Sihon that God hardened his mind and heart in order "that he might deliver him into thy hand" (Deut. 2:30). But there is also mention of hardening within the nation of Israel. This is often indicated in terms that point to a continuation in sin. Sin is not an incidental occurrence which soon belongs to the past; it is trespassing, and calls forth the reaction of God's holiness and wrath. It then can happen that He abandons His entire people, or individuals among them, and thus reveals His holy, majestic justice (Rom. 1:24). We see such a judicial act of God in what Stephen relates concerning the golden calf when he says: "But God turned, and gave them up to serve the host of heaven" (Acts 7:42). The text in Isaiah has drawn much attention in this connection because it plays an important role in the New Testament. After Isaiah was called to service, he was told to say to his people: "Hear ye indeed, but understand not; and see ye indeed, but perceive not. Make the heart of this people fat, and make their ears heavy, and shut their eyes; lest they see with their eyes, and hear with their ears, and understand with their heart, and turn again and be healed" (Isa. 6:9-10).

It is almost incomprehensible that this passage has been quoted as "proof" for the hardening of the reprobate from eternity. In Isaiah 6 there is indeed mention of an act of judgment, but in that act of God the issue is not the self-evident purpose of preaching as seen in the light of reprobation. Rather, this passage has bearing on the sins of Israel. It cannot be denied that hardening is indicated as the purpose of Isaiah's mission, but this word can be understood only if it is seen as a righteous judgment against the sin of the people. The hardening effect of his preaching is inseparably connected with that. Furthermore, Isaiah does not stabilize this hardening in his thinking, but answers prayerfully: "How long, Lord?" — a question whose import is completely contrary to that interpretation which maintains that there is no mystery in Isaiah 6 since a child can understand that it does not mean to be a serious offer of grace.[52] It is precisely this chapter which speaks of a holy remnant (Isa. 6:13). And it is Israel which laments: "O Jehovah, why dost thou make us to err from thy ways, and hardenest our heart from thy fear? Return for thy servants' sake, the tribes of thine inheritance" (Isa. 63:17).

It is understandable that particularly Isaiah 6 comes so clearly to the fore in the New Testament. Hesse remarks that this chapter remains difficult to harmonize with religious experience and therefore stands by itself.[53] But he does point to the New Testament continuation of Israel where it stands before Christ as the fulfillment of the salvation of God. With that, we are confronted with a much discussed parallel in connection with the purpose of preaching, especially in the parables.

Christ said that He gave the meaning of the parable of the sower to His disciples so that they could understand the mysteries of the Kingdom, but "to the rest in parables; that seeing they may not see, and hearing they may not understand" (Luke 8:9-10).

There has been much discussion about this quotation from Isaiah, especially in connection with variations in the Synoptic Gospels, and the discussion has been concentrated on God's part in hardening man's heart. Here we must be careful not to minimize the seriousness of the problem. We may not authoritatively judge these Scriptural references on the basis of a self-

---

52. Hoeksema, *Een Kracht Gods,* p. 84.
53. Hesse, *op. cit.,* p. 60.

constructed concept of God.   Such passages tell of God's acts against and through sin, of which Scripture frequently speaks.[54] Moreover, every attempt to weaken Christ's words must be rejected; they must be understood in their profound significance. At the same time, it must be remembered that we are not to give them a "hard" meaning which does not actually belong to them. We may plead for recognition of God's sovereignty, but we must beware that no deterministic interpretation is attached to it.

When we read of the purpose of the parables, for instance in John, "For this cause they could not believe, for that Isaiah said again . . ." (John 12:39), we see why this deterministic view has some plausibility.   Does Jesus not speak of a "not being able to," which can only be interpreted as an excuse?   One can see these words about powerlessness in a deterministic light, and then further compare this hardening, this blinding, to that other blinding, of which Scripture says that the god of this age has blinded the minds of the unbelieving (II Cor. 4:4).   To be sure, they are placed opposite each other, the divine and the satanic blinding, but they can nevertheless be viewed structurally and causally as on the same level.   But in this manner all light that shines here is extinguished.

In Scripture the issue in hardening is never an arbitrary, causal matter.   The divine hardening is closely related to the message of salvation, to the preaching of the gospel which evokes a decision.   Not only in the parables are we confronted with decision.   Christ Himself spoke of His coming in these words: "For judgment came I into this world, that they that see not may see; and they that see may become blind" (John 9:39).   This word "that" places the coming of Christ before us in its "crisis" character, in its dual orientation: illumination and blinding.   This is not a matter of parallelism, because this duality is inseparably connected with the message of salvation.

The gospel does not leave unchanged the person who does not listen and remains disobedient; it compels him to go the way of estrangement and judgment.   In that way we see the ripening process, and when it is said that "they could not believe," that inability is not the result of a decree by a *potentia absoluta* but the holiness of the judgment of God, which is increasingly real-

54. At various occasions Scripture mentions a progressive process, a ripening, a deterioration, without mentioning the acts of God explicitly. We think of the words regarding the last state of a man becoming worse than the first (Luke 11:23-27; II Peter 2:20ff.).

ized in such unbelief. It is a terrible misconception when one interprets the "either-or" of many Scripture passages (fall-resurrection, illumination-blinding, life-death) in the light of a symmetry between election and rejection. The "either-or," deterministically interpreted apart from Christ and His gospel, is contrary to the whole intent of Scripture.

The New Testament teaches an "either-or" only in connection with Christ and His salvation. It does not teach a parallelism, but a stumbling-block and foolishness (I Cor. 1:23), a savor of death unto death and a savor of life unto life (II Cor. 2:16). All abstraction is foreign to this contrast where Paul first praises God that He spreads everywhere the fragrance of the knowledge of Christ. The same gospel gives a fragrance of Christ among those who are saved and those who are on their way to perdition.[55] That is why it is incorrect to employ this passage to repudiate a general offer of salvation.[56] For then the function of the gospel is completely misunderstood. There is no symmetry; rather, there is a profound distinction which can be understood only in the light of the gospel. "Corresponding to the dual character of the gospel, He becomes as its herald at the same time judgment to those that oppose Him.[57]

When Isaiah 6 is quoted in connection with the parables, we see the judgment of God's acts in connection with sin. It cannot be denied that Christ speaks in the parables with finality with respect to the hardening of the heart. The conjunction "that" may certainly not be tampered with, nor the duality in John 9:39. But neither may it be used only formally, and by itself, and pressed into a general discussion of the purpose of preaching, as if it were a direct means to that goal. Rather, "that" can be correctly understood only in connection with the message, the mystery of the Kingdom of God, the coming of Christ into the world as a crisis. The language of the parables is not to be interpreted as an obscure way of revealing an objective purpose, namely, hardening of the heart. Rather, such language reveals that unbelief can lead only to progressive hardening of the heart. In the way of faith and communion with Christ there is a progressive increase and ever deeper understanding, but in the way of unbelief there

---

55. F. W. Grosheide in his Commentary on II Corinthians, p. 98.
56. See H. Hoeksema, *Een Kracht Gods*, p. 94, who poses this thesis: "It is a savor of life unto life and a savor of death unto death and that according to the express intent of God."
57. Kittel, *T.W.N.T.*, V, 494.

is progressive estrangement which makes the unbeliever ripe
for the judgment.

He who detaches this hardening from the decisive soteriological significance of Christ has nothing left but the causality of
reprobation and hardening of the heart, so that he no longer can
get the correct perspective on God's judicial acts or man's responsibility with respect to his ever increasing sin. The gospel, however, is far removed from determinism, even in those texts regarding the hardening of man's heart. For according to the
gospel human inability comes about only through sinful response
to the preaching of the gospel. That is why we should reflect on
that hardening with "fear and trembling." It is impossible to
draw conclusions from it apart from the way of faith, confession
of sin, and prayer, and simply say: "God hardens. Why
dost Thou harden our hearts?" That can be asked only in
prayer and supplication, as did Israel when it recognized its sins
and called for new favor. Otherwise we do not understand
God's judgment and His wrath, and the problem may arise as to
which part of the hardening is God's and which ours. One can
speak of God's hardening only after every excuse has been replaced by a confession of sins and a prayer for His return. The
reasoning from causality then becomes impossible, because hardening is not the result of a fateful decree but an act of God which
manifests its judgment upon man's sinful self-determination.
And for that reason hardening is forever distinguished from fate.
Behind fate stands the impersonal power of determinism, but
behind hardening of the heart stands a God who repeats: "Do
not harden your hearts!"

In this light, all passages about hardening are far removed even
from a semblance of determinism. We see that nowhere more
clearly than when Christ Himself, who knew of the prophecy
of Isaiah 6, is saddened about the hardening of hearts (Mark
3:5). Both His sadness and His wrath must be seen in the light
of His saving act unto salvation.

This is different from a determinism with a conception of God
all its own, whereby the overcoming of the hardening of the
heart is quite impossible. In the gospel we meet another
kind of determinism. It is more tremendous and more serious
than any other determinism imaginable. Its power and seriousness never have the character of fatality because they manifest
themselves in and through man's sin. With recognition of sin,
the hardening of heart is therefore never seen as fate but as

punishment for leaving God's ways. And therein the irrevocability of hardening as a human act becomes evident.[58] In the
hardening, there is nothing left on which man can fall back as
a last resort in order to return. The power of hardening is too
great for that. Man — also believing man — must be warned
against it as against sinning against the Holy Spirit.

Hardening can never be broken by man in his own power.
There is no other therapy that can bring about a change
except the divine healing in Christ and the superior power of the
Spirit. For man's heart is cunning, deadly, more than anything
else. Only in God's mercy lies the power, when the Word of
God as the sword of the Spirit revokes the irrevocable in an
act of grace. Therein lies the perspective of preaching, a perspective that certainly does not become uncertain because of the
doctrine of free election but rather is possible through and because of the election of God.

And in connction with hardening of the heart there can be no
conflict between election and preaching. That would be the case
only if we should consider the act of hardening as an impersonal determination apart from the gospel. But when the connection with the gospel is understood, everything becomes different, because of the voice of Him who hardens. For then the
gospel does not become merely an announcement of the salvation
of God, but a calling voice which, promising and warning, goes
out to man. In this unity, the seriousness of hardening and of
judgment is by no means minimized, but the irrevocability of it
is broken in the presence of grace, in the warning of the gospel
against hardening with that seriousness with which Scripture
warns against crucifying afresh the Son of God and putting Him
to an open shame (see Heb. 6:6).

The Church of Christ is compelled thus to preach the gospel.
It knows that its salvation did not come from its own flesh and
blood and that the change of the heart of stone is not an act of
the individual, but God's saving cure. If hardening is to be
overcome, we must see in the light of Scripture that what is
impossible with man — because of the nature of hardening — is
possible with God. The Church knows that the *non posse non
peccare,* which assumes its most serious form in hardening of
the heart, cannot be remedied by man himself. That is why the
Church can go out into the world which lies in darkness. It will

58. Cf. J. Ridderbos on Deut. 29:3, in *Korte Verklaring,* II, 87.

thereby not overestimate the world, but address it in its sin. But the Church does not, because of the world's sin, stop preaching salvation, and it does not therefore abandon the world. It may not do that on the basis of election, since the Church itself knows that it too has been called out of darkness into the light by a free and sovereign election. This constant reminder is the only guarantee the Church has against all passiveness and against all deterioration of its missionary calling in the world.

The act of God in the preaching of the gospel by man is not an accidental means God has resorted to. He calls men to this task, to give testimony to that light that has become their salvation. And it is by no means true that the doctrine of election leaves no room for the preaching of the gospel. Rather, that preaching finds its decisive and only foundation in the free mercy of God.

CHAPTER EIGHT

SUPRA- AND INFRALAPSARIANISM

I T is necessary to occupy ourselves with that well-known dispute within the Reformed doctrine of election which is usually called the struggle between supra- and infralapsarianism.

This controversy of the seventeenth century often reveals profound aspects, and although it was usually regarded as an intra-confessional dispute, the controversy sometimes revived with great sharpness as each opposing side discovered in the view of the other a total theological concept that exerted its influence on the understanding of the gospel as a whole. And it was certainly not because it wished to penetrate more deeply into the mystery of God's election, but rather to keep peace, that the Synod of Utrecht in 1905 saw itself compelled to give a brief synopsis of this theological dispute. But also afterwards it has become clear that this difference in view does not belong merely to the past, for in the controversy about the Covenant questions were raised which were very reminiscent of those problems of the past even though the concepts *supra* and *infra* were not used. And for those who thought that this was only a matter of scholastic hairsplitting, it must come as a great surprise that Barth in his doctrine of election discusses this old struggle very thoroughly and attempts to trace its deepest motives.[1]

But in spite of this renewed interest, many are aware of the fact that we face here a subtle controversy which owes its existence to a trespassing of the boundaries set by revelation. The terminology employed (supra-infra) sounds strange, and it has been asked whether theology has not become a *gnosis* which can never become quite transparent to the Church and can never really affect the Church's belief.

---

1. About the supra-infra controversy see, among others, K. Dijk, *De Strijd Over Infra- and Supralapsarisme in de Gereformeerde Kerken in Nederland*, 1912; *Om 't Eeuwig Welbehagen*, 1924; *Van Eeuwigheid Verkoren*, 1952; J. L. Hulst, *Supra en Infra*, 1892; K. Barth *Kirchliche Dogmatik*, II, 2, (1942), 136ff.; J. G. Woelderink, *De Uitverkiezing*, 1951; L. v. d. Zanden, *Praedestinatie*, 1949.

There is also the fact that in the discussion of this dispute we often hear of partialities, both in supra and infra, and of the insolubility of this struggle. But we cannot brush these questions aside by appealing to the simplicity of the gospel. The Reformed churches have been responsibile for keeping this struggle alive, and if we now think that this burden is really too heavy, and that at least this one problem of the many can be thrown off, it will be at least necessary to see why that is possible and also necessary. This matter is all the more urgent since it touches upon the doctrine of election — the heart of the Church — and no speculation is permissible here.

Is it perhaps true that this controversy never reached a satisfactory solution because it was purely speculative? In other words, must we indeed choose between supra and infra? Or is it possible to say with Spanheim that in the pulpit we are supra, but in preaching and teaching infra?[2] This strange way of putting the problem evokes the question whether we are here really confronted by a dilemma of faith and if we are not obeying the teaching of Scripture if we refuse to make a choice here.

The urgency of these questions is all the more obvious since the Synod of Utrecht in 1905 gave a short synopsis of this dispute and said "that our Confessions, certainly with respect to the doctrine of election, follow the infralapsarian presentation," but that "this does not at all imply an exclusion or condemnation of the supralapsarian presentation."[3] The word "presentation" in both cases strikes our attention because it suggests specific approaches from both sides which do not necessarily exclude each other.

The apparent intention is to call for peace, and a confessional and therefore religious schism between infra and supra is denied. On the one hand it is said that it is not permissible to present the supralapsarian view as the official doctrine of the Reformed Church, but on the other hand it is not permissible to interfere with someone who adheres to the supralapsarian view. The word "view" which replaces the earlier "presentation" indicates again a certain outlook, an approach with an unmistakable subjective element which is subject to variation without affecting the heart

2. Bavinck, *Gereformeerde Dogmatiek*, II, 346. A. G. Honig calls this *"insincere"* (*Handboek der Gereformeerde Dogmatiek*, p. 268).
3. *Acta* 1905, p. 207.

of the Church. The Synod of Utrecht in 1905 did not intend
to give a definite solution to this problem but, rather, warned
its members to speak as little as possible of such matters which
go beyond the understanding of simple believers, and it gave the
concrete advice to adhere as closely as possible in preaching and
catechetical teaching to the presentation given by the Confessions.[4]

But even this attempt to keep peace, with its many qualifications
and concessions, still confronts us with questions about the
nature of this curious dispute, questions which are so urgent
because they are directly related to the Confessions of the Church.
Why was it said that the Confessions give an infra presentation
but at the same time that a certain freedom must be allowed to
the supra position?

The first thing to do is to give a description of the controversy.
From the terms supra and infra it appears already that the point
at issue is the relation between predestination and the fall (*lapsus*).
The Latin words from which the struggle derived its name may
give it a rather speculative appearance, as though to create the
impression that we are far away from the simplicity of faith;
but they may not prevent us from inquiring concerning the deepest motive of this controversy.[5]

Many descriptions of this dispute present the point at issue
as a difference of opinion regarding the order of God's decrees.
In this connection the impossible and unsatisfactory aspects of
both these solutions is brought out, and the question arises whether
this problem of order does not presuppose a transposition of
the temporal succession into the eternity of God's counsel, and
whether that does not harbor the *vitium originis* of this insoluble
problem.

It is quite apparent that there is more to this than meets the
eye, otherwise the two sides would have come to a solution much
sooner. Can it really be only a logical problem, a matter of sharp
and consequent thinking, of speculation about the "eternity" of
God's counsel in the historical terms of "before" and "after"?
The history of this dispute indicates clearly that much more is
involved than a mere question regarding order. Dijk was therefore quite correct when he opposed the opinion that the actual

---

4. *Ibid.*, p. 208.
5. Cf. A. Kuyper, *E Voto*, II, 168 on the contention that this is an aca-
    demic problem.

point at issue lies in the "order."[6] At least that was not the original problem. Only in the later development of the doctrine of election the element of succession began to play an important role.

Originally it was a matter of different interpretations of the relationship between predestination and the fall. The question arose whether in the counsel of God the fall of man had been willed by Him. According to Dijk, two different answers were given: the answer of Luther, Zwingli and Calvin, who all taught that the fall was comprised in the counsel of God, and the answer of Bullinger, who did not dare to go that far, but wanted to speak only of *praescientia*.

In this connection there was also a difference in the interpretation of rejection. According to the first view, rejection was ultimately based on the good pleasure of God, while according to the second view it was primarily connected with sin (*praevisio peccati*). "And this," says Dijk, "is the fundamental difference between supra and infra." He calls the view according to which the problem is a matter of succession, "incomplete."[7] Bullinger, as a representative of the original infra position, saw rejection as an act of God's justice against sin, which therefore preceded the *justitia*, and upon which the divine answer of the *justitia* followed. This shows clearly that the relation between predestination and the fall is at stake. But at the same time it becomes understandable how later on out of this original controversy a modified controversy could issue. For when it was more and more generally understood that the concept of *praescientia* did not offer a solution for the relationship between the counsel of God and sin, the fall was considered part of the counsel of God. But at the same time the logical question arose as to how that was to be understood, for there was apriori an unhesitant adhering to the doctrine that God was not the author of evil, and that it was impossible to think of a predestination to evil. What, then, was to be the interpretation of the fall being part of God's counsel? Was rejection as a part of the counsel of God a reaction against sin, or had rejection apriori no bearing on that sin? It was in connection with these questions that the difference between supra and infra received its aspect of a problem of succession.

6. K. Dijk, *De Strijd*, Chapter I.
7. *Ibid.*, p. 30.

In my opinion it can thus be said that the problem Bullinger met returned in the later form of the controversy as the infra view, but as a view which had bearing only on what had been decided within the counsel of God. To be sure, the later infra concept did not seek the solution in the *praescientia,* but the problem is the same. Bullinger's question whether sin could have been part of the counsel of God continued to live in the question how that had happened and how that was to be understood. From this issued the question concerning the succession of God's decrees, in which the relation between predestination and fall again became a problem, albeit now within the counsel of God.

The difference between supra and infra has often been formulated thus: the object of predestination according to the supra position is the *homo creabilis et labilis,* and according to the infra position the *homo creatus et lapsus.* This formulation is correct but it must be remembered that this *homo creatus et lapsus* is not a concrete, already existing mankind, but man as he appears in the counsel of God as already created and fallen.

In the supra position the first decree is that of predestination, which is thought to precede the decree of creation and fall. The later decrees of God (creation and fall) are then subsumed under this first decree of God. They form, so to speak, the means by which that primary predestination decree becomes realized. The decree to election and rejection precedes all other decrees. In this decree man does not yet figure as fallen man, so that God's primary goal is not connected with sin. To be sure, in this position there is also a connection between sin and ultimate rejection (the judgment), but this happens in time, in history, and sin does not play any part in the apriori decree. Hence, rejection is, in the counsel of God, more an act of God's sovereignty than of His justice. God's primary plan, His first apriori decree — also as decree to rejection — is a decree of His eternal pleasure.

In the infra position the situation is different, especially the connection between the decree to rejection and that to creation and fall. In this position the relation between sin and judgment (on earth) are considered as being part of the counsel of God.

According to this position the decree to creation and fall logically precedes the decree to rejection and election, so that in the counsel of God rejection presupposes a fallen mankind. This rejection then changes its nature, and is more an act of His justice than of His sovereignty. This does not imply that the infra position denies the sovereignty of God, but in it the idea of God's wrath and reaction (God's justice) is dominant and central just as God's mercy is in election.

Bavinck has pointed out that the supralapsarian presentation "has not been incorporated in a single Reformed Confession"[8] but that the infra position has received an official place in the Confessions of the churches.[9] It is not difficult to understand what Bavinck means when we remember that in the Reformed Confessions predestination is continually brought to bear on the fallen human race. We read in Lord's Day 21 of the Heidelberg Catechism, for instance, that the Son of God has chosen a Church to life eternal out of the human race, and in Article 16 of the Belgic Confession that God preserves from perdition all whom He in His eternal and unchangeable counsel out of mere goodness has elected. To be sure, there is mention here of saving from perdition as the act of God which refers to the elect, but the infra position is evident from the emphasis on God's merciful election. Nothing is said of a separate decree of predestination preceding other decrees, for example, those of creation and fall. We notice the same thing in other Confessions, for instance, in the *Confessio Helvetica Posterior,* where we read of God's sovereign predestination out of mere grace,[10] and in the *Confessio Gallicana,* which speaks of God's goodness and mercy by which God elects and saves from corruption and damnation." Also other Confessions speak in the same manner.[12] In itself, however, this does not yet imply a decidedly infralapsarian presentation, because there is usually no mention at all of any succession in the decrees of God, but election is rather presented as having a bearing on

8. Bavinck, *op. cit.,* pp. 327f.; K. Dijk, *op. cit.,* p. 279
9. *Ibid.,* pp. 329, 346; see also the position of Utrecht, 1905.
10. Müller, *Bekenntnisschriften,* p. 181.
11. "We believe that God in His eternal and immutable counsel elects out of this corruption and general condemnation into which all men have fallen those whom he has chosen in His goodness and mercy in the Lord Jesus Christ" (Müller, *op. cit.,* p. 224).
12. For instance, *Erlauthaler Bekenntnis* (1562): *"Ex eadem massa hominum . . . ex peccatoribus quos voluit juxta beneplacitum in sese elegit et praedefinivit ad vitam aeternam ex morte aeterna"* (Müller, *op. cit.,* p. 276).

the perdition from which God saves. Dijk has continually and
correctly pointed this out,[13] although there are exceptions when
the infra position comes more explicitly to the foreground.[14]

But with that we are confronted with a very peculiar state of
affairs, namely, that the Reformed Confessions are called infra
(follow the infra presentation), but do not intend to exclude
the supra entirely. What did the Synod of Utrecht in 1905
mean by saying that it is not permissible to present the supralapsarian view as *the* doctrine of the Reformed Churches, when
it did not add that the infra is the doctrine of the Churches,
although this view seems to be found in the Confessions? Are
we confronted here with an impossible compromise, or is there
a pure and responsible motive for the purpose of keeping peace?

The complexity of the situation is accentuated still more when
we read what Bavinck says, namely, that the infra position has
been officially adopted in the confession of the Church,[15] while
later on in his analysis of supra and infra he says that each view
errs at a certain point. They both are guilty of one-sidedness
and neither of the two is quite satisfactory.[16]

Nowhere in the field of symbolics and dogmatics are we confronted with such problems regarding the official formulation of
the Church as we are with regard to supra and infra. One wonders whether it is possible at all to shed any light on these
remarkable complications.[17]

For that purpose we must first of all investigate why those
who are really inclined to one or the other view sometimes make
such vague statements. Bavinck has attempted to show that the
two views are not completely contrary to each other, and Dijk
writes: "Although the supra presentation is the one of the Ref-

---

13. K. Dijk in *De Strijd,* Chapter V, points out that the *Confessio Gal-
    licana* was adopted by the Synod of La Rochelle in 1561, of which
    Beza was the chairman (p. 284).
14. E. g., the *Formula Consensus* of 1645 regarding the order of the
    decrees: creation, allowing of the fall, election (Dijk, *ibid.,* p. 293).
    "Gomarus hardly could have subscribed to the *Formula Consensus.*"
15. Bavinck, *op. cit.,* p. 329.
16. *Ibid.,* pp. 351-52. A. G. Honig, *op. cit.,* p. 268, says, "Both can be criti-
    cized, and that is the reason why neither of the two views can be
    adopted as the correct one."
17. The so-called Five Theses (regarding doctrines about which dif-
    ferences have occurred in recent years in the Reformed Churches
    in the Netherlands) are far more positive in expressing an opinion.

ormation, no one will maintain that the infra presentation is contrary to Calvin's teachings."[18]

According to Dijk, there is no contrast of principles. Each uses the other's terms to such an extent that there is no infra that does not turn to the supra, while both not only appeal to Scripture, but have a right to do so. No doubt Dijk refers here to the supra and the later infra, because both saw the fall as part of the counsel of God. Only concerning supra and the later infra does Dijk mean to say that they together do justice to the riches of revelation.[19]

Bavinck, too, says that there are points of contact, and he thinks the matter is one of approach. There is no difference regarding the decrees proper and their content, but while infra adheres to the historical-causal order, supra emphasizes the apriori sovereignty. The infra, says Bavinck, appeals to all those passages in Scripture "where election and rejection have bearing on a fallen world and are presented as acts of mercy and justice," while supra refers to those texts that speak of God's sovereignty. But since each of them appeals to "a certain group of texts" and does not do justice to other passages, they suffer from one-sidedness.[20]

The infra presentation must be praised for its modesty, but it does not give complete satisfaction because if God made the decree of rejection after that of allowing sin, the question still arises why God has permitted sin. If that allowing is more than *nuda praescientia,* then the fall must ultimately have been part of God's counsel and therefore it "rests" in God's sovereign pleasure. But in that case the infra concept says the same as the supra.[21]

However, these objections against the infra position do not alter the fact that the supra "is at least as unsatisfactory," because it gives only the "appearance of a solution." It embraces only hypothetical persons in election and rejection and even — as with Comrie — a hypothetical Christ. Bavinck finds this error inherent in the concept of supra. Furthermore, the supra concept leads to making eternal punishment the object of God's will in the same manner and in the same sense as life eternal, and to making sin "in the same manner and the same sense" a means

18. K. Dijk, *op. cit.,* pp. 48ff.
19. *Ibid.,* pp. 50ff.
20. *Ibid.,* p. 347.
21. *Ibid.*

to perdition as redemption in Christ is the means to salvation.[22]
For that reason Bavinck calls the infra position modest,[23] tem-
perate, sober, and a mild form of the doctrine of predestination in
comparison with the supra, which also gets itself entangled in
antinomies.[24]

Abraham Kuyper, too, has reflected on the difference between
supra and infra. His criticism of supra is sharp: it is a theory
which is open to severe criticism, especially because thus the
fall into sin is not only deduced from man, but forms a link in
the divine decree; moreover, it evokes the idea of a divine
creating in order to destroy. Kuyper speaks of this as a horrible
thought, in flagrant opposition to the concept of God's inscrutable
mercies."[25]

But that does not mean that Kuyper therefore chooses the infra
presentation. For, says Kuyper, the infra presentation entails
almost equal objections, because it seeks the solution in the
praescientia, the foreseen fall.[26] Neither in supra nor in infra
does he see a solution, and he further mentions the unyielding
fact "that the connection between God's eternal decree and the
fall is inscrutable to us."[27]

We cannot, says Kuyper, deduce the fall from the decree, for
that eliminates sin; nor can we deduce the decree from the
fall, for then there is no longer a decree of the counsel, with
the result that there is no room left for God.

"All systems that have tried to find a solution for this mystery
end either with a weakening of man's consciousness of sin and
guilt, or with a weakening of the sovereignty and self-sufficiency
of God." According to Kuyper, we must conclude with the
acknowledgment that the connection between God's sovereignty
and man's sin "is not revealed to us."[28]

22. *Ibid.,* p. 349.
23. *Ibid.,* p. 347.
24. *Ibid.,* pp. 320ff.
25. A. Kuyper, *E Voto,* II, 170f.
26. The original infra (Dijk).
27. *Op. cit.,* p. 172.
28. *Ibid.* All this must be considered in connection with the discussion
    of L. J. Hulst in *Supra en Infra, Een Woord van Verdediging en Toc-
    lichting der Confessioneele Gereformeerde Leer en Practijk Omtrent
    de Predestinatie en het Genadeverbond* (Grand Rapids, 1892), which
    is especially directed against Kuyper and supralapsarianism.

When we ponder all this, there is one conclusion which forces itself upon us, namely, that the heart of the matter concerns the "relation" between God's counsel and man's fall into sin. Bullinger's questions, his concerns and fears, have remained, even though in the later concept of infra the fall is considered part of God's counsel. The very words "supra" and "infra" already indicate this core of the dispute.

What else could infra mean when its adherents speak of going "above" the fall and of remaining "below" the fall? To be sure, one can say of the supra as well as of the later infra that they both went beyond the fall to the counsel of God, but it is nevertheless understandable that the terms supra and infra continued to be used to indicate the difference. For the problem remained, even in the acknowledgment of the all-comprising counsel of God, and it made its influence felt.

In order to describe the problem more closely, some have advocated changing the term supralapsarianism to "supracreationism." Otto Ritschl, for instance, wrote: "Strictly speaking, this theory could be more correctly called supracreationism."[29] But there are objections here. For, although supra — and infra, for that matter — goes beyond creation, it is nevertheless quite understandable that the terms in this controversy are focused on the *lapsus,* on man's fall. To be sure, the question concerning the meaning and significance of creation entered in — whether creation did not have its own God-given purpose[30] and hence was not more than just a "means" to realize God's primary decree — but the main concern was nevertheless the question concerning the relation between predestination and fall, so that Ritschl's proposal obscures rather than clarifies the problem.

Once we have seen that the struggle between supra and infra does not primarily concern the problem of order but that this problem arose out of reflection on predestination and fall, the question returns whether supra — infra is indeed an unavoidable dilemma. Is there such a drastic difference? Is there a clear

---

29. O. Ritschl, *Dogmengeschichte des Protestantismus* (1926), III, 295. Ritschl says, however, that the term acquired "its correct significance" over against infra.
30. K. Schilder has spoken of the infra-supra controversy in connection with Lord's Day 9 (*Heidelbergse Catechismus,* III, 455ff), because with supra-infra the question arises how God evaluates world history and time. Cf. I, 309ff.

indication in the many vague formulations and in the peace attempt of 1905 that we are here confronted with an insoluble problem?

The problem cannot be solved by an analysis of succession. The problem of time and succession in supra and infra (the order of God's decrees) is part of an altogether different problem. Neither supra nor infra are interested in an abstract time problem, but rather in the background of history and human life, creation, fall, and redemption; and, in all that, especially in the reality of man's fall and sin.

Infralapsarianism especially has always feared that this reality, in all its destructive and sinful power, becomes vague in a pre-destination decree to salvation and to destruction which precedes the decree of creation and the "allowing" of the fall. It is feared that such a conception, by which everything (also the fall and sin) serves the purpose set by the predestination decree, destroys the character of the doctrine of predestination. To avoid that, the decree of creation and of allowing the fall are placed before the predestination decree. In this way the attempt is made, not to isolate these decrees from God's omnipotence but to emphasize the reality of sin in its negative, antithetical character. Election and rejection are for that reason brought to bear on this reality of sin, and although in the infra concept, too, the issue is one of presupposed fall and sin in the counsel of God, the reality of sin is accentuated by the order in which the decrees are placed. Fall and sin are no longer means, but first of all factors of rebel-lion and violation of God's holiness. Furthermore, the adherents of this viewpoint wish to stress the connection between God's decree and sin, so that God's mercy and justice are brought to bear on the reality of the human race. It cannot be said, in my opinion, that the Reformed Confessions are infra in the sense that they make explicit pronouncements on the order of the decrees of God, but they evidence great sympathy for the infra presentation when predestination is continually mentioned in such a manner that it is brought to bear on sin and guilt. That is not only the case in the Heidelberg Catechism, Lord's Day 21, and in Article 16 of the Belgic Confession, but also in the Canons. That is especially the case when with respect to the decree of rejection the Canons say that this decree does not make God the author of sin, but declares Him to be an awful, irrepre-hensible, and righteous Judge and Revenger thereof (CD, I, 15).

This shows clearly the relation between the decree to rejection and sin.

The inclination toward the infra concept in the Confessions is shown by the fact that always reference is made to sin and perdition whenever predestination is mentioned. In the supra concept the condemnation in time is directly related to sin because actual judgment presupposes guilt, but not to the decree to rejection itself. This connection is not present, because the decree of predestination is thought to precede all merits and demerits, hence also the decree to creation and the "decree" of the fall. But that the Confessions follow the infra presentation does not imply an obvious and exclusive choice with respect to the succession of God's decrees. Rather, *in abstracto* no reflection on the decrees and their order is intended, but salvation from perdition is seen in the perspective of eternal election (BC, 16). Exactly on that account we see that Reformed theology sometimes contains criticism of infra as well as of supra, but also an unmistakable appreciation for what is called the infra-presentation in the Confessions. That, in my opinion, is the only possible explanation for the peculiar fact that Bavinck, for example, calls the confessions "infra" while at the same time he criticizes the infra as well as the supra presentation. Apparently Bavinck did not intend a criticism of the Confessions themselves, for the Reformed Confessions do not speak about the order of the decrees.[31]

It can therefore be said that in spite of the contrast between supra and infra the Church has been kept from making a definite confessional statement with respect to succession in the decrees of God. If that had actually been done in the so-called infra presentation, it would have been illogical not to reject the supra. And that this did not happen is the bright spot in the struggle between supra and infra, for now we can take a responsible attitude toward the Confession with its "infra presentation" and at the same time understand that the problem of succession in the theological supra and infra is a self-created and therefore insoluble problem which does not touch upon the essential faith of the Church.

31. The matter is discussed by Dijk, who presents striking historical data which shed light on the state of affairs. Regarding the only time that the difference between supra and infra was discussed at the Synod of Dort, see Dijk, *op. cit.,* p. 168.

It may never be forgotten that the Synod of Utrecht in 1905 spoke of doctrines "which go far beyond the understanding of the simple." It may even be asked whether this body went far enough when it gave the advice to refrain as much as possible from preaching about such questions. It seems that in this "as much as possible" there still is some feeling that the problem of succession has significance for the pulpit.

To this it may be said that the quite general criticism of the idea of succession in infra and supra virtually excludes this possibility. Here we agree with Van der Zanden, who says that "we cannot speak of before and after in God's eternal decrees as we do in time, hence the difference between supra and infra can be called imaginary because it implies the application of a temporal order to eternity."[32]

But he who cannot and will not make a choice here can still accept the emphases of the Confessions where they fully honor the implication of predestination regarding the fallen human race. That makes it impossible for us abstractly to discuss the decrees of God. Infra — for all the inacceptability of its problem of succession — has made that more clear to us than supra. It is the pattern of the infra position which is followed in the Confessions, and that is why Utrecht in 1905 gave the advice to adhere as closely as possible to the presentation of the Confessions.[33]

We find the infra motif in Article 16 of the Belgic Confession when it speaks of election from perdition. Salvation is confessed in connection with sin and guilt. There is no apriori mention of the counsel of God; but the depth and the stability and the eternal source, not out of us, but out of God, are confessed in the light of salvation as it is revealed in history. W. H. Gispen says: "From these words it is clear that the Confession does not go beyond the fall and that it does not use preconceptions of God, His sovereignty, etc., but that it adheres closely to history and Scripture, to the revelation of God." For that reason Gispen correctly goes beyond the problems of succession in both supra and infra when he remarks: "It is therefore not the most important question whether God in predestination has accepted man as already created and fallen or as not-yet-created and therefore before the

32. L. v. d. Zanden, *Praedestinatie in Christus,* p. 39; cf. K. Schilder, *op. cit.,* I, 310.
33. *Acta* 1905, p. 208.

fall, but the most important thing is that man's salvation is seen in the light of God's mercy."[34]

It is clear that the problems of succession cannot shed any light. For if supra and infra were taken seriously in this respect, one would have to conclude that in God there are a number of independent decrees. The concept of succession in the doctrine of predestination is a clear form of humanization of God. This judgment is not based on an abstract contrast between time and eternity, but on the simplicity, the majesty, the mercy, and the glory of God. Our rejection of the concept of succession is based on the Biblical testimony regarding the election in Christ. In that light it is impossible to speak *in abstracto* of a predestination decree which is realized by another independent decree to create and to ordain the fall. Nor may that be done for the sake of emphasizing God's sovereignty, as if God's attributes were honored and praised by positing one fundamental attribute on which all others are based. To be sure, the confession of God's sovereignty belongs to the essence of Christianity, and the Church has had to be continually on its guard against attempts to minimize God's sovereignty. But the Church may never defend God's sovereignty by isolating it, for that would unavoidably result in speaking of primary and secondary attributes of God. It has often happened that in speaking thus the Church has confused the concept of God so that this concept revealed the traits of arbitrariness.

Nor is it possible to defend an isolated, apriori decree, whereby God's plan in creation and through sin is not yet immediately transparent, by referring to the glory of God as though this were revealed in a separate predestination decree. Scripture never speaks abstractly of God's glory. That glory meets us in the hymn of praise of creation, but especially where "glory to God" is sung in the fields of Ephratha. And that glory is certainly not meant as a contrast to the salvation which He grants. What is revealed in history and through sin is not the glory of abstract sovereignty,[35] but the glory of sovereign love and loving sovereignty.

34. W. H. Gispen, *De Geloofsbelijdenis der Nederlandse Gereformeerde Kerken* (1932), pp. 90, 98.
35. The manner in which O. Ritschl has associated Beza (and also Calvin) with the French interpretation of the glory of God (*op. cit.,* II, 293; cf. 290-91) is based on a simplistic tradition which suggests that this *gloria* as "philautie" obtains humanized traits.

That is what the infra position correctly recognizes. But to express this insight, infra has chosen a form — that of succession — in which the doctrine of the unity of God's decrees and acts is in jeopardy. The idea of succession takes the form of a preceding decree of creation and a preceding "ordinance" of the fall from which emerges "after that" the decree of predestination. And thus — in spite of the good intentions of the infra presentation — the election in Christ is obscured, and the abstraction of the preceding decree of creation threatens to overshadow the unity of God's decrees and acts.

For that reason it can be said that some benefit resulted from the struggle between supra and infra in that they kept each other in check, that the one was something like a conscience to the other even though it was against the background of the concept of order. At least this background served as a warning.

In the struggle at and around the Synod of Dort we hear of the *phrases duriores* in connection with supralapsarianism. After what we have said about that in Chapter I, we now can add that infralapsarianism also has its dangers. These dangers are not speculative (*praedestinatio ad peccatum!*), but they have to do with historicizing the acts of God. Bavinck's criticism of infra as well as of supra is striking, especially when he points out that the infra position at times has given the impression that the "allowing" of the fall is part of the counsel of God. When Reformed theology occasionally points out the relative correctness of the supra, it does so with an eye to this particular danger in the infra concept.

The Synod of Utrecht in 1905 was also unwilling to choose either supra or infra. It only indicated — and that was sufficient — the infra motif (the orientation of predestination to the fallen human race) as *the* way for preaching and catechetical teaching. We do not hesitate to add that this way is the only safe way for theological reflection too. But this infra motif can degenerate when it attempts to inquire into the counsel of God by way of the concept of succession, so that the mystery in the unity of God's acts is obscured. And that this danger is not imaginary appears from the fact that under the influence of the concept of succession the solution has at times been sought in the *praescientia*.[36] In the concept of succession of both supra and

---

36. K. Dijk points out that Turretin cannot get away from the doctrine of the *praevisio* (*De Strijd*, p. 42). See Chapter II of the present volume regarding the power of the *praescientia* concept.

infra the dual danger ultimately becomes unavoidable: an explanation is given of the relation between God's counsel and sin, and that which can be understood only in the way of faith is rationalized.

Abraham Kuyper once described the difference between supra and infra by saying that infra looks at the counsel of God from the point of view of man, whereas supra looks at it from the point of view of God. And that, to him, constituted the insolubility of the controversy.[37] If this were actually the difference between supra and infra, then new questions would arise; first of all, whether man may look at the counsel of God from the side of God; and secondly, whether in that case the Synod of Utrecht should not have warned against supra. When Kuyper says of the infra that "it stood squarely on the level plane below" we may ask whether that is humanly not the only place from where we can understand anything at all of God's mystery, the mystery of election. For that "from the human side" means that man is a subject to revelation in time, and that in the light of that revelation he understands more and more of the height and depth, length and breadth of salvation, but that this is possible only by being subject to revelation in time. There is not another way, for instance, the way of deduction which proceeds from God's side and from the counsel of God. If the essence of supra lies in that, then the Synod of Utrecht made an irresponsible attempt to keep peace, because it did not repudiate the two possibilities: "from God's side" and "from man's side." But it is not very likely that Kuyper meant such a contrast. He probably had in mind another distinction which has often played a role, namely, that between the apriori and the aposteriori treatment of predestination.[38] Bavinck points out that the Reformed position usually employed the apriori order, since it mentioned predestination already in the *locus de Deo* instead of waiting until the *locus de salute*. And, says Bavinck, in this synthetic apriori method is involved a deeply religious matter.

Clearly Bavinck does not intend here to defend speculation, as if it were quite all right and possible to proceed from the counsel of God. Bavinck is not concerned with an apriori de-

37. A. Kuyper, *Gemecne Gratie,* II, 95.
38. Bavinck, *op. cit.,* II, 321; cf. analytic-synthetic.

duction, based on the counsel of God and apart from revelation, but — also in the *locus de Deo* — with the teaching of Scripture. All he intends to reject is an anthropological construction of the doctrine of salvation which would shift the doctrine of predestination from the *locus de Deo* to the *locus de salute*. In the *locus de Deo,* too, he thinks it possible to speak responsibly of predestination without falling into abstraction.[39]

It all depends on how predestination is discussed. The term apriori (as opposed to aposteriori) can give the impression of abstraction and speculation. But it can, and also does, mean that God's acts, His sovereign and merciful works, are discussed — of course, from man's point of view. And now we see that the infra presentation, too, is no less apriori than the supra, in that it proceeds from the revelation regarding God's decrees.[40]   And for that reason, supra and infra cannot be simply contrasted as apriori and aposteriori.

Both want to proceed from God's revelation. It is understandable, however, that frequently the supra presentation has been connected with the apriori approach because it places the preceding decree of predestination by itself and does not connect it with redemption from sin and perdition until afterwards. Thus, the supra position indeed obtains specifically apriori traits, even though it intends to have this primary decree logicailly, not temporally, precede the other decrees. These a-priori traits open the way to speculation for the *epigones,* and election and rejection are at times spoken of in a manner hardly distinguishable from determinism. The opposition of the infra adherents is not concerned with a preference for an apriori doctrine, but with a defense against the possibility of abstraction and a plea for the original relation of God's counsel to salvation and redemption. Only in this way can the controversy be understood.[41] The point at issue in this controversy is the a-priority as such. The difference becomes transparent as soon as one decree is considered independently and apart from the other. For in so far as either supra or infra makes one decree

---

39. He correctly points out that abstraction and petrification may invade dogmatics later on just as well as at the beginning.
40. Cf. Barth, *K. D.,* II, 2, 143, regarding the place of the doctrine of election in the dogmatics of infralapsarianism.
41. The matter of apriori-aposteriori has played a role in connection with the treatment of predestination by Calvin in the various editions of the *Institutes.*

primary, they become involved in problems which generate a-
priori and aposteriori motifs.[42]

When the Synod of Utrecht in 1905 emphatically pointed
out and warned against absolutizing the infra, it made a con-
tribulation to peace without propagating a compromise.

It is necessary to pay attention to Karl Barth's extensive
analysis of the controversy.[43] He first indicates what he thinks
to be common to the two presentations, namely, that they emphasize the freedom of God's grace over the individual, and they consider predestination as a stable system which is then realized
in history by way of the symmetrical balance between election
and rejection, which originates from and is given with the
decretum absolutum.

To a certain extent Barth appreciates the supra as well as the
infra motifs. Supra is not as speculative as it may seem at first
sight. If one wants to call its adherents "theistic monists,"
then it is at any rate "a Biblical-Christian monism" to which they
adhere. They are concerned with the contemplation of the works
of God. Supra does not want to make that dependent on other
decrees and ordinances, and for that reason it serves "the glorification of free grace" more than infra. But infra, too, may
claim appreciation, especially with respect to "its greater reserve
regarding the reality of the fall and the presence of evil in the
world," as becomes evident from the reference to a decree to
"allow" evil, and from the thesis that sin is not simply a
"means" to realize the decree of predestination. Infra wants to
avoid the danger of supra by leaving the mystery of evil unsolved, and by not making it a component part, a necessity of
nature. Infra recognizes evil in its enigmatic character and
obscurity, more so than supra does.

We could summarize Barth's view thus: supra recognizes and
indicates the danger of dualism; infra the danger of monism.
But Barth does not plead for neutrality, nor does he advocate
choosing according to personal preference; he is of the opinion
that supra is relatively more correct. The criticism of supra
amounts to no more than an indication of its dangers, without
thereby proving that supra is unacceptable as such. Furthermore, says Barth, all of these dangers are really connected with

42. We find a remarkable illustration of this in H. de Cock, *Is de Leer
    der Aboslute Predestinatie Uitgangspunt of Resultaat van de Leer
    der Gereformeerde Kerken?*, 1868.
43. *K. D.*, II, '2, 136-157.

the mutual presuppositions of both supra and infra (the stable
system of election and rejection of the individual). By accepting
a *decretum absolutum,* the supra thesis becomes indeed dangerous and even untenable. But if supra is detached from these
suppositions and the doctrine of election is understood Chris-
tologically, and seen in connection with God's first decree in
Jesus Christ — the triumph of light over darkness — then
supra is to be preferred to infra. For then Jesus Christ becomes
the actual object of predestination, and the object of the supra
presentation can be realized: the predestination in election and
rejection of Christ as the "sum of the gospel."

On the other hand, infra always represents the point of view
derived from the dangers of supra. Hence, it presupposes a
decree of creation and a decree of the fall which precede the
actual predestination. This view cannot really be corrected
but only criticized as leading to the dualism of a natural theology. That is why infra is less able to shed light on the problems that lie at the basis of both supra and infra. The infralapsarians "have offered nothing in the way of a better solution to the problem of the *objectum praedestinationis.*"

It is clear, in the light of the preceding discussion, that we
cannot possibly accept this criticism of the infra presentation.
It strikes us that Barth somewhat retracts his original appreciation for infra. The question is whether the reserve which
Barth originally appreciated in the infra presentation does not
actually render a positive contribution to the pure doctrine of
predestination. For that caution concerned the reality of the
fall and of evil in the world. Precisely at this point much
deeper matters are at stake than simply a contradiction derived
from the dangers of supra. Infra has rendered undeniable
service as a positive warning against and a legitimate rejection
of the idea that sin is a "means" to the realization of the predestination decree. It is correct that this rejection took place
in the form of an objectionable arrangement of succession, but
that does not justify a lack of appreciation for the positive
element in this defense. And for that reason, it is incorrect to
see infra as a gateway to natural theology. Its succession-con-
cept — first creation and fall — can give that impression, but the
deepest motive is not to make creation independent of the counsel
of God, but to warn against "monism," which — also on the basis
of succession — makes the decree of predestination independent
so that it can no longer fully and legitimately relate this decree

to creation, fall, and redemption. That positive warning gives us the sense in which the Reformed Confessions are said to be infralapsarian.

Not independence of creation was the deepest concern of infra, but rather the reality of sin as opposition to God. The interest of infra is not directed at the domain of an *oeconomia naturalis providentiae* as such, but at the significance of creation and the disturbance of sin. The infralapsarians cannot and do not see creation and fall as simply a means to realize God's prime decree. By this rejection, infra can the better avoid a symmetry between election and rejection.

Ultimately infralapsarianism does not solve anything, but it indicates a view of the counsel of God which does not hold God causally responsible for everything, including sin and hell, although it confesses the superiority of God's decrees and acts over evil. Supralapsarianism also tries to avoid this causality, but it cannot really do so legitimately. This supra position can merely say "nevertheless, God is not the author of evil," while infra finds a stouter defense in its (faulty) succession concept. And that, we think, is why Barth's criticism of infra and his relative plea for supra betrays a misrepresentation of doctrinal history. He interprets the hesitation of infra negatively, as being a reaction without any real contribution to the solution of the problem. Actually, it is much more than a negative reaction. Its reserve is essentially related to the inscrutability of God's counsel, and at the same time it points to the superiority of God's plan, and to the place of man before God, a place from which man does not as a spectator survey God's works at one glance but from which he is called to God's electing grace.

After paying some attention to this struggle, it is a joy to find that variations in theological thinking cannot prevent a meeting of minds in the Church of God. The call to peace and tolerance which came from Utrecht in 1905 was in the interest of the Church. That does not mean that the struggle between supra and infra was either valueless or without dangers. But it is striking that in the way of faith — with which doctrine is concerned — things often become clearer than in the way of theologizing. It cannot be denied that the problem of supra and infra, the succession of God's decrees, has found no echo in the Church, and that the controversy, as far as I know, has not entered into the preaching of the gospel. That is not true, however, regarding the background problem from which infra issues, and which especially concerns the place of sin in God's counsel and world rule. This issue concerns not merely theology but the Church and each individual believer as well.

Here aberrations can arise which may be injurious to the Church. One may make monistic deductions from God's all-encompassing counsel, and thus see sin "implied" and "ordained" in such a manner that one loses sight of the teaching of Scripture concerning the destructive power of evil. Sin then seems unavoidable and "necessary" — a mode of thinking which always leads to silent or expressed excuses. God's counsel with respect to sin is then interpreted causally, and thus one ultimately becomes receptive to the idea that evil is ordained and that this accounts for the tragic fate of man.

Out of reaction the other side wishes to defend man's independence. But this leads to a conception which is not monistic but dualistic. It is so impressed by the power of evil and the destructive potentialities of sin that it comes to consider evil, if not the equal, then at least the relatively independent opponent of God's plan for the world, so that it almost overshadows the absolute power of God. What is sin? "Is this dark realm, with its forbidding mysteries, in which depth-psychology aimlessly pokes about, this realm which might justly be called chaos and demonry — is it nature, is it super-nature, is it both or . . . what is it?"[44]

It is clear that both the aspect of triumph and of threat are closely linked to the question concerning the reality of sin in the world. Hence it is that theology, if it refuses to be satisfied with simplistic conclusions, repeatedly encounters this reality, and not in the *locus de peccato* only! That is certainly true with respect to the doctrine of election, as we may discover most clearly in the problems of infralapsarianism. If infra is reserved and even hesitant, that is not because it lacks courage to think logically, but because it believes that man may not deduce his sin from God. This hesitancy does not concern the majesty and glory of God's counsel over all things; it concerns a refusal to explain sin in terms of a causality in God. Infralapsarianism fervently desires to make clear that God is not the author of sin and it is always careful not to introduce in a roundabout way a causality

44. J. Bernhart, *Chaos und Dämonie. Von den göttlichen Schatten der Schöpfung* (1950), p. 22.

on the basis of the symmetry between election and reprobation.

The most striking aspect of this reservedness is that infralapsarianism is nevertheless able to maintain what can be called the essence of the doctrine of election.   There is no hesitation when it comes to confessing God's election from before the foundation of the world, without human merit and without *praevisa fides*.[45] The hesitation originates when it becomes impossible to draw lines of "causality" from man's religious relation to God.   It is especially the infra adherents who see through the seeming logic of referring belief and unbelief back to God, and this explains the infra emphasis in the Confessions, to which the Synod of Utrecht in 1905 so urgently referred.

The danger of infra is its susceptibility, especially at this point, to a dualism which renders God's counsel both independent and relative.   He who sees these dangers and avoids them, will always return to that reserve which neither deducts sin causally from God, nor forgets that God's counsel is independent of man's activity.

It was especially Bavinck who occupied himself with these questions when he reflected on what he called the incorporation of sin in the counsel of God.   He, too, spoke of God's will, but he always surrounded his words with reservations.   He rejected dualism — sin as an independent power over against God — but also every form of predestination *ad peccatum*.   Bavinck's solution was to emphasize the seriousness of sin, which in a certain sense only is willed and determined by God, but not in the same manner as grace and salvation.[46]   Sin is made subservient to the revelation of God's attributes and thus it does not violate God's counsel.   In all of Bavinck's discussions we notice the same reservedness.   When he discusses the idea that there is *necessitas* in sin rather than chance or arbitrariness, but *felix culpa* by virtue of God's purpose, then he adds that in spite of the truth and attractiveness in this presentation, it cannot and may not be accepted, because it still makes God the author of sin.

45. It is striking that Kuyper here takes the side of supra.   He writes that Scripture reveals "that the actual salvation of the elect will be the fruit and result of an eternal love which created them according to this election, formed them according to this election, and will save them according to this election, (*E Voto*, II, 172).   Dijk writes that Kuyper takes the supralapsarian point of view.

46. Bavinck, *op. cit.*, II, 354.

Over against that he places the unreasonableness of sin. Sin is not necessary for the existence of man and still less for the existence of God. If sin often serves to reveal the good more clearly, that happens only by virtue of God's wisdom and sovereignty. There is, indeed, a relation between sin and the counsel of God, but it is not the relation of causality.

Nor can the concept of "allowing sin" bring the solution. This concept actually removes sin from God's counsel and providential government.[47] When Bavinck himself begins to formulate — after rejecting the *permissio* — we notice his hesitations. They become, as it were, tangible: God is at the most the negative cause, not *causa efficiens,* but *causa deficiens.* His only concern is to reject aberrations and to think in terms of God's superiority, His counsel, and His acts in and over and through evil. He has "allowed" sin but He "would not have condoned it if He had not been able to rule it in an absolutely holy and sovereign manner." As the Almighty, He did not fear its existence, because He knew He could rule absolutely over sin. Here the way becomes visible on which man, although he does not see the connection,[48] can walk before the eyes of God. For now there is on the one hand the impossibility of excuse, and on the other hand the refuge of God's grace.

Thus theology refrains from taking a way other than the one on which every believer may walk. Perhaps it is precisely at this point that the deepest motifs of supra and infra touch each other without conflict. They are motifs of the simplicity (unity) of God's almighty counsel on the one hand, and of the rebellion *contra,* but not *praeter, voluntatem Dei* on the other. In this harmony between supra and infra motifs the concept of succession has fallen away, and there is no reason to create a distance between the preacher and the theologian.

The prospect and the call for the Church remain safeguarded. We confess that "now we see in a mirror, darkly," and "now I

---

47. *Ibid.,* III, 34-41.

48. Bavinck has made one more statement in which, I think, he goes a step further and which reminds us of the *felix culpa:* "If He had not granted its existence, there would have always been room for the thought that He was not in all His attributes above a power of which the possibility was implied in creation" (III, 42). I would bring the same objections against this attempt of explanation as those which I mentioned against Barth's speaking of sin as the *Nichtige.* See my *Triumph of Grace in the Theology of Karl Barth.*

know in part" (I Cor. 13:12), but in so doing we do not merely set limits to our knowledge. For these limits are established in the love and hope of the believer, who one day will know fully face to face. Within this boundary it is possible truly to walk, not by sight, but by faith (II Cor. 5:7).

CHAPTER NINE

ELECTION AND THE CERTAINTY OF SALVATION

THERE is good reason to discuss separately the relationship between election and the certainty of salvation. This relationship, to be sure, has already come to the foreground several times, and each time it was clear how intimately this matter of certainty is related to the election of God. When we now devote a chapter to this relationship, we are aware of the danger of an individualism which is interested only in man's personal life and certainty. In spite of this danger, the subject is very legitimate, and it has come to the fore again and again in the history of the doctrine of election.

It has arisen especially with the question whether the confession of free and sovereign election is not a threat rather than a comfort to the certainty of salvation. Besides, how often do we not actually experience, in the practice of faith, a certain tension between election as the far-removed act of God and our own assurance? Many attempt to escape this tension by consciously or unconsciously pushing the doctrine of election into the background. Since the election of God does not give any solid support, they look for something that can better afford them a strong foundation for the joyfulness of faith. They look for some compensation against the ever threatening aspects of the election of God in all its inscrutability.

It is obvious that compensation is often sought in man himself, *qua* believer; for things outside of man, such as the Bible, the Church, the Word and sacraments, are also threatened by the all-inclusive fact of predestination and therefore cannot counterbalance the tormenting uncertainty.

In this state of affairs the final question is whether it is possible to escape the tensions of the doctrine of election by way of self-contemplation and self-analysis, in an attempt to find the possible effects of the election of God in one's self. Or the question may be asked: Can one conclude, on the basis of good works, the apriori certainty of salvation and election?

With that we are confronted with the important question: What is the relationship between the doctrine of election and life, and how is the election of God manifested and effected, especially in sanctification?

When we spoke in a previous chapter of Christ as the mirror of election and as the Book of Life, we pointed out that the pastoral message which is thus oriented does not seem to touch the hearts of the believers very much, and that much uncertainty remains. Is it perhaps true that the reference to Christ, which the Reformation so strongly emphasized, proves to be one-sided and to have an impoverishing effect after all? Is there a last vacuum which the comfort and solace of the *sola gratia* cannot fill? Does the way of certainty of salvation consist only in holding up the mirror of merciful election, or are there other factors, subservient or perhaps even dominant, which play a role here?

These oft-repeated questions are summarized in one: Are there specific signs and marks of election which are so clear that they can remove the last trace of doubt? Are there still other mirrors besides the one, Jesus Christ? Or does this very question already obscure His light and violate the *sola fide — sola gratia?* Is not the concern with such "signs" or "marks" already a symptom of crisis, of the lack of true certainty in the clear evidence of faith? Can certainty ever be found, or even be affirmed, except in the one source, Jesus Christ Himself? Is there still another direction — the direction of experience and works — or is every seeking in that direction nothing but a sign that faith has deteriorated?

These questions arose again and again in connection with a momentous struggle concerning the so-called *syllogismus practicus,* a struggle which, as we shall see, is closely linked with the correct insight into the doctrine of election.

The question that occupies us can be formulated thus: Does sanctification and the presence of good works provide a sign of election so that one may legitimately infer from that sign the certainty of election? Can good works form a "basis" of certainty so that it is possible — *syllogismus practicus* — to deduce a trustworthy conclusion from it?

It need not surprise us that the *syllogismus practicus* has been the object of much contention, for it involves many further questions. If those signs are a basis for certainty, what then is the relationship of this basis to that other which is indicated to us

in the *sola gratia,* in Jesus Christ Himself, and in His grace (I
Cor. 3:11)? Can we ever find a foundation of certainty in ourselves, and will this not eliminate any other foundation of our
salvation?[1] Can the man who seeks certainty find it in self-contemplation and self-analysis as well as in Jesus Christ? At stake
in these questions is the direction of the eye of faith, which is also
of decisive importance to the ministry of the Word. It has often
been asked whether the very mention of this *syllogismus practicus* does not reveal a profound crisis in the doctrine of election,
and whether this *syllogismus practicus* is not simply an escape
from the hidden election to the tangible proof in one's own life.
Is it then still possible to regard our salvation as coming solely
from on high, sovereignly and graciously?

That the *syllogismus practicus* is sometimes seen in direct
connection with the doctrine of election is revealed most clearly
in Max Weber's influential discussion of Calvinism.[2] Although
he was mainly concerned to indicate the connection between
Calvinism and capitalism, he also made some penetrating obser-
vations on the structure of Calvinism in relation to certainty and
election. He pointed out that it was precisely Calvinism which
led to great activity in the Christian life, especially in man's
vocation; and he was of the opinion that this vocational zeal
originated in the attempt to arrive at certainty regarding one's
own election on the basis of the fruits of faith, on the basis of
sanctification, especially in one's vocation. Weber arrived at this
conclusion because he saw in the background of Calvinism a
source of uncertainty for the believer, a terror and torment
which originate from the accepted doctrine of God's absolute
freedom of election. In this fear human activity became the means
to escape the impasse of the inscrutable and hidden election.
According to Weber, the characteristic Calvinistic doctrine is
that of election.[3] This doctrine, he says, led "in its pa-

---

1. Cf., the Form for the Lord's Supper which speaks of "the sacrifice of
Christ as the only basis and foundation of our salvation."
2. M. Weber, *Gesammelte Aufsätze zur Religions-soziologie,* I, 1947[4].
For information regarding Weber's views see: E. Troeltsch, *Die
Soziallehren der christlichen Kirchen und Gruppen,* 1923; G. Klingenburg, *Das Verhältnis Calvins zu Butzer untersucht auf Grund der
wirtschafts-ethischen Bedeutung beider Reformatoren,* 1912; P. A.
Diepenhorst, *Calvijn en de Oeconomie,* 1904; A. A. v. Schelven, "His
torisch Onderzoek naar den Levensstijl van het Calvinisme" in *Uit den
strijd der Geesten* (1944) pp. 239ff.; W. L. von Gunsteren, *Kalvinismus
und Kapitalismus,* 1934.
3. Weber, *op. cit.,* pp. 93-127.

thetic inhumanity" to a feeling of inner loneliness on the part of the individual. Man had no choice but to go his lonely way and then "meet with a fate that was determined from eternity." Neither preaching nor the Word and sacraments could remedy this loneliness and save man from the impasse of uncertainty. There was not one means by which grace could be afforded him concerning whom God had determined not to be gracious. For the Calvinist all communication with God took place in "deep inner isolation." But if one should think that this doctrine of election necessarily led to quietism and fatalism, he would be grossly mistaken, for, said Weber, just the opposite was true.

Calvinism certainly did not lead to a devaluation of human activity; on the contrary, it stimulated it tremendously. Weber points out that this activism was closely related to the question that arose from the doctrine of election, namely, Am I elected, and how can I become certain of this election? That, says Weber, was not yet a problem for Calvin, who believed that the only way leading to certainty of salvation was the way of trust in Christ. But that changed with the *epigones* and especially in "the broad stratum of everyday men," for with them the problem of the knowledge of election became acute. Wherever the doctrine of predestination was accepted, it was of necessity followed by the question about the marks of election, according to Weber.

The ministry had to take notice of this tormenting question, and had to seek and provide an answer for it. It could do so only by pointing to real and indubitable signs of election. One such sign lay in "restless and unceasing professional activity," and it became the way "to work away the effects of religious fear."

Over against Lutheranism with its *unio mystica*, Reformed doctrine taught that the actual entrance of God into the soul was impossible because of the divine transcendence, and that communion with God could become conscious only by God working in us. Our acting in faith became, *in concreto*, legitimate only as worked by God.

In other words, a religious emphasis was placed on this human activity. Faith had to reveal itself in the objective effects of election in order to lay a foundation for the certainty of salvation and election. Real faith could be known from those fruits of belief which served to increase God's glory, and although good works could not serve to acquire salvation, they were indispensable as "signs" of election.   They could serve "to get rid of the fear concerning salvation."   Systematic self-control thus became a duty of the highest order.   Logically speaking, one would expect the doctrine of predestination to lead to fatalism, but psychologically speaking, the opposite was true. Attention was focused on the acts of the Christian, which were directly and concretely related to the certainty of salvation and election.

When the Lutherans objected that this was a form of salvation by works they were not correct theoretically, but practically this seemed to be the case "for the everyday life of the average Reformed Christian."   For there never was "a more intensive form of religious appreciation of man's moral acts than that which Calvinism evoked from its adherents."   The act, as sign of divine election, became so very important that men began to direct all their attention to it.   No magic of Church or ministry could eliminate the tension generated by the doctrine of election and take away the fear of the *deus absconditus*.   Only action could open a way of escape.   It was the way of total Christianization of life, to the glory of God.   The doctrine of predestination thus became the background of puritanical morality.   The high tension was discharged in the concreteness of everyday life; not in the quietude of meditation, but in one's vocation.   What was lacking in Lutheranism, namely, constant self-control, became law here; the planned regulation of life was the psychological result of the doctrine of election, which in itself was an abyss.   The *mysterium tremendum* did not lead to quietism, but to activity.

We are not concerned here with the historical aspects of Weber's thesis, and certainly not with the questions which have occupied Van Schelven and others, who reproached Weber by saying that he ascribed to Calvinism what was much more characteristic of Puritanism and Pietism.   More important to us is what lies at the root of Weber's argument, namely, his view of the connection between election and certainty.   He supposed that this connection was completely determined by the tension arising from the doctrine of election, that this tension could be relieved only by activity, and that this activity was not a basis for salvation but a principle of recognition.

This raises the question, not whether there is a connection between faith and sanctification, but whether this connection is such that certainty can be based on the manifest works of man, and whether this does not contradict the confession of the *sola fide*, and further whether this connection may not even be impossible on the basis of the doctrine of election. These questions concern at the same time the nature and the legitimacy of the *syllogismus practicus* in Reformed thinking. Since this formulation has undoubtedly played an important role in Reformed theology, the question cannot be avoided as to its connection with the doctrine of election. We are thereby confronted by a question that touches the core of the doctrine of election.

It is striking how much attention in our time has been devoted to the *syllogismus practicus*. This renewed interest goes hand in hand with a greater interest in the so-called "Further Reformation," the significance of which has been indicated by Van Ruler, Van Genderen, Van der Linde, and others.[4] Although this "Further Reformation" has at times been interpreted as an aberration of the original Reformation, many now hold that especially in its doctrine of the signs of election its emphasis is legitimately Reformed and represents a valuable point of view over against the danger of petrification in orthodoxy.

We are not interested here in passing historical and doctrinal judgment on this "Further Reformation,"[5] but in the logical questions that arise here. Theologians of the Further Reformation are principally concerned with the danger of calling upon man to accept God's promises, without taking sufficient account of the reality of the Holy Spirit, and God's indwelling in the hearts of the believers. The salvation of God, it is said, is not something that is realized in a special sphere of the Word which lies

4. I mention, among others, A. A. van Ruler, "De Bevinding" (*Kerk en Theologie*, 1st ed., 1950, pp. 71ff.), "De Grenzen der Prediking" (*ibid.*, 4th ed., 1953, pp. 84ff.), "De Bevinding der Prediking" (*Schrift en Kerk*, 1953, pp. 161ff.) ; J. van Genderen, "Het Practisch Geloofssylogisme en Zijn Referaat: De Nadere Reformatie" (*Wapenveld, Maandblad C. S. F. R.*, 5th ed., 1955, No. 4; S. v. d. Linde, *De Betekenis van de Nadere Reformatie voor Kerk en Theologie*, 5th ed., 1954, pp. 215ff.).
5. The term "Further Reformation" does not imply criticism of the Reformation. "It does not pretend to go beyond it, but expects nothing but good from the full development of that Reformation" (Van der Linde, *op. cit.*, p. 216). It is fully on the side of the Reformation and Calvin. Van Genderen speaks of "an ethical supplement of the Reformation and the furthering of its principles in the spirit of Calvin (*op. cit.*, p. 8). This movement is not a correction of the Reformation but its continuation. Van Ruler speaks of the spiritual "consequence of the Reformation" (*Kerk en Theologie*, 1950, p. 74).

beyond man (*extra nos*), but in the depth of man's heart and in the fullness of the *gratia interna*. For a correct insight into salvation we need not only a Christological, but also a pneumatological point of view,[6] especially in connection with the matter of certainty. Precisely in this connection, the significance of the signs comes at once to the foreground. The movement emphatically denies that its views of the signs can be interpreted as an irreligious departure from the Reformation. Rather, it points out that something happens when salvation comes, and that man is most existentially and in the depths of his being involved in this salvation.

It does not surprise us, therefore, that attention is again called to the *syllogismus practicus,* and that after a period of emphasizing the *extra nos* (over against experiential theology and subjectivism) again a plea is made for the consideration of the *in nobis,* even by Karl Barth, who emphatically defends the *syllogismus practicus.*[7] The important question is whether the emphasis on the syllogismus practicus is an indication of a crisis in which the attempt is made to compensate for the uncertainty of election by emphasizing experience or sanctification, or whether it has a legitimate Biblical foundation which cannot be disregarded except at the expense of the certainty of salvation.

In our consideration of this question, we at once touch upon the oft-discussed Question and Answer of the Heidelberg Catechism (Lord's Day 32) which speaks of the necessity of good works. Besides the motives of gratitude and of winning others for Christ, it mentions that of assurance (". . . each of us may be assured in himself of his faith by the fruits thereof").

The whole controversy around the *syllogismus practicus* centers around the question whether the Catechism is indeed in this respect Biblical and Reformed. Not so long ago, a certain Bruins in a dissertation on Chalmers stated that "it is not correct to make, as Lord's Day 32 of the Catechism does, the certainty of salvation co-dependent on good works as the fruits of faith." This

---

6. Van Ruler (e.g., in "De Bevinding," p. 75) speaks of the duality of the Christological and the pneumatological point of view. Compare his criticism of Dr. H. Schroten's *Christus, de Middelaar, bij Calvijn* (*ibid.,* p. 73). Regarding the relationship between the Christological and pneumatological in Van Ruler, see my *Het Werk van Christus* (1953), pp. 236ff. S. van der Linde wrote his dissertation on *De Leer van den Heiligen Geest bij Calvijn* (1943). For Christology and pneumatology see Van der Linde, *Kerk en Theologie* (1954), p. 219.

7. *K. D.,* II, 2, 367-75.

criticism is not an isolated case but finds an emphatic defender in Wilhelm Niesel, who has asserted that in the *syllogismus practicus* the attention of the believer is drawn aside and that thus the purity of the Reformed emphasis on *sola fide* is abandoned. According to Niesel, attention is no longer solely on the revelation of God in Christ. The Catechism, in Lord's Day 32, gives the impression that Christ "first directs our attention to ourselves and our works, and from there to Himself." It is the way of self-contemplation. "The Catechism does not solely and exclusively call attention to the Word and sacraments by which alone Christ will be present with us, but it ascribes to the born-again man a significance which he cannot possess in Calvin's theology, which holds so closely to the Word and to Christ."[8] According to Niesel, the *syllogismus practicus* ascribes to regenerate man a role in the shadow of the doctrine of predestination. Evidently he discovers in it an element of competition with regard to the exclusive, absolute trust in Christ and His salvation, and hence an obscuring of the liberating *sola fide*.

It is of decisive importance for the doctrine of election that we investigate this interpretation of the *syllogismus practicus* to see whether it does indeed weaken the gospel message, and whether the *syllogismus* is possibly a result of the tensions which arise in connection with the Calvinistic doctrine of election.

Although Lord's Day 32 of the Heidelberg Catechism stood in the center of the controversy over the *syllogismus practicus,* the Canons should also be mentioned since they especially deal with election. Especially CD, II, 12 has been cited: "The elect in due time, though in various degrees and in different measures, attain the assurance of this their eternal and unchangeable election, not by inquisitively prying into the secret and deep things of God, but by observing in themselves with a spiritual joy and holy pleasure the infallible fruits of election pointed out in the Word of God — such as a true faith in Christ, filial fear, a godly sorrow for sin, a hungering and thirsting after righteousness, etc. (II Cor. 13:5)." This passage shows still more clearly the relation between election and certainty, and it speaks emphatically of "observing." Some have regarded this observing as a faithless analysis and induction from which certainty is to come, and they have for that reason interpreted CD, II, 12 as a serious aberration from the original Reformed

---

8. W. Niesel, "Syllogismus practicus?" in *Festgabe für E. F. Müller* (1933), pp. 158-79.

view in so far as it places the reborn man in the foreground.
Barth, who emphatically defends the *syllogismus practicus* against
Niesel, thinks of CD, II, 12 as "difficult to take" and as an
"obvious aberration" from Calvin.[9] For it has led to giving
"prominence to the self-evidence of the life of the elect as a sign
of empirical self-contemplation and self-judgment, in order actually to disregard the testimony of Jesus Christ."

It is clear that in principle we are confronted with the same
question in both CD, II, 12 and Lord's Day 32, namely, in how
far man's life is, and can be, of significance with respect to the
certainty of salvation.

Sometimes a distinction has been made between the *syllogismus
practicus* (the conclusion from good works) and the *syllogismus
mysticus* (the conclusion from faith and experience).[10] But it is
clear that in both instances we are confronted with the same
question, namely, the *syllogismus,* the "conclusion" which is drawn
from what is actually present in the believers. We can, therefore, concentrate our attention on the question whether this
syllogismus is — consciously or unconsciously — a moving away
from a crisis, the crisis of the "hidden" election.

Undoubtedly it is true that there is a danger of shifting the
emphasis from grace and the salvation of God, from the promise
in Word and sacrament, to man, the believing, active, reborn
man. And it is unmistakable that this shift has often taken place
in the history of Church and theology because man — uncertain
in regard to his election — began to analyze himself in order to
find "signs" of election. His eye was thereby no longer first of
all on God's promise and its truly trustworthy character, but on
what had been accomplished in him, in order to conclude —
either practically or mystically — his election therefrom.

Weber's presentation of the Calvinistic doctrine of predestination may be a caricature, but the problem he brought up is
certainly not imaginary or without real significance. For frequently this way has indeed been taken, and the shifting of
emphasis has become very real, so that uncertainty has loomed
dark and disquieting in the background. Men have wondered
whether there are not indeed evidences that go deeper than the
"promise" — a promise which escapes practical application.
Where is certainty to be found if preaching, Word, and sacrament cannot impart subjective certainty? Has man any choice

---

9. *K.D.*, II, 2, 370.
10. Van Ruler, *op. cit.*, p. 83.

left but to walk the way of analysis and induction and from there to deduction?

To summarize the problem once again: Is it not understandable that Beza used a formulation, often criticzed by the opponents of the *syllogismus practicus,* namely, that when man is in doubt regarding his election, he must look at the effects, which reveal his spiritual life and election, just as the body reveals that it lives when we observe it?[11] Was not Beza, it is asked, precisely the man who spoke of election in a supralapsarian manner, and was it not for precisely that reason necessary for him — when doubts arose — to point to the effects in order to obtain thus the certainty which could not be ascertained in a different way? Was that not why Beza spoke of "beginning sanctification," and could he still maintain the *sola fide?*

Niesel is of the opinion that in this way the promise is made powerless, and Barth thinks that good works thus become the main witness.[12]

We are not, however, concerned here with possible aberrations from the *syllogismus practicus,* but with the question whether it can be interpreted in a positive manner, and whether it actually is consistent with the Reformation principle of *sola fide.*

The complexity of this problem already appears from the fact that Niesel does not think that there is evidence of the *syllogismus practicus* in Calvin's teaching, while Barth believes there is. We must, therefore, turn directly to Calvin's commentary on I John, where appears a passage crucial to the controversy about the *syllogismus practicus.* "We know that we have passed out of death into life, because we love the brethren" (I John 3:14). Niesel calls special attention to Calvin's commentary. He begins by noting that Calvin, in his search for certainty regarding salvation, points out the *signa posteriara,* the resulting signs which are certain indications of salvation. But by those *signa* Calvin means the Word, the testimony, the calling of God. According to Calvin, the way of investigation is "that we begin with God's calling and end with it" (*Inst.* III, xxiv, 4). Through His calling, God affirms with a sign all that we are permitted to know of His counsel. God Himself is a sufficient witness to the hidden grace in us. He is such in His outward

---

11. I am merely concerned with an illustration here. Van Genderen is of the opinion that not full justice is done to Beza.
12. *K. D.,* II, 2, 369.

Word (*ibid.,* III, xxiv, 3) and we must look unto Christ
(III, xxiv, 5). Not in ourselves, but in Christ we must seek
assurance. Nowhere, according to Niesel, do we find mention
of any certainty which we may seek in ourselves,[13] and he finds
this thought confirmed by Calvin in his polemics with Rome with
reference to II Peter 1:10. According to Calvin this text is not
concerned with the obtaining of assurance, but with the reality
of sanctification which issues from faith as fruit issues from
a tree.

According to Niesel, there is not one trace of a *syllogismus
practicus* in Calvin. But he is also aware that Calvin sometimes
uses language which approaches the *syllogismus,* especially where
he says that the saints often strengthen and comfort themselves
by reflecting on their integrity (*Inst.* III, xiv, 19). That does
not mean (and Niesel agrees here) that Calvin thinks that
believers trust in their good works. For the foundation of salvation man must not look unto his works, but unto God's goodness. But if man's conscience looks to God in such a way, then
it is also confirmed by regarding his works in so far as they are
a testimony that God lives in him and rules him. Man's trust
must first be in God's mercy — without any *meritum* — but that
does not mean that the believer is not strengthened in his faith
by the signs of God's goodness toward him. All gifts — also
those of good works — are like rays shining from God's countenance. They show that we have been given the grace of having
been adopted as His children. That is why Niesel must acknowledge that with Calvin good works have "a certain significance."[14]
One can agree with Niesel that for Calvin man's good works
remain subordinate to the promise of God and that they do
not provide the ultimate foundation of certainty. But for Niesel
that means that Calvin does not actually teach the *syllogismus
practicus* but only makes a concession to Rome when he says
that man's works are indeed signs of the state of grace, but only
after the acknowledging of salvation in Christ. And Niesel
adds: "And ultimately he really cancels this little concession
again." It seems, then, that Niesel does not take Calvin quite
seriously at this point.[15] He particularly emphasizes the fact

13. Niesel, *op. cit.,* p. 141.
14. *Ibid.,* p. 164.
15. From *Inst.* III, ii, 38, it is clear how unsatisfactory Niesel's argument
    really is.

that according to Calvin we might equally deduce God's wrath from our works (cf. *Inst.* III, xiv, 29), for they are full of sin. For that reason alone they can never be the foundation of certainty.

It is clear, however, precisely because Calvin emphasizes this, that there must be a reason for him to attach significance to man's works within the concept of the *sola fide* — *sola gratia*. That takes us to Calvin's exegesis of I John 3:14, a passage which he certainly does not see as a threat to the *sola fide*.

According to Calvin, John does not speak here of the foundation, but of the sign of certainty. This sign indeed strengthens man's belief, but God's mercy is and remains the sole foundation. When someone would therefore deduce from I John 3:14 that in order to obtain certainty, we must rest in our works and trust in them, then Calvin considers this a confusion between sign and foundation. When there is light, we know for certain that the sun is shining; but only after man's belief has a foundation can there be mention of helping, confirming, and strengthening it. We see the same point in Calvin's commentary on I John 3:19. Love is not a foundation for certainty, but a sign and a means to strengthen faith. Here again Niesel speaks of a concession by Calvin which he later on negates when he warns not to trust one's works and when he continually points to Christ only. Niesel obviously interprets that as a warning against the *syllogismus practicus*. He comes to the conclusion that Calvin nowhere teaches the *syllogismus practicus,* and Niesel therefore opposes Klingenburg, who finds in Calvin a necessary "accompanying symptom" of secondary importance,[16] namely, the strengthening of faith. Niesel rather thinks that Calvin does not refer to man's good works, but to the sacrament.[17]

It seems to be impossible, however, to maintain such an interpretation of Calvin. To say that Calvin made a "concession to Rome" and later retracted it, is unsatisfactory. What Niesel interprets as a retraction of the "concession" (by pointing to Christ) is not a criticism on the part of Calvin of the *syllogismus practicus* but the safeguarding of the *syllogismus* against mutilation. In his warnings not to trust in good works, Calvin does

16. Klingenburg, *op. cit.*, p. 69.
17. Niesel, *op. cit.*, p. 174.

not retract anything, but he rejects an incorrect application of the *syllogismus practicus,* as it later came to be called.[18]

From the above discussion it is quite evident what is the central question concerning the *syllogismus practicus.* Does the *syllogismus practicus* really look away from Christ (Niesel)? This is a serious matter for Niesel, since for him the *syllogismus* does not strengthen and affirm certainty, but rather endangers it. Logically it leads to despair. He finds that the *syllogismus* always comes to the fore when man's attention no longer solely focuses on Christ. Man begins to look for other sources of certainty, because the one source and fountain is no longer sufficient to him and he must finally receive certainty from his own life. But that is utterly impossible. According to Niesel, one must choose between *sola fide* and *syllogismus.*

It is very interesting to note that again in our day much attention is devoted to the *syllogismus practicus,* particularly by those who emphatically want to maintain the *sola fide.* We think here of Barth, who disagrees with Niesel that the *syllogismus practicus* contradicts the *sola fide.* He finds evidence of the *syllogismus practicus* in Calvin, and speaks of this recognition as not only useful but in its place also necessary.[19] According to Barth, we are not dealing with a speculative problem, but with a real problem: the recognition of what Calvin calls the *adminicula.* When Calvin speaks of the significance of good works, he is not concerned with a "foundation other than Christ," Barth says, but with the human "act and behavior in which man comes to rest in Christ as the only foundation."

Because Christ lives in the believers through faith, it becomes unavoidable that we interpret the life of the believer — the life of faith — "as an accidental but not necessary affirmation of the one decisive witness." To be sure, Barth affirms, Christ is the one, true, and decisive foundation for certainty, but the believer receives certainty of this foundation "in the form of his own decision, of his own faith and confession, and of his own (corresponding) existence." Man, the believer, is truly involved in the sole foundation. He goes wrong only when he makes his life

18. The unsatisfactory analysis of Niesel is also evident when he describes Calvin's point of view by saying that "he [Calvin] did not deem it advisable to generalize and incorporate into dogma single apostolic conclusions which he found in the Epistle of John" (*op. cit.,* p. 173).
19. *K. D.,* II, 2, 369-370.

the foundation; but faith in Christ gives the believer the right to look unto "the work of the electing God in man." And this is not only allowed, it is even mandatory.

According to Barth, this life of faith becomes a testimony to faith. Man in all his concreteness becomes a witness himself, dependent and "secondary," to be sure, but as such necessary. This testimony is given to him, but then he also receives it from himself. "As long as I live as one who is elected, I become and am certain of my election." Because this witness is dependent, it can only be a matter of *adminiculum* in man's good works, inconclusive and secondary. The issue is not the works proper, but the fruits of the tree, the fruits of faith.

"Self-witness" may never lead to placing the primary foundation there, as a sign of empirical self-consideration and self-evaluation. It did not become such until after Calvin. On the one side, Barth sees Beza, for whom good works become the main witness, and on the other side, he sees the *Consensus Bremensis* of 1595, which declares that man, when in doubt regarding his certainty of salvation, must not look at what is in him, but only at the infallible promises of the Word of God,[20] a view which eliminates not only the indecisiveness of the *syllogismus* with Beza, but also Calvin's real problem.[21] Over against this it must be maintained, says Barth, that there is coherence between our election in Christ and the reality of His work in us through the Holy Spirit, in order thus to find the way to the *syllogismus practicus* which is to be sharply distinguished from any form of self-analysis outside of faith.[22]

We now approach the core of the problem concerning the *syllogismus practicus* in connection with election. How, and in which sense, have man's good works significance for one's assurance of salvation?[23] Can they really become an unambiguous indication of election, or do they rather lead to more doubt? How is it possible to look solely unto the goodness and mercy of God — without regarding one's works — and still, for the

20. See Müller, *Bekenntnisschriften* (1903), p. 758.
21. Barth, *K. D.,* II, 2, 371.
22. Barth tries to explain how these variations could have originated. He is of the opinion that in the Reformed doctrine of election Christ as the "means" to salvation can no longer become the main witness (cf. Chapter V).
23. Cf. G. Oorthuys, "De Betekenis van het Nieuwe Leven voor de Zekerheid des Geloofs Volgens Calvijns Institutie" (*Onder Eigen Vaandel,* XIII).

confirmation and strengthening of our faith, attach significance to good works?

It is quite understandable that on the basis of the *sola fide* the *syllogismus practicus* has at times been abandoned. For the dangers of moralism threaten in connection with the *syllogismus practicus,* and of mysticism in connection with the *syllogismus mysticus.* And the "signs" have often been more esteemed than God's revelation and trustworthy promise. Does it not betray a lack of courage of faith to reserve a place for this function of good works along with the *sola fide?* And is it indeed possible to ascribe such a function to good works, which after all, according to our Christian confession, are polluted with sin (HC, Q. 24)? Has not this confession its implications for the problem of certainty? Is it not rather true that our works will again make the certainty uncertain? Can certainty ever be evoked and strengthened apart from belief in the forgiveness of sins? How can our good works become a witness, even a secondary witness? Do they not remain witnesses on the debit side rather than on the credit side? All these questions arise automatically when we discuss the *syllogismus practicus,* and they can be summarized in these words: (1) Can good works have this function? (2) Is such a function of good works indeed necessary for the certainty, which after all issues from the indisputable trustworthiness of God's promises and the convincing power of the Holy Spirit?

First of all we wish to point out that it is impossible to accept the *syllogismus practicus* if it is understood as a logical conclusion, made apart from faith, and based on a neutral analysis of one's life, whether mystical or practical.

So understood, it shifts the emphasis from *sola fide,* and therefore can never bring about true certainty of salvation. Schilder was correct when he pointed out in this connection that Scripture even speaks of pagans who by nature do what the law requires, which shows that we can never conclude that we are elected on the basis of a neutral analysis of our works which conform to the law.[24] Man can easily overestimate himself in such a neutral self-analysis and reach a conclusion that could not stand before God.

Man's heart is deceitful above all things, and exceedingly corrupt. Who can know it? (Jer. 17:9). This is true especially

24. K. Schilder, *Heidelbergse Catechismus,* I, 178.

regarding the analysis of one's own life. For that reason, such an analysis can never lead to certainty. It would only be the rationalistic form of the *syllogismus practicus,* which is in flagrant contradiction to the teaching of the Reformation and especially of Scripture. It is, apart from faith and promise, utterly impossible to come to the conclusion: I believe. Besides, a peculiar reasoning here takes place, namely, reasoning from the content of faith proper, which then has to be examined as to its presence (or absence) and its activity. This process of thinking resembles the Roman Catholic reasoning when it draws rational conclusions from the creation. The rationalistic *syllogismus practicus* draws a causal conclusion very similar to the conclusion of the *theologia naturalis.*

This kind of syllogism is merely a reasoned conclusion, and it is understandable that it leaves man's heart cold and untouched, and that it presently evolves into a new *tentatio,* when the question arises — must arise — whether the "conclusion" is correct or maybe based on self-deception and illusion.

Over against that it must be posed that the *syllogismus practicus* is possible only if it is understood as the syllogism of faith.[25] To be sure, that evokes other questions, but at any rate it is clear that this principle puts us on an altogether different basis than the one of rational conclusions drawn from the observed empirical reality of our lives. That was the intention of Calvin's *postquam.* Niesel's citation of Calvin, where the latter argues against Scholasticism is important here: "Hence we may judge how pernicious is the scholastic dogma that we can have no stronger evidence of the divine favour towards us than moral conjecture, according as each individual deems himself not unworthy of it. Doubtless, if we are to determine by our works in what way the Lord stands affected towards us, I admit we cannot even get the length of a feeble conjecture: but since faith should accord with the free and simple promise, there is no room left for ambiguity" (*Inst.* III, ii, 38).

That is linked up with the fact that man's works can never be the foundation for certainty. Calvin is convinced "that no believer ever performed one work which, if tested by the strict judgment of God, could escape condemnation: and moreover, that were this granted to be possible (though it is not), yet the act being vitiated and polluted by the sins of which it is certain

25. J. van Genderen, "Het Practisch Syllogisme."

that the author of it is guilty, it is deprived of its merit" (*ibid.*, III, xiv, 11).

All this is so clear and convincing in the light of the gospel that the question can be asked whether this does not imply a negative solution of the syllogistic problem. In this state of affairs is not faith, resting on God's promise, the only thing? Does not Calvin's *postquam* definitely preclude the *syllogismus practicus*? Is not the idea of the *syllogismus* violated when now there is mention of faith? How can this "conclusion" obtain a place within faith and its certainty? Is not certainty already determined, and is it still necessary to "conclude" from good works?

The answer to all these questions is that by virtue of the *sola fide* a place has indeed been reserved and had to be reserved for the *syllogismus practicus*. It seems to me that Lord's Day 32 of the Heidelberg Catechism clearly indicates this. There the Catechism is not concerned with a causal and rationalistic deduction in the sense that right in the middle — and, moreover, at the beginning of the part that treats of gratitude — a neutral, empirical analysis of a life of good works suddenly emerges. That is precluded by the very fact that Lord's Day 33 gives as definition of good works that they issue from true faith, and that definition rules out every neutral phenomenological analysis. Furthermore, it is striking that Question 86 proceeds from the *sola gratia* (without any merit of ours . . . by grace alone"), and that the *sylogismus practicus* stands between two other motives for the necessity of good works, namely, gratitude and the winning of our neighbor for Christ. The statement about assurance of our faith by the fruits thereof follows the confession that Christ, after He has redeemed us by His blood, also renews us after His own image by His Holy Spirit, that we with our whole life may show ourselves thankful to God for His benefits. This order rules out the possibility that in the *syllogismus practicus* we suddenly have a new and other way of salvation, or, at least, a new way of our own to assurance. Apparently the Catechism does not see, no more than does Calvin, any distance or contradiction between syllogism and *sola gratia.*

It is clear that the syllogism may not be taken out of the context of the Catechism which already in Lord's Day 1 speaks of the fact that the Holy Spirit assures us of eternal life, and later says that the Holy Spirit by the gospel works in our hearts a firm confidence (Q. 21) and that He comforts us (Q. 53).

The only question is, therefore, how we are to understand the syllogism of faith. The word "syllogism" may give the impression that we are dealing here with a logical figure, a logical conclusion as such, a deduction which can be made on the basis of certain premises, namely, that on the basis of the presence of good works (or of other experiences) we may conclude the fact of election. But Lord's Day 32 does not speak of that kind of syllogism. It has been asked whether, in order to avoid confusion, it would not be better to drop the use of the word "syllogism" altogether. That this has not been done is probably due to the fact that in the word "syllogism" something is seen that can serve to indicate the relation between good works and assurance. It is also clear, however, that the matter is not primarily verbal. The real point is the significance which man's good works have (according to Calvin and the Catechism) for the assurance of salvation.

When we look for this connection we may say that the whole problem of the *syllogismus practicus* is connected with and originates from the Biblical connection between justification and sanctification by the Holy Spirit. We really need not be divided regarding the connection between the Christological and the pneumatological point of view.[26] In this unbreakable connection, and the concomitant significance, function, and seriousness of sanctification, lies the only legitimate interpretation of the *syllogismus practicus*. Here we touch directly upon the connection between election and assurance of salvation.

He who loses sight of the connection between God's salvation — in His electing mercy — and the sanctification of life, becomes the victim of a serious misinterpretation of the *sola fide*. Out of reaction against the teaching that man's works are meritorious, sanctification may at times be in disrepute[27]; nevertheless the light of Scripture makes this connection so clear

---

26. I have been asked what I mean by the statement that the work of the Spirit "is not a second mystery along with the mystery of reconciliation" (in *The Triumph of Grace*). This expression does not imply any devaluation of the work of the Spirit, but only a rejection of the scheme: possibility-realization, in which the relatedness of the work of the Spirit to that of Christ is denied. I indicated this by saying that the work of the Spirit is filled with the mystery of reconciliation.

27. Cf. W. Stählin, *Allein. Recht und Gefahr einer polemischen Forme!* (1950) pp. 22ff.

that it cannot possibly be overlooked.[28]   One may object, however, that although this connection is clearly indicated in man's
being judged according to his works, it is not directly meaningful
for the noetic problem of our own personal certainty.   Indeed, there
are many passages in Scripture which speak of judging others, for
instance, when Jesus says that there is a correlation between
the good tree and the good fruit, and between the bad tree and
the bad fruit, and that the tree is known by its fruit (Matt.
12:33), without explicitly speaking of man's passing judgment
on his own life.[29]

And the *syllogismus practicus* is concerned precisely with one's
own individual life.   It is therefore no wonder that often specific
attention is paid to those words in the epistle of John which stress
the element of knowing in connection with brotherly love.   These
words are remarkable: "We know that we have passed out of
death into life, because we love the brethren" (I John 3:14).
In the first place, it is clear that John's statement does not at all
suggest a shift of emphasis.   That is impossible in view of the
love that is the burden of this epistle.   There is only one
direction in which the eye of faith may look.   It is the love of
God which forms the only basis for boldness (I John 4:17).
"Herein is love, not that we loved God, but that he loved us"
(I John 4:10).   But that does not at all imply that this love is
inactive and has no effect on everyday life.   Rather, in that new
life it becomes evident who this new person is — in Christ.   The
children of God and the children of Satan are recognizable:
he who does not do justice is not of God, nor he who does not
love his brother.   There is a connection between the love of
God and the concrete act of love.   This connection is also
definitely concerned with a command, with the imperative:
"Beloved, if God so loved us, we also ought to love one another"
(I John 4:11), but this imperative is not a vague and distant
possibility, it is also reality: "Whosoever is begotten of God
doeth no sin" (I John 3:9), and there are *perfecta* in this epistle
which are full of this reality: "Ye have overcome the evil one"
(I John 2:13).

For that reason John can speak of these relations as correla-

---

28. Cf. my *Faith and Sanctification* (1952) especially the chapter "Sola
    Fide and Sanctification" and Ernest Gaugler, *Die Heiligung im Zeugnis
    der Schrift* (1948).
29. Matthew 7 deals with the judgment of false prophets.

tions and thus indicate that in the concrete act of love the transition has become manifest — so manifest that the believer himself can discern it in the form of its manifestation.

We have here not only a principle by which false prophets in sheep's clothing are recognized and unmasked as wolves (Matt. 7:15), but a "knowing" and seeing into one's own life. That life becomes manifest as it is and remains in Him, manifest both before the eyes of God and before man's own eyes. And the ultimate foundation of the *syllogismus practicus* lies in this concrete, profoundly real manifestation.

The concept of the *syllogismus practicus* is not based exclusively on that one passage in John regarding "knowing," however; this epistle is filled with evidence for assurance. We read in I John 2:3, "And hereby we know that we know him, if we keep his commandments." Again and again John indicates the great change: darkness is passing away and the true light already shines (I John 2:8). He who says that he is in the light, but hates his brother, is in darkness, but he who loves his brother, abides in the light (I John 2:9-10). That light is not a hidden thing, not even for the believer himself. This does not imply proud perfectionism (I John 1:8-10), nor building on and trusting in one's own works, but it is all very real and concrete by virtue of the love of God which "herein" is perfect in us (I John 4:12). And on that is also based the boldness of which John writes: "Hereby shall we know that we are of the truth." And this is preceded by the warning: "My little children, let us not love in word, neither with the tongue: but in deed and truth" (I John 3:18).

It is striking — in connection with the many discussions — that the *syllogismus practicus* is here related to the self-accusation of man's heart: "Hereby shall we know that we are of the truth, and shall assure our heart before him: because if our heart condemn us, God is greater than our heart and knoweth all things" (I John 3:19-20). Who is not reminded here of what Calvin says concerning our good works, namely, that they also can make us reflect on God's wrath? It is clear, therefore, that John is not concerned with a neutral analysis and conclusion. The heart can indeed condemn, and who then would still dare to draw neutral conclusions on the basis of the inclinations of the heart?

Such a conclusion is for John not the answer to the accusing heart. The solace lies in the fact that God is more than our heart and that He knows all things. In the same connection we read of our discerning and of God's knowing.[30] The way of knowledge and discernment has been paved — the true light is already shining — but it is impossible to stay on this way without the merciful knowledge of God.[31] It is not a way which we can travel by ourselves as a matter of course. Knowing that we are in the truth is not the result of our autonomous self-knowledge. The syllogism of faith implies the knowledge of our own weakness, and this knowledge does not disappear when realizing it. The outlook is not changed in the *syllogismus practicus*. The knowledge of one's own life — in the light that is already shining — has nothing to do with such a shift. For, as "knowing," it is and remains only a comfort and solace because of Him who is greater than our heart. This Greater is no longer a threat as one would expect because of His being greater and because of His knowledge of all things, but a solace.[32]

In this connection we wish also to mention the Canons of Dort (I, 12). Are the Canons here concerned with a syllogism (*syllogismus mysticus*) that seeks the foundation for certainty in man's life, in his experience, in his faith, in his fear of God, in his sorrow for sin, and in his hunger and thirst after righteousness? Or does this "observing" stand in the light of the manifest change in I John?

The opposite has often been affirmed, and the Canons have been interpreted as shifting attention from Christ to reborn man. J. J. Woldendorp, for instance, has said that for this reason the Canons are in need of further revision. They do not direct our attention to the righteousness of Christ and justification by faith

30. Almost all commentaries refer to Peter's word to Christ: "Thou knowest all things" (John 21:17).
31. There has been much dispute concerning the relation between I John 3:20 and 21 (the heart that does and does not accuse). Is there not a contradiction when verse 21 says that we have boldness if our heart does not accuse us? Does it not imply restlessness and lack of boldness when our heart does accuse (v. 18)? Almost all commentaries are somewhat hesitant here, and the exegesis of this passage is and remains very difficult.
32. Calvin is of the opinion that "greater" means that it is impossible to escape God's judgment because nothing is hidden from Him.

alone, but rather to man who, in the horror of his questioning as to whether he is elected, has to be comforted with the indications of his own life and experience.[33]

But the statement in the Canons (I, 12) does not stand by itself. It is not at all a "strange body." In CD, I, 13 we read of the sense and the certainty of election, and in I, 16 of those "in whom a living faith in Christ, an assured confidence of soul, peace of conscience, an earnest endeavor after filial obedience, a glorying in God through Christ, is not as yet strongly felt," and of those who "cannot yet reach that measure of holiness and faith to which they aspire." And in V, 5 we even read of "sometimes for a while" losing "the sense of God's favor."

On the basis of these and similar statements Woldendorp comes to the conclusion that the Canons have deviated from the correct path (the *justificatio impii*). "Man becomes certain of his election to the extent that he believes and seriously attempts to do the will of God. That means that together with faith the serious attempt to obtain sanctification of life becomes the inner basis of the certainty of salvation or of personal election."

Evidently Woldendorp sees and reads in these words the same thing that Niesel sees in the *syllogismus practicus,* namely, the radical shift of attention from justification to reborn man. He sees the development of theology after Dort as its result. The message of Christ's righteousness is exchanged for "the tinsel of human reason."

This is a very unreasonable judgment of the Canons. We see how easily an anti-psychological attitude — on the basis of the *extra nos* — can lead to a misjudgment of man's situation in which justification by grace alone is preached. The Canons do not intend to sanction weakness, temptation, and doubt, but they point out the therapy after having diagnosed the illness. There is a strong pastoral element in many of the Canons' expressions, for instance, when it reminds us of God's promise that He will not quench the smoking flax and not break the bruised reed (CD, I, 16). The interest in believing, struggling and doubting man can, of course, be taken as a psychological approach, but it is also possible that the Canons realize the struggle in man's heart against the power of the Spirit, and

33. J. J. Woldendorp, "Heeft de Dordtsche Synode een Nadere Hervorming van Node?" in *Onder Eigen Vaandel,* Vol. V (1930), pp. 25-46

that here legitimate and pastoral words are spoken to offer help and guidance in this struggle.[34]

When we consider the various expressions, we notice that the Canons are concerned with leading believers to the assurance of salvation. In CD, I, 12 they emphatically warn against inquisitively prying into the secret and deep things of God. They block this road completely. CD, I, 13, too, speaks of the certainty of election, but in such a manner that God's children find additional matter for daily humiliation before God, for adoring the depth of His mercies, for cleansing themselves, and rendering grateful returns of ardent love to Him. When CD, I, 16 speaks of "not as yet strongly feeling the assurance of faith," then it comfortingly adds that believers ought not to be alarmed "at the mention of reprobation," and at the same time it points out the way they must walk and on which they can long for more abundant grace.

Woldendorp attempts to interpret the "psychology" of the Canons as an obscuring of justification. But they actually again and again emphasize justification, grace, and forgiveness. They nowhere indicate a foundation in man himself when he is in doubt and temptation; on the contrary, they point out God's election, not as an abstract thing but as the mystery of God's love which becomes manifest in life, and for that reason is known in many essential connections. Woldendorp disregards these connections altogether. When the Canons speak of these connections he, as Böhl before him, sees nothing in them but Osiandrism, even though Scripture presents God's salvation in precisely these connections. And these connections are also significant in the problem of certainty.

In Article V, 5 of the Canons (Rejection of Errors) it is said over against the doubts of Roman Catholicism that the certainty of future perseverance is deduced "not from a special and extraordinary revelation, but from the marks proper to the children of God and from the very constant promises of God." He who isolates this statement in the Canons could think that they here give priority to the signs, and secondarily add the promise of God. But it is striking that as Scriptural proof Romans 8:39

---

34. Cf. A. A. van Ruler's valuable remarks in "De Bevinding in de Prediking" (*Schrift en Kerk*, p. 166) with respect to what must be remembered in preaching when it calls man to faith; see also J. Ridderbos, "Versterking van het Geloof uit de Goede Werken" (*Gereformeerd Theologish Tijdschrift*, 1939, pp. 163-68).

is given, which says that no creature can separate us from the love of God which is in Christ Jesus and that precisely here the connections of I John are recalled: "He that keepeth his commandments abideth in him, and he in him. And hereby we know that he abideth in us, by the Spirit which he gave us" (I John 3:24).

The Canons speak here, regarding the question of certainty, of the connection between sanctification and assurance. For that reason I think one should not draw rash conclusions from the order, marks — promise, especially not since we read in CD, V, 10 that certainty does not originate "from any special and extraordinary revelation but from . . . the very constant promises of God," which He has most abundantly revealed in His word for our comfort; from the testimony of the Holy Spirit, witnessing with our spirit that we are children and heirs of God (Rom. 8:16); and, lastly, from a serious and holy desire to preserve a good conscience and to perform good works."[35]

Precisely because the connection does not contain competing motifs, the Canons' alternate manner of speaking is not without significance and not illegitimate.[36] It would be illegitimate if there were an idea of competition, but then there would be no room either at the beginning or at the end for "marks." But if the idea of competition is absent — and the entire structure of the Canons teaches us that it is — then the connection between election, certainty, and sanctification may be legitimately indicated.

This connection is found in Amos' words: "You only have I known of all the families of the earth; *therefore* I will visit upon you all your iniquities" (Amos 3:2). If one thing is clear in Scripture, it is that it is impossible to walk the way of certainty apart from sanctification. How would life, based on the electing grace of God, be possible apart from that sanctification which is the purpose of election? And how could assurance remain when sin and disobedience cause estrangement from the electing God?

At the time when the Reformed heritage — the *sola fide* —

---

35. Cf. my *Conflict with Rome* (1957), p. 193.
36. Cf. Van Genderen's series of articles, "Verkiezing en Prediking" in *Eenheid des Geloofs*, 6th ed., No. 5, in which he discusses the formulations of the Canons and speaks of "some hesitation." He regrets that the Canons do not fully indicate the significance of election in Christ for man's certainty of faith, and he says that that only will shed full light on CD, I, 12.

had still to be defended against the teaching of the meritoriousness of good works, the Canons did not in reaction minimize
the significance of sanctification, but so strongly emphasized it
that they considered it the basis for certainty.

Thereby they sounded a warning against all rashness, also
against "the usual effects of rash presumption or of idle and
wanton trifling with the grace of election" in those who refuse
to walk in the ways of the elect (CD, I, 13) This is one of the
important theses of the Canons regarding the issue under discussion. It is not at all a matter of a vicious circle: "first election
then sanctification," and then again: "first sanctification, then
election," but it is a matter of honoring the connections of Scripture by which we understand that the election of God is not an
objective act of God, and that only in the way of sanctification
man can be, and remain, certain of his election. Only he who
considers the *simul peccator et justus* an objective situation of
the believers in which there is no place for the *gratia interna,*
can continue to oppose the connection between election and
certainty, and can consider the *syllogismus practicus* a contradiction of the *sola fide.*

At this point it is certainly not inappropriate to remind ourselves of the passage which is often discussed in connection with
the *syllogismus practicus,* namely, II Peter 1:10: "Wherefore,
brethren, give the more diligence to make your calling and
election sure: for if ye do these things, ye shall never stumble."
Especially that "make sure" has drawn much attention, and
the question is asked how that is possible since election itself is
sure and unchangeable, and must be known by us as such. Niesel
has pointed out that Calvin did not relate this text to the *syllogismus practicus* because Calvin saw in it only a call to sanctification, without relating this sanctification to the question of
certainty.

However this be,[37] we think that we are here dealing with
the same connection between sanctification, election, and certainty, and there is no reason to think that the expression "make
sure" concerns others and not believers. The context, too, indicates that we are to think of the certainty of the believer. "For
if ye do these things, ye shall never stumble" (II Pet. 1:10),
and "thus shall be richly supplied unto you the entrance into

37. Cf. *Inst.* III, 15, 8.

the eternal kingdom of our Lord and Saviour Jesus Christ"
(v. 11).

Therefore, it is not in the least necessary that the *syllogismus
practicus* lead to pride and self-justification. This necessity does
not exist for the very reason that the syllogism refers to the
grace, the power, and indwelling of the Holy Spirit. We are here
simply warned against drawing rash conclusions. Precisely the indwelling of the Spirit was for Paul an urgent reason to make a
fervent call to sanctification. Imperative and indicative coincide
here most marvelously: "Know ye not that your body is a temple of the Holy Spirit which is in you, which ye have from God?
and ye are not your own" (I Cor. 6:19). Paul speaks of this
indwelling and power of the Spirit in connection with election
(Rom. 8:28-29), sanctification (Rom. 8:27, 29), glorification
(Rom. 8:30), and weakness (Rom. 8:26). It is the Holy Spirit
who searches the hearts of men and who makes intercession for
the saints according to the will of God (Rom. 8:27).

The simplicity and unity of God's work is so clearly evident
that no justice is done to Scripture when Niesel speaks of some
isolated expressions and calls them "secondary." For, truly,
the connections are present everywhere, and are by no means
secondary but essential, although by "secondary" we might con-
ceivably imply a warning against isolating such expressions.
Therefore, when Van Genderen says that the *syllogismus practicus* occupies such a modest place in Scripture, then he does
not minimize its significance, but warns against seeing it in
wrong connections.

The *syllogismus practicus* does not imply a second foundation
besides the only one that is laid, but the realization of sanctification in everyday life, of which Scripture speaks even warningly
in connection with the last things: "Follow after . . . the sanctification without which no one shall see the Lord" (Heb.
12:14). He who sees herein a new law has not understood
sanctification or justification, and certainly not the election of
God.

It is not a discrepancy when the Heidelberg Catechism, which
in Lord's Day 32 formulates the *syllogismus practicus,* says in
Lord's Day 44 that God has the law preached so that we
more and more should come to know our sinful nature, and
should so become the more earnest in seeking remission of
sins and righteousness in Christ. He who has to some extent
seen this connection will also understand the relation between

God's good pleasure in election and that will of God which the believers must recognize and which comprises the good, the acceptable, and the perfect (Rom. 12:2). Believers are exhorted to prove what God's will is after their attention has been called to God's ways and acts in the history of Israel and the nations. "For he that herein [the Holy Spirit] serveth Christ is well-pleasing to God" (Rom. 14:18).

Here every possibility to act impurely in the course of history is removed. The Word of God reaches beyond all human dilemmas, and shows us the connection between God's good pleasure and this well-pleasingness before His eyes.[38] This connection is most concretely manifested in the way of faith, which is the way of sanctification, of that sanctification in which the election of God can only be understood in unshakable certainty. This does not minimize the *sola fide;* on the contrary, the *sola fide* is thus fully honored. For the "impossible" of Lord's Day 24 is closely linked up with the "necessary" of Lord's Day 32. From this connection the question inevitably arises whether much uncertainty does not originate from a probing for certainty as an isolated problem, since certainty is only found in the way of sanctification.

In the defense against rendering salvation objective and ignoring the work of the Spirit in man, daring formulations have at times been employed to vindicate the *syllogismus practicus.* Van Ruler speaks of incorporating the believer's experience in preaching, and says that the signs of sanctification must also be mentioned, and he adds that the hearer thereby can judge his eternal status. When the signs are incorporated, then "the figure of the conclusion must also be admitted."[39] This conclusion is described in these words: "Man can then from the signs conclude his eternal status and even 'climb up,' by way of induction, to his eternal election." As a matter of fact, says Van Ruler, "man's faith-relation to God then takes on the form of the syllogism," which is the only possibility for a pneumatology which does not stop at a call to faith. Of course, Van Ruler himself sees the danger of a Protestant parallel to the Vatican decision of 1870, which on the natural level proceeded from induction and conclusion to the existence of God. And it

---

38. The opposite of the *syllogismus practicus* is the connection between estrangement from God in a sinful life and false certainty. Amos 5:18 warns against that. See also Jeremiah 7.

39. A. A. van Ruler, *Schrift en Kerk,* p. 183.

certainly is not his intention to deny what Calvin advises, namely, to turn the eye of faith to Christ, and to Him alone. With this "climbing up" and induction we may think for a moment that we have arrived in the midst of a danger zone, but Van Ruler gives a further explanation which makes it clear that he — with Van der Linde[40] — does not intend this conclusion to be simplistic. The "climbing up" and the induction and the entire faith-relation to God are all one syllogism, meant to be sharp formulations against any form of pneumatologic docetism. And when Van Ruler becomes more explicit, he says that the Word is judge,[41] and that man accepts that fact "in the presence of God as witness, hence in the *epiklese,* so that God be present; then, praying, struggling, believing and reasoning, he makes, in a sanctified judgment, his decision."[42] The conclusion is shaped through and on the basis of the *coram Deo.* It remains in the light of faith, prayer, and struggle. It is that conclusion "in which operates the *dynamis* of the faith that takes God at His Word."[43]

The *syllogismus practicus* does not lead us outside the way of faith by seeking compensation in man's own life in the face of the crisis of uncertainty regarding election; rather, it occurs before the eyes of Him who is more than our heart and who therefore can comfort us in the "firstfruits" of the Spirit.

It will always be necessary to distinguish between the conclusion, the syllogism, and any type of reasoning which operates independently of God's judgment over our lives. The conclusion can only have meaning and value through and on the basis of the *coram Deo.* It remains in the light of faith, prayer, and struggle. It is a testing which does not take place without the assistance of the divine testing (cf. Jer. 9:7, 11:20), and which loses its essence if we think the prayer for divine scrutiny superfluous.

The relationship between election and certainty led us to the opposite of Weber's vision, who in the "following after" sanctification (Heb. 12:14) suspected the disquiet and tension of man's loneliness in the face of the electing God. There is a connection between the doctrine of election and of sanctification, but this

---

40. S. van der Linde, *Kerk en Theologie,* 1954.
41. Cf. CD, 1, 12.
42. A. A. van Ruler (with reference to W. á Brakel), *op. cit.,* p. 183.
43. *Ibid.,* p. 184.

connection is of an altogether different nature than Weber thought. It is not a connection in which sanctification becomes a compensation whereby man — as a last resort — may deduce his personal election from his sanctification. It is, rather, a connection which originates from the revelation and the reality of election itself. Where this connection is not understood and regarded, there the secret of God's gracious election disappears. It then becomes a *mysterium tremendum* or an inscrutable fate[44] and it does not manifest itself in the fullness of man's life. It ends in a rash presumption which prevents man from walking in the ways of the elect (CD, I, 13), or in a self-awareness which is in conflict with the essence of election. For it is precisely election which reveals all self-justification as a terrible misconception, as a caricature of the *syllogismus practicus*.

44. Cf. E. G. van Teylingen, "De Leer der Verkiezing en de Geloofspractijk," a very informative article on the structure of the doctrine of election (in *Enigheid des Geloofs*, 4th ed., No. 1).

CHAPTER X

THE GREAT MISCONCEPTION

MORE than once we came across various misconceptions
regarding the doctrine of election. We recall the fatal
misinterpretation which identifies the election of God with
a causal-deterministic system, and the various types of fatalism
which rob the message of election of its comforting character.
Another misconception is connected with the hiddenness of election. It is thought that there is only one way left open, namely,
to seek the certainty of salvation outside the revelation in Christ.
And, finally, there is the tendency to ascribe arbitrariness to God's
election.

When in this last chapter we discuss the great misconception,
we are referring to something quite different. We do not mean
to minimize those mentioned above; rather, we wish to point
to that great misunderstanding which so directly concerns the
nature of divine election that for many generations it has fallen
like a shadow over the doctrine of election. It is the formidable
danger which even Scripture warns us against and which therefore becomes an urgent warning in the message of election. We
are thinking of that misunderstanding of election whereby man
takes his election for granted so that it becomes an occasion
for subtle self-justification. Election is accepted as a matter of
course and it is no longer seen as truly free, sovereign, and
gracious.

Essentially, of course, there is no contrast between election
and being elected. Scripture speaks both of the election of
God and of the elect.[1] But this fact can be mutilated when
being elected is abstracted from the grace of God and from
His *gracious election*. When that happens, the whole picture

1. Th. C. Vriezen in *Die Erwählung Israels nach dem Alten Testament*,
1953, has made a sharp distinction between God's election and being
elected. Evidently he attacks man's pretentiousness whereby he abstracts
his being elected from God's electing activity. The criticism against
this pretentiousness is correct but does not justify the distinction.

of election and the elect is suddenly deformed. The humility which in Scripture is the correlate of election, and which is incorporated in the warning which is part of the message of God's electing act, changes into self-awareness, self-justification, and self-distinction. God's gracious and free election is obscured by man's pretentiousness. Even though election is not denied, but indeed presupposed, it no longer dominates all of man's life as being a *gracious* election. It becomes only the background of an arrogated human right.

We shall have to discuss this deformation more fully, but first be it observed that the doctrine of election is often attacked because it is said to create this sense of pride.

To test the truthfulness of this serious accusation we may start with that one word from the passage on which all theories of the doctrine of election converge, namely, the word "us" in Paul's letter to the Ephesians: "even as he chose us in him" (Eph. 1:4). Does not the word "us," which corresponds to "we," unavoidably create a sectarian outlook upon the "world" round about us and does it not cause us proudly to consider ourselves righteous and to set all others at nought (Luke 18:9)? This question arises because there are people who at least seem to have such an arrogant attitude because of their election. But the question must be viewed in connection with the fact that Scripture itself presents people who, in direct relation to God's electing act, are indicated as "elect" (Luke 17:7).

From these words of Scripture it is quite evident that the election of God cannot be more seriously misinterpreted than when it is seized as a basis for self-exaltation and pretentiousness. The entire Scriptural testimony is one regarding election and the elect. God's election is sovereign and gracious, and hence not based on any human quality. It can therefore never lead to self-exaltation.[2] That is why there is an unfathomable abyss between an arrogated election and the election of God (cf. Rom. 8:33). Precisely the election in Christ, which, according to Calvin, precludes any merit on man's part, points out the abyss by virtue of the harmony which exists between the election in Christ and the justification of the *wicked*.

The Canons, in the struggle with the Remonstrants, repeatedly

---

2. Cf. N. H. Snaith, *The Distinctive Ideas of the Old Testament* (1947), Chapter 6 ("The Election - Love of God"), especially pp. 138ff.

concentrate on this very point; for instance, when they say that the believers find additional matter for daily humiliation before God on account of their certainty of election (CD, I, 13). This correlation is unbreakable on the basis of the *gracious* election, and this election puts its stamp on the understanding of the word "elected" in Scripture. Here we are far removed from an awareness of election motivated by self-exaltation and self-estimation, and based on one's own qualities.[3] It is correct to refer in this connection to the election of Israel, which was not based on anything empirically present in Israel, but on God's love (cf. Deut. 7:6ff.). When Lord's Day 21 of the Heidelberg Catechism speaks of the Son of God who gathers a Church chosen to everlasting life (Q. 54), then Lord's Day 23 speaks, without taking a big leap, of "mere grace without any merit" and of our not being acceptable to God on account of the worthiness of our faith (Qq. 60, 61). The emphasis is always on the sovereign and gracious character of the salvation of God, which as electing grace precludes all self-esteem, and which, if self-esteem does arise, brands it as illegitimate.[4]

This decisive point of view regarding the nature of election applies to the individual as well as to the Church.[5] We are repeatedly struck by the lack of tension between the election of the individual and the election of the Church. The emphasis of Scripture is definitely not on the individual in his estrangement and isolation, although he, too, is fully presented in the light of this comfort (cf. Rom. 16:13), when we see him with his own experience and his personal confession incorporated into the great community of the Church. The *pro me* has its place in the fellowship, as it does in the Psalms of the Old Testament and in the creed of the Church.[6] There is

---

3. Cf. J. R. Wiskerke, *Volk van Gods Keuze* (1955), pp. 30ff.
4. F. M. Th. Liagre Böhl, in *Mission und Erwählungsgedanke. Opera Minora* (1953), p. 88, says that the conviction of being an elected nation is not limited to Israel. He mentions also Egyptians, Greeks, and Romans. "But in these cases the election idea was based on an aristocratic consciousness of superiority."
5. Cf. Chapter III, "Election and Arbitrariness."
6. Cf. the variation in the Heidelberg Catechism: the plural "us" is at times replaced by "I" as in Lord's Day 1, regarding our only comfort, and in Q. 44, regarding temptation; cf. also Q. 59. There are many examples in the N. T. See E. von Dobschütz, "Wir and Ich bei Paulus" (*Zeitschrift für systematische Theologie,* 1933, pp. 251-77).

a definite strain of individualism in the song of praise of the Church; but it does not have that narrowness which places the individual in the center and esteems the election of the others secondary.

Precisely by virtue of the gracious election, the tension between the individual and the community is eliminated. Indeed, how could an individualistic emphasis ever be legitimate in a Church which knows that he who loves his neighbor has fulfilled the law (Rom. 13:8), and that each must count the other better than himself (Phil. 2:3)? Though believers may be dispersed over many regions (I Pet. 1:1), the salvation of God unites them as an elect race, a holy nation, a people for God's own possession (I Pet. 2:9).

This unity, which breaks through all isolation, is the unity and oneness in Christ. Because He is the elect cornerstone (I Pet. 2:6), there is an elect people. The one is no longer without the other, and yet the life of the individual does not dissolve into the community. That is why the election in Christ can never be placed in an individualistic or collectivistic framework. This dilemma disappears by virtue of the objectivity and finality of election, and by virtue of the richness of the community, which, together with all the saints, is able to comprehend the breadth and length and height and depth, and to know the love of Christ.[7] The prominence of the category "people" in "people of God," therefore, does not imply a narrowing of the believer's individuality, but its fulfillment and riches.

Just as the communion between Jews and Greeks does not imply a generalization but communion in Christ, so the communion of the people of God does not threaten the individual's joy, because election is not based on man's works. Both in the fellowship and in individual life, election rules out all pretentiousness, all self-exaltation, and all self-election (cf. Gal. 3:28).

Hence election in Christ characterizes and marks the whole life of the community that knows of electing grace. This community understands that God chose the base things of the world, and the things that are not, that He might bring to nought the things that are (I Cor. 1:28). This community understands something of the history of Israel, of the teaching concerning

7. Cf. how "us" predominates in the Catechism and in the Lord's Prayer. See N. Dahl, *Das Volk Gottes*, 1941; A. Oepke, *Das neue Volk Gottes*, 1950; Kittel, *T.W.N.T.*, on *laos*.

the "others," of the fact that God's sovereign election cannot be deduced and is not a matter of course.[8]

Only thus is it possible to understand the legitimate meaning of "us" in the doctrine of election, and only thus does "us" escape the traits of proud self-distinction, because this "us" has meaning only by virtue of God's election, which is sovereign and cannot be deduced.[9]

Nevertheless, the question arises again and again whether "us" does not automatically imply self-distinction, and whether it indeed can be limited in its function and working in the hearts of the believers. Does not "us" imply a pronounced judgment upon "others"?

Kuyper once said that the Hebrew *bachar* (to elect) does not so much mean "choosing from," as the divine granting of His good pleasure, and that for this reason the New Testament uses not only the word *eklegein* but also other words. The apostles felt that this one word did not convey the whole idea. Nevertheless, says Kuyper, *eklegein* requires our attention. But we should not interpret it as a preference based on something in man, but as a preference resulting from God's choice.[10]

That confronts us again with the question concerning the nature of the word "us" in the doxology on the election in Christ. No matter which way we look at election, whether we base it on Christ or on what Scripture says about Israel's election in Deuteronomy, the question always arises: What is the meaning of God's sovereign, distinguishing election?

8. In this connection we are reminded of the statement of CD, I, 8, regarding the decree of election which is not multiple but "one and the same decree respecting all those who shall be saved, both under the Old and the New Testament." This does not imply a generalization of the history of salvation, but refers to the "aforementioned election" which is described in CD, I, 7, where the phrase "neither better nor more deserving than others" is an obvious reference to Deut. 7.
9. We are also reminded of the frequent use of "we" in Scripture, e.g., Rom. 5:1, especially when it is contrasted with "others," as in Heb. 10:39ff.
10. A. Kuyper, *E Voto*, II, 166-67. Cf. A. H. de Hartog, *Voorbeschikking en Uitverkiezing* (1934), pp. 16ff., concerning "searching out" and "selecting." Cf. Th. C. Vriezen, *op. cit.*, pp. 36ff., on *bachar*. Vriezen indicates the problem when he says that the idea of separation is implied in election, although he adds that the separation is not an end in itself but that it has a purpose. Cf. Ps. 147:19-20 for the distinction between Jacob and the other people; Amos 3:2: "You only have I known among all the families of the earth." This word "comes very close to the election-concept" (Vriezen, *op. cit.*, p. 37).

Reflection on the meaning of this "us" and its results in the depths of man's heart and life is not an academic exercise. Rather, we maintain that at precisely this point the great misunderstanding has originated. That which is absolutely evident on the basis of God's revelation regarding His sovereign and gracious election has repeatedly been misinterpreted in the course of history. This misunderstanding stands as a stark reality before us in the history of Israel.

When we read the Old Testament, we discover in the light of God's sovereign and gracious acts that Israel repeatedly misunderstood its election. But we obscure this fact when we say that Israel interpreted God's election as a "being elected." It is not this wherein Israel's misunderstanding consisted, for the election of God implies this being elected. Psalm 147 clearly summarizes the distinction: "He showeth his word unto Jacob, his statutes and his ordinances unto Israel. He has not dealt so with any nation" (Ps. 147:19-20). The reality is clear: "You alone have I known from all the families of the earth" (Amos 3:2). Israel's being elected is identical with its being God's possession, as is repeatedly emphasized (Deut. 14:2, 26:18, Ps. 135:4). Possession, separation, election: therein is expressed the reality of being elected (Lev. 20:24, 26; I Kings 8:53).

The misunderstanding lies elsewhere, namely in the fact that this being elected as fruit of God's election is not seen in its real nature but as a fact which paves the way for pretentiousness and vainglory. When it is no longer understood what the Canons say about the connection between election and increasing humility, then the nature of God's electing act is misinterpreted. We see that in Israel, where this misconception exists alongside of an "acknowledging" of God. False self-glory lies at the root of its religion and its covenant. Judah enters the gates of the house of the Lord in order to bow before Him, but it is Judah whom Jeremiah has to admonish right at the gates of the temple: "Trust ye not in lying words, saying, The temple of Jehovah, the temple of Jehovah, the temple of Jehovah, are these" (Jer. 7:4). This very trust and certainty is shattered by the prophetic word (Jer. 7:8), exactly when Judah stands before God, at the house over which the name of God has been invoked, and when Judah says: "We are safe!" Its false security is exposed to the scathing criticism of the prophet's words; God reminds Judah of what He did with Shiloh because of the wickedness of His people Israel (Jer. 7:12).

The religious practice of the people lacks the one thing necessary: God spoke to them, rising up early and speaking, but they refused to hear. He called but they did not answer (Jer. 7:13). They have a feeling of certainty, of safety, but terrible is the judgment: "I will cast you out of my sight, as I have cast out all your brethren, even the whole seed of Ephraim" (Jer. 7:15). The situation of the people is dark. From this false sense of security originates idolatry and deceitfulness (Jer. 7:16ff., 8:4). There is no repentance, no knowledge of the Lord's justice, no ashamedness (Jer. 8:5, 7, 9, 12). They think they have peace, but it is no peace (Jer. 8:11, 15). Only prophetic criticism is in place here: "Let not the wise man glory in his wisdom, neither let the mighty man glory in his might, let not the rich man glory in his riches; but let him that glorieth, glory in this, that he hath understanding and knoweth me, that I am Jehovah who exerciseth lovingkindness, justice, and righteousness in the earth: for in these things I delight" (Jer. 8:23, 24).

Everything is at stake when visitation comes upon all them that are circumcised in their uncircumcision (Jer. 9:25), and suddenly they find themselves considered as of a kind, without distinction: Egypt and Judah, Edom and the Ammonites,[11] for "all the nations are uncircumcised, and all the house of Israel is uncircumcised in heart." An appeal to Israel's election is no longer of any avail, for the essence of election has been misunderstood, the mark of grace in it has been ignored.

The prophetic criticism does not imply that God is abandoning His election as an experiment that has failed; rather, He shows what it actually is in contrast with Israel's perversion of it. Israel's false sense of security is a caricature of the security which God's election entails. Israel's security is an abstracted security, like that in the corrupt days of Micah, when the people confidently said: "Is not Jehovah in the midst of us? no evil shall come upon us" (Micah 3:11). Especially in the prophecy of Amos we see the same misunderstanding brought out. Judgment is pronounced upon the surrounding peoples but after that also upon Judah and Israel (Amos 2:4, 6). Israel's distinctiveness, its consciousness of exclusiveness, has led to wrong conclusions. Those are the people to whom the word of the prophet is directed.

11. Cf. G. Ch. Aalders, *Korte Verklaring* (on Jeremiah), I, 123.

We may ask, How can Amos preach a God who is more
severe with His own people than with strange nations?[12] The
answer is: God elected and knew Israel! That is why He
punishes sin. That indeed is the opposite of any simple conclusion regarding being elected. Jehovah's conclusions are different from His people's. And when the people continue to draw
rash conclusions, all pretentiousness is beaten down, also that
which is most closely linked up with God's electing activity: "Are
ye not like the children of the Ethiopians unto me, O children
of Israel?" (Amos 9:7). "This text at once does away with
a prejudice which through false conclusions from the election had
become part and parcel of Israel's thinking."[13] Both God's election and Israel's national existence were considered by them as
the antithesis of other nations. Israel interpreted election apart
from faith and thus drew illicit conclusions from it.

But God transcends such logic and "conclusions," and as a
matter of fact places Israel on a level with the Cushites. The eyes
of the Lord Jehovah are upon the sinful kingdom (Amos 9:8).
He issues a command against all the sinners "of my people."
The core of the contention between Jehovah and Israel is the
diverging conclusion from election. "Israel has no claim upon
special consideration because of election, nevertheless God has a
special claim upon Israel's obedience because of that election."[14]

We see the same crisis in Hosea when "my people" changes to
"not my people" (Hos. 1:9). To be sure, this *loammi* is not
the end, and soon the light shines through the judgment again,
but it is God's light. The *ammi* is God's unspeakable miracle,
not a self-evident human truth upon which conclusions can be
built, or which justifies human arrogance. "Ye are not my people
and I will not be your God" contains "a negation of the covenant
formula, which He uses not without a purpose"; it is a definite
severance of the covenant relationship, an *ultima abdicatio*.[15]

Hosea, and with him all the true believers in the Israel of the
ten tribes, are, so to speak, pushed back to the pre-Mosaic period
of revelation, to the status of the patriarchal era when God had
not yet revealed Himself to the patriarchs in the full riches of
His covenant-name Jehovah.[16]

---

12. C. van Gelderen, *Amos,* p. 55.
13. A. Weiser, on Amos, p. 174; cf. Van Gelderen, *op. cit.,* p. 279.
14. Weiser, *op. cit.,* p. 123.
15. *Ibid.,* p. 9.
16. Van Gelderen, *op. cit.,* p. 34.

We meet with the same trend of thought in the New Testament when the Jews think and act on the basis of the pretentious, national idea that they are Abraham's seed. The misconception which prevents them from understanding God's election in its true meaning is characterized by Christ as imagination. "Think not to say within yourselves, We have Abraham to our father" (Matt. 3:9). They misinterpret God's sovereign freedom, and over against the Jewish arrogance Christ indicates what God can do, namely, raise up children unto Abraham out of stones. That is Christ's criticism, not of the actuality of election but of the Jews' misconception of it. Their misrepresentation has been variously described as rendering election objective, abstract, materialistic, etc. But the central idea is obvious. God's grace, as the brief characteristic of election, has been replaced by human pretentiousness. When Oepke says: "The synagogue made of the *mysterium tremendum* and *fascinosum* a ground for a boastful claim," he touches with that word "boast" the core of the matter. Therein lies the abstraction and materialization. Every aspect of the revelation regarding God's election can thus be incorporated in this viewpoint, even the idea of the "others"; but everything is at the same time a perversion of election. The attitude towards those "outside" election is, on the basis of legalism, fanatically and proudly perverted, whereas the true attitude is one of the deepest humility before God's saving grace.[17]

This externalized and legalistic approach to God's election, which completely by-passes the real nature of it, makes the dynamic forces which lie in the salvation of God for the nations of none effect. We touch here upon the tremendous problem of particularity and universality. The misconception consists in the fact that the seclusion of Israel in its particularity (Gen. 12:3, Amos 3:2, Ps. 147:19-20) is particularistically interpreted, so that the grand perspectives for other nations disappear. In the New Testament, not in contrast but in harmony with the Old, particularism is definitely rent asunder on the basis of its fulfillment in the Kingdom of God, and it is revealed as a radical misconception. Many unfruitful and objectionable consequences issue from this particularism. In its dark isolationism it shuts the door to the world and believes God's ways to end where they have just begun.[18]

---

17. Oepke indicates Pharisaism as "the consequent application of a wrong notion concerning the 'others' by the synagogue" (*op. cit.,* p. 142).
18. See A. Kuyper, *De Gemeene Gratie,* I, Chap. XLII.

Now we might ask whether the force of this argument is not diminished by the missionary activity of the Pharisees, of which we read in the New Testament. Is this, perhaps, an instance where the universal aspects of the Old Testament are taken into account by the synagogue? We remember at once Christ's severe pronouncement, precisely in connection with the proselytizing of the Pharisees: "Woe unto you, scribes and Pharisees, hypocrites! for ye compass the sea and land to make one proselyte; and when he is become so, ye make him twofold more a son of hell than yourselves" (Matt. 23:15). What does this kind of universality, this "apostolate" of the Pharisees, mean? Is it a dispensing of Israel's blessing over all the nations? Has it something to do with the joyful song of Israel, "Oh praise Jehovah, all ye nations, laud him, all ye peoples. For his lovingkindness is great toward us; and the truth of Jehovah endureth for ever. Praise ye Jehovah" (Ps. 117)?

Election has not stranded in such Old Testament expressions; rather, they open wide the windows to the nations, and Israel understands the meaning and the purpose of its election. The "us" of God's lovingkindness is incorporated in the invitation to the nations and thus it is legitimate and inviolable.

The "mission" of Pharisaism, however, is different. From the formal-phenomenological standpoint we apparently cannot detect any illegitimate traits in it, because it sports election, safety, and apostolic ardor. But it all depends whether election is understood in its character of free grace. Where this grace is legalistically interpreted, legalism infects all of life, and thus its mission ultimately becomes nothing but a revelation of the arrogance of a falsely understood election, so that this mission is unrecognizably mutilated. In spite of such formal traits as apostolic journeying over land and sea, such mission becomes grossly introverted.

Real universalism — salvation offered to all people — has here become lost. The lines of this "apostolate" return to its center. The degradation of legalism makes this mission a questionable matter which outwardly, indeed, resembles the New Testament apostolate, but which is separated from it by a deep abyss. For this movement is not full of the good tidings, but of disaster for those whom it reaches and wins.

It is not the message of God's salvation which they hear, the salvation for lost sinners, but they are drawn by a propaganda which obscures the actual salvation. When the gladness — the *eu-aggelion* — has departed from the tidings, only a formal skeleton of real mission is left. Grace has been eliminated from it. The fundamental shortcoming of Pharisaism is not a lack of fervor. They even thought to offer service unto God when they cast certain people out of the synagogue. But when Jesus came, not to be ministered unto, but to minister, they rejected Him (Mark 10:45). What, then, remains left to proclaim to the nations?[19] Which other service are they to preach to the world than this kind of service of Jesus Christ? If all that remains is their religion, their kind of service, then where is the real mystery of the gospel and how can they thus be a light unto the nations "that thou mayest be my salvation unto the ends of the earth" (Isa. 49:6)?

He who misconceives of revelation and the salvation it offers can not engage in mission work because the sovereign freedom of grace has been removed from it. The glad tidings are then no longer seen and consequently not brought to others, the poor, the miserable, and the lost.[20] That is why the conflict between Jesus and the Pharisees' mission is identical with the one regarding Christ's intercourse with publicans and sinners.

The New Testament sheds far more light upon divine election than one would think, judging by the few places where the word "elect" occurs. The light of election beams forth in the "preference" of Christ for the lost, for publicans and sinners. This electing preference is explained by the Pharisees as the violation of the holy *thora*. They think it a shame that Jesus enters the home of sinners, and that He eats and drinks with them. But that is precisely the essence of Christ's mission on earth, and He reveals therein the good pleasure of the Father. Pharisaism no more understands that than the elder son in the parable understands the love of his father for the younger son. Both he and Pharisaism have only one point of view: "Lo, these

---

19. Cf. Grosheide, in his commentary on Matt.: "There was no spiritual gain, for they were initiated into the doctrine and practice of the Pharisees" (p. 346).

20. On Jewish missions, see A. Oepke, "Internationalismus, Rasse und Weltmission im Lichte Jesu, *Zeitschrift für systematische Theologie* (1933), 10th ed., pp. 290ff.; L. Goppelt, *Christentum und Judentum im ersten und zweiten Jarhhundert* (1954), p. 80.

many years do I serve thee, and I never have transgressed a commandment of thine" (Luke 15:29).[21]

How could they therefore understand the free, sovereign, and gracious election, and the connection between election and prayer (cf. Ps. 65:3, Luke 18:11ff.)? They replace penitence and mercy by sacrifices (Matt. 9:13), but over against this utter misconception of salvation, the message of election shines forth that the last shall be first, and the first, last (Luke 13:30, Mark 10:31). "Verily, I say unto you, that the publicans and the harlots go into the kingdom of God before you" (Matt. 21:31). This precedence does not violate the teaching of the *thora;* rather, it fulfills it, and all the windows to salvation are opened: "Many shall come from the east and the west, and shall sit down with Abraham, and Isaac, and Jacob, in the kingdom of heaven; but the sons of the kingdom shall be cast forth into the outer darkness" (Matt. 8:11-12).

The conflict between Jesus and the Pharisees was ultimately a conflict concerning the gracious election of God.[22]

The danger is not imaginary that we see Pharisaism merely as a local phenomenon, limited to the Jews of Jesus' time. But the very nature of the misconception of the electing grace of God indicates that the opposite is true.[23] In Pharisaism we meet far more than simply that hypocrisy which in the Church has been designated with the simple term "Pharisaism." Rather, we are dealing with that resistance against gracious election which is identical to the resistance against the foolishness of the cross. It is that form of religion which boasts an extensive insight into covenant and law, but which has not understood the depth of the covenant and the fulfillment of the law. The result of this misunderstanding is false self-exaltation — even in prayer — which in turn results in blindness concerning God[24] and one's neighbor, and which creates its own antithesis re-

---

21. The universality of the Pharisees was narrower than the temporary limitedness of the message in the New Testament. The limitedness appears, for instance, in Matt. 10:5; cf. Mark 7:27. Nevertheless, there are perspectives of universality even in this limitedness. See in this connection John 12:20-24.

22. The entire N. T. shows how much the Pharisees were blinded in their understanding of salvation and of the divine commandment. Cf. Goppelt, *op. cit.,* pp. 43ff., and H. H. Henson, *Christian Morality* (Gifford Lectures), (1937), Chapter IV ("Jesus and Judaism").

23. Cf. A. Oepke, *op. cit.,* p. 149.

24. Cf. Mark 7:6.

garding the multitude that knows not the law and therefore is accursed (John 7:49).

Hence, not only in historical Pharisaism, but wherever salvation and forgiveness, penitence and mercy, are no longer correctly understood, there the characteristics of self-exaltation, pride, pretentiousness, self-election, self-justification, and false antithesis appear immediately. They are a threat wherever the message of grace is heard. When Paul speaks of the apostasy of Israel, which paved the way for the salvation of the nations, he warns: "Be not high-minded, but fear" (Rom. 11:20). This high-mindedness is the opposite of continuing in God's goodness (Rom. 11:22). The law of the *ekloge* is not just a thing of the past (cf. Rom. 9:11). Just as Christ says to the Pharisees that God is able to raise children unto Abraham out of stones, so Paul writes to the believers that God is able to graft in again those Jews who do not continue in their unbelief. But in the same verse he warns those who might become high-minded (Rom. 11:21, 22), whereby they would prove that they had not understood the meaning and purpose of election.

It is no wonder that the Canons speak of the relationship between God's election and the believer's humility, nor that Calvin, the theologian, who so emphatically stresses the freedom of God's election, speaks of those who are humble before God: "What means is there of humbling us if we do not make way for the mercy of God, by our utter indigence and destitution?" (*Inst.* III, 12, 6).

It has often emphatically been maintained that no better refutation of the "great misunderstanding" can be given than by stating that all of election is election to service. This service is then placed over against the egocentric and anthropocentric misunderstanding of election. This point of view is illustrated especially by the reference to God's redemptive-historical election of Israel to service for the purpose of realizing the coming of the Kingdom of God.

This idea is often advanced in opposition to the traditional idea of election to salvation. We find a clear example of this in Van Dijk. Proceeding from the election of the people of Israel, he first concludes that election in the Old Testament "is election to service in the life of revelation, in the Kingdom of God." All God's special election activity is directed toward the one goal — His Kingdom. "God elects not by excluding others, but for the sake of others" and He does so by electing nations and individuals in His service.[25] But according to Van Dyk, this election to service is not just an adumbration of the election to salvation, for also in the New Testament all election is election to service. The point at issue in the election of God is only our work, our place and service in the Kingdom of God, and not the beginning of our new life."[26]

We find similar ideas in the writings of T. C. Vriezen and H. H. Rowley. Vriezen speaks especially of Israel. God's object with electing a people is first of all a matter of the divine economy of salvation. The purpose of election is not the salvation of the individual, but "it places a whole nation in the world as a place of the revelation of His Kingdom." There is a connection between election and the Kingdom of God, but not between election and salvation. Vriezen poses this "fact" so emphatically that he even says: "If one thing is needful, it is that the Christian doctrine of election turn from the question of the certainty of salvation, and point out that the Biblical concept of election is a call to service in the Kingdom of God."[27] Rowley, too, emphasizes the service of the elect, its "purpose," and its meaning. "Whom God chooses, He chooses to service." There is great variety in service, but "it is all service for God." With Van Dijk and Vriezen, he says very positively that "the divine election concerns exclusively the divine service."[28]

It seems to me that the dilemma between "elected to service" and "elected to salvation" is unacceptable, and that it cannot be maintained in the light of what Scripture teaches. The main purpose of the dilemma seems to be to oppose an understanding of election which is selective and exclusive, and to stress instead that election always contains a commission.[29]

It is clear that this dilemma cannot be refuted by denying the relation between the election of God and this service, this mis-

---

25. I. van Dijk, "De Leer der Verkiezing in het N. T." (*Gezam. Geschr.* 1917, I, 232).

26. *Ibid.*, p. 262.

27. Vriezen, *Die Erwählung Israels nach dem A. T.* (1953), p. 34.

28. Rowley, *The Biblical Doctrine of Election* (1953), p. 42. Cf. pp. 44 and 62; "only in terms of purpose and election" (p. 68); "their election is for service and it is valid only as far as and so long as they fulfill that purpose" (p. 11); "rather for service than for privilege" (p. 170). No "favouritism" (p. 172); "purposeful service" (p. 174).

29. Vriezen, *op. cit.*, p. 109.

sion, or even by considering it to be of little importance. Scripture shows us clearly that we may not ignore the importance of this connection. Its significance, therefore, has never been denied by those who emphasize the aspect of election to salvation. When Kuyper, for instance, posed the question: Elected for what purpose? he first of all referred to Jesus' statement to His disciples: "Ye did not choose me, but I chose you, and appointed you, that ye should go and bear fruit" (John 15:16). Kuyper even says that the doctrine of election must be considered from this angle "if it is to be Scriptural, defended in the spirit of the Reformation, and maintained as an indispensable power for practical life."[30] Not man's salvation, but the consummation of the Kingdom is central.

Kuyper could have taken over many of the remarks made by Van Dijk, Vriezen, and Rowley in his rejection of anthropocentric piety which does not know the *gloria Dei* and does not understand that the question is whereunto we are elected. He remarks, for example, that "by being and doing this, we shall at the same time be saved." But there is one great difference: Kuyper nowhere speaks of the "exclusiveness" of the connection between election and service, task, calling, and he avoids the dilemma of either service or salvation. The emphasis on election to service may be necessary over against the misunderstanding of election, but that does not imply that we may oppose service to salvation. We are confronted with the undeniable fact that God's salvation in Scripture is always directly connected with His election, as in Romans 8 and Ephesians 1, where the certainty of salvation is linked with gracious election and with the keeping of God's love for all time. Furthermore, the expression "election unto salvation" occurs in Scripture itself where Paul says "God chose you from the beginning unto salvation" (II Thess. 2:13). That there is no mention here (or elsewhere) of anthropocentrism is evident from the fact that this election is directly conjoined with sanctification by the Holy Spirit. But there is no dilemma. Paul's thanksgiving for the Thessalonians' election unto salvation is connected with the love of the Father, with eternal comfort and good hope (II Thess. 2:16). But for Paul it does not end in a vacuum of passivity and self-indulgence, but in activity. "Now our Lord Jesus Christ . . . establish [your hearts] in every good work and word" (II Thess. 2:17). There

30. Kuyper, *Uit het Woord* (1875), II, 258, 261.

is here not the slightest contrast between the service and salvation
in connection with election.[31]

The misinterpretation of election does not lie in relating it to
God's salvation, but in isolating it from the call to sanctification
and from the task and the mission in the Kingdom of God. That
does not imply that he who stands outside of salvation and has
not yet approached the electing God in faith and penitence can
ever maintain that his life and opposition are independent of and
outside the realm of God's activity. God's purpose is being fulfilled
by and in spite of man's sinful deeds. They are subservient to
the fulfillment of God's counsel for the salvation of the world.[32]

In this connection Rowley has spoken of "election without
covenant," citing the examples in the Old Testament where the
nations are made subservient to God's plan even in their activity
against Him (Amos 6:14). But Rowley himself recognizes the
difference between these instances and the election "that leads to
a permanent relationship between the elect and God." It is impossible to concentrate the various aspects of election into the one
concept of "service" (in the sense of being subservient), in order
to contrast service with salvation. For the service to which the
elect are called is more than an unconscious being subservient
to God (e.g., Cyrus, Isa. 45:4), so that Rowley himself admits:
"Far higher, too, is the purpose of the election of Israel than any
election that lay outside of the Covenant."[33]

Of decisive importance, therefore, is the correct understanding
of the gracious and therefore purposeful election. The "us" in
connection with the election of God confronts us with one of the
most profound questions of the entire doctrine of election. Confessing this "us" is legitimate — precisely because it is connected with
God's election — only when it is absolutely disconnected from all
self-exaltation. This thought leads us to the problem which is not
always brought up in regard to election but which is nevertheless
closely related to it: the problem of the antithesis. It is, of course,
impossible to trace here all the aspects of the problem of the antithesis, but it is necessary for a moment to consider the profound ques-

---

31. Cf. K. Dijk, *Om 't Eeuwig Welbehagen* (1924), p. 343, who correctly
    calls II Thess. 2:13 unambiguous and also refers to Acts 13:48 ("unto
    life eternal"). Cf. his *Van Eeuwigheid Verkoren*, p. 110, where he also
    mentions, besides Van Dijk, Chant. de la Saussaye, Jr., Gunning, and
    Roozemeyer.
32. Cf. my *The Providence of God*, E T (1952).
33. Rowley, *op. cit.*, p. 138.

tions related to the word "us" and other questions regarding the problem which is usually called the reality of the antithesis.

The antithesis is frequently interpreted on the basis of a caricature which has been made of it, and which indeed actually exists. We have already seen it in Pharisaism, which thrived on a sharp but false antithesis over against the multitude which did not know the law. We might call it a legalistic or moralistic antithesis. Such an antithesis is detached from God's activity as a whole and is therefore in flagrant contradiction to the Old Testament and God's purpose with Israel. The divinely intended and posited antithesis — Israel and the nations — is here robbed of its essence when it is not understood that in Israel is contained the blessing for the nations. The legalistic antithesis is without this blessing, and this antithesis is no less illegitimate when the promises are fulfilled and the Kingdom has come. Just as Christ says that the Comforter will come, who will convince the world because it does not believe in Him (John 16:9), so the antithesis carries its absolute Christological character and mark, as Christ Himself calls out at the crossroads of all decisions: "He that is not with me is against me" (Matt. 12:30, Luke 11:23). That is the great distinction between the "yes" and the "no" to Him who is the Light of the world. The *skandalon* lies in His cross. Here men stand over against each other because of the most profound choice of their life, men who have so much in common with each other but who nevertheless separate in spite of this solidarity. It is a decision which has priority over all other decisions.

This unmistakable divergence in the depths of man's heart is not left unmentioned in the New Testament. On the contrary, it points to it with great seriousness. It illustrates this antithesis which makes itself felt in all directions, even as far as the terror of persecution for Christ's sake. It does this in many ways, and places — over against faith, the offense; over against illumination, the blindness; over against resurrection, the fall; over against life, death; over against the longing to do God's will, the longing after this world.

This antithesis would never have been denied or made relative (for Scripture speaks quite plainly here), if it had not been for the many caricatures of it by presumptuous men. This truly horrible caricature, against which Augustine, Luther, and Calvin — on the basis of the election of God — seriously warned, has led some theologians to emphasize men's solidarity in sin over against the antithesis. On the basis of this solidarity they hardly acknowledge any antithesis, because the antithesis seems almost permanently and directly connected with self-exaltation and pride. These theologians think that true humility of the Christian life can be urged only if the antithesis is left unmentioned. They insist that man should be made to look at his solidarity in sin. This will forever prevent him from arriving at a *positive* antithesis. They accuse the Church of overestimating itself and of underestimating the world. They insist that the Church is so absorbed in its idea of the antithesis that it no longer has an eye for the "majority" of the world, and thus is in danger of perishing in self-complacency."[34]

When we listen to this criticism, which is much more than a necessary warning against Pharisaism with its legalistic antithesis, it is first of all necessary to think of the Scriptural testimony which does not weaken the reality of the antithesis but still radically eliminates all occasion for self-glory. The structure of the Biblical message is a good deal more complex than can be comprehended in the dilemma: either antithesis or solidarity. The distinction between Israel and other nations already contains a warning against false and vain self-glory which obscures the significance of the distinction. Psalm 147 does not contradict the warning and humiliation contained in Deuteronomy 7; instead, it harmonizes fully with it. Not glory as such but false glory perishes under the judgment of God. It is possible in self-glory and self-distinction over against others to pervert salvation. It is possible to maintain an antithesis which cannot stand before the face of God. It is possible to forget that God chooses "the things that are not that he might bring to nought the things that are (I Cor. 1:28), and thus continue to glory in one's own distinctiveness. All these possibilities often became facts in Israel's history. And they did so when Israel lost the right conception of God's election. Israel then no longer saw the solidarity from which it was elected out of mere grace and not because of its priority or its advantage over others. To be sure, Pharisaism does not altogether ignore election, but election nevertheless becomes the forgotten or at least misunderstood chapter.

The constant warning of the Word of God is not that we must speak no more of the reality of the antithesis, but that the antithesis

---

34. We touch here upon the current discussion concerning Dietrich Bonhoeffer. See K. Kroon, *Stenen voor Stenen. Gesprek over Kerk er Humanisme,* 1953; H. J. Heering, "Mönnichs Pelgrimage" (*Wending,* 1954, pp. 457ff.).

must be correctly understood as being legitimate only by virtue of the grace of election. Precisely here we are confronted with the real touchstone of the antithesis in the world.

One may, however, admit that this connection is essential, but still consider it hardly plausible that it — the connection between the humility spoken of in the Canons and the antithesis — can be experienced *in concreto*. Moreover, does not this connection concern the unreachable, ultimate, and deepest stirrings of the heart, which are beyond all control? And do we in reality not often see the shadows of an antithesis which shows little of that deep humility which election evokes? Are we indeed able to understand and judge the real essence of the "us" and the "we," both in ourselves and in others?

In answer to these questions we are first of all reminded of the fact that God searches man's heart. He truly knows this heart, no matter in what form it reveals the antithesis. His all-seeing eye detects at once every camouflage of humility.[35] However, this does not refer only to the things that go on in the depths of man's heart. For his deepest feelings come to expression in his life, so that the Pharisee clearly reveals himself in his legalistic antithesis, in his mission, and in his prayer. On the occasions when the heart pours itself out, like a river over the fields, it reveals what it is and whether it understands the relation of the antithesis to God's gracious election. This evident connection is closely linked up with the fact that the antithesis does not concern a stable situation resulting from two opposite and opposing worlds, namely, light and darkness. Much rather, the situation in the antithesis between *pro* and *contra* is perpetually in motion, both in individuals and nations. And precisely that being in motion determines the direction of the struggle the antithesis entails.

This struggle is of an altogether different nature than when two persons are engaged in a battle of life and death. For in the antithesis, because of the offense of the cross, there is always the possibility of reconciliation, of peace after the struggle, just as the gulf between Jews and Gentiles is bridged in Christ and the adding of the Gentiles is part of the mystery which is now revealed. If we see this reconciliation in the antithesis as an easy way to dissolve the antithesis in the solidarity, then we misjudge

35. See George Wehrung's "Selbstgefühl und Demut" (*Zeitschrift für systematische Theologie*, 1954, pp. 347ff.).

the real antithesis in which reconciliation does not lie in our
hands nor can be anticipated by us. If we think we can and may
do that, then we by-pass the cross and we finally no longer
understand the seriousness of the *kerygma* and of the call to
confession. Then, because of the fading of the antithesis, we no
longer understand the joy of the angels over the one sinner who
repents (Luke 15:10). And the dynamics of the preaching of
the gospel, of the witnessing to the ends of the earth, are
destroyed.

This fading of the antithesis may at times have resulted from the
protest against false glory, but nevertheless it cannot therefore
be defended. A misconception of election cannot be corrected by
a new misconception.

It seems to me that the New Testament shows this clearly.
On the one hand it does not weaken or eliminate the antithesis
because of the solidarity of sin, and on the other hand it indicates
the contrast in such a way that it both by warning and threatening eliminates all self-exaltation. Both aspects are decisive and
issue from the gracious election of God.[36]

The reality of the contrast precludes high-mindedness because
otherwise the Church would forget its own origin and reason for
existence. Regarding solidarity D. van Swigchem correctly says:
"This solidarity in sin does not mean an elimination of the fundamental distinction but the demand that the believer must always
be aware that the new law of life is a grace."[37] The Bible does
not present election as a way to self-exaltation, but to true humility. It is precisely the Church which understands the meaning
of "therefore!" in Amos 3:2 and the searching of Jerusalem with
lamps (Zeph. 1:12). And because of this solidarity in sin which
is understood in the reality of the antithesis — and only there —
it is understandable that the Church knows God's calling which
came to her in the preaching of the gospel. What we before
indicated as the connection between election and preaching finds
its concrete form in the New Testament.

36. This can also be said regarding the position of Israel in the Old
    Testament. Cf. the continuous demarcation with respect to the nations
    and their sins as in Ezra 9:1ff., 10:2 (the mixed marriages); cf. also
    Malachi 2:11.
37. See D. van Swigchem, *Het Missionair Karakter van de Christelijke
    Gemeente Volgens de Brieven van Paulus en Petrus* (1955), e.g., p. 55,
    regarding the reality of the contrast, which works through in life
    and which is also recognizable; and pp. 60, 61.

The point at issue in the antithesis which is redemptive-historically concentrated in the *skandalon* of the cross is not a contrast of man's natural heart.[38] What is meant is not the kind of breach which came between Cain and Abel, or any quarrel or hatred caused by egotism. Rather, in the antithesis we are confronted with a truly unique contrast. This uniqueness finds its origin in God's mercy, and that is the reason why it finds its true expression not in isolation from the world, but in turning toward the world.[39] Therein the Church resembles its heavenly Father, who makes His sun to rise on the evil and the good alike (Matt. 5:45).

Constantly mindful of having been called out of darkness herself, the Church cannot help but be concerned about the conversion of others, no matter how estranged and lost. This by no means implies a weakening of the distinction between good and evil, faith and unbelief, Church and world. Rather, the Church, because of the seriousness of this antithesis, goes out into the world to witness. She does not do so despairing that the world cannot be saved, for then she would forget her own former lost condition as well as the sovereign election of God which called her from her darkness to His marvelous light. Every trace of a proud and legalistic antithesis is absent here. It is replaced by an apostolic fervor which never and nowhere generalizes but which, in the antithesis, knows itself compelled by the love of Christ (II Cor. 5:14). When Peter calls the Church an elect race which must show forth the excellencies of God, then he adds the profound and meaningful reminder: "who in time past were no people, but now are the people of God: who had not obtained mercy, but now have obtained mercy" (I Pet. 2:10).

And when the Church of Christ understands her election, not as a *fatum* or a *dominium absolutum,* but as a sovereign, gracious, undeserved election, then she also understands her service to the Lord in the world, a service which is indissolubly connected with her election.[40] Every term of the Christian vocabulary now returns; most certainly *pro rege* and *soli Deo gloria,* no matter how often misused. To be sure, the words may be used carelessly, and only seemingly resemble the true apostolic spirit because of

---

38. Cf. HC, Q. 5, "prone by nature to hate."
39. Cf. Van Swigchem, *op. cit.,* p. 222.
40. Van Swigchem correctly speaks in this connection that it is a matter of course that Christ's Church turns itself toward its environment (*op. cit.,* p. 225). Cf. H. R. Boer, *Pentecost and the Missionary Witness of the Church* (1955), Chapter V.

a wrong understanding of election. But, on the other hand, they can also be rightfully used in the Christian life when election is understood correctly. The Christian life finds its expression in the election because it found therein, in Christ, its origin.

All the longing in the Old Testament for the salvation of the nations is here fulfilled. Though the antithesis become an oppressive reality for the Church, in the horrible form of matryrdom for Christ's sake, even then the Church is not filled with despair concerning the world. It is filled, rather, with expectation and intercession for its salvation in Him who came to seek that which was lost.

Only because of the reality of salvation in Christ is it possible to live out of the election of God, to find comfort in it, and to know oneself to be called. When election is rightly understood, then it does not call forth a natural sentiment, but heartfelt concern about the darkness of a God-forsaking life. I know of no clearer statement in this connection than the one made by Paul when, weeping, he says of the "others" that they are the enemies of the cross of Christ (Phil. 3:18); enemies — that is the word which reveals the antithesis in its stark reality. Because they are enemies, their end will be perdition, but even over against that darkness Paul's "we" is spoken, also with respect to the end, the eschatological expectation of Jesus Christ (Phil. 3:20). But he speaks this word concerning the enemies with tears. It contains both "a sorrowful lamentation" and a "fierce wrath,"[41] and precisely therein lies the unity of the antithesis and the concern in the life of Paul, who knows himself to be the object of the divine mercy and who elsewhere says that Christ died for us when *we* were yet *enemies* (Rom. 5:10).

In this chapter we have discussed that misunderstanding of election which transposes the mystery of sovereign and gracious election into a pretentiousness, which flagrantly contradicts that gracious election.

This misconception is by no means just an intellectual error which does not see the correlations in the Word of God. On the contrary, this misconception is a revelation of the craftiness of man's heart by which the mystery of God's love, of His sovereign grace, is transposed into a form of thinking and living

41. E. Lohmeyer, *Die Briefe an die Philippenser, Kollosenser und Philemon* (1953), p. 153.

in which man finds an excuse for no longer living exclusively by the grace of God. In this misinterpretation man wagers everything. He may retain the appearance that he is filled with zeal for the Church's apostolate, mission, and universality, but the salvation which gives these things meaning and value has been eliminated from it.

The doctrine of God's election is truly not without reason called the heart of the Church.[42]

This doctrine has often been mutilated and speculatively interpreted to the detriment of many, but when we have seen through this deformation then we shall desire to proceed very carefully. We shall have to realize that many threatening dangers surround this "heart" of the Church. Precisely when there are misrepresentations, then there is the danger of the vehement reaction. The history of the dogma of election could for a large part be described in terms of this reaction. Often the pendulum has swung from determinism to indeterminism, from the arbitrariness concept to the denial of divine sovereignty, from a terrifying doctrine of rejection to a denial of all rejection. All this reveals the estrangement of man's thinking, which no longer understands that both God's sovereignty and His grace, both His love and His justice, go together. The way back is not a way of rational transparency. The knowledge of the electing God is not the outcome of rational considerations, but it is found only when man walks in the way of this truth. And only in this way can we by the abundant power and guidance of the Holy Spirit be prevented from falling again, either on the right hand or on the left, in the abyss of misconceptions. Thus we can be saved, too, from the threatening dangers which surround the concept of the word "us," and we may take our place in a world where it is not our task to scrutinize God's inscrutable ways with men. In this world we see, more and more, the way before us which leads to communion in Christ, and in this communion we understand that salvation does not originate from man's own flesh and blood, but that salvation is according to the election of grace and is to be preached to the utmost ends of the earth.

Only thus will it be possible to get rid of the complexities with which our thinking has obscured the doctrine of election. For then it is possible to understand that far beyond these complications lies the apex of simplicity, namely, that good pleasure of

42. A. Kuyper, *Predicatiën* (1913), p. 43.

God which led Christ to utter His prayer of thanksgiving which is not without reason preserved both for our admonition and comfort: "I thank thee, O Father, Lord of heaven and earth, that thou didst hide these things from the wise and understanding, and didst reveal them unto babes: yea, Father, for so it was well-pleasing in thy sight" (Matt. 11:25-26).

INDEX OF PERSONS

INDEX OF SCRIPTURE